T0270797

Digital Forensics and Cyber Crime Investigation

In the ever-evolving landscape of digital forensics and cybercrime investigation, staying ahead with the latest advancements is not just advantageous—it's imperative. *Digital Forensics and Cyber Crime Investigation: Recent Advances and Future Directions* serves as a crucial bridge, connecting the dots between the present knowledge base and the fast-paced developments in this dynamic field. Through a collection of meticulous research and expert insights, this book dissects various facets of digital forensics and cyber security, providing readers with a comprehensive look at current trends and future possibilities. Distinguished by its in-depth analysis and forward-looking perspective, this volume sets itself apart as an indispensable resource for those keen on navigating the complexities of securing the digital domain.

Key features of this book include:

- **Innovative Strategies for Web Application Security**: Insights into Moving Target Defense (MTD) techniques.
- **Blockchain Applications in Smart Cities**: An examination of how blockchain technology can fortify data security and trust.
- **Latest Developments in Digital Forensics**: A thorough overview of cutting-edge techniques and methodologies.
- **Advancements in Intrusion Detection**: The role of Convolutional Neural Networks (CNN) in enhancing network security.
- **Augmented Reality in Crime Scene Investigations**: How AR technology is transforming forensic science.
- **Emerging Techniques for Data Protection**: From chaotic watermarking in multimedia to deep learning models for forgery detection.

This book aims to serve as a beacon for practitioners, researchers, and students who are navigating the intricate world of digital forensics and cyber security. By offering a blend of recent advancements and speculative future directions, it not only enriches the reader's understanding of the subject matter but also inspires innovative thinking and applications in the field. Whether you're a seasoned investigator, an academic, or a technology enthusiast, *Digital Forensics and Cyber Crime Investigation: Recent Advances and Future Directions* promises to be a valuable addition to your collection, pushing the boundaries of what's possible in digital forensics and beyond.

Digital Forensics and Cyber Crime Investigation

Recent Advances and Future Directions

Edited by
Ahmed A. Abd El-Latif
Lo'ai Tawalbeh
Manoranjan Mohanty
Brij B. Gupta
Konstantinos E. Psannis

CRC Press
Taylor & Francis Group
Boca Raton London New York

CRC Press is an imprint of the
Taylor & Francis Group, an **informa** business

Designed cover image: ShutterStock Images

First edition published 2025
by CRC Press
2385 NW Executive Center Drive, Suite 320, Boca Raton FL 33431

and by CRC Press
4 Park Square, Milton Park, Abingdon, Oxon, OX14 4RN

CRC Press is an imprint of Taylor & Francis Group, LLC

Library of Congress Cataloging-in-Publication Data
Names: Abd El-Latif, Ahmed A., 1984– editor. | Tawalbeh, Lo'ai, editor. | Mohanty, Manoranjan (Editor), editor. | Gupta, Brij, 1982– editor. | Psannis, Konstantinos E., editor.
Title: Digital forensics and cyber crime investigation : recent advances and future directions / edited by Ahmed A. Abd El-Latif, Lo'ai Tawalbeh, Manoranjan Mohanty, Brij Gupta and Konstantinos E. Psannis.
Description: First edition. | Boca Raton : CRC Press, 2025. | Includes bibliographical references and index.
Identifiers: LCCN 2024020918 (print) | LCCN 2024020919 (ebook) | ISBN 9781032075396 (hardback) | ISBN 9781032075419 (paperback) | ISBN 9781003207573 (ebook)
Subjects: LCSH: Computer crimes—Investigation. | Digital forensic science.
Classification: LCC HV8079.C65 D535 2025 (print) | LCC HV8079.C65 (ebook) | DDC 363.25/2—dc23/eng/20240517
LC record available at https://lccn.loc.gov/2024020918
LC ebook record available at https://lccn.loc.gov/2024020919

ISBN: 978-1-032-07539-6 (hbk)
ISBN: 978-1-032-07541-9 (pbk)
ISBN: 978-1-003-20757-3 (ebk)

DOI: 10.1201/9781003207573

Typeset in Sabon
by Apex CoVantage, LLC

Contents

Preface

In the dynamic field of digital forensics and cybercrime investigation, continuous advancement and adaptation are not just beneficial but necessary. *Digital Forensics and Cyber Crime Investigation: Recent Advances and Future Directions* aims to bridge the gap between the current state of knowledge and ongoing developments in this rapidly evolving field. This book is a compilation of in-depth research and insights from experts, structured into chapters that each tackle a specific aspect of digital forensics and cyber security.

- **Chapter 1: Secure Web Applications Based on Moving Target Defense** This chapter delves into the concept of Moving Target Defense (MTD) as a strategy to secure web applications. It discusses the challenges and solutions, offering a perspective on the new trends shaping the future of web security.
- **Chapter 2: Blockchain-Based Data Security in Smart Cities** Focusing on smart city infrastructures, this chapter explores how blockchain technology can be leveraged to enhance data security and trustworthiness, ensuring the integrity and reliability of urban digital systems.
- **Chapter 3: Recent Advances in Digital Forensics and Cybercrime Investigation** A comprehensive overview of the latest advancements in the field, this chapter provides insights into the evolving techniques and methodologies in digital forensics and cybercrime investigation.
- **Chapter 4: Detailed Evolution Process of CNN-Based Intrusion Detection in the Context of Network Security** Here, the focus is on the development and application of Convolutional Neural Networks (CNN) in intrusion detection systems, highlighting their significance in the context of network security.
- **Chapter 5: Crime Scene Investigations through Augmented Reality** Augmented Reality (AR) is revolutionizing crime scene investigations. This chapter discusses the recent advances in AR technology and its future directions in forensic science.
- **Chapter 6: Chaotic Watermarking for Tamper Detection** The chapter introduces the concept of chaotic watermarking as a method for tamper detection in digital multimedia, emphasizing its role in enhancing the robustness and security of digital content.
- **Chapter 7: Secure Health Features: Implementing Hyperledger Fabric in Blockchain-Driven Healthcare Management Systems** This chapter addresses the implementation of Hyperledger Fabric in blockchain-driven healthcare systems, focusing on the security features and benefits it brings to health data management.
- **Chapter 8: Security Threats and Countermeasures for Digital Images in Smart Systems** An exploration of the security challenges associated with digital images in smart systems, this chapter outlines the potential threats and the countermeasures necessary to safeguard digital imagery.

- **Chapter 9: Deep Learning Model for Digital Forensics Face Sketch Synthesis** This chapter discusses the application of deep learning models in the synthesis of forensic face sketches, a tool that has significant implications in criminal investigations.
- **Chapter 10: Forgery Detection Based on Deep Learning for Smart Systems** Focusing on forgery detection in smart systems, this chapter explores the application of deep learning techniques, discussing recent advances and the importance of dataset collection.
- **Chapter 11: Deep Learning-Based Forensics and Anti-Forensics** A dual perspective on the use of deep learning in both forensic analysis and anti-forensic techniques, highlighting the ongoing arms race in digital forensics.
- **Chapter 12: Cyber Synergy: Unlocking the Potential Use of Biometric Systems and Multimedia Forensics** The final chapter delves into the potential of combining biometric systems with multimedia forensics in cybercrime investigations, providing a futuristic view of cyber synergy.

Each chapter in this book is not only a window into the current state of affairs in digital forensics and cyber security but also a lens focusing on future possibilities. Our aim is to provide a comprehensive resource for practitioners, researchers, and students in the field, contributing to the ongoing discourse and development in digital forensics and cyber-crime investigation.

Acknowledgments

We would like to extend our profound gratitude to everyone who played a pivotal role in creating *Digital Forensics and Cyber Crime Investigation: Recent Advances and Future Directions*. These individuals' collective wisdom, invaluable insights, and unwavering dedication have been instrumental in shaping this comprehensive volume.

First and foremost, our heartfelt thanks go to the authors and reviewers of each chapter. Their profound expertise, meticulous reviews, and dedicated efforts have been the cornerstone of this work, imbuing it with depth and substance. This book would have lacked its rich content and critical perspectives without their contribution.

We are also immensely thankful to the staff at CRC Press. Their consistent encouragement, persistent assistance, and tireless support have been crucial in navigating the complexities of publishing. Their technical expertise and professional guidance have been invaluable in bringing this project to fruition.

A special acknowledgment goes to our families, who have provided us with an endless reservoir of love, unwavering support, and constant prayers. Their presence has been a source of strength and inspiration in the creation of this book and in all aspects of our lives.

Finally, we extend our deepest appreciation to the Almighty, who has given us the courage and resilience to face life's challenges and complete this significant work. We are forever grateful for the strength and wisdom granted to us throughout this journey.

Editors

Dr. Ahmed A. Abd El-Latif (SMIEEE, MACM) is an associate professor of computer science at Menoufia University, Egypt, and at EIAS Data Science Lab, College of Computer and Information Sciences, Prince Sultan University, Saudi Arabia. He received the BSc degree with honor rank in mathematics and computer science in 2005 and MSc degree in computer science in 2010, both from Menoufia University, Egypt. He received his PhD in computer science & technology at Harbin Institute of Technology (H.I.T), Harbin, P. R. China in 2013. He is an associate professor of computer science at Menoufia University, Egypt, and at EIAS Data Science Lab, College of Computer and Information Sciences, Prince Sultan University, Saudi Arabia. In more than 17 years of his professional experience, he has published more than 280 papers in journals/conferences, including 14 books, with more than 10,000 citations. He was also selected in the 2023, 2022, 2021, and 2020 Stanford University's ranking of the world's top 2% of scientists. He is involved in government and internationally funded R&D projects related to the widespread use of artificial intelligence for 5G/6G networks. He received many awards, including the State Encouragement Award in Engineering Sciences 2016, Arab Republic of Egypt; the best Ph.D. Student award from Harbin Institute of Technology, China 2013; Young Scientific award, Menoufia University, Egypt 2014. He is a fellow at the Academy of Scientific Research and Technology, Egypt. His areas of interest are cybersecurity, 5G/6G wireless networks, post-quantum cryptography, artificial intelligence of things, AI-based image processing, information hiding, dynamical systems (Discrete-time models: Chaotic systems and Quantum Walks). He is the leader of the mega-grant program "Research of Network Technologies with Ultra-Low Latency and Ultra-High Density Based on the Widespread Use of Artificial Intelligence for 6G Networks". Dr. Abd El-Latif is the chair/co-chair of many Scopus/EI conferences. He is the EIC of the *International Journal of Information Security and Privacy* and series editor of *Advances in Cybersecurity Management* (https://www.routledge.com), as well as academic editor/ associate editor for a set of indexed journals (Scopus journals' quartile ranking).

Dr. Lo'ai Tawalbeh (IEEE SM) completed his PhD in electrical and computer Engineering from Oregon State University in 2004 and MSc in 2002 from the same university with GPA 4/4. Dr. Tawalbeh is currently an associate professor in the department of Computing and Cyber Security at Texas A&M University, San Antonio. Before that he was a visiting researcher at the University of California, Santa Barbara. Since 2005, he has taught/ developed more than 25 courses in different disciplines of computer engineering and science with a focus on cyber security for the undergraduate/graduate programs at New York Institute of Technology (NYIT), DePaul University, and Jordan University of Science and Technology. Dr. Tawalbeh won many research grants and awards worth more than $2 million. He has more than 80 research publications in refereed international journals and conferences.

Dr. Manoranjan Mohanty has a PhD in soil science from the University of Queensland, Australia. He has a specialization in crop growth simulation and soil carbon modeling in agricultural systems. With a masters degree in agricultural sciences, specialization in soil science and agricultural chemistry from the ICAR-Indian Agricultural Research Institute, Dr. Mohanty began his career as a scientist in 1999 at the ICAR-Indian Institute of Soil Science, Bhopal in soil science, soil physics, and soil and water conservation under the Ministry of Agriculture and Farmers' Welfare. Dr. Mohanty was instrumental in developing and implementing various projects with national and international bodies and organizations.

Dr. Brij B. Gupta is Director of the International Center for AI and Cyber Security Research, Incubation and Innovations, and Full Professor with the Department of Computer Science and Information Engineering (CSIE), Asia University, Taiwan. In more than 17 years of his professional experience, he has published more than 500 papers in journals/conferences, including 35 books and 10 patents with more than 20000 citations. He has received numerous national and international awards including the Canadian Commonwealth Scholarship (2009), Faculty Research Fellowship Award (2017), MeitY, GoI, IEEE GCCE outstanding and WIE Paper awards and Best Faculty Award (2018 & 2019), NIT KKR, respectively. Dr. Gupta was recently selected for the 2022 Clarivate Web of Science Highly Cited Researchers in Computer Science. He was also selected in the 2022, 2021 and 2020 Stanford University's ranking of the world's top 2% of scientists. He is also a visiting/adjunct professor with several universities worldwide. He is also an IEEE Senior Member (2017) and was selected as 2021 Distinguished Lecturer in IEEE CTSoc. Dr. Gupta is also serving as Member-in-Large, Board of Governors, IEEE Consumer Technology Society (2022–2024). Dr. Gupta is also leading IJSWIS, IJSSCI, STE and IJCAC as Editor-in-Chief. Moreover, he is serving as lead editor of a book series with CRC and IET Press. He also served as TPC members in more than 150 international conferences, as well as serving as associate/guest editor of various journals and transactions. His research interests include information security, cyber physical systems, cloud computing, blockchain technologies, intrusion detection, AI, social media, and networking.

Dr. Konstantinos E. Psannis was born and raised in Thessaloniki, Greece. He is a professor of communication systems and networking in the department of Applied Informatics, School of Information Sciences, University of Macedonia, Greece; director of Mobility2net Research & Development & Consulting JP-EU Lab; member of the EU-JAPAN Centre for Industrial Cooperation and Visiting Consultant Professor, Graduate School of Engineering, Nagoya Institute of Technology, Nagoya 466-8555, Japan. Konstantinos received a degree in physics, Faculty of Sciences, from Aristotle University of Thessaloniki, Greece, and a PhD degree from the School of Engineering and Design, Department of Electronic and Computer Engineering of Brunel University, London, UK. Konstantinos was awarded the British Chevening Scholarship. The Chevening Scholarships are the UK government's global scholarship program, funded by the Foreign and Commonwealth Office (FCO) and partner organizations. The program makes awards to outstanding scholars with leadership potential from around the world to study at universities in the UK.

Dr. Psannis' research spans a wide range of Digital Media Communications, media coding/synchronization and transport over a variety of networks, both from the theoretical as well as the practical points of view. His recent work has been directed toward the demanding digital signals and systems problems arising from the various areas of 6G-enabled-ubiquitous Big Data/AI-IoT/Clouds/Digital Twins/AI-Predictive analytics and communications. This work is supported by research grants and contracts from various government organizations. Dr. Psannis has participated in joint research works funded by Grant-in-Aid for Scientific Research, Japan Society for the Promotion of Science (JSPS), KAKENHI Grant, The Telecommunications Advancement Foundation, and the International Information Science Foundation as a Principal Investigator and Visiting Consultant Professor at Nagoya Institute of Technology, Japan. Konstantinos E. Psannis was invited to speak on the EU-Japan Co-ordinated Call Preparatory meeting, Green & Content Centric Networking (CCN), organized by European Commission (EC) and National Institute of Information and Communications Technology (NICT)/ Ministry of Internal Affairs and Communications (MIC), Japan (in the context of the upcoming ICT Work Programme 2013) and International Telecommunication Union. (ITU-founded in 1865), SG13 meeting on DAN/CCN, Berlin, July 2012, amongst other invited speakers. Konstantinos received a joint-research Award from the Institute of Electronics, Information and Communication Engineers, Japan, Technical Committee on Communication Quality, July 2009, and joint-research Encouraging Prize from the IEICE Technical Committee on Communication Systems (CS), July 2011. Dr. Psannis has more than 90 publications in international scientific journals and more than 110 publications in international conferences, 23 book chapters, 25 editorial-special issues, 11 technical reports and received more than 5900 citations (h-index 31, i10-index 71). He has several highly cited papers powered by Web of Science—Clarivate. Dr. Psannis supervises four post-doc students, 12 PhD students and more than 250 M.Sc. Theses.

Contributors

Novi Susatediyo Adi
Marine Research Center
Ministry of Marine Affairs and
  Fisheries
Indonesia

Saksham Arora
CSE Department
Chandigarh College of Engineering and
  Technology
Chandigarh, India

Varsha Arya
Department of Business Administration
Asia University
Taiwan

Ayushi
CSE Department
Chandigarh College of Engineering and
  Technology
Chandigarh, India

Ritika Bansal
Insights2Techinfo
India

Eshita Badwa
CSE Department
Chandigarh College of Engineering and
  Technology
Chandigarh, India

Shavi Bansal
Insights2Techinfo
India

Vanshika Bhardwaj
Chandigarh College of Engineering and
  Technology
Chandigarh, India

Totok Ruki Biyanto
Institut Teknologi Sepuluh
  Nopember
Indonesia

Amit Chhabra
Chandigarh College of Engineering and
  Technology
Chandigarh, India

Vanshika Chilkoti
CSE Department
Chandigarh College of Engineering and
  Technology
Chandigarh, India

Kwok Tai Chui
Hong Kong Metropolitan University
  (HKMU)
Hong Kong

Francesco Colace
University of Salerno
Italy

Gerry Firmansyah
Department of Computer Science
Esa Unggul University of
  Jakarta
Indonesia

Akshat Gaurav
Ronin Institute
Montclair
New Jersey, USA

Sahil Garg
CSE Department
Chandigarh College of Engineering and
  Technology,
Chandigarh, India

Brij B. Gupta
Asia University
Taiwan

Harkiran Kaur
Chandigarh College of Engineering and
   Technology
Chandigarh, India

Sudhakar Kumar
Chandigarh College of Engineering and
   Technology
Chandigarh, India

Chun Yuan Lin
Department of Computer Science and
   Information Engineering,
Asia University
Taiwan

Anupama Mishra
Computer Science & Engineering,
   Himalayan School of Science &
   Technology
Swami Rama Himalayan University
Dehradun, India

Kshitij Mishra
cybercrypticworld
India

Prayitno
Politeknik Elektronika Negeri Surabaya
Indonesia

Priyanshu
CSE Department, Chandigarh College of
   Engineering and Technology
Chandigarh, India

Princy Pappachan
Asia University
Taiwan

Mosiur Rahaman
Department of Computer Science and
   Information Engineering
Asia University
Taiwan

Ikbal Rachmat
Department of Communication Science
Esa Unggul University
Jakarta, Indonesia

Ritika Saini
Chandigarh College of Engineering and
   Technology
Chandigarh, India

Domenico Santaniello
University of Salerno
Italy

Sunil Kr Sharma
Indian Railway
Kolkata, India

Amanpreet Singh
Chandigarh College of Engineering and
   Technology
Chandigarh, India

Gurmehar Singh
Chandigarh College of Engineering and
   Technology
Chandigarh, India

Sunil K. Singh
Chandigarh College of Engineering and
   Technology
Chandigarh, India

Krishana Singla
CSE Department
Chandigarh College of Engineering and
   Technology
Chandigarh, India

Sreerakuvandana
Department of AI-ML and Cyber Security
Jain University
Bangalore, India

Ruchika Thakur
CSE Department
Chandigarh College of Engineering and
   Technology
Chandigarh, India

Agung Mulyo Widodo
Universitas Esa Unggul
Indonesia

Yuvraj
Chandigarh College of Engineering and
   Technology
Chandigarh, India

Chapter 1

Secure Web Applications Based on Moving Target Defense

Challenges, Solutions, and New Trends

Anupama Mishra, Brij B. Gupta, Domenico Santaniello, and Kshitij Mishra

1. INTRODUCTION

In the current digital environment, the exponential growth of web applications has fundamentally altered the manner in which organizations, enterprises, and individuals connect with the virtual world, discussed by authors Albanese et al. (2018). Web applications, including e-commerce platforms and social networking sites, have become indispensable components of our everyday existence. Nevertheless, as per author Li et al. (2022), the growing dependence on web applications has rendered them highly susceptible to exploitation by cybercriminals and threat actors who intend to introduce malicious content. Figure 1.1 presents the number of attacks by country, which shows the severity of the cyber security threat.

Also, the threat landscape for web applications is continuously evolving, with new attack vectors, tactics, and threat actors emerging that include:

Advanced Persistent Threats (APTs): As per authors Ren et al. (2023) and Sharma et al. (2023), APTs are becoming more sophisticated, utilizing custom malware and targeted attacks against high-value web applications. These threats may require more advanced MTD strategies. APTs are highly experienced and well-resourced adversaries that launch intelligent attacks. These attacks can take months or even years to organize and carry out, and they are frequently directed at certain companies or people. APTs frequently have several stages, and the attackers employ a range of methods, such as malware, social engineering, and zero-day exploits to obtain access to their targets.

AI-Enhanced Attacks: As per authors (Cho et al., 2020; Roy et al., 2019), the latest statistics (2023):

Threat actors are incorporating artificial intelligence and machine learning into their attacks, making them more adaptive and difficult to detect. Web applications will need AI-based MTD solutions to counter these threats. Attacks fueled by artificial intelligence provide a serious risk to businesses of all sizes because of their capacity to:

Automate repetitive work: Artificial intelligence can automate time-consuming chores like scanning for vulnerabilities, exploiting holes, and spreading malware. This enables attackers to focus on more strategic areas of their operations, which in turn frees up more time for them (Martin et al., 2021; Sengupta et al., 2017).

Enhance decision-making: Artificial intelligence systems are able to evaluate huge volumes of data in order to detect patterns, correlations, and abnormalities. This enables attackers to make informed judgments regarding their targets, attack paths, and resource allocation.

Personalize attacks: Artificial intelligence can adapt attacks to specific targets by evaluating their networks, user behavior, and security posture, which significantly increases the likelihood that the attack will be successful.

DOI: 10.1201/9781003207573-1

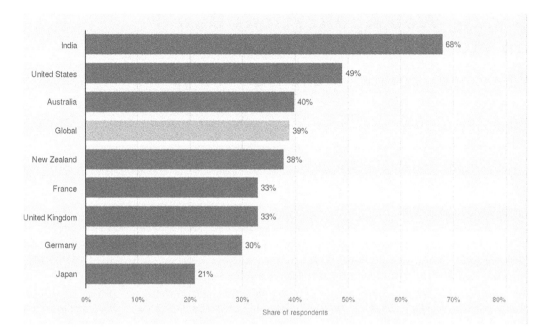

Figure 1.1 Number of attacks by country

Elude detection: Artificial intelligence is able to modify its behavior in real time based on the feedback it receives, which makes it more difficult for traditional security systems to identify and stop attacks.

Exploit vulnerabilities in emerging technologies: It is possible to employ artificial intelligence to devise new attack tactics and to exploit holes in developing technologies, such as cloud computing, Internet of Things devices, and even AI-powered systems. These vulnerabilities can be exploited by using AI.

Supply Chain Attacks: As per authors Wolff et al. (2021): A supply chain attack is a type of cyberattack directed at a company or organization by compromising a third-party vendor or supplier that has access to the target's systems or data. This can be performed in a few different ways: by inserting malicious code into software or hardware; by gaining access to the network of the provider and utilizing that network to conduct an attack on the target; or by hacking into the network of the third party. One more possibility is to directly enter the network of the target in order to access it. Attacks against the supply chain are growing more common as firms become more dependent on external vendors and suppliers. Because these attacks generally make use of flaws in the systems or software provided by the supplier that the victim is typically ignorant of, it can be extremely difficult to recognize and prevent them from occurring.

A huge attack on the supply chain that took place when SolarWinds was targeted in 2020. During this particular cyberattack, cybercriminals were successful in breaking into Solar-Winds' software supply chain. Software for management of information technology is provided by SolarWinds to a diverse range of customers, including the federal government of the United States. The hackers implanted malicious code into the popular network monitoring tool SolarWinds Orion, and SolarWinds' customers were given access to the compromised version of the application. SolarWinds Orion is widely used in the industry. The cybercriminals were able to break into the networks of SolarWinds' customers, which included the networks of the Department of State, the Department of Homeland Security, and the National Security Agency of the United States of America.

The NotPetya malware was responsible for carrying out one of the most major cyberattacks ever launched against a supply chain in the year 2017. Their targets were businesses and organizations located all over the world. NotPetya was designed to spread itself throughout supply chains, and it was successful in accomplishing this goal. As a result, it was able to infect a wide variety of enterprises, including governmental agencies, medical facilities, and financial institutions. Damages totaling billions of dollars and operations in every region of the world were hampered as a direct effect of the strike.

Zero-Day Exploits: The term "zero-day exploits" refers to a specific kind of cyberattack that makes use of a software vulnerability that is not known either to the developer of the product or to the vendors of antivirus software. This indicates that the vendor has zero days' notice to repair the vulnerability, and that means that attackers can use it to get access to susceptible systems before the company has the opportunity to correct it.

Because defenders have no means to learn about or fight against zero-day attacks until after they have been utilized, combating these types of cyberthreats is one of the most challenging aspects. As a result, zero-day attacks are extremely useful for stealing data, installing malware, or interrupting operations. An attack using a zero-day vulnerability will likely require the following steps:

Discovery refers to the process by which attackers unearth a vulnerability in software that has not previously been reported to the software manufacturer or to antivirus software vendors.

The next step in the process is known as exploiting, and it involves attackers developing a piece of code that takes advantage of the vulnerability.

Attackers generally send phishing emails, engage in social engineering, or attack other vulnerabilities in order to deliver the exploit to the target machine.

The target system is compromised when the exploit is put into action, which grants the attackers access to the compromised system.

Exfiltration occurs when an adversary removes data, installs malicious software, or disrupts business processes.

There are many different variations of zero-day exploits; however, the following are some of the most common examples:

SQL Injection is a type of exploit that occurs when a program improperly sanitizes user-supplied data before inserting it into a SQL query. This can leave the application vulnerable to attacks. This opens the door for attackers to include malicious code the query, which then gives the database the ability to carry out the attack.

Cross-Site Scripting, sometimes known as XSS, refers to a class of vulnerabilities that arise when an online application fails to adequately escape user-supplied input. This might give attackers the ability to insert malicious JavaScript code into the web page, which would then allow the malware to be run by the user's browser.

Future attacks discussed by authors Yamin et al. (2021) may exploit unknown vulnerabilities (zero-days) that do not have patches or signatures. Because Web applications frequently process sensitive user information, financial transactions, and valuable intellectual property, security is an absolute necessity. Traditional security measures, such as firewalls and intrusion detection systems, have proved insufficient in addressing the evolving nature of web-based threats.

Moving Target Defense (MTD) is a dynamic cybersecurity strategy that aims to increase the cost and complexity of cyberattacks by continually changing the attack surface and system parameters. As per author Sengupta et al. (2020), this approach challenges the predictability of attackers, making it harder for them to exploit vulnerabilities and gain unauthorized access. MTD encompasses a range of techniques and practices to achieve dynamic security,

Table 1.1 Moving target defense timeline

Year	Milestone	Description
2000	Concept introduced	The concept of moving target defense (MTD) is introduced as a new approach to cybersecurity.
2005	Early R&D	Initial research and development efforts begin to explore the feasibility and potential of MTD.
2010	Gaining traction	MTD starts to gain traction in the cybersecurity community as organizations recognize its potential benefits.
2015	Vendors emerge	Commercial vendors begin to offer MTD solutions, making the technology more accessible to organizations.
2020	Mainstream adoption	MTD adoption accelerates as organizations seek to improve their security posture.
2023	Continuous evolution	MTD continues to evolve with new techniques and technologies to address the ever-changing cybersecurity landscape.

and it can be particularly valuable in the context of web application security. Table 1.1 presents a timeline of the developments in this area.

1.1 Motivation

This chapter investigates modern web application safety strategies. A new cybersecurity paradigm aims to undermine an attacker's advantage over a system by altering its attack surface. Figure 1.2 presents the number of cyberattacks in different areas. This strategy increases the level of uncertainty that possible attackers face, which makes it more difficult for them to locate and exploit weaknesses. MTD principles are the reason for motivation, which includes:

Dynamic Infrastructure: MTD involves altering the infrastructure of a system, including server configurations, network settings, and service locations. This dynamic infrastructure introduces uncertainty and variability to the attacker, as the system's structure is continually changing.

Component Rotation: Key components such as IP addresses, encryption keys, and server-side technologies are frequently rotated. This rotation strategy ensures that even if attackers discover one component, it will become invalid shortly afterward, disrupting their efforts.

Adaptive Access Control: MTD incorporates adaptive access controls that continuously assess user behavior and adapt permissions and privileges in real time. This enables the system to respond to anomalies and potential threats effectively.

If we apply the ideas of MTD to web applications, we may be able to address the security issues with a solution for web applications.

1.2 Scope of the Chapter

The chapter will explain MTD's dynamic web application architecture, including dynamic infrastructure, component rotation, and adaptive access control. Scalability, performance overhead, administrative complexity, and legacy system compatibility issues while adopting MTD for online applications will be discussed. This chapter covers MTD web application security best practices, including continuous monitoring, threat intelligence integration, automation, and user and entity behavior analytics.

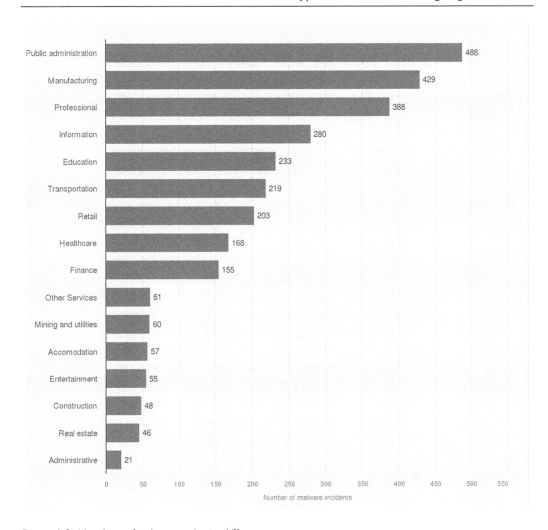

Figure 1.2 Number of cyberattacks in different areas

2. APPLICABILITY TO WEB APPLICATIONS

The implementation of MTD principles can effectively increase the security of online applications by overcoming the inherent issues associated with their static nature. Figure 1.3 presents the components of MTD. As per authors Mercado-Velázquez et al. (2021), the potential utility of MTD in the context of online applications encompasses:

Dynamic Web Application Architecture: This refers to the design approach employed in the development of web applications, wherein the server configurations, databases, and application components undergo frequent modifications. This architectural framework allows adaptability and flexibility, enabling seamless adjustments to the underlying infrastructure and software components as required. By embracing a dynamic architecture, organizations can effectively accommodate evolving business needs and technological advancements, ensuring the optimal performance and robustness of their web applications. The implementation of this strategy effectively disrupts the established patterns that are commonly

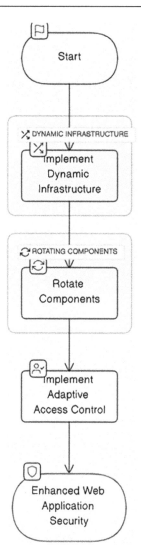

Figure 1.3 Components of MTD

exploited by attackers, thereby significantly increasing the difficulty for them to leverage known vulnerabilities.

Rotating Components: Within the field of web applications, the term "Moving Target Defense" (MTD) refers to the practice of periodically altering important pieces such as IP addresses, session tokens, encryption keys, and database credentials. MTD is an acronym for "Moving Target Defense: Web Applications." The incorporation of a rotation mechanism is an essential component of a security system because of the significant impact reduction it affords if the system is compromised by adversarial actors. The rotation mechanism efficiently slows the progression of attackers by rendering any compromised piece obsolete as quickly as possible. This contributes to an improvement in the overall security posture of the system.

Adaptive Access Control: This is an essential component of the safety of web applications. Web applications can effectively monitor user activity in real time by utilizing systems for adaptive access control. These techniques are intended to identify any anomalies or suspicious activity that may point to the existence of possible security risks (Zhang et al., 2023). The basic purpose of adaptive access control is to automatically modify access credentials in response to observed patterns of behavior on the part of users. This method ensures that users are provided with appropriate levels of access based on their actions and activities within the application by considering their history of previous interactions. Adaptive access control systems can detect any departures from typical patterns thanks to continuous monitoring of user activity. This could include unusual login times, access attempts from unfamiliar locations, or abnormal data access patterns. By detecting these anomalies, the system can take immediate action to mitigate potential risks. Upon detecting an anomaly, adaptive access control mechanisms can respond by either temporarily restricting access privileges or triggering additional authentication measures to verify the user's identity. These measures may include multi-factor authentication or challenge-response mechanisms. Dynamic access control is a robust security measure that effectively mitigates unauthorized actions and proactively adjusts to emerging threats (Kanellopoulos et al., 2019).

Applying Moving Target Defense principles to web application security offers several notable benefits, as presented in Figure 1.4:

- **Increased Resilience:** By continuously shifting the attack surface, MTD strengthens the resistance of web applications against malicious hacking attempts. Attackers have to deal with a constantly changing environment, which makes it difficult for them to organize and carry out attacks.
- **Reduced Attack Surface:** The vulnerability of web applications can be reduced by changing the infrastructure dynamically and rotating the components that make up the program. As a result, this narrows the window of opportunity for attackers to take advantage of vulnerabilities.
- **Enhanced Detection and Response:** The ability to more quickly detect harmful behavior can be achieved through the use of adaptive access control and continuous monitoring. In turn, this leads to speedier response times, which in turn helps mitigate possible dangers before they cause a major impact.
- **Improved Security Posture:** Not only does MTD make it difficult for attackers to be successful, but it also makes it abundantly evident that the business places a high priority on maintaining its security. This preventative stance has the potential to discourage would-be attackers and improve the security posture overall.
- **Compliance and Regulatory Alignment:** MTD practices can be brought into alignment with compliance standards if they demonstrate a commitment to security and a dynamic defensive plan, both of which are frequently anticipated by regulatory authorities as a necessity.

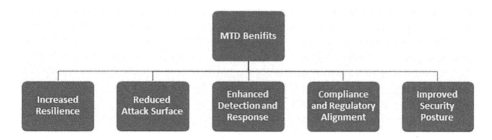

Figure 1.4 MTD benefits

3. IMPLEMENTING MTD IN WEB APPLICATIONS

The establishment of a dynamic architecture is required in order to implement Moving Target Defense (MTD) in online applications. This type of design has the potential to effectively disrupt the predictability of attackers and improve security. Because of its dynamic architecture, the web application is subject to regular modifications and adaptations in a variety of elements, which makes it a difficult target for those who wish to cause harm to it.

3.1 Dynamic Infrastructure

The establishment of a dynamic infrastructure is an essential component of MTD, which is utilized in online applications. This procedure involves making constant adjustments to the core configurations of the servers, as well as the settings of the networks and the placements of the various service components. When a dynamic infrastructure is put into place, there is a degree of unpredictability and volatility that is introduced; as a result, potential attackers face obstacles in their efforts to establish a strong position. In this chapter, the strategies that may be used to achieve dynamic infrastructure in web applications are discussed.

Server Rotation: This prevents attackers from taking advantage of static server settings for an extended length of time by requiring regular rotation of web servers and their configurations.

Load Balancing: These methods are utilized so that requests from users are dynamically distributed across a number of different servers. This approach successfully reduces the risk of having a single point of failure and adds another layer of complexity for potential attackers to deal with.

Content Delivery Networks (CDNs): One of the factors contributing to the growing unpredictability of the architecture of a web application is the distribution of content. Content Delivery Networks, often known as CDNs, can efficiently send network traffic toward multiple servers that have been strategically placed in a variety of geographical regions.

Cloud-Based Resources: When cloud services are used, scalability can be increased effectively, resources can be distributed in a flexible manner, and new server instances can be quickly deployed in response to changing demand.

3.2 Rotating Components

Component rotation is a fundamental notion of MTD, and it applies specifically to the context of online applications. Important parts of the system, like IP addresses, encryption keys, session tokens, and database credentials, are periodically changed so that known attack avenues are rendered ineffective. With this method, it is guaranteed that even if an adversary manages to corrupt a specific component, that element will become obsolete within a short amount of time. The following techniques might be utilized in order to rotate the components:

   IP Address Rotation: Changing the IP addresses of web servers and database servers at regular intervals makes it difficult for attackers to establish persistence in the network. This is accomplished using a technique known as IP Address Rotation.

   Renewal of Session Tokens: Introducing an element of unpredictability into user sessions and lowering the efficiency of session hijacking attacks can be accomplished by renewing session tokens for users at certain intervals or when particular events take place.

Rotating Encryption Keys: The practice of rotating encryption keys for data both while it is in transit and while it is at rest ensures that even if an adversary is successful in obtaining an older key, they will not be able to decipher the most recent data.

Database Credential Rotation: Changing database access credentials on a regular basis can help prevent unauthorized users from gaining access to a database.

3.3 Adaptive Access Control

Adaptive access control mechanisms play a crucial role in implementing MTD for web applications (K. et al., 2023). These mechanisms continuously monitor user behavior, detect anomalies, and adjust access privileges in real time. By adapting access control dynamically, web applications can protect against unauthorized actions and adapt to emerging threats (Dahiya & Gupta, 2021). Some key aspects of adaptive access control include:

Behavioral Analysis: In MTD, the role of behavioral analysis is essential because it offers insights into the activity of the system and identifies irregularities that may point to the presence of potential dangers. MTD makes it difficult for attackers to establish a foothold and maintain persistence within the network.

Monitoring and analyzing a wide variety of data sources is required for behavioral analysis in MTD. These data sources include:

Network Traffic: Monitoring patterns of network traffic, including volume, protocol usage, and destination addresses, might indicate suspicious activity such as illegal access attempts or data exfiltration.

System Logs: Analyzing system logs, which include event logs, application logs, and error logs, can uncover odd behavior, such as unanticipated file access, unauthorized configuration changes, or aberrant process executions.

Monitoring Endpoint Activity: It includes user actions, application usage, and system resource consumption, and can detect suspicious behavior, such as unauthorized program installations, strange data access patterns, or aberrant system resource usage spikes.

Scanning for Vulnerabilities: Conducting vulnerability scans on a regular basis allows the identification of potential attack vectors that cybercriminals may exploit in order to obtain access to a system or execute malicious malware.

Threat Intelligence: Improving the detection of sophisticated attacks by incorporating threat intelligence data, such as known attack patterns, indications of compromise (IOCs), and threat actor tactics, methods, and procedures (TTPs), is possible. MTD systems can recognize patterns and anomalies by doing an analysis on this data. These patterns and anomalies may signal the presence of potential risks. After collecting this data, it is possible to use it to set off alarms, begin investigations, or immediately begin taking corrective steps.

Real-Time Alerts: Within MTD, real-time notifications serve a multitude of purposes and are an essential component in the process of strengthening cybersecurity protections. In the first place, they keep a watchful eye out for anything suspicious and make sure it's reported as soon as possible. This rapid notification gives security teams the ability to quickly analyze and respond, perhaps foiling attempts before they can cause significant damage. In addition, these warnings are invaluable tools for the prioritization of threats. They provide information that is contextual, which assists security staff in identifying the most pressing problems and devising solutions to those problems. These alerts have a wider range of applications than only security; for example, they can be used to monitor system performance and bring attention to performance abnormalities or problems. Because it is proactive, MTD systems may be maintained and optimized in a timely manner thanks to this feature. In conclusion, the study of alerts makes a substantial contribution to the collection of threat information. This analysis provides insights into the tactics, methods, and procedures (TTPs) used by attackers, which in turn enriches the overall understanding of the threat landscape. In their most basic form, real-time alerts in MTD serve the purpose of a dynamic and necessary component, which integrates without any hiccups into the more comprehensive cybersecurity architecture to improve both readiness and resilience.

User Profiling: Creating and maintaining profiles of individual users and the activity patterns they engage in is part of the process of user profiling in MTD. This information can be utilized to recognize abnormal patterns of behavior, which may point to the presence of a possible danger. In MTD, user profiling can be based on a wide variety of data sources, including the following:

Login Events: It is possible to uncover potentially malicious behavior by monitoring login events, which include timestamps, user IDs, and originating IP addresses.

Monitoring the Patterns of System Usage: This monitors patterns such as file access, application usage, and resource consumption and can detect aberrant activity such as illegal file alterations, strange data access patterns, or excessive resource utilization.

Monitoring Network Activity: Monitoring network activity, including traffic volume, protocol usage, and destination addresses, might show suspicious activities such as unauthorized data exfiltration or communication with known malicious IPs.

User Preferences: By analyzing user preferences, such as desktop configurations, software installs, and browser settings, one might spot deviations from usual behavior that may indicate a compromised account.

Access Policy Adjustments: Adaptive access control has the capability to modify user permissions in an automated fashion, thereby restricting access if suspicious activity is identified.

4. CHALLENGES IN IMPLEMENTING MTD FOR WEB APPLICATIONS

The implementation of Moving Target Defense (MTD) is an approach that has the potential to be beneficial for enhancing the safety of web services. The challenges are presented in Figure 1.5. However, the adoption of MTD is accompanied by a wide variety of challenges that must be overcome. The thorough analysis and successful resolution of these issues are required in order to ensure the successful deployment of MTD in the realm of online applications (Singh & Gupta, 2022).

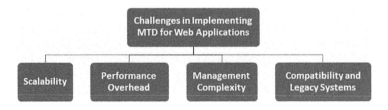

Figure 1.5 Challenges of MTD

4.1 Scalability

Scalability is one of the key issues that must be overcome when using MTD for online apps. It's possible for scalability-related complications to arise as a result of the dynamic architecture, component rotation, and adaptive access control techniques. In this sense, challenges include the following:

Resource Management: Because the infrastructure is in the process of dynamically changing, it is necessary to have efficient resource management in order to guarantee that there are adequate resources available to support the components that are either increasing or rotating.

Scalable Monitoring: Continuous monitoring and behavioral analysis of users and the application's components can produce a vast volume of data. This can be a challenge for scalable monitoring systems. It is crucial to have scalable solutions in place for the collection, analysis, and storage of this data.

Response to Traffic Spikes: When abrupt traffic spikes occur, web applications are required to dynamically scale their infrastructure in order to manage the additional load. This might put a strain on the resources that are already available.

4.2 Performance Overhead

The implementation of MTD may result in performance overhead, which may influence both the response times and the user experience provided by web apps (Bilge & Dumitraş, 2012). Among the most important aspects connected to performance are the following:

Latency: The introduction of latency can be caused by frequent changes in infrastructure and the rotation of components, as the requests made by users may need to be redirected or reauthenticated.

Utilization of Resources: There is a possibility that resources that are committed to security duties, such as continuous monitoring and behavior analysis, could drain resources away from program functionality, which could have an impact on performance.

Striking the Right Balance Between Robust Security and User Experience: It is essential to find the optimal balance between the user experience and robust security.

4.3 Management Complexity

Especially for large-scale web applications, the administration of MTD best practices can be a complicated process. Managing MTD for web applications presents a number of challenges, including the following per Nguyen and Debroy (2022):

Configuration Management: Frequent changes in infrastructure and component rotation necessitate painstaking configuration management in order to guarantee that these changes take place seamlessly and without causing any disruptions.

Updates to Security Policies: Both security policies and access controls should be continually updated and altered to meet changing threats. It can be difficult to ensure that these changes are in accordance with the security policies of the firm.

Monitoring and Analysis: In order to monitor and analyze the data efficiently, continuous monitoring and behavioral analysis both demand highly developed tools and staff with specialized knowledge.

4.4 Compatibility and Legacy Systems

Many web applications are built on existing frameworks and may depend on legacy systems. The following challenges can occur:

Legacy Infrastructure: There may be compatibility concerns with legacy systems and MTD since legacy systems do not always support the dynamic modifications and rotation that are required by MTD.

Integration Challenges: Because older systems and third-party services might not simply adapt to the dynamic security controls, integrating MTD practices can be a challenging and time-consuming endeavor.

Costs of Replacement: The process of upgrading or replacing legacy systems in order to enable MTD can be time-consuming and expensive, making it a considerable problem for enterprises that have a large amount of legacy infrastructure.

Addressing these challenges necessitates careful planning, resource allocation, and a deep understanding of the specific needs and constraints of the web application and the organization. Overcoming these obstacles is essential to effectively implement MTD for web applications and achieve the intended benefits in terms of enhanced security.

5. SOLUTIONS AND BEST PRACTICES

Implementing Moving Target Defense for web applications requires a combination of solutions and best practices to address the challenges and enhance security. The implementation of these strategies has the potential to greatly enhance the efficacy of MTD. Figure 1.6 depicts the type of solutions that are discussed here:

5.1 Continuous Monitoring

MTD entails the continuous monitoring and examination of various system elements, network data flow, user actions, and security incidents in real-time (Behera et al., 2023). Several important elements of continuous monitoring encompass:

Real-time Alerts: In order to generate notifications as quickly as possible in the event of potentially suspicious behaviors or security occurrences, real-time alerts should be established within the systems.

Behavioral Analysis: Continuous monitoring is a process that analyzes both the behavior of system components and the behavior of users on a continuous basis. Behavioral analysis can be performed on both user and component behavior. The method establishes

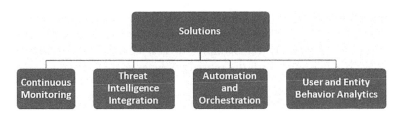

Figure 1.6 Type of solutions and adaptability

normative benchmarks for expected behavior and recognizes instances of behavior that deviate from these standards.

Log and Event Analysis: The constant collection, analysis, and correlation of log data and security event information is necessary in order to detect potential risks.

Incident Response: It is essential to enact a reliable incident response procedure in order to guarantee prompt and effective action in reaction to newly found hazards.

5.2 Threat Intelligence Integration

The incorporation of threat information into procedures related to Mitigation and Threat Detection is of the utmost importance to maintain a proactive stance against developing threats. Threat intelligence offers significant insights into contemporary attack methodologies, weaknesses, and malevolent entities. Per Gupta et al. (2020), the most effective strategies in this domain encompass:

Threat Feeds: Web applications may be helped in proactively modifying their defensive measures if they subscribe to threat intelligence feeds that provide up-to-date information regarding prevalent threats and vulnerabilities. These feeds can deliver this information in real time.

Intelligence Sharing: The practice of sharing intelligence comprises participating in joint endeavors and exchanging information with other members of the same industry, as well as members of cybersecurity communities and government agencies. The gathering of actionable threat intelligence can be significantly aided by this method.

Machine Learning and AI: In the context of threat intelligence analysis, the application of machine learning and artificial intelligence can be helpful in facilitating the detection and mitigation of emerging and dynamic risks.

5.3 Automation and Orchestration

The efficient and effective implementation of MTD relies heavily on the utilization of automation and orchestration. These methods provide prompt and synchronized reactions to identified dangers and alterations in the web application's surroundings. There are several important factors that need to be considered, including:

Automated Responses: By implementing automation, one can more easily support rapid responses to detected threats, such as the segregation of components that have been impacted or the adjustment of access rules.

Orchestration of Security Tools: Orchestration systems have the potential to improve the integration and coordination of various security technologies and procedures, leading to a reduction in the amount of time needed to provide a response.

Policy Enforcement: Automation and orchestration, which provides a consistent implementation of security regulations and allows for dynamic adaptability, can be used to fulfill the goal of enforcing security policies.

5.4 User and Entity Behavior Analytics

User and Entity Behavior Analytics (UEBA) plays a crucial role in the implementation of MTD strategies for web applications. The primary focus of UEBA is the comprehension of user and entity behavior, with the objective of detecting and characterizing abnormal actions. The implementation of UEBA can be optimized by following a set of recommended practices (Arya, 2023).

Baseline Establishment: The user's text is already academic in nature. The initial phase of establishing a baseline model. To enhance threat detection, it is essential to establish benchmarks for both regular user behavior and entity activity, which can serve as reference points for identifying any variations that may suggest potential security risks.

Anomaly Detection: The application of machine learning algorithms is employed to identify deviations from predefined baselines, hence facilitating the timely identification of potentially suspicious activity.

User Profiling: The concept of user profiling refers to the practice of gathering and analyzing data about individuals in order to gain insights into their characteristics and preferences.

Integration With Access Control: Integrate UEBA solutions with adaptive access control mechanisms to dynamically adjust permissions in response to identified anomalies.

It is imperative to integrate these solutions and optimal methodologies into the execution of MTD for online applications in order to provide a resilient and flexible security framework. Web applications may effectively protect against a constantly changing and developing threat environment by employing a range of strategies. These include ongoing monitoring, the integration of threat intelligence, the automation of reaction mechanisms, and the application of behavior analytics.

6. ADVANCED TECHNOLOGIES AND MTD

Advanced technologies will shape the future of MTD and web application security. These technologies include:

Artificial Intelligence (AI) and Machine Learning (ML): Within MTD, AI and ML will be utilized to improve threat detection and response in order to keep users safe. The behavior of users and systems will be continuously analyzed by AI algorithms to identify abnormalities and anticipate potential dangers.

Blockchain Technology: When used for web application security, blockchain has the potential to increase trust and data integrity while simultaneously minimizing the number of vulnerabilities that are caused by data tampering.

Quantum Computing: As quantum computing moves closer to being a practical reality, it can present a risk as well as an opportunity. Quantum computing can break currently used encryption algorithms, but it could also lead to the development of new cryptographic methods that improve the security of web applications.

IoT and Edge Computing: New entry points for malicious actors are created because of the growth of Internet of Things (IoT) devices and edge computing. To ensure the safety of the entire ecosystem, MTD will need to expand its coverage to include newly developing technologies (Fatemidokht et al., 2021; Gaurav et al., 2023; Rahman et al., 2022).

7. REGULATORY AND COMPLIANCE IMPLICATIONS

Regulatory and compliance requirements will continue to play a significant role in shaping web application security and MTD. Future trends in this area include:

Stricter Data Protection Regulations: It is anticipated that new and more stringent data protection legislation will arise, making it necessary for web applications to employ robust security measures, such as MTD, to secure sensitive user data.

Industry-Specific Compliance: There is a possibility that special compliance requirements relating to web application security will be introduced by various businesses. It will be necessary for organizations to connect their MTD strategy with the sector-specific rules.

Data Breach Reporting: It is possible that regulators will compel data breaches to be reported more quickly and transparently. MTD procedures have the ability to assist firms in more effectively detecting and responding to breaches, hence decreasing potential liabilities.

International Collaboration: It is possible that international cooperation on security standards and MTD best practices could result from efforts made on a global scale to address cyber threats.

8. CONCLUSION

This chapter discussed the crucial intersection between web application security and MTD. It emphasized web application problems, MTD principles, and MTD strategy implementation. Web apps are used to communicate with consumers, conduct business, and store sensitive data; therefore, protecting them is crucial. By adding dynamic aspects that make it difficult for attackers to exploit vulnerabilities and obtain unauthorized access, MTD may help solve web application security issues. Web applications are attractive targets for cyberattacks due to their static nature and easy attack paths. MTD is a dynamic cybersecurity method that makes web application security unpredictable and adaptable. Web applications using MTD require dynamic infrastructure, component rotation, and adaptive access control. Web application MTD implementation challenges include scalability, performance overhead, administration complexity, and legacy system compatibility. MTD adoption requires continuous monitoring, threat intelligence integration, automation, and UEBA. As we move forward, firms must remain aware of threats, use innovative technologies, and comply with regulations. By adopting MTD principles and best practices, enterprises may strengthen their web applications, improve security, and respond to changing cybersecurity threats. They'll be better equipped to defend against new threats and protect their digital assets, users, and data.

REFERENCES

Albanese, M., Jajodia, S., & Venkatesan, S. (2018). Defending from stealthy botnets using moving target defenses. *IEEE Security & Privacy*, 16(1), 92–97.

Arya, V. (2023). *Building Cyber-Resilient Communication Technologies: Strategies for Enhanced Security* (p. 1). Insights2Techinfo. https://insights2techinfo.com/building cyber-resilient-communication-technologies-strategies-for-enhanced-security/

Behera, T. K., Bakshi, S., Sa, P. K., Nappi, M., Castiglione, A., Vijayakumar, P., & Gupta, B. B. (2023). The NITRDrone dataset to address the challenges for road extraction from aerial images. *Journal of Signal Processing Systems*, 95(2–3), 197–209.

Bilge, L., & Dumitraş, T. (2012, October). Before we knew it: An empirical study of zero-day attacks in the real world. In *Proceedings of the 2012 ACM Conference on Computer and Communications Security* (pp. 833–844). Insights2TechInfo.

Cho, J. H., Sharma, D. P., Alavizadeh, H., Yoon, S., Ben-Asher, N., Moore, T. J., & Nelson, F. F. (2020). Toward proactive, adaptive defense: A survey on moving target defense. *IEEE Communications Surveys & Tutorials*, 22(1), 709–745.

Dahiya, A., & Gupta, B. B. (2021). A reputation score policy and Bayesian game theory based incentivized mechanism for DDoS attacks mitigation and cyber defense. *Future Generation Computer Systems*, 117, 193–204.

Fatemidokht, H., Rafsanjani, M. K., Gupta, B. B., & Hsu, C. H. (2021). Efficient and secure routing protocol based on artificial intelligence algorithms with UAV-assisted for vehicular ad hoc networks in intelligent transportation systems. *IEEE Transactions on Intelligent Transportation Systems*, 22(7), 4757–4769.

Gaurav, A., Gupta, B. B., & Panigrahi, P. K. (2023). A comprehensive survey on machine learning approaches for malware detection in IoT-based enterprise information system. *Enterprise Information Systems*, 17(3), 2023764.

Gupta, B. B., Perez, G. M., Agrawal, D. P., & Gupta, D. (2020). *Handbook of Computer Networks and Cyber Security* (Vol. 10, pp. 3–978). Springer.

Kanellopoulos, A., & Vamvoudakis, K. G. (2019). A moving target defense control framework for cyber-physical systems. *IEEE Transactions on Automatic Control*, 65(3), 1029–1043.

Li, S., Qin, D., Wu, X., Li, J., Li, B., & Han, W. (2022). False alert detection based on deep learning and machine learning. *International Journal on Semantic Web and Information Systems (IJSWIS)*, 18(1), 1–21.

Martin, P., Fan, J., Kim, T., Vesey, K., & Greenwald, L. (2021, November). Toward effective moving target defense against adversarial AI. In *MILCOM 2021–2021 IEEE Military Communications Conference (MILCOM)* (pp. 993–998). IEEE.

Mercado-Velázquez, A. A., Escamilla-Ambrosio, P. J., & Ortiz-Rodriguez, F. (2021). A moving target defense strategy for internet of things cybersecurity. *IEEE Access*, 9, 118406–118418.

Nguyen, M., & Debroy, S. (2022). Moving target defense-based denial-of-service mitigation in cloud environments: A survey. *Security and Communication Networks*, 2022.

Rahman, M. A., Mukta, M. Y., Asyhari, A. T., Moustafa, N., Patwary, M. N., Yousuf, A., & Gupta, B. B. (2022). Renewable energy re-distribution via multiscale IoT for 6G-oriented green highway management. *IEEE Transactions on Intelligent Transportation Systems*, 23(12), 23771–23780.

Ren, R., Fang, J., Hu, J., Ma, X., & Li, X. (2023). Risk assessment modeling of urban railway investment and financing based on improved SVM model for advanced intelligent systems. *International Journal on Semantic Web and Information Systems (IJSWIS)*, 19(1), 1–19.

Roy, A., Chhabra, A., Kamhoua, C. A., & Mohapatra, P. (2019, November). A moving target defense against adversarial machine learning. In *Proceedings of the 4th ACM/IEEE Symposium on Edge Computing* (pp. 383–388). Association for Computing Machinery.

Sengupta, S. (2017, May). Moving target defense: A symbiotic framework for AI & security. In *Proceedings of the 16th Conference on Autonomous Agents and MultiAgent Systems* (pp. 1861–1862). International Foundation for Autonomous Agents and Multiagent Systems.

Sengupta, S., Chowdhary, A., Sabur, A., Alshamrani, A., Huang, D., & Kambhampati, S. (2020). A survey of moving target defenses for network security. *IEEE Communications Surveys & Tutorials*, 22(3), 1909–1941.

Sharma, A., Gupta, B. B., Singh, A. K., & Saraswat, V. K. (2023). Advanced persistent threats (APT): evolution, anatomy, attribution and countermeasures. *Journal of Ambient Intelligence and Humanized Computing*, 1–27.

Singh, A., & Gupta, B. B. (2022). Distributed denial-of-service (DDoS) attacks and defense mechanisms in various web-enabled computing platforms: Issues, challenges, and future research directions. *International Journal on Semantic Web and Information Systems (IJSWIS)*, 18(1), 1–43.

Wolff, E. D., Growley, K. M., & Gruden, M. G. (2021). Navigating the solarwinds supply chain attack. *The Procurement Lawyer*, 56(2).

Yamin, M. M., Ullah, M., Ullah, H., & Katt, B. (2021). Weaponized AI for cyber attacks. *Journal of Information Security and Applications*, 57, 102722.

Zhang, T., Xu, C., Lian, Y., Tian, H., Kang, J., Kuang, X., & Niyato, D. (2023). When moving target defense meets attack prediction in digital twins: A convolutional and hierarchical reinforcement learning approach. *IEEE Journal on Selected Areas in Communications*, 41(10), 3293–3305.

Chapter 2

Blockchain-Based Data Security in Smart Cities

Ensuring Data Integrity and Trustworthiness

Priyanshu, Sunil K. Singh, Sudhakar Kumar, Sahil Garg, Saksham Arora, Sunil Kr Sharma, Varsha Arya, and Kwok Tai Chui

I. INTRODUCTION

1.1 Signifying Data Security in Smart Cities

The revolution of urban landscapes into smart cities has immensely impacted the collection, processing, and utilization of data[1] in this era of digital transformation. This chapter explores the crucial importance of data security within the intricate web of smart cities. It delves into the central role of data in enhancing urban efficiency, sustainability, and the overall quality of life, and sheds light on the driving forces behind this smart city revolution. Permeating the urban environment are myriad sensors, devices, and systems that generate diverse forms of data; all of which is vital for smart city operations. The significance of data security[2] becomes increasingly crucial as the volume and diversity of data continue to grow. Emphasizing the importance of preserving citizens' and stakeholders' trust, this section illuminates the complex obstacles and susceptibilities that come with this data-inundated terrain. These issues vary from cyberattacks to privacy violations and the possibility of data breaches. Furthermore, the chapter underscores the repercussions of sub-par data protection and stresses the significance of upholding both legal and moral commitments.

Within smart cities, blockchain technology is a promising solution for tackling data security challenges. Its decentralized, tamper-resistant ledger can provide transparency and improve data integrity and trustworthiness. This section is key in setting the stage for the exploration of these benefits to urban data. The section concludes by outlining the broader objectives of the chapter, guiding readers through the forthcoming sections that delve into the technical, operational, and strategic aspects of blockchain-based data security in the smart city context.

In essence, "Signifying Data Security in Smart Cities" serves as the gateway to understanding the intricate relationship between data security and the smart city evolution, emphasizing the critical role of maintaining data integrity and trustworthiness while introducing blockchain as a transformative solution in this dynamic landscape.

1.2 Scope and Focus of the Chapter

This chapter intricately delves into the complex interplay of blockchain technology and data security within the dynamic landscape of smart cities. The scope is comprehensive, commencing with a foundational exploration of data integrity—unveiling its essence and elucidating indispensable strategies for maintaining trustworthiness in the multifaceted smart city environment. The technical architecture[3] of blockchain takes center stage, providing an in-depth understanding of its core components, consensus mechanisms, and decentralized ledger architecture. The narrative unfolds the transformative potential of blockchain as a robust and immutable foundation for elevating data security within the distinctive

DOI: 10.1201/9781003207573-2

context of smart cities. Moving forward, the chapter meticulously explores the pivotal role of smart contracts—self-executing, code-based agreements—in safeguarding data security and integrity. Concurrently, it delves into various data governance models inherent within blockchain, adding layers of understanding to the governance structures that underpin data integrity. The narrative strategically advances the implementation of blockchain for data security in smart cities, offering nuanced insights into specific use cases tailored to urban infrastructures[4]. Practical considerations come to the forefront, addressing challenges and presenting innovative solutions that optimize data security while upholding critical facets of system performance, reliability, and scalability. Real-world case studies serve as tangible examples, reinforcing the transformative benefits of blockchain technology in reshaping the paradigm of data security in smart cities. The chapter concludes with a forward-looking perspective, anticipating emerging blockchain technologies, scalability enhancements, and the evolving landscape of data security. In essence, this technical compass guides computer science practitioners, researchers, and technology enthusiasts through the profound and intricate relationship between blockchain and data security, emphasizing the central role of blockchain in ensuring data integrity and trustworthiness within the intricate web of smart city ecosystems.

2. LITERATURE REVIEW

Blockchain's integration into smart city infrastructure has prompted a surge in research exploring its potential for ensuring data integrity, trustworthiness, and privacy within IoT environments. This section provides a comprehensive review of influential works that delve into blockchain-based solutions for securing data in smart cities. By examining various studies, frameworks, and initiatives, this review aims to provide critical insights and assess the contribution made toward fortifying data security and governance within the dynamic landscape of IoT-powered urban spaces.

Table 2.1 presents a selection of pivotal works in this domain, highlighting their main findings and nuances compared to our research. Each study presents distinctive perspectives on leveraging blockchain technology to address security, privacy, and data access control challenges. Analyzing these works provides a panoramic view of the evolving discourse on blockchain's role in fortifying the integrity and trustworthiness of data streams, explaining both advancements and challenges in existing research.

3. DATA INTEGRITY AND TRUSTWORTHINESS

3.1 The Essence of Data Integrity

Maintaining proper data accuracy, consistency, and reliability is the core idea behind data integrity, ensuring it remains unaffected by the passage of time. This serves as a critical component of several fields like information systems[11,12], data storage, and records. Table 2.2 shows the methods that are crucial for data integrity:

Maintaining and achieving data integrity is fundamental, particularly in regulated industries where verifiable, complete, and accurate data is a must-have at all times. By ensuring the accuracy, completeness, and quality of data over time and formats, your organization could save considerable time, effort, and money that would have been wasted if crucial decisions were based on incorrect or incomplete data. Investing in sufficient time and resources for data management strategies can offer a prominent competitive edge through clean and

Table 2.1 Literature review on blockchain-based data security in smart cities ensuring data integrity and trustworthiness

Authors	Year	Comparison to our chapter	Main findings
Rashid Ali [5]	2020	Aligns with our chapter's focus on data integrity and trustworthiness, though it lacks specific use cases demonstrating real-world application.	Introduces a blockchain-based framework aiming at trust establishment in IoT-based smart cities. It emphasizes secure data handling and proposes a system to ensure trustworthiness of IoT data.
Alexander A. Varfolomeev [6]	2020	Explores access control mechanisms but lacks detailed scalability aspects. Our chapter covers scalability enhancements and emerging technologies.	Proposes a blockchain framework for ensuring secure and reliable data access control within smart cities. Focuses on access rights management and integrity using blockchain technology.
Imran Makhdoom [7]	2019	Emphasizes privacy preservation but offers limited discussion on scalability and emerging technologies. Our chapter provides a more comprehensive view.	Presents PrivySharing, a blockchain-based framework addressing privacy concerns in sharing IoT data in smart cities. Introduces a multi-channel blockchain system for preserving data privacy and security.
Mohammad Saidur Rahman [8]	2022	Focuses on interoperability and data integrity but lacks discussion on data governance models compared to our chapter.	Proposes a hierarchical blockchain platform, Blockchain-of-Blockchains (BoBs), for ensuring data integrity and blockchain interoperability in smart cities. Addresses managing IoT data in smart city organizations and introduces a decentralized hierarchy of blockchains.
Driss el Majdoubi [9]	2020	Focuses on data privacy, but its discussion on scalability and emerging technologies is limited. Our chapter covers these aspects in greater depth.	Introduces "SmartPrivChain," a blockchain-based system aimed at preserving privacy and security within smart city environments. Focuses on data privacy through smart contracts and compliance with privacy laws like GDPR.
Sophocles Theodorou [10]	2019	Provides a broad overview but lacks detailed exploration into specific blockchain models or governance structures. Our chapter offers a more detailed analysis of various blockchain-based data security models and governance approaches.	Investigates the potential of blockchain-based systems to enhance security and privacy in smart cities. Explores blockchain and smart contracts for e-governance and examines existing e-residency models.

Table 2.2 Methods for data integrity

Methods	Description
Accuracy	Data must be free of errors and inconsistencies to ensure that it reflects reality and what is intended. Misinformation can lead to wrong decisions and actions.
Consistency	Data should be integrated and consistent, both within the dataset itself and between different datasets. Conflicts can be caused by duplicate data, inconsistent data, or incorrect data entry.
Reliability	Reliable information can be trusted to be accurate and reliable. It should be consistently available and accessible when needed.
Security	Data integrity includes safeguarding data from unauthorized access, modification, or deletion. Security measures like encryption and access controls help protect data from tampering or corruption.
Validation	Data validation processes check data for conformity to predefined rules or standards. Validation helps prevent the input of invalid or inconsistent data.
Following regulations	Some industries find themselves needing to follow regulations for data integrity practices. The people running these organizations must adhere to these rules in order to not receive any legal consequences or financial backlash.

healthy data. The Big Data era rewards organizations that employ data effectively and prioritize data integrity, enabling informed decision-making, better data quality, and prevention of data loss or corruption.

3.2 Ensuring Trustworthy Data in Smart Cities

Promoting transparency, protecting privacy, and maintaining the integrity of data-driven systems and services is crucial in smart cities. To ensure trustworthy data, consider the following strategies in Table 2.3:

Table 2.3 Strategies to ensure trustworthy data in smart cities

Strategies	Description
Data governance framework	Establishing a framework for data governance is crucial. A comprehensive approach should include defining policies and procedures and outlining responsibilities and expectations for managing data. The framework must ensure compliance with regulations and structured data handling.
Data security measures	Robust measures for safeguarding data are a must. Security audits at regular intervals, strict access controls, and encryption are all effective means to protect against breaches, banking threats,[13] cyber threats, and unauthorized access that compromise the confidentiality and integrity of sensitive data.
Data privacy protection	When it comes to protecting data privacy, it's important to gather only the necessary information, utilize anonymization and pseudonymization approaches, and gain informed consent before handling personal data. By incorporating these strategies, one can uphold the privacy of individuals and conform to privacy regulations.

(Continued)

Table 2.3 (Continued)

Strategies	Description
Data quality assurance	Establishing a framework for data quality assurance is paramount, but how do we get there? Processes for monitoring and validating data are key components to ensure data reliability, consistency, and accuracy. These aspects are vital to trustworthy information that decision-making relies upon.
Transparency and community engagement	Resident awareness of data practices is essential to maintaining transparency in data governance initiatives. Active community involvement and input should be encouraged to promote responsible access to data. Data collection, sharing, and usage also require continual dissemination of information to residents to build trust.

Smart cities require reliable data to thrive, making data integrity a top priority for smart cities. The connectivity of these cities and their reliance on innovative tech to optimize operations and citizen experiences means data security, privacy, and accuracy take on greater importance. To establish confidence with all invested parties, thorough data management practices, cybersecurity measures, and governance frameworks must be in place. Selecting the optimal data center is also crucial.[14] To pave the way for their long-term success, smart cities require the cooperation of various entities such as governments, private sectors, and the community.[15] The key to tackling the hurdles linked with data integrity and privacy is forming a comprehensive plan that entails ethical data practices, efficient communication,[16] and state-of-the-art technologies. Not only can smart cities unlock the full potential of data-driven innovations, but they can also foster trust as a crucial foundation through these strategies.

4. ROLE OF BLOCKCHAIN

4.1 Introduction to Blockchain Technology

A blockchain is a sequence of blocks, as shown in Figure 2.1, that could be regarded as a public ledger, with all committed transactions stored in that list. This chain grows as new blocks are appended to it continuously. Each of the blocks in a blockchain are immutable. Any change to one block would mean that all the blocks following that block must be changed. A block in a blockchain consists of a block header and a block body (see Figure 2.2). The block header contains the following:

(i) Block version: This indicates the rules which should be followed for that block's validation.
(ii) Merkle tree root hash: The hash value of all the transactions in the block.
(iii) Timestamp: Current time as seconds in universal time since January 1, 1970.
(iv) nBits: Target threshold of a valid block hash.
(v) Nonce: A 4-bit number which usually starts with 0 and increases for every hash calculation.
(vi) Parent block hash: A 256-bit hash value that points to the previous block.

4.2 How Does the Blockchain Maintain its Decentralized Nature?

The blockchain is deployed on a network. The network is a connection between the nodes that run that blockchain. All the nodes (or systems) have a copy of the blockchain stored on them. When a new block is added, all the nodes in the blockchain take part in reaching a consensus of whether the node will be added to the blockchain or not and whether it is correct or

Figure 2.1 Blocks of a blockchain

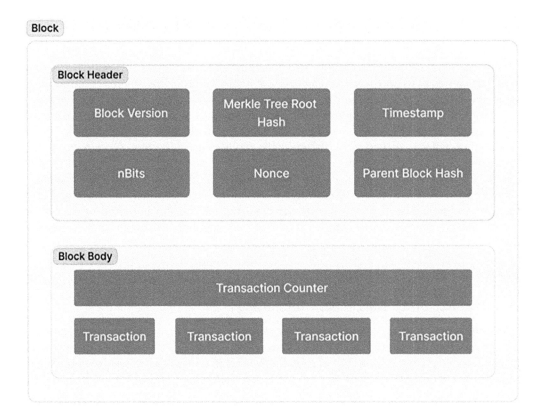

Figure 2.2 Block of a blockchain

not. There are various consensus approaches for this purpose; the two most popular among them are:

a) **POW (Proof of Work):**
The PoW algorithm sets a mathematical puzzle or cryptographic hash function[17, 18] that miners must solve. This puzzle requires miners to find a specific value, called a "nonce," which, when combined with the transaction data and the previous block's hash, results in a hash value with specific characteristics, often starting with a certain number of leading zeros.
Miners continuously iterate through different nonce values and calculate the hash of the block until they find a hash that meets the defined criteria (e.g., a hash with the required number of leading zeros). This process is computationally intensive and involves trial and error.

The network adjusts the difficulty of the puzzle periodically to ensure that new blocks are added at a relatively consistent rate, typically every 10 minutes in Bitcoin. This adjustment is based on the total computational power (hash rate) of the network, making it more challenging as more miners join, and easier if miners leave.

When a miner successfully solves the PoW puzzle and finds a valid nonce, they broadcast the new block to the network. Other nodes in the network can easily verify the solution by applying the same hash function to the block's contents and confirming that the resulting hash meets the required criteria.

Once the new block is added to the blockchain, it becomes part of the longest chain (the one with the most accumulated PoW) and is considered the consensus version of the blockchain. All nodes in the network then continue to build on top of this new block.

According to Gervais et al.[19], PoW blockchains can achieve a throughput of 60 transactions per second without significantly affecting the blockchain's security.

b) **PoS (Proof of Stake):**

In a PoS blockchain network, participants who wish to become validators must lock up a certain amount of the network's native cryptocurrency as collateral. This locked-up cryptocurrency is called a "stake." The amount of stake held by each participant is a key factor in determining who gets the opportunity to create new blocks and validate transactions. Validators take turns proposing new blocks in a deterministic or pseudo-random order based on their stake and other factors determined by the specific PoS protocol. They can include transactions in the blocks they propose. They are responsible for checking the validity of transactions within the block they propose. They verify factors such as the authenticity of transactions, the availability of sufficient funds for transfers, and adherence to network rules. Once a block is proposed, validators in the network vote on its validity. In some PoS systems, validators may also vote on the order of transactions within the block. If a supermajority of validators (e.g., two-thirds or more) agree that a block is valid, it is added to the blockchain. They are incentivized to act honestly and responsibly. If one of them acts maliciously and tries to submit a fraudulent transaction, their staked currency can be partially or fully slashed as a penalty.

4.3 How Difficult Is It to Alter the Blockchain?

Each block in a blockchain contains a hash of the parent block and Merkle tree root hash. This hash calculation includes a lot of computation and considers the complete blockchain within them. Any change in any of the blocks would lead to the need to recalculate the hash in all the children blocks and the altered block itself. This process becomes computationally very expensive. Even if a block is somehow altered in a blockchain, the decentralized nature of the blockchain prevents this malicious change from affecting the main blockchain. The change is broadcasted to all the blockchains in the network but the other nodes check whether that blockchain matches or not. It will fail for many nodes; hence the change will be rejected and the attacker will be banned from the blockchain. To take this over, more than 50% of the nodes should accept this change which is very difficult to achieve in a well-established blockchain.

4.4 Role of Smart Contracts

Smart contracts are programs that run on a blockchain and execute actions based on pre-defined conditions. They are designed to automate the execution of agreements without the need for intermediaries or central authorities. A smart contract consists of code and data that reside at a specific address on the blockchain. The code outlines the functions and logic of the contract, whereas the data stores the contract's state and variables. The code and data of a contract are immutable or unchangeable once deployed. A user interacts with a smart contract by addressing the contract and sending a transaction, specifying any parameters or value to send, and the function to call. After validation and execution by nodes of the network, following consensus protocol rules, the blockchain logs the transaction's result as a contract state. Depending on the blockchain platform, a range of programming languages can be used to create smart contracts. For instance, Solidity is a higher-level language reminiscent of both JavaScript and C++ and is utilized by Ethereum. Different languages, like Rust, Go, or Python, may be employed by alternate platforms.

Decentralized applications, token creation, voting systems, and more are just a few examples of the countless ways smart contracts can be utilized, including escrow services. They can also communicate with other smart contracts or external sources of information, such as oracles. Smart contracts enable trustless and transparent transactions among anonymous parties, without the risk of fraud, censorship, or downtime.

4.5 Blockchain for Data Security in Smart Cities

Data security is very important in the context of a smart city. As the name goes, a smart city will be smart and thus be deeply connected to the internet. Any service booking can be done through the internet; banking and any other money transaction should be enabled through the internet. The city will be dotted with IOT devices[20] and sensors. Smart electric meters, smart home apps, smart traffic lights, and smart parking are just a few examples where IOT devices will rule[21, 22]. For securing the city and the data, we need to secure the network on which it is established. Thus we need to have an established framework for this to be executed.

For this, one of the frameworks is proposed in the paper "Securing Smart Cities Using Blockchain Technologies" (2016)[23]. Another framework is proposed in "PrivySharing: A Blockchain-Based Framework for Privacy-Preserving and Secure Data Sharing in Smart Cities" (2019)[24]. In these frameworks, they define how to handle the data generated in the smart cities and how to use blockchain to protect the data while providing all the services expected in a smart city.

5. SMART CONTRACTS AND DATA GOVERNANCE

In the vibrant landscape of smart cities, where data reigns supreme, the symbiotic relationship between smart contracts and data governance emerges as a pivotal focus. This section embarks on a technical journey to dissect the profound impact of smart contracts, the self-executing, code-based agreements, within the intricate web of smart city infrastructure. We delve into the core concepts, functionality, and applications of smart contracts in the context of data security, integrity, and governance.

5.1 Smart Contracts in Smart City Infrastructure

Smart contracts, often lauded as the digital nerve center of blockchain technology, occupy a central stage in the grand orchestration of smart city governance. At their essence, smart contracts are self-executing code-based agreements that reside on the blockchain, ushering in a new era of automation, transparency, and efficiency. In the context of data security and integrity, they play an instrumental role in shaping urban dynamics.

This segment is initiated by exploring the fundamental principles that underpin smart contracts within smart city infrastructure. From transparent and automated billing for city services to real-time data integrity checks, smart contracts are the digital guardians of governance. Real-world use cases within the urban landscape provide tangible examples of how

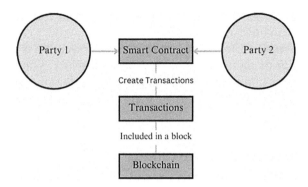

Figure 2.3 Smart contracts using blockchain

smart contracts revolutionize processes, ensuring accountability, accuracy, and the efficient execution of agreements.

Key Components of Smart Contracts

At the heart of smart contracts lie their key components, essential for technical understanding. These components include:

a) **Code Logic:** Smart contracts are written in programming languages, often specific to the blockchain platform. This code governs the terms, conditions, and actions to be executed automatically when predefined conditions are met.

b) **Decentralized Ledger:** Smart contracts operate within a decentralized ledger, ensuring that all transactions and contract states are recorded transparently and immutably.

c) **Cryptographic Security:** The integrity of smart contracts is preserved through cryptographic algorithms. Digital signatures and cryptographic hashes ensure the security of both the contract and its data.

d) **Oracles:** Oracles serve as external data sources that provide real-world data to the smart contract. They enable the contract to react to external events or conditions.

5.2 Automation and Trust in Smart Contracts

Smart contracts, as the linchpin of blockchain technology, are distinguished by their core attributes of automation and trustworthiness. A closer technical examination of these aspects unveils the inner workings that make smart contracts an indispensable component of smart city infrastructure.

5.3 Technical Foundations of Automation

Predefined Conditions: Smart contracts operate based on predefined conditions and rules. These conditions are written into the contract's code, outlining the specific actions to be executed when certain conditions are met. For instance, in a utility billing scenario, a smart contract may stipulate that when a customer's monthly consumption reaches a certain threshold, a payment is automatically triggered.

a) **Code Execution:** The code of a smart contract is self-executing. When the conditions specified in the contract are met, the contract's code is executed automatically without the need for intermediaries or manual intervention. This technical facet ensures that processes are streamlined and free of human error.

b) **Blockchain Consensus:** The trust in smart contract execution is bolstered by the consensus mechanism of the underlying blockchain network. Once conditions are met, nodes in the network validate the execution, ensuring that it adheres to the contract's code. This consensus process occurs in a decentralized and tamper-resistant manner, reinforcing the reliability of smart contracts.

5.4 Technical Aspects of Trustworthiness

a) **Transparency:** Smart contracts are deployed on public or private blockchains, making their code visible to all network participants. This transparency is a technical feature that ensures that all parties can review the contract's terms and logic, thus eliminating hidden clauses or unexpected behavior.

b) **Immutability:** Once a smart contract is deployed on the blockchain, its code and the transactions it processes are recorded in an immutable ledger. This means that the contract's execution history is tamper-proof and can be audited at any time. Immutability enhances the technical trustworthiness of smart contracts.

c) **Cryptographic Security:** Smart contracts rely on cryptographic mechanisms to ensure data and code security. Digital signatures authenticate the parties involved, and cryptographic hashes are used to secure the code and data within the contract. These technical security measures provide an additional layer of trust.

5.5 Data Governance Models in Blockchain

Smart contracts, often lauded as the digital nerve center of blockchain technology, occupy a central stage in the grand orchestration of smart city governance. At their essence, smart contracts are self-executing, code-based agreements that reside on the blockchain, ushering in a new era of automation, transparency, and efficiency. In the context of data security and integrity, they play an instrumental role in shaping urban dynamics.

5.5 Consensus Mechanisms and Data Validation

Blockchain networks rely on consensus mechanisms to validate data transactions and maintain a unified ledger. The technical consensus process, whether through Proof of Work (PoW), Proof of Stake (PoS), or other methods, ensures that data alterations are subject to agreement among network participants. This robust and decentralized validation system minimizes the risk of data tampering and fraud. In the context of smart cities, this technical safeguard is paramount to maintaining the integrity of data generated by urban sensors and systems.

Mathematical Formulation

1. Let G be the set of network participants.
2. C(G) represents the consensus mechanism applied, such as PoW or PoS.
3. For a given data transaction T, the consensus process can be expressed as:

$C\ (G, T) \Rightarrow$ Validation.

5.6 Blockchain Data Immutability and Auditing

One of the fundamental technical features of data governance in blockchain is data immutability. Once data is recorded on the blockchain, it cannot be altered or deleted without consensus from the network. This technical characteristic facilitates auditability, enabling stakeholders to review the complete history of data entries and changes. In smart cities, where transparency and accountability are vital, the technical immutability of data ensures that data governance remains tamper-proof and verifiable.

Mathematical Formulation

1. Let D be the set of data entries on the blockchain.
2. $\forall d \in D$, where d is a data entry, $\exists t \in T$ such that: $d = T(t)$
3. t represents a timestamp associated with a data entry.

5.7 Permissioned Blockchains and Data Access Control

In some smart city scenarios, permissioned blockchains are employed, allowing only authorized participants to access and modify data. This technical control over data access is facilitated through cryptographic keys and access permissions. Data governance models in permissioned blockchains offer a granular level of control, ensuring that only trusted parties can interact with specific data sets. This technical access control mechanism is essential for managing sensitive urban data, such as public records or personal information.

5.8 Smart Contracts for Automated Data Policies

Within blockchain-based data governance, the technical innovation of smart contracts plays a pivotal role. These self-executing agreements are coded with predefined data governance policies. When data-related conditions are met, smart contracts automatically enforce policies, whether it's granting or revoking data access permissions or triggering data archiving processes. This technical automation ensures that data governance is not only comprehensive but also consistently adhered to, reducing human errors, and ensuring policy enforcement.

5.9 Data Privacy Techniques

To address data privacy concerns within smart cities, data governance models incorporate technical privacy-preserving techniques. Zero-knowledge proofs, data anonymization, and differential privacy are among the tools used to protect sensitive information while allowing data to be accessed and used in a technically secure and privacy-compliant manner. These techniques provide a nuanced approach to data governance, addressing the complex and evolving landscape of data privacy laws and regulations.

a) **Zero-Knowledge Proofs (ZKPs):**
   Mathematical Foundation: Zero-Knowledge Proofs are based on mathematical formulations that include:
   (i) **Zero-Knowledge Property:** $\forall V$, $\exists P$: V receives the proof from P, and after verification, V knows nothing about the secret except its validity.
   (ii) **Soundness Property:** The probability of a dishonest prover convincing the verifier of a false statement is negligible.

Technical Application: Zero-Knowledge Proofs are technically applied to ensure data privacy during authentication processes. For instance, in zk-SNARKs, the mathematical formulation involves constructing a succinct non-interactive zero-knowledge argument for a statement. zk-SNARKs use algebraic curves and cryptographic operations for these calculations.

b) **Data Anonymization:**

Mathematical Foundation: Data anonymization techniques, such as k-anonymity, rely on mathematical concepts such as equivalence classes. For k-anonymity, the mathematical formulation involves grouping data into clusters where each cluster contains at least k-1 similar data points.

Technical Application: In smart cities, data anonymization is technically implemented by quantifying the degree of anonymity. For example, to achieve k-anonymity, the algorithm ensures that no individual in the dataset is uniquely identifiable, and each data point belongs to a cluster of at least size k.

c) **Differential Privacy:**

Mathematical Foundation: Differential privacy is based on mathematical constructs, particularly Laplace or Gaussian mechanisms, which add noise to data queries.

1. Let ε represent the privacy parameter.
2. The differential privacy guarantee can be expressed as:

$$\Pr\left(\text{Query}(D_1) \in S\right) \le e^{\varepsilon} * \Pr\left(\text{Query}(D_2) \in S\right)$$

Technical Application: In smart cities, differential privacy is technically implemented through noise addition to query results. For instance, when calculating statistics on sensitive data, Laplace noise is added to ensure that the results are statistically accurate but do not reveal individual data points.

d) **Homomorphic Encryption:**

Mathematical Foundation: Homomorphic encryption is grounded in mathematical concepts such as lattice-based cryptography and algebraic structures like rings and fields. The mathematical formulation involves operations that can be performed on encrypted data without decryption.

Technical Application: In smart cities, homomorphic encryption is technically applied to allow computations on encrypted data. For instance, encrypted traffic data can be analyzed using homomorphic encryption without revealing the individual vehicle details.

e) **Secure Multi-Party Computation (MPC):**

Mathematical Foundation: Secure Multi-Party Computation relies on cryptographic protocols and mathematical algorithms, including secret sharing and protocols like the Yao's Millionaires' Problem. The mathematical formulation includes sharing secrets among parties and jointly computing functions over the shared secrets.

Technical Application: In smart cities[21], Secure MPC is technically applied to enable multiple parties to collaborate on data analytics while keeping their raw data private. For example, in the technical execution of the Yao's Millionaires' Problem protocol, parties share encrypted data and perform operations on the shared data without revealing the actual values, facilitating secure comparisons.

These mathematical foundations and technical implementations underpin data privacy techniques in smart cities, ensuring that sensitive information remains confidential while still facilitating data-driven insights and decision-making. In the technically complex and data-rich environment of smart cities, these techniques are essential for protecting data privacy and maintaining public trust.

5.10 Interoperability and Data Integration

Smart cities often employ a diverse array of systems, databases, and data sources. Technical interoperability is a critical aspect of data governance models within blockchain technology. These models are designed to seamlessly integrate with existing urban infrastructure, ensuring that data governance is comprehensive and covers all data generated by various sources, from IoT devices to administrative databases.

5.11 Technical Accountability and Compliance

The technical accountability within data governance models is reinforced through audit trails. Every data transaction, access, or modification is recorded in a technically verifiable audit trail. This provides a robust layer of accountability, ensuring that data governance policies are consistently applied and adhered to. It also facilitates compliance with legal and regulatory requirements.

Data governance models within blockchain technology, enriched with technical features like consensus mechanisms, data immutability, and smart contracts, serve as the technical guardians of data integrity and trustworthiness in smart cities. These models provide a structured framework for data management, ensuring that data is secure, auditable, and accessible to authorized parties while preserving privacy and complying with evolving data protection standards. In the data-driven landscape of smart cities, this technical foundation is indispensable for responsible and transparent data governance.

6. IMPLEMENTING BLOCKCHAIN FOR DATA SECURITY

As discussed in Section 3.2, data security is crucial, and we have already reviewed two established frameworks in this space. We will now explore what goes into implementing blockchain in a smart city, including the various considerations and limitations involved.

First, we need to define what the use cases of blockchain would be in a smart city, then we will move onto the list of considerations we need to keep in mind. Then we move onto the list of challenges in implementation of blockchain technology and the solutions we can integrate to overcome them.

6.1 Use Cases in Smart City

Several use cases have already been defined in the article "Smart City and IOT" (2017)[21]. These examples include Smart Electricity Meters, Smart Home Apps (e.g. Nest and Smart-Me), Smart Environment Meters, Smart Finder, Smart Traffic Lights, etc. Some of the other use cases in a smart city are mentioned in Table 2.4.

There can be many other use cases, but those listed in Table 2.3 are just an example showing how a blockchain when built can handle the service compliance of the government.

6.2 Considerations in Blockchain Integration

A proper survey needs to be done before implementing anything; hence assessing the needs, checking the scalability of the system, integrating the existing systems, making user-friendly interfaces, and most importantly encryption and data security. An appropriate consensus mechanism needs to be established. A lot of consensus mechanisms are explained by researchers B. Lashkari (2019) and P. Musilek (2019) in their article "A Comprehensive Review of

Table 2.4 Use cases of blockchain in smart cities

Problems	Blockchain solution
Supply chain management	Implementing blockchain and having all the records of each step of the process in a pseudo-anonymous view can increase transparency, traceability, and accountability.
Public transportation coordination and payments	Integrating blockchain in public transportation can streamline ticketing[25] and reduce fraud and corruption. It can also improve the management of the vehicle fleets and maintenance records.
Identity management	Blockchain provides a secure and decentralized identity management system. Citizens can have control over their digital identities and access to services can be granted based on verified and immutable credentials.
Contracts and enabling trust Without fraud	Smart contracts as explained in detail in Section 4.1 can automate and enforce agreements between parties in a transparent and tamper-proof way.
Property and land registry	Extending the previous use-case, property and land registry can be done on blockchain, which ensures transparency and unforgeable records. It reduces fraud, streamlines transactions, and facilitates easier access to ownership information.
Healthcare data management	Using IoT and blockchain to manage and maintain healthcare[26–29] data ensures patient records can be stored securely and access can be granted with patient consent through smart contracts only.[30]
Crisis and emergency response	Blockchain can be used to create a secure and transparent system for managing emergency response data, ensuring real-time communication, resource allocation, and coordination between different agencies.
Tourism and city services	Blockchain can streamline tourism-related transactions, verify the authenticity of services, and provide a transparent platform for managing bookings.

Blockchain Consensus Mechanisms"[24]. Creating appropriate and robust smart contracts for all the services and having proper identity management systems in place are crucial for blockchain integrations. This will lead to huge costs that will be required to run the blockchain and develop all the applications.

Blockchains have a huge environmental impact; considering that is also very important when setting up the infrastructure of the blockchain. Energy expenditure on the blockchain is a massive pain point. If running a blockchain becomes very costly, the project could fail.

6.3 Challenges and Solutions

When implementing blockchain, we will face a lot of challenges. Many of these considerations we have already seen in Section 5.2. Here we will see more about the challenges we face and the solutions to those challenges. Many of the challenges have been discussed in the article "Blockchain-based Initiatives: Current state and challenges."[31] They are classified by sector. Broadly, the challenges faced by most of the industries in the implementation are shown in Table 2.5:

Table 2.5 Challenges and solutions to blockchain

Challenges	Solutions
Public blockchain networks face scalability issue	Exploring more scalability solutions such as sharding[32] and layer 2 protocols (e.g., lightning network[33]) can help.
Integrating with existing systems	Develop standardized APIs, middlewares, and interoperability protocols
Energy consumption	Choosing the correct consensus protocol is very important. The importance is highlighted in Section 5.2.
User adoption	Conducting awareness campaigns and educating the stakeholders about the blockchain benefits is the key to widespread adoption.
Security concerns	Regularly auditing smart contract code, following best security[34] practices, and implementing robust encryption can help prevent most of the security concerns.
Heavy cost	Conduct a cost-benefit analysis to justify blockchain adoption. Seek public-private partnership, grants, or funding opportunities to support the project.
Linux-based security considerations	Leveraging Linux security best practices, employing secure APIs, and ensuring compatibility with Linux systems can enhance the overall security posture of blockchain implementations.[35]

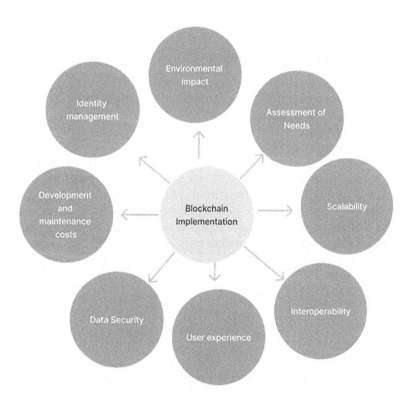

Figure 2.4 Considerations in implementing blockchain

7. CASE STUDIES AND TRENDS

In recent years, the concept of smart cities[15] has emerged as a beacon of progress and efficiency in an era marked by the relentless advancement of urbanization and the proliferation of interconnected technologies. These cities leverage cutting-edge technologies to enhance the quality of life for their residents, optimize resource allocation, and foster sustainable growth[36]. However, the seamless operation of smart cities relies heavily on the secure management and exchange of vast amounts of sensitive data. Ensuring the confidentiality, integrity, and availability of this data is a paramount concern. To address this critical challenge, blockchain technology has become an instrumental tool, providing a robust framework for data security and integrity.

7.1 Applications and Real-World Examples of Blockchain Implementation

Blockchain technology has been implemented in various domains, including smart cities, to enhance data security and integrity. For instance, a paper published in IEEE Xplore[23] proposes a security framework that integrates blockchain technology with smart devices to provide a secure communication platform in a smart city. The framework ensures the confidentiality, integrity, and availability of sensitive data, which is crucial for the seamless, privacy protection, and security of operational data processes. These examples illustrate the trans-operation of smart cities. Blockchain technology has found application in various sectors beyond cryptocurrency. Here are some applications of Blockchain Implementation with real-world examples:

Applications of Blockchain Implementation

a) **Supply Chain Management:** Transformative changes are occurring within the supply chain management system with the introduction of blockchain technology. The different stages involved in the supply chain, such as retail, distribution, logistics, procurement, and production, are witnessing this evolution. VeChain is an example of a platform employing smart contracts to automate procurement processes, leading to greater transparency and efficiency. On the blockchain, manufacturing specifications can be recorded, offering the benefit of traceability and swift identification of product sources when problems arise. Information on transportation and logistics, as well as warehouse operations, can easily be documented and provide immediate insight into the status and location of products. Smart contracts that automate returns processes are simplified through blockchain technology, increasing authenticity and trust for consumers who access product information via product QR codes.

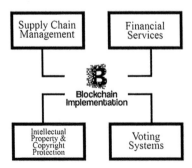

Figure 2.5 Applications of blockchain implementation

b) **Financial Services:** The revolutionary potential of blockchain technology is evidenced in financial services, particularly seen in Ripple's cross-border payment system. The usual cross-border transaction system is riddled with obstacles like sluggishness, high expenses, and many middlemen. It presents a solution that offers secure global reach and fast cross-border payment processes. Despite the need for regulations and adoption hurdles, there is an increasing interest in integrating blockchain into existing banking infrastructure, as its benefits for the financial sector are undeniable.

c) **Voting Systems:** Incorporating blockchain technology into the voting process results in greater security, transparency, and trust. Identifying details of voters are confirmed by blockchain, creating a secure digital identity. By using a clear online platform, cast votes are converted into unchangeable blocks on the blockchain after thorough verification by decentralized nodes. Through this method, records which are resistant to tampering are created, which helps to address problems like lack of transparency and fraud in traditional systems. Benefits include greater security, traceability, and transparency in the history of voting. Smart contracts operate automatically, which limits the occurrence of errors. Platforms such as Follow My Vote strive to maximize the effectiveness of blockchain to create secure and efficient voting systems. Although there are several challenges to overcome such as adopting new technology, ensuring all voters can access the system, and privacy issues, blockchain technology provides the potential for creating a fairer voting experience.

d) **Intellectual Property and Copyright Protection:** Intellectual property and copyright protection undergo a drastic change with the help of blockchain technology. Creative works can now be registered on the blockchain, creating a transparent and secure ownership record. Copyright terms can be automated via smart contracts, thus ensuring fair compensation. Decentralization reduces the risks of infringement, and intermediaries become unnecessary. Legal disputes can be resolved effortlessly with tamper-resistant records of each transaction. By implementing blockchain, content creators now have an efficient way to manage their intellectual property. Challenges still need to be tackled for the worldwide adoption of blockchain technology, including legal recognition.

Real-World Examples of Blockchain Implementations

Table 2.6 Applications and real-world examples of blockchain in smart cities

Applications of blockchain implementation	Real-world examples
Supply chain management	Maersk and IBM's TradeLens collaboration is a prime example of blockchain's integration into global supply chain management.
Financial services	Utilizing Distributed Ledger Technology (DLT), the Australian Securities Exchange (ASX) has implemented its Clearing House Electronic Subregister System (CHESS) as a unique illustration of blockchain integration in the financial services sector.
Voting systems	Voatz is a transparent voting mobile app that uses blockchain technology to ensure anonymity of users. This voting system is a prime example of blockchain technology in real-world use.
Intellectual property and copyright protection	Using blockchain technology, KodakOne can manage and protect image rights in a transparent and secure manner.

7.2 Current Trends in Smart City Data Security

Data security has always been a hot topic when dealing with networks, especially in public networks. We have discussed data security throughout this chapter. Gharaibeh et al. (2017)[37] have surveyed smart city data management and security and have listed the challenges they found in the survey. They also list a survey of various research and methodologies they found that are being implemented to solve those challenges.

In terms of current trends in smart cities, most of the implementation is centralized. IOT devices are employed dotting the cities. The data is communicated to a central server which is open to risk of attacks. Also, the IOT devices and sensors placed are cheap ones which often do not have enough capability to encrypt data using modern cryptographic algorithms and hence transmit data in a vulnerable manner.

Some of the security threats are[37-39]:

1. Masquerade attack
2. Replay attack
3. Man-in-the-middle attack
4. Sybil attack
5. GPS spoofing
6. Broadcast and transaction tampering
7. DoS
8. Malware
9. Brute force
10. Timing attack
11. Node security
12. Routing attacks

Public Key Infrastructure (PKI), identity certificates, cryptography, Precise Positioning System (PPS), CRL and Elliptic Curve Digital Signature Algorithms (ECDSA) are some of the current solutions to the problems as cited in[37].

Blockchain, as described in the previous sections and with the proper measures taken, is a far better alternative to the current technologies. Blockchain makes the data public yet tamper-proof. Smart contracts prevent the trust from being broken and removes dependence on third parties. For the rest of the security threats related to the network, we need to have more robust network protocols in place for solving them.

8. FUTURE TRENDS AND CONSIDERATIONS

Blockchain technology has the potential to revolutionize the way we approach data security in smart cities[15]. According to a recent study, blockchain's decentralized and transparent nature can provide adequate security for a wide range of purposes. The use of blockchain in smart cities can help share resources across different, unauthenticated enterprises, and enable efficient use of information collected from various resources to engage in operational processes without requiring access to the data.

In terms of future trends and considerations, blockchain technology is expected to play an increasingly important role in securing IoT-based networks[40-42] in smart cities. Blockchain can provide trustworthy mechanisms for data acquisition and verification, which is essential for ensuring the integrity and authenticity of data in smart cities.

8.1 Emerging Blockchain Technologies

In the realm of smart cities, blockchain technology is pivotal for ensuring data security. In the academic world, a bibliometric analysis of 148 publications spanning 76 journals from 2016 to 2020 highlights a significantly increasing interest in the intersection between blockchain applications and smart cities. According to the results, blockchain can serve as a fundamental technology that has copious possibilities in smart cities.

Smart cities can leverage blockchain technology to enhance data security in various ways. Notably, a research study suggests a secure communication network for a smart city, integrating blockchain technology with smart devices to establish a robust security framework[43]. This innovative approach ensures secure communication among smart devices by storing and managing their public keys on the blockchain platform. This eliminates the need for intermediaries and guarantees transparent and secure data sharing within the smart city ecosystem.

In some research[44], a suggestion was put forward for a secure communication network in a smart city. This proposal integrates blockchain technology with smart devices to create a security framework. Whenever required, smart devices could then communicate on this platform securely. The public keys of these devices would be stored and managed by blockchain, guaranteeing that communication between them is secure. Secure data sharing among entities within a smart city ecosystem can be facilitated through the use of blockchain technology. Intermediaries become unnecessary, as blockchain allows for transparent and secure data sharing. Data security can be upheld in a smart city through the use of blockchain technology. By being resistant to tampering, blockchain enables data to be stored securely and prevents unauthorized changes or deletions.

Social media[45, 46] and blockchain technology are merging to form a transformational realm where data control and decentralization reign supreme. By serving as a distributed and decentralized ledger, blockchain potentially addresses the issues of centralization and data privacy that plague conventional social media platforms. Through the application of cryptographic methods, users have more control over the data they possess, thus increasing transparency and security. Blockchain's incorporation of cryptocurrencies and tokens on social media platforms brings fresh opportunities for monetizing content and establishing decentralized economies in these digital domains. Potent tools from blockchain technology challenging traditional monetization models include direct payments to content creators and microtransactions. The timestamping and data-securing ability of blockchain presents itself as a potent tool in the quest to combat fake news and misinformation. This, in turn, encourages users to have faith in information shared on social media. By automating a variety of processes, smart contracts[47] from blockchain can introduce self-executing agreements ranging from content rewards to advertising contracts. Reducing fake accounts and enhancing user profiles are two potential outcomes that make blockchain's role in identity verification especially promising. Of course, there are also challenges to overcome, such as scalability, user adoption, and regulatory considerations. These factors serve as a reminder that careful navigation is required to fully realize the potential of the social media-blockchain convergence.

8.2 Scalability and Performance Enhancements

Different techniques can be employed to enhance the scalability and performance of cloud-based blockchain data security for Smart Cities. Cloud computing[48] has transformed traditional mobile computing and is responsible for the huge increase in on-demand services. Through mobile computing based on cloud computing, mobile device functions can be virtualized, reducing power consumption[49]. A few strategies have been presented in various research papers. One way to reduce computational overhead and increase transaction throughput is by choosing an appropriate consensus algorithm, like Proof of Stake (PoS) or Delegated Proof of Stake (DPoS). Total Commit and Transaction Off-chains (TCTOC) is proposed as a synthesis of two solutions in the paper[49] for improved transaction management.

Scalability Solutions for Blockchain[50] and *A Survey of Blockchain Scalability Issues and Opportunities*[51] have identified several methods to efficiently distribute traffic and reduce congestion on the blockchain, such as caching mechanisms, data compression, and load balancing. Smart contract efficiency, optimization, and keeping up with the latest consensus protocol upgrades are additional crucial factors.

For handling sensitive data, a hybrid solution that utilizes both public and private blockchains has shown itself to be effective. To keep up a thriving cloud blockchain infrastructure in Smart Cities[52], it's crucial to have dependable disaster recovery strategies, easily adaptable storage solutions, and continuous monitoring, testing, and optimization.

8.3 The Evolving Landscape of Data Security

The information security environment is constantly evolving and is affected by technological developments, legislative changes, and changing cyber threats. Ransomware and data deletion attacks in particular are on the rise. As organizations migrate, concerns remain about the security of shared models in the cloud. Use the recommended zero-point safety model to be accurate and minimal[53]. Artificial intelligence[54] and machine learning[55,56] can be helpful in identifying risks, loop unrolling[57], and stock market prediction[58,59] and they also serve as a helpful tool for cybercriminals. Strict data protection regulations (e.g. GDPR, CCPA) increase privacy concerns. Integrating neural network[60] into blockchain is used for decentralized and secure AI-driven consensus and decision-making[61]. Through neural network analysis, precise predictions are likely to be achieved in the Indian subcontinent[62–64]. Supply chain and biometric security and employee training are critical. Modernization is essential for organizations to create effective defenses against cyber threats[65–67].

9. CONCLUSION

In summary, this chapter has provided a rigorous technical examination of the convergence of blockchain technology and data security in the context of smart cities. The smart city ecosystem, characterized by its complexity and dynamism, places an absolute premium on data integrity and trustworthiness. We initiated our exploration by underlining the nuanced importance of data security in smart cities, which have undergone a rapid transformation driven by the pursuit of enhanced urban efficiency, sustainability, and an improved quality of life. Data, emanating from a multitude of sensors, devices, and systems, serves as the lifeblood of smart city operations. However, this proliferation of data has ushered in myriad challenges, including concerns related to privacy, cyber threats, and the specter of data breaches. Blockchain technology emerged as a formidable solution to address these data security challenges. We dissected the fundamental components of blockchain, ranging from its consensus mechanisms to its decentralized ledger architecture. This technology was revealed as a transparent and tamper-resistant foundation for urban data, promising heightened data integrity and trustworthiness. Our exploration extended to the symbiotic relationship between blockchain technology and data governance. The transformative role of smart contracts, code-based agreements that execute automatically, took center stage in preserving data security and integrity. We also delved into the diverse data governance models intrinsic to blockchain, shedding light on their pivotal role in upholding data integrity. Practicality and implementation considerations were at the forefront as we transitioned to the strategic deployment of blockchain for data security in smart cities. Specific use cases tailored to the unique challenges of smart cities were elucidated, accompanied by innovative solutions aimed at optimizing data security while upholding critical aspects of system performance, reliability, and scalability in a data-rich urban environment. Importantly, this exploration was not confined to theoretical constructs but was substantiated through real-world case studies. These case studies underscored the tangible benefits of blockchain technology in reshaping the paradigm of data security, further validating its burgeoning significance.

As we gaze into the future, the role of blockchain in ensuring data security within smart cities is set for continued growth and innovation. Emerging blockchain technologies, scalability enhancements, and the ever-evolving landscape of data security reaffirm the enduring relevance of blockchain's immutable ledger and cryptographic principles.

In an environment characterized by perpetual evolution, this chapter stands as a technical compass for computer science practitioners, researchers, and technology enthusiasts. It offers a comprehensive understanding of the central role of blockchain in safeguarding data integrity and trustworthiness within the intricate web of smart city ecosystems. Through its technical lens, this chapter illuminates the intricate and profound relationship between blockchain and data security, underscoring the pivotal position of blockchain technology in ensuring data integrity and trustworthiness in the intricate and data-rich milieu of smart cities.

REFERENCES

1. Rajput, R. K., Goyal, D., Pant, A., Sharma, G., Arya, V., & Rafsanjani, M. K. (2022). Cloud data centre energy utilization estimation: Simulation and modelling with iDR. *International Journal of Cloud Applications and Computing (IJCAC)*, 12(1), 1–16. http://doi.org/10.4018/IJCAC.311035
2. Gupta, B. B., Perez, G. M., Agrawal, D. P., & Gupta, D. (2020). *Handbook of Computer Networks and Cyber Security* (Vol. 10, pp. 3–978). Springer.
3. Kumar, S., Singh, S. K., Aggarwal, N., Gupta, B. B., Alhalabi, W., & Band, S. S. (2022). An efficient hardware supported and parallelization architecture for intelligent systems to overcome speculative overheads. *International Journal of Intelligent Systems*, 37(12), 11764–11790.
4. Aggarwal, K., Singh, S. K., Chopra, M., Kumar, S., & Colace, F. (2022). Deep learning in robotics for strengthening industry 4.0.: Opportunities, challenges and future directions. In N. Nedjah, A. A. Abd El-Latif, B. B. Gupta, L. M. Mourelle (Eds.), *Robotics and AI for Cybersecurity and Critical Infrastructure in Smart Cities. Studies in Computational Intelligence* (Vol. 1030, pp. 1–19). Springer.
5. Ali, R., Qadri, Y. A., Zikria, Y. B., Al-Turjman, F., Kim, B. S., & Kim, S. W. (2020). A blockchain model for trustworthiness in the internet of things (IoT)-based smart-cities. In F. Al-Turjman (Ed.), *Trends in Cloud-Based IoT. EAI/Springer Innovations in Communication and Computing*. Springer. https://doi.org/10.1007/978-3-030-40037-8_1
6. Varfolomeev, A. A., Alfarhani, L. H., & Oleiwi, Z. C. (2021). Secure-reliable blockchain-based data access control and data integrity framework in the environment of smart city. *IOP Conference Series: Materials Science and Engineering*, 1090, 012127.
7. Makhdoom, I., Zhou, I., Abolhasan, M., Lipman, J., & Ni, W. (2020). PrivySharing: A blockchain-based framework for privacy-preserving and secure data sharing in smart cities. *Computers & Security*, 88, 101653.
8. Rahman, M. S., Chamikara, M. A. P., Khalil, I., & Bouras, A. (2022). Blockchain-of-blockchains: An interoperable blockchain platform for ensuring IoT data integrity in smart city. *Journal of Industrial Information Integration*, 30, 100408.
9. Majdoubi, D. E., El Bakkali, H., & Sadki, S. (2020). Towards smart blockchain-based system for privacy and security in a smart city environment. In *2020 5th International Conference on Cloud Computing and Artificial Intelligence: Technologies and Applications*, Marrakesh, Morocco (pp. 1–7). CloudTech. http://doi.org/10.1109/CloudTech49835.2020.9365905

10. Theodorou, S., & Sklavos, N. (2019). Blockchain-based security and privacy in smart cities. In *Smart Cities Cybersecurity and Privacy* (pp. 21–37). Elsevier.

11. Kumar, S. S., Singh, S. K., Aggarwal, N., & Aggarwal, K. (2021). Efficient speculative parallelization architecture for overcoming speculation overheads. In *International Conference on Smart Systems and Advanced Computing (Syscom-2021)* (Vol. 3080, pp. 132–138). Springer.

12. Xiao, J., Liu, X., Zeng, J., Cao, Y., & Feng, Z. (2022). Recommendation of healthcare services based on an embedded user profile model. *International Journal on Semantic Web and Information Systems (IJSWIS)*, 18(1), 1–21. http://doi.org/10.4018/IJSWIS.313198

13. Sharma, A., Singh, S. K., Kumar, S., Chhabra, A., & Gupta, S. (2021, September). Security of Android banking mobile apps: Challenges and opportunities. In *International Conference on Cyber Security, Privacy and Networking* (pp. 406–416). Springer International Publishing.

14. Elrotub, M., & Gherbi, A. (2022). Multi-cloud service brokers for selecting the optimal data center in cloud environment. *International Journal of Cloud Applications and Computing (IJCAC)*, 12(1), 1–19. http://doi.org/10.4018/IJCAC.309935

15. Singh, R., Singh, S. K., Kumar, S., & Gill, S. S. (2022). SDN-aided edge computing-enabled AI for IoT and smart cities. In *SDN-Supported Edge-Cloud Interplay for Next Generation Internet of Things* (pp. 41–70). CRC Press.

16. Gupta, A., Singh, S. K., Chopra, M., & Gill, S. S. (2022). An inquisitive prospect on the shift toward online media, before, during, and after the COVID-19 pandemic: a technological analysis. In *Advances in Data Computing, Communication and Security: Proceedings of I3CS2021* (pp. 229–238). Springer Nature Singapore.

17. Kumar, S., Singh, S. K., & Aggarwal, N. (2023). Speculative parallelism on multicore chip architecture strengthen green computing concept: A survey. In *Advanced Computer Science Applications* (pp. 3–16). Apple Academic Press.

18. Kumar, S., Singh, S. K., Aggarwal, N., & Aggarwal, K. (2021). Evaluation of automatic parallelization algorithms to minimize speculative parallelism overheads: An experiment. *Journal of Discrete Mathematical Sciences and Cryptography*, 24(5), 1517–1528.

19. Gervais, A., Karame, G. O., Wüst, K., Glykantzis, V., Ritzdorf, H., & Capkun, S. (2016). On the security and performance of proof of work blockchains. In *Proceedings of the 2016 ACM SIGSAC Conference on Computer and Communications Security*. https://doi.org/10.1145/2976749.2978341

20. Raj, M. G., & Pani, S. K. (2022). Chaotic whale crow optimization algorithm for secure routing in the IoT environment. *International Journal on Semantic Web and Information Systems (IJSWIS)*, 18(1), 1–25. http://doi.org/10.4018/IJSWIS.300824

21. Kim, T., Ramos, C., & Mohammed, S. (2017). Smart city and IOT. *Future Generation Computer Systems*, 76, 159–162. https://doi.org/10.1016/j.future.2017.03.034

22. Tiwari, A., & Garg, R. (2022). Adaptive ontology-based IoT resource provisioning in computing systems. *International Journal on Semantic Web and Information Systems (IJSWIS)*, 18(1), 1–18. http://doi.org/10.4018/IJSWIS.306260

23. Biswas, K., & Muthukkumarasamy, V. (2016). Securing smart cities using blockchain technology. In *2016 IEEE 18th International Conference on High Performance Computing and Communications; IEEE 14th International Conference on Smart City; IEEE 2nd International Conference on Data Science and Systems (HPCC/SmartCity/DSS)*. https://doi.org/10.1109/hpcc-smartcity-dss.2016.0198

24. Lashkari, B., & Musilek, P. (2021). A comprehensive review of blockchain consensus mechanisms. *IEEE Access*, 9, 43620–43652. https://doi.org/10.1109/access.2021.3065880

25. Chopra, M., Kumar, S., Madan, U., & Sharma, S. (2021, December). Influence and establishment of smart transport in smart cities. In *International Conference on Smart Systems and Advanced Computing (Syscom-2021)*. Springer.

26. Zaidan, A. A., Alsattar, H. A., Qahtan, S., Deveci, M., Pamucar, D., & Gupta, B. B. (2023). Secure decision approach for internet of healthcare things smart systems-based blockchain. *IEEE Internet of Things Journal*, 10(24), 21647–21655.

27. Secure blockchain enabled Cyber–physical systems in healthcare using deep belief network with ResNet model.

28. Tiwari, H. (2023) *Revolutionizing Healthcare: Federated Learning* (p. 1). Insights2Techinfo. https://insights2techinfo.com/revolutionizing-healthcare-federated-learning/

29. Mengi, G., & Kumar, S. (2022). *Artificial Intelligence and Machine Learning in Healthcare* (p. 1). Insights2Tecinfo. https://insights2techinfo.com/artificial-intelligence-machine-learning-in-healthcare/

30. Vats, T., Singh, S. K., Kumar, S., Gupta, B. B., Gill, S. S., Arya, V., & Alhalabi, W. (2023). Explainable context-aware IoT framework using human digital twin for healthcare. In *Multimedia Tools and Applications* (pp. 1–25). Springer.

31. Alam, S., Shuaib, M., Khan, W. Z., Garg, S., Kaddoum, G., Hossain, M. S., & Zikria, Y. B. (2021). Blockchain-based initiatives: Current State and challenges. *Computer Networks*, 198, 108395. https://doi.org/10.1016/j.comnet.2021.108395

32. Zamani, M., Movahedi, M., & Raykova, M. (2018). RapidChain. In *Proceedings of the 2018 ACM SIGSAC Conference on Computer and Communications Security*. https://doi.org/10.1145/3243734.3243853

33. Poon, J., & Dryja, T. (2016). The bitcoin lightning network: Scalable off-chain instant payments.

34. Gupta, B. B., Gaurav, A., & Panigrahi, P. K. (2023). Analysis of security and privacy issues of information management of big data in B2B based healthcare systems. *Journal of Business Research*, 162, 113859.

35. Singh, S. K. (2021). *Linux Yourself: Concept and Programming*. CRC Press.

36. Bouncken, R. B., Lapidus, A., & Qui, Y. (2022). Organizational sustainability identity: 'New work' of home offices and coworking spaces as facilitators. *Sustainable Technology and Entrepreneurship*, 1(2), 100011. https://doi.org/10.1016/j.stae.2022.100011

37. Gharaibeh, A., Salahuddin, M. A., Hussini, S. J., Khreishah, A., Khalil, I., Guizani, M., & Al-Fuqaha, A. (2017). Smart cities: A survey on data management, security, and enabling technologies. *IEEE Communications Surveys & Tutorials*, 19(4), 2456–2501. https://doi.org/10.1109/COMST.2017.2736886.

38. Appati, J. K., Nartey, P. K., Yaokumah, W., & Abdulai, J. (2022). A systematic review of fingerprint recognition system development. *International Journal of Software Science and Computational Intelligence (IJSSCI)*, 14(1), 1–17. http://doi.org/10.4018/IJSSCI.300358

39. Gaurav, A., Gupta, B. B., & Panigrahi, P. K. (2023). A comprehensive survey on machine learning approaches for malware detection in IoT-based enterprise information system. *Enterprise Information Systems*, 17(3), 2023764.

40. Kumar, R., Sinngh, S. K., & Lobiyal, D. K. (2023, April). Routing of vehicular IoT networks based on various routing metrics, characteristics, and properties. In *2023 International Conference on Computational Intelligence, Communication Technology and Networking (CICTN)* (pp. 656–662). IEEE.

41. Kumar, R., Singh, S. K., & Lobiyal, D. K. (2023). Communication structure for vehicular internet of things (VIoTs) and review for vehicular networks. In *Automation and Computation* (pp. 300–310). CRC Press.

42. Bouneb, Z. E. (2022). A distributed algorithm for computing groups in IoT systems. *International Journal of Software Science and Computational Intelligence (IJSSCI)*, 14(1), 1–21. http://doi.org/10.4018/IJSSCI.300363

43. Singh, M., Singh, S. K., Kumar, S., Madan, U., & Maan, T. (2021, September). Sustainable framework for metaverse security and privacy: Opportunities and challenges. In *International Conference on Cyber Security, Privacy and Networking* (pp. 329–340). Springer International Publishing.

44. Yetis, R., & Sahingoz, O. K. (2019). Blockchain based secure communication for IOT devices in Smart Cities. In *2019 7th International Istanbul Smart Grids and Cities Congress and Fair*. ICSG. https://doi.org/10.1109/sgcf.2019.8782285

45. Aggarwal, K., Singh, S. K., Chopra, M., & Kumar, S. (2022). Role of social media in the COVID-19 pandemic: A literature review. In *Data Mining Approaches for Big Data and Sentiment Analysis in Social Media* (pp. 91–115).

46. Kar, R. (2022). To study the impact of social network analysis on social media marketing using graph theory. *International Journal of Software Science and Computational Intelligence (IJSSCI)*, 14(1), 1–20. http://doi.org/10.4018/IJSSCI.304437

47. Narayan, N., Jha, R. K., & Singh, A. (2022). A differential epidemic model for information, misinformation, and disinformation in online social networks: COVID-19 vaccination. *International Journal on Semantic Web and Information Systems (IJSWIS)*, 18(1), 1–20. http://doi.org/10.4018/IJSWIS.300827

48. Osuolale, F. A. (2022). Reactive hybrid model for fault mitigation in real-time cloud computing. *International Journal of Cloud Applications and Computing (IJCAC)*, 12(1), 1–23. http://doi.org/10.4018/IJCAC.295240

49. Mayila Mve, W. J., & Ramaiah Yeluripati, G. (2023). Total commit and transaction off-chains (TCTOC): A blockchain scalability solution. In *2023 3rd International Conference on Electrical, Computer, Communications and Mechatronics Engineering (ICECCME)*, Tenerife, Canary Islands, Spain (pp. 1–5). http://doi.org/10.1109/ICECCME57830.2023.10252248.

50. Peñalvo, F. J. G., Sharma, A., Chhabra, A., Singh, S. K., Kumar, S., Arya, V., & Gaurav, A. (2022). Mobile cloud computing and sustainable development: Opportunities, challenges, and future directions. *International Journal of Cloud Applications and Computing (IJCAC)*, 12(1), 1–20.

51. Monrat, A. A., Schelén, O., & Andersson, K. (2019). A survey of blockchain from the perspectives of applications, challenges, and opportunities. *IEEE Access*, 7, 117134–117151. http://doi.org/10.1109/ACCESS.2019.2936094.

52. Sahoo, L., Panda, S. K., & Das, K. K. (2022). A review on integration of vehicular ad-hoc networks and cloud computing. *International Journal of Cloud Applications and Computing (IJCAC)*, 12(1), 1–23. http://doi.org/10.4018/IJCAC.300771

53. Singh, S. K., Sharma, S. K., Singla, D., & Gill, S. S. (2022). Evolving requirements and application of SDN and IoT in the context of industry 4.0, blockchain and artificial intelligence. In *Software Defined Networks: Architecture and Applications* (pp. 427–496).

54. Gupta, A., Singh, S. K., & Chopra, M. (2023). Impact of artificial intelligence and the internet of things in modern times and hereafter: An investigative analysis. In *Advanced Computer Science Applications* (pp. 157–173). Apple Academic Press.

55. Zhang, Y., Liu, M., Guo, J., Wang, Z., Wang, Y., Liang, T., & Singh, S. K. (2022, December). Optimal revenue analysis of the stubborn mining based on Markov decision process. In *International Conference on Machine Learning for Cyber Security* (pp. 299–308). Springer Nature Switzerland.

56. Sharma, K., Anand, D., Mishra, K. K., & Harit, S. (2022). Progressive study and investigation of machine learning techniques to enhance the efficiency and effectiveness of industry 4.0. *International Journal of Software Science and Computational Intelligence (IJSSCI)*, 14(1), 1–14. http://doi.org/10.4018/IJSSCI.300365

57. Singh, I., Singh, S. K., Singh, R., & Kumar, S. (2022, May). Efficient loop unrolling factor prediction algorithm using machine learning models. In *2022 3rd International Conference for Emerging Technology (INCET)* (pp. 1–8). IEEE.

58. Chopra, M., Singh, S. K., Aggarwal, K., & Gupta, A. (2022). Predicting catastrophic events using machine learning models for natural language processing. In *Data Mining Approaches for Big Data and Sentiment Analysis in Social Media* (pp. 223–243). IGI Global.

59. Peñalvo, F. J. G., Maan, T., Singh, S. K., Kumar, S., Arya, V., Chui, K. T., & Singh, G. P. (2022). Sustainable stock market prediction framework using machine learning models. *International Journal of Software Science and Computational Intelligence (IJSSCI)*, 14(1), 1–15.

60. Gupta, A., Singh, S. K., Gupta, B. B., Chopra, M., & Gill, S. S. (2023). Evaluating the sustainable COVID-19 vaccination framework of India using recurrent neural networks. *Wireless Personal Communications*, 1–19.

61. Kaur, P., Singh, S. K., Singh, I., & Kumar, S. (2021, December). Exploring Convolutional Neural Network in Computer Vision-based Image Classification. In *International Conference on Smart Systems and Advanced Computing (Syscom-2021)*. Springer.

62. Chopra, M., Singh, Dr. S. K., Gupta, A., Aggarwal, K., Gupta, B. B., & Colace, F. (2022). Analysis & prognosis of sustainable development goals using big data-based approach during COVID-19 pandemic. *Sustainable Technology and Entrepreneurship*, 1(2), 100012. https://doi.org/10.1016/j.stae.2022.100012

63. Martín, J. M., & Salinas Fernández, J. A. (2022). The effects of technological improvements in the train network on tourism sustainability. An approach focused on seasonality. *Sustainable Technology and Entrepreneurship*, 1(1), 100005. https://doi.org/10.1016/j.stae.2022.100005

64. Ortigueira-Sánchez, L. C., Welsh, D. H. B., & Stein, W. C. (2022). Innovation drivers for export performance. *Sustainable Technology and Entrepreneurship*, 1(2), 100013. https://doi.org/10.1016/j.stae.2022.100013

65. Singh, I., Singh, S. K., Kumar, S., & Aggarwal, K. (2022, July). Dropout-VGG based convolutional neural network for traffic sign categorization. In *Congress on Intelligent Systems: Proceedings of CIS 2021* (Vol. 1, pp. 247–261). Springer Nature Singapore.

66. Gupta, P., Yadav, K., Gupta, B. B., Alazab, M., & Gadekallu, T. R. (2023). A novel data poisoning attack in federated learning based on inverted loss function. *Computers & Security*, 130, 103270.

67. Mishra, A., Gupta, B. B., Peraković, D., Yamaguchi, S., & Hsu, C. H. (2021, January). Entropy based defensive mechanism against DDoS attack in SDN-Cloud enabled online social networks. In *2021 IEEE International Conference on Consumer Electronics (ICCE)* (pp. 1–6). IEEE.

Chapter 3

Recent Advances in Digital Forensics and Cybercrime Investigation

Sreerakuvandana, Agung Mulyo Widodo, Totok Ruki Biyanto, Princy Pappachan, and Francesco Colace

1. INTRODUCTION

Digital forensics is a branch within cybersecurity which focuses on recovery and the investigation of any material that can be found in digital devices and in cybercrimes. Initially, digital forensics was a synonym for computer forensics, but today the discipline has expanded its application to cover the investigation of all devices that store digital data. As the reliance on computer systems and cloud computing increases, digital forensics has emerged to be a crucial aspect of law enforcement and various businesses. Given the importance digital forensics has earned today, it is essential to look into the many realms of digital forensics and cybercrime, along with understanding the technicalities and the implications these fields have on law, society and the legal system.

The way digital forensics have developed is evidence of how quickly technology is advancing. When digital forensics first started out, its main focus was on recovering data from computer hard drives (Harbawi & Varol, 2016). However, the field of digital forensics expanded along with the technology. These days, it covers a broad spectrum of electronic gadgets, such as cell phones, cloud storage and even Internet of Things (IoT) devices. This growth is a direct result of cybercrime becoming more diverse, encompassing anything from identity theft and financial fraud to cyberterrorism and espionage.

To fully comprehend the subtleties of digital forensics, one must have a thorough understanding of the state of cybercrime today. Cybercrimes vary a lot in their nature, ranging from email scams to sophisticated ransomware attacks. The motives behind these scams and crimes are plenty, ranging from financial gain to political objectives (Alawida et al., 2022). This is where digital forensics become particularly useful. Typically, digital forensics involve the practice of identifying, acquiring, and analyzing any electronic evidence. Almost all the criminal activity carried out today has some element of electronic evidence. Digital forensic experts can provide the much-needed assistance to investigate of these crimes (Gaurav et al., 2021). One important element of digital forensics is the ability to analyze the suspected cyberattacks with the only objective of identifying, mitigating and eradicating any further cyberthreats, thus making digital forensics one critical aspect of the incident response process. Digital forensics is also useful in the aftermath of an attack, providing information that may be required by legal or law enforcement teams (Gupta & Agrawal, 2021). Electronic evidence from these crimes is gathered from sources ranging from computers to mobile devices to Internet of Things (IoT). Advancements in information technology have allowed it to be used as a criminal tool to perform, hide and serve as an aid in unethical activities. This is particularly relevant given how common computers are among the general public and how they allow individuals to appear anonymous even when they use computer systems to commit crimes. These are termed "cybercrimes". Focus on digital forensics in terms of apprehending and convicting computer criminals has increased recently (Lillis et al., 2016). Many

DOI: 10.1201/9781003207573-3

computer crime cases had remained unsolved before the development of reliable procedures and techniques in computer forensics. There are several reasons why cases end in acquittal, but the most obvious one would be that the authorities lack the instruments and expertise necessary to guarantee the successful gathering of digital evidence. The repercussions of these cybercrimes are also profound, affecting individuals and sometimes even the government, causing financial and reputational damage. To counter these, advancements in digital forensics play a very pivotal role. Experts in the field employ a variety of tools, such as recovering deleted files, decrypting encrypted data and trying to trace any anonymous online activity that potentially involve threats.

Digital forensics does not merely concern itself with digital and computing environments. In fact, it has a larger impact on society as computers and computerized devices are now a part of everyone's daily lives, making digital evidence critical to solving various types of crimes and legal issues. Massive volumes of data are generated by all connected devices. Numerous gadgets record everything that their users do in addition to the autonomous tasks that they carry out, like network connections and data transfers. This covers a wide range of devices in both the public and private domains, such as traffic lights, automobiles, cell phones, routers and personal computers.

However, digital forensics also has its fair share of challenges. The quick development of forensic methods continually evolves, and cybercriminals often use very nuanced and sophisticated techniques to escape any detection, including encryption and the darknet platforms. An additional layer of complexity is introduced by the legal and ethical considerations that arise in digital investigations. The cyber law field is constantly debating topics like jurisdictional limits, privacy concerns and the admissibility of digital evidence in court.

Integration of Artificial Intelligence (AI) and machine learning is one major development in digital forensics. Essentially, these technologies have the potential to automate even complex tasks like pattern recognition and detecting anomalies in large datasets (Alawida et al., 2022). Predictive policing, which enables law enforcement to stop cybercrimes before they happen, can also benefit from AI. But there are also important concerns regarding bias, dependability and ethical application raised by the use of AI in forensics. IoT, or Internet of Things, is one that has grown exponentially with the expansion of various IoT devices and applications. While some of these IoT devices are passive and are made active only when needed, others are connected and accessible over internet from almost anywhere. This proliferation of IoT devices as well as 5G technology has the potential to result in even more enhanced data generation, thus creating opportunities and challenges for digital forensics (Atlam et al., 2020).

In summary, the fields of cybercrime investigation and digital forensics are dynamic and always changing. We will examine the most recent developments in digital forensics tools and methods, the varieties of cybercrime and the difficulties faced by experts in the field as we delve deeper into this chapter. We will also look at how digital forensics will develop in the future and consider how the industry can keep evolving to meet the ever-changing issues of cybercrime.

2. LITERATURE REVIEW

It is now apparent that the internet, mobiles and computers have dramatically altered the way we think about the world. The proliferation of technology into modern society has had a massive impact on the behavior of humans. Essentially, the world around us is also being restructured around the use of CMCs, thus affecting the way we interact with entities such as business, government, politics and even education. At the same time, it is also creating a divide between generations based on the involvement of individuals in their use of technology (Gupta & Quamara, 2020).

2.1 Evolution of Digital Forensics

While it is impossible to state when the history of computer forensics began, it is widely accepted that the area of computer forensics began to evolve about 30 years ago. As computers became highly accessible to the public, so did the potential for their misuse. Computer crimes in the early days involved unauthorized access to systems and financial fraud (Gupta et al., 2020). Law enforcement and military investigators were among the first in the United States to notice that criminals were getting more sophisticated. When there was a suspicion of a security breach, government officials in charge of safeguarding private, secret and sensitive data conducted forensic investigations to not only identify the specific breach but also figure out how to prevent similar ones in the future. Information security, which protects data and assets, and computer forensics, which concentrates on responding to high-tech crimes, eventually combined. In the decades that followed, the field took off and is still expanding today. Law enforcement and the military maintain a significant presence in the fields of information security and computer forensics at the local, state and federal levels (Frąckiewicz, 2023). Private businesses and organizations have adopted similar strategies, either by employing specialists in internal information security and computer forensics or by contracting these specialists or services as needed. Notably, there has been an explosion in e-discovery because of the private legal sector's recent recognition of the necessity of computer forensic testing in civil litigation. The field of computer forensics is expanding daily (Gupta et al., 2022). Novel and robust forensic software solutions continue to be developed by software companies. Additionally, law enforcement teams are continuing to identify and educate people in the response to technology-related crimes.

In the 1980s, digital forensics came up with a set of specialized tools to counter cybercrimes. The 1990s saw major advancements in digital forensics, driven by the complexity of the computer systems and the growth of the internet. Digital forensics had to change when the World Wide Web was launched in 1991 because it gave cybercriminals access to a whole new set of opportunities. Several significant cases during this time period demonstrated the value of digital evidence in criminal investigations. Digital forensics continued to evolve at a very rapid pace. The proliferation of mobile devices such as tablets, phones, etc. only added further to the complexity. This meant investigators now had to be mindful of the new vast array of data sources such as text messages, call logs, GPS activity and social media activity of the user in question. Along with this, the new millennium also saw the rise of state-sponsored cyberterrorism and cyberattacks. This called for even more robust and newer digital forensic methods. In recent years, digital forensics has become quite sophisticated and specialized. The field today consists of network forensics, cloud forensics and mobile device forensics. The increasing significance of digital forensics has also prompted the creation of specialized educational curricula and professional certifications, assisting in guaranteeing that practitioners possess the know-how and abilities needed to meet the intricate problems of the digital era. Rapid technological progress and the growing need to combat cybercrime have shaped the development of digital forensics. Digital forensics, from its humble origins in the 1970s to its current state of sophistication, has been instrumental in identifying and stopping illegal activity in the digital sphere. The importance of digital forensics in preserving the security and integrity of our digital world will only increase as our reliance on digital gadgets and the internet grows.

2.2 Cybercrime: An Overview

Although the exact beginning date of cybercrime is up for debate, most experts concur that it began to gain traction in the late 1980s, when email started to become a widely used technology. Phishing is a modern manifestation of the widespread practice of using emails to spread viruses or carry out scams, which was a common element of early cybercrimes.

Cybercrime has a long history that begins with the inception of computer networks. When the first computer viruses were developed in the 1970s, they were some of the first cases ever documented. These early viruses were mostly used for practical jokes or academic experiments, and they were comparatively safe (Hildebrandt, Kiltz, & Dittmann, 2013). But they also created the framework for future cybercrimes that were more potent and malicious. As personal computers became more commonplace in the 1980s, so did the occurrence of cybercrime. During this time, hacking into computer networks, stealing confidential data and disseminating increasingly complex viruses were some of the early instances of cybercrime. One of the first laws passed to address these new cyberthreats was the Computer Fraud and Abuse Act of 1986 in the United States.

Cybercrime underwent a sea change with the introduction of the internet in the 1990s. The internet's widespread use has given cybercriminals access to a hugely expanded new area for their illegal activity. Identity theft, cyberstalking and online fraud all increased during this time. Law enforcement efforts are complicated by cybercriminals' ability to target victims beyond their physical location due to the anonymity and global reach of the internet. During the 1990s, one notable instance of cybercrime was the "ILOVEYOU" virus. Under the guise of a love letter, this malware infected millions of computers globally, resulting in damages worth billions of dollars. It brought attention to how destructive and widespread cybercrimes can be.

However, the New Millennium's arrival of social media brought with it a whole new realm of opportunity for cybercriminals to prey on. Suddenly, individuals everywhere were voluntarily disclosing their personal information online, frequently with public access. This easy prey provided fuel for an entire horde of identity thieves, who frequently exploited their illicitly obtained but inadequately safeguarded profits to obtain credit cards, bank accounts and other resources.

The period of 2010 and beyond saw cybercrime become more advanced and riskier. Cyber criminals were seen to use even more sophisticated tools like ransomware. This involves encryption of a victim's data leading to the demand for ransom for its release. With this, state-sponsored cyberattacks also became common. The rise of social media and mobile phones opened a door of opportunity for cybercrimes like cyber bullying and unauthorized access to one's personal data. Cryptocurrencies like Bitcoin gave rise to newer crimes like cryptojacking, where the criminals illegally mine cryptocurrencies using computing resources.

The field of cybercrime is always changing as we advance in the digital era. With millions of connected devices potentially vulnerable to hacking, the Internet of Things (IoT) offers a new frontier for cybercrimes. Another new threat is the use of artificial intelligence (AI) by cybercriminals, who can use it to automate attacks and create phishing schemes that work more effectively.

The growing relationship between cybercrime and other types of criminal activity is another cause for concern. For instance, the trafficking of drugs, people and terrorists is increasingly made possible by cybercrimes.

Figure 3.1 illustrates the approximate growth, which will be driven by increases in the number of internet users and connected intelligent devices. The graph shows the growth trend for the devices connected to the internet.

The use of digital technology such as computers and mobile devices to commit criminal activities is referred to as cybercrime. "Cyber criminal" is the name given to malicious actors who exploit the computer systems, its hardware, software and the network vulnerabilities for stealing any data to disrupting the business operations of a target. There are a range of cybercrimes that are recognized:

a. Phishing: Phishing involves impersonating any legitimate company or person to trick the user into revealing sensitive or personal information such as bank account details or education certificates.

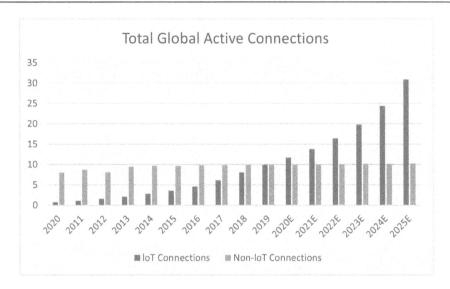

Figure 3.1 An estimate of the number of device connections by 2025

b. Hacking: Another common cybercrime is hacking. In this, the computer system or account gets unauthorized access to inflict further damage.

c. Malware: Malware is the spread of malicious software such as viruses and ransomware within a third party's device or the network. This is also done with the intention to gain access to the target's personal or sensitive information.

d. Identity theft: This involves stealing personal data such as name, address, etc., in order to assume someone else's identity.

Figure 3.2 discusses a range of cybercrimes that exist and the ones that are rampant.

Cybercrimes have the potential to impact businesses, society and the individual in a variety of ways. Financial loss is often the most common issue. Both individuals and businesses can suffer economic damage. This may involve stealing bank details. Personal effects include stress and anxiety for the individual. Business disruption also happens with cybercrime, wherein there is a denial of service for a company for as long as possible. This takes the shape of website downtime, leading to lost customers and profits.

There are a range of case studies that illustrate the range and nature of cybercrimes. Ranging from hacking and phishing to ransomware and espionage, every kind of cybercrime poses a unique challenge to everyone. One needs to understand these crimes and their real-world implications so that an effective strategy can be built to combat them.

2020 Twitter Bitcoin Scam: In July 2020, a significant security breach at Twitter resulted in the compromise of multiple prominent accounts, such as those of Bill Gates, Elon Musk and Barack Obama. The attackers posted phony tweets promising to double any amount sent, enticing followers to send Bitcoin to a given address. Significant questions were raised by this incident regarding the security of social media sites and the possibility of disseminating widespread false information.

Microsoft Exchange Server Attack (2021): Several zero-day vulnerabilities were discovered in Microsoft Exchange Server software early in 2021, impacting tens of thousands of businesses globally. Attackers were able to install malware, gain access to email accounts and make backdoors for later use thanks to this vulnerability. Because of this attack's widespread nature, critical infrastructure needs strong cybersecurity protections.

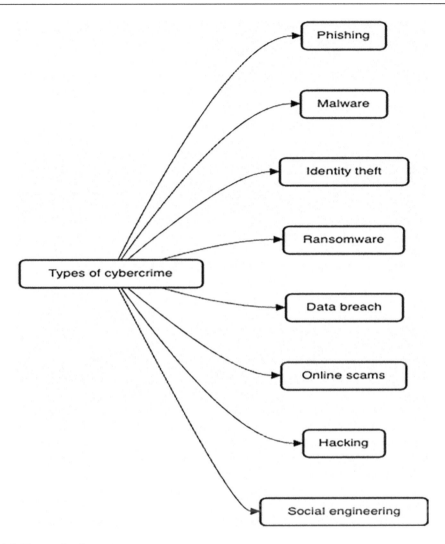

Figure 3.2 Types of cybercrime

Microsoft Bing AI Chatbot Leak: In 2023, there was an incident involving a data leak involving Microsoft's Bing AI chatbot. Sensitive information was unintentionally made public by the AI chatbot, which engages with users through conversational AI. This event brought to light the possible dangers of artificial intelligence and machine learning.

Growth in Frauds Concerning Cryptocurrencies: 2023 witnessed an increase in related cybercrimes due to the growing popularity of cryptocurrencies. These included hacking of cryptocurrency exchanges, investment scams and phishing attacks directed toward cryptocurrency wallets.

As technology advances, cybercrime also changes to get around current defenses. Early versions first appeared as viruses and scams enabled by email in the 1980s. The emergence of AI-driven phishing and social engineering, ransomware as a service (RaaS), commercial spyware and extortionware are some of the current trends in cybercrime.

Cybercriminals and those entrusted with stopping them are engaged in a never-ending game of cat and mouse, as evidenced by the history and development of cybercrime. As technology develops, cybercriminals' strategies and techniques also advance. It takes constant vigilance, adaptation and cooperation between law enforcement, governments and the private sector to stay ahead of these changing threats.

Cutting-edge tools like artificial intelligence (AI) and machine learning, which can identify and stop cyberattacks, hold the key to the prevention of cybercrime in the future. But because cybercrimes have no national boundaries, a global strategy is also necessary. In order to combat cybercrime, international collaboration and information sharing will be essential.

3. DIGITAL FORENSIC PROCESS

Experts in forensics use a methodical and organized procedure called digital forensics to investigate cybercrimes. There are multiple steps in this process, and each is essential to the integrity and accomplishment of the research: Identification, Preservation, Collection, Analysis and Presentation. Gaining insight into the intricacies and difficulties of digital forensic investigations can be achieved by thoroughly comprehending each step.

a. Digital evidence is gathered during the collection phase, usually by seizing physical assets like computers, hard drives and phones. It is crucial to ensure that no data is lost or damaged while being collected. You can prevent data loss by creating copies of the original data or storage media.
b. Data extraction and identification are part of the examination phase. Three steps make up this stage: prepare, extract and identify. When preparing to extract data, you can work on a live or dead system. For example, you can turn on a laptop and work directly on it, or you can connect a hard drive to a lab computer. During the identification phase, you must determine which data points are relevant to the investigation. Forensic investigators define the investigation's scope, which is determined by the specifics of the case. For example, email servers and end-user devices may be the main targets of email phishing attacks. In order to make sure that the evidence gathered is acceptable in court at this point, investigators also need to be aware of the legal and jurisdictional boundaries. In order to stop data from being written to the storage devices, write-blockers are frequently used. Another common procedure is to create a forensic image, which is a precise, bit-by-bit replica of the digital evidence. Because of this, data analysis can be done by investigators without jeopardizing the authenticity of the original evidence.
c. The analysis process uses the collected data to prove or disprove the case initially made by examiners. This includes understanding who created the data, who edited the data, how was the data made and when these activities occur. Analysis is the most complex of the process. It is carried out in a controlled environment with the use of specialized software tools. These tools useful for recovering any deleted file, decrypting of encrypted data and helping to analyze the internet history. In addition to technical proficiency, the analysis phase calls for a sharp investigative mindset. Investigators must work to piece together digital evidence and reconstruct the events in order. This may entail correlating data from various sources and searching for hidden or obfuscated information. This stage can be especially difficult and time-consuming in situations involving complex cybercrimes.
d. In the last step, reporting, synthesis of data and analysis of format happens for the whole thing to make sense for all. This report is deemed important because it contains all the information that the stakeholders can understand. Testifying in court is another aspect of the reporting stage in legal contexts. Under cross-examination, forensic investigators need to be able to defend their conclusions and provide an explanation of their

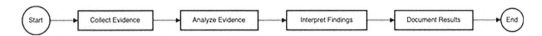

Figure 3.3 Digital forensic process

methodology. At this point, it is essential to have the ability to explain complicated technical concepts clearly and succinctly. Figure 3.3 illustrates the process.

Forensic experts have several obstacles and factors to navigate during these stages. Keeping up with the quick speed of technological change is one of the main challenges. Unexpected challenges in the gathering and analysis of evidence can arise from new gadgets and technologies as well as the growing usage of cloud services and encryption.

Ethical and legal concerns are also critical. Adhering to legal standards for search and seizure and respecting privacy rights are essential to guaranteeing the admissibility of evidence. Additionally, forensic specialists need to keep up with any changes to laws and rules that impact on their work. Nonetheless, digital forensic process is a cornerstone when it comes to fighting cybercrime. Essentially, it involves the use of technical expertise, their investigative skills and knowledge of the legal system. Staying abreast of the changes is essential in order to ensure that the digital investigations are effective, especially given that the technology keeps changing rapidly every day.

3.1 Advancements in Digital Forensic Tools

Rapid technological advancements have played a major role in the significant transformation of the field of digital forensics in recent years (Vincze, 2016). These developments have ushered in a new era for cybercrime investigation, with forensic specialists now equipped with state-of-the-art instruments and technologies to better tackle the difficulties presented by crafty cybercriminals. This section examines how investigation processes have been enhanced by recent developments in digital forensic tools.

Evolution of Digital Forensic Tools

Until the 1990s, digital forensics was referred to as computer forensics, and the first forensic technicians were law enforcement officers.

In terms of the digital world, digital forensics is a much younger field than forensic science itself, which has been around for over a century (including the first fingerprints ever recorded). This is primarily because digital forensics gained popularity after the introduction of personal computers in the 1980s. Around 1984, FBI labs produced some of the first tools used in digital forensic investigations. The FBI's specialized CART (Computer Analysis and Response Team) led the forensic investigations and assisted with digital investigations. In the past, the recovery and analysis of data in digital forensic investigations was primarily dependent on simple software. These instruments frequently had a narrow focus and found it difficult to keep up with how quickly digital technology was developing. Digital forensic tools have developed into sophisticated solutions that can handle a wide range of devices and platforms, complicated encryption and large volumes of data (Sachdeva, Raina, & Sharma, 2020).

Advanced Data Recovery and Analysis

Data recovery and analysis is one area where digital forensics has made some of its biggest strides. Data can be recovered from a wide range of sources using modern forensic tools, including smartphones, cloud storage, IoT devices and damaged or erased hard drives. These tools can recover data that was previously believed to be permanently lost by using sophisticated algorithms to reconstruct data from fragments. Tools like Encase Forensic and Magnet AXIOM, for instance, have revolutionized the industry and set new benchmarks. They provide services like timeline analysis, which assists investigators in piecing together events by generating a timeline of user activities, and artifact recovery, which can retrieve valuable data from files and applications.

Cloud Forensics

Cloud-based services have brought change to the way a company does its business. Companies embrace cloud migration through which businesses can host their software and their applications on inexpensive servers, thus saving time, money and the hassle of having to manage dedicated hardware. However, these cloud-based technologies are convenient and inexpensive. Cloud forensics is focused on crimes occurring primarily involving the cloud. These include data breaches and identity thefts. When cloud forensics is implemented, the owner essentially gets to protect and preserve their evidence. Cloud-based services like Dropbox, iCloud and Google Drive can have data accessed and extracted using cloud forensic tools like Oxygen Forensics and Cellebrite UFED. Additionally, they make it possible to analyze data from social media platforms, which is useful in some types of investigations.

Mobile Forensics

Mobile forensics is the process of obtaining digital evidence from mobile devices through established methods. Mobile forensics, in contrast to traditional digital forensics procedures, is limited to the recovery of data from mobile devices, including tablets, smartphones and Android phones. Law enforcement can greatly benefit from the wealth of information found on mobile devices, including location data, text message histories and web search histories. In this regard, tools like Cellebrite's UFED and MSAB XRY have been very helpful. They can get around some security measures on smartphones, making data that would not normally be accessible possible. Considering how important cell phones are to most people, this feature is essential.

Network Forensics

Network forensics concerns monitoring and analyzing the network traffic in order to detect and investigate cybercrimes. Advancements in network forensic tools have also exponentially improved the ability to trace and analyze data transmissions that occur over networks. These tools help in identifying any unauthorized access, data breaches and other such security concerns. Tools that offer in-depth analysis of network traffic include Wireshark and SolarWinds Network Performance Monitor. By allowing forensic specialists to record and examine data packets as they are transferred across a network, they can assist in spotting questionable activity and tracking down the origin of cyberattacks.

AI and Machine Learning in Digital Forensics

Digital forensics now features both Artificial Intelligence and Machine Learning (ML). With the help of these, it is now possible to enable the automation of complex and other time-consuming tasks like pattern recognition and anomaly detection (Jarrett & Choo, 2021).

Both AI and ML help in analyzing larger datasets very efficiently and quickly. For example, tools like IBM's Watson will analyze unstructured data from a range of sources. Forensic tools that are driven by AI also learn from previous investigations thus improving accuracy and efficiency with time.

Forensic Imaging Tools

To preserve the integrity of digital evidence, forensic imaging tools are crucial. These imaging tools have become so advanced that they now allow for the creation of exact copies of storage devices making sure that the original data is not changed in the process of investigation. These tools can handle a variety of storage media. Forensic imaging software such as DD and FTK Imager is frequently utilized. They can make bit-by-bit copies of hard drives, flash drives and other storage devices, retaining all data, including files that have been hidden or erased.

Cryptocurrency Tracing

The importance of forensic tools for monitoring and examining cryptocurrency transactions has increased with the rise of cryptocurrencies. These instruments can track the flow of cryptocurrency across the blockchain, assisting in the discovery of illegal activities such as money laundering. CipherTrace and Chainanalysis are some of the tools used in this field. These tools provide a detailed analysis of cryptocurrency transactions; they also help investigators trace the flow of funds and aid in identifying wallet addresses associated with the criminal activity that has taken place.

Automated Reporting and Visualization

A common feature of contemporary digital forensic tools is automated reporting and visualization. This feature is especially helpful for clearly presenting complex digital evidence. These days, tools produce comprehensive reports and visual aids, such as charts and graphs, that can aid court cases.

In spite of these developments, the field of digital forensics still faces difficulties. The copious amounts of data, variety of devices and platforms and advanced tactics utilized by cybercriminals persist in presenting formidable obstacles. Furthermore, rigorous adherence to ethical and legal standards is necessary to ensure that digital evidence is admissible in court.

In the coming years, the field of digital forensics will likely keep developing quickly. More and more AI and ML integration will be possible, providing even more advanced analytical capabilities. Furthermore, the industry will have to change to accommodate new and exciting technologies like 5G networks and quantum computing.

The field of cybercrime investigation has seen a transformation, thanks to developments in digital forensic tools. These tools have improved data recovery and analysis capabilities while also allowing forensic specialists to stay up to date with the constantly changing strategies used by cybercriminals. The methods and instruments of digital forensics will develop along with technology, guaranteeing that those tasked with investigating cybercrimes will have the means to effectively counteract these threats (Ghazinour et al., 2017).

3.2 Challenges in Digital Forensics

In the field of digital forensics, experts face a lot of challenges that further complicate the process of investigation. These challenges typically stem from various factors, including rapid advancements in technology and the complexity of digital environments and legal and ethical considerations (Mishra et al., 2021). The following section discusses these challenges, focusing on encryption, cloud computing, large data sets and legal and ethical considerations.

1. Encryption: One major hurdle in the field of digital forensics is encryption. Encryption is essential for protecting data from unwanted access, but it also makes forensic investigations very difficult.

   a. Robust Encryption Algorithms: With today's remarkably resilient encryption algorithms, decrypting data without the right key is extremely challenging, if not impossible. This makes it difficult to obtain important evidence.
   b. End-to-End Encrypted Communication: Applications such as WhatsApp and Signal that provide end-to-end encrypted communication shield the message content from view by anybody but the parties involved in the conversation. While this encryption safeguards user privacy, it also obstructs legal monitoring and inquiry.
   c. Decrypting Without Keys: It can be a difficult and time-consuming task for forensic experts to figure out how to decrypt data without the original encryption keys.

2. Cloud Computing: Cloud computing has typically transformed the way in which data is stored and accessed and the introduction of new challenges for further investigations.

   Data Location and Jurisdiction: One of the main issues with cloud computing is the possibility of data dispersal across several servers located in various regions, possibly even across international borders. This makes the investigation process more difficult because it involves several legal systems and jurisdictions.

   Access to Cloud Data: Collaboration between cloud service providers is frequently necessary to obtain access to data kept on cloud servers. Legal barriers or providers' reluctance to share data can impede this process.

   Broken Data: Information stored in the cloud may be broken up and dispersed throughout different places, which makes it challenging to put together and properly analyze.

3. Large Datasets: Data volume is a major concern given the data present in modern digital systems, as it may pose a significant challenge to investigators. Finding pertinent evidence in the massive amounts of digital data generated by the increase in data storage capacities makes it a difficult task.

   Complex Data Analysis: Advanced methods and tools are needed to analyze big data sets. Working with unstructured data or data in different formats and sources adds to the complexity.

   Limitations on Time and Resources: Large data sets can require a lot of time and resources to handle and analyze. It needs a lot of processing power and skilled labor, neither of which are always readily available.

4. Legal and Ethical Considerations: To make sure that the evidence gathered is acceptable in court and that people's rights are upheld, digital forensic investigations must handle a challenging terrain of ethical and legal issues.

   Privacy Concerns: It is critical to respect people's right to privacy. Except in cases where it is legally justified, investigators must make sure that their actions do not violate the individual's right to privacy.

Legal Compliance: All applicable laws, including those pertaining to international regulations, data protection and search and seizure, must be complied with by digital forensic operations. It can be difficult to navigate these legal frameworks, particularly when laws have not kept up with the advancements in technology.

The Custody Chain: For digital evidence, maintaining an appropriate chain of custody is essential. Any flaw in this procedure could raise concerns regarding the reliability and admissibility of evidence.

Ethical Hacking: Forensic experts may also sometimes have to employ techniques similar to ethical hacking in order to collect evidence. However, one must remember to carefully balance this against ethical considerations.

5. *Rapid Technological Advancements:* Digital forensic specialists are constantly faced with new challenges due to the rapid advancements in technology.

Keeping Up with New Technologies: To stay current with emerging technologies, forensic specialists need to regularly upgrade their knowledge and equipment. What is useful now might not be in a few years.

Devices for the Internet of Things (IoT): The growth of IoT devices brings with it new kinds of data and possible sources of evidence, each posing unique forensic difficulties.

6. Advanced Persistent Threats (APTs): APTs or Advanced Persistent Threats are sophisticated and prolonged cyberattacks where attackers typically gain access to a network and stay undetected for long periods.

Detection and Analysis: Identifying and detecting APTs is extremely difficult given their sophistication. These attacks employ advanced techniques to escape detection and subsequently hide them.

Digital forensics presents a wide range of intricate challenges. Experts in digital forensics have to maneuver through a constantly changing terrain, which includes technological obstacles like encryption and massive data sets as well as ethical and legal issues. Digital investigations are further complicated by the swift progress of technology and the worldwide scope of cybercrimes. A multifaceted strategy, including ongoing technological innovation, legal reforms, international cooperation and strict ethical standards, is needed to address these challenges. It will be essential to adjust to these challenges as the field of digital forensics develops in order to effectively investigate and prosecute cybercrimes.

4. CYBERCRIME LAWS AND REGULATIONS

One of the major reasons a comprehensible and exhaustive legal framework may be needed is because of the penetration of cybercrimes in the digital age. The laws and regulations specifically aim at combatting the various forms of cybercrime, ranging from hacking and data breach to online fraud and cyberterrorism. The following section outlines the international cybercrime laws and discusses the effectiveness and limitations of the current act.

4.1 Overview of International Cybercrime Laws

Because of the many legal, cultural and technological contexts, cybercrime laws differ greatly between nations. Nonetheless, several significant international initiatives and agreements seek to offer a coordinated strategy for battling cybercrime.

The Convention of Budapest: Known formally as the Convention on Cybercrime, it is the first international agreement that aims to combat computer and Internet crime by bringing national laws into compliance, enhancing investigative methods and fostering international cooperation (Pollitt, 2010). Many nations had ratified it as of 2023, with the notable exceptions being China, India and Russia.

Directives of the European Union: The EU has put into effect directives such as the NIS Directive, which focuses on network and information security, and the General Data Protection Regulation (GDPR), which contains provisions for data security and penalties for data breaches.

American States: Cybercrime is covered by several federal laws in the United States, such as the Cybersecurity Information Sharing Act (CISA), the Electronic Communications Privacy Act (ECPA) and the Computer Fraud and Abuse Act (CFAA). These laws address a variety of issues, including data protection and privacy as well as illegal access to computer systems.

Other National Laws: Aspects of the Budapest Convention are frequently mirrored in the cybercrime laws of other nations, such as the UK, Australia, Canada and Japan, with particular modifications made to fit their unique national circumstances.

Effectiveness of the Current Cybercrime Laws

There have been several successes and difficulties with cybercrime laws, which are still being debated.

Success in Prosecution and Deterrence: Cybercrime laws have frequently been effective in bringing offenders to justice and discouraging would-be online offenders. Strong laws have been demonstrated by high-profile cases involving identity theft, hacking and online fraud, in which offenders have been brought to justice.

Adaptation to Emerging Threats: Some legislation, especially in developed nations with advanced technology, have shown remarkable flexibility in responding to the ever-changing nature of cybercrime, including the introduction of new threats such as ransomware and cryptojacking.

4.2 Limitations of the Current Laws

Although the current laws have been successful and efficient, the current cybercrime laws face a lot of challenges.

1. Jurisdictional Challenge: The fact that cybercrimes fall under different jurisdictions is one of the main obstacles. Due to the fact that cybercrimes frequently cross national borders, investigations and prosecutions may become more difficult.
2. Rapid Technological Advancements: The rate of technological development frequently surpasses the capacity of laws to keep up. Cybercrimes are constantly evolving, and laws might not be able to fully address these new dangers.
3. Enforcing cybercrime laws can be difficult because of the anonymous nature of the internet and the sophisticated methods cybercriminals use to avoid detection.
4. Legal and Ethical Issues: Laws pertaining to data access and surveillance may give rise to issues with civil liberties and privacy that are both legal and ethical. It is an ongoing challenge to strike a balance between the protection of individual rights and the necessity for security.
5. Global Consensus: It is challenging to reach an international agreement on cybercrime laws. Diverse national viewpoints on matters such as data sovereignty, privacy and freedom of expression impact the development and implementation of these legal frameworks.

4.3 Case Studies of Cybercrime Legislation

Understanding some of the specific case studies and special cases can provide insights into their effectiveness and shed light on the limitations of cybercrime laws.

The WannaCry ransomware attack of 2017 brought attention to data privacy laws and the need for international cooperation in combating cybercrime. It raised awareness and improved national security protocols, but it also exposed the challenges associated with tracking down and prosecuting individuals abroad (*What Is WannaCry Ransomware?*, 2023). The Facebook-Cambridge Analytica data scandal brought data privacy laws, especially the General Data Protection Regulation (GDPR), into sharp relief (Wong, 2019).

4.4 Future Directions in Cybercrime Legislation

In the future, a few areas will be crucial to the development of cybercrime laws.

Harmonization of Laws: To effectively combat cross-border cybercrimes, there is an increasing need to harmonize cybercrime laws across various jurisdictions.

Updating Laws to Reflect Technological Advancements: It is essential that laws be updated continuously to reflect advancements in technology. Addressing cutting-edge technologies like AI and IoT is part of this.

Public-Private Partnerships: Creating more efficient policies and legislation to combat cybercrime requires enhancing cooperation between the public sector, private businesses and academic institutions.

Knowledge and Education: Raising public and organizational knowledge and education about cyber laws can help with prevention and guarantee improved compliance.

Laws and regulations pertaining to cybercrime are essential to combating digital crime. Even though these laws have been formulated and enforced with great success, difficulties still exist. Obstacles include jurisdictional concerns, the need for international cooperation and the speed at which technology is developing. The legislative frameworks that oversee the digital world must also change with it, ensuring they remain strong, flexible and efficient in the face of constantly evolving cyberthreats.

5. FUTURE DIRECTIONS IN DIGITAL FORENSICS AND CYBERCRIME

The domains of digital forensics and cybercrime are ripe for major changes as we maneuver through the constantly changing technological terrain. Along with new threats and technologies, developments in predictive analytics will play a major role in shaping future directions in these domains. This section delves into these facets, providing perspectives on potential developments in the future.

5.1 Predictive Analytics in Digital Forensics

Predictive analysis plays a very pivotal role when it comes to shaping the future of digital forensics (Chang et al., 2013). Predictive analytics uses data, statistical algorithms and machine learning techniques to anticipate possible cyberattacks before they happen.

   a. Behavioral Analysis for Threat Detection: Using data patterns, predictive analytics can find unusual behavior that could point to a cyberthreat. Predictive models track system logs, user activity and network traffic to anticipate possible security incidents.

b. Improving Investigative Procedures: Predictive analytics can aid in the quicker and more effective identification of possible evidence sources in digital investigations. It can expedite the investigation process by ranking data sources according to historical cases and current patterns.
c. Predictive Policing in Cybersecurity: To tackle cybercrime, law enforcement organizations are starting to apply predictive policing techniques. These techniques can forecast the chance of cybercrimes in particular domains or industries.

5.2 Emerging Threats in Cybercrime

With technology continuing to advance, newer types of cyberthreats emerge, thus posing challenges to professionals of cybersecurity and digital forensics.

a. AI-powered Cyber Attacks: Cybercriminals' use of AI is a growing threat. Robust cyberattacks can be automated by AI, increasing their effectiveness and difficulty to identify. Artificial intelligence (AI) can be used in cybercrimes such as identity theft and disinformation campaigns, as demonstrated by deepfake technology, which uses AI to produce realistic-sounding fake audio and video.
b. The Evolution of Ransomware and Cryptojacking: More complex ransomware attacks are targeting larger organizations and extorting larger ransom payments. In a similar vein, cryptojacking—the unlawful use of another person's computer resources for cryptocurrency mining—is growing in popularity.
c. IoT Device Security Flaws: There are more opportunities for cyberattacks due to the growing number of IoT devices. Because many IoT devices don't have strong security, they can be hacked and used maliciously.

Figure 3.4 illustrates the total number of cases the FBI IC3 tracked the total number of complaints and losses from 2001 to 2019 (Jarrett & Choo, 2021). There has also been an increase of an average of 44.4% yearly in total losses apart from what is noted in Figure 3.3.

Figure 3.5 depicts the risks of a compromised cybersecurity practice and shows how multifaceted these are. The lines on the graph vary significantly across those three metrics, defying the notion that the number of records exposed, the number of people impacted, and the number of data compromises all increase over time.

These sharp variations are mostly the result of significant data breaches that have occurred over the past few years. The data commentary by Statista, which was released in April 2023, highlights the fact that significant rises in these compromises are mostly industry-specific. The largest data breaches as of 2022 occurred in the sizable industries of manufacturing, financial services and healthcare.

5.3 Emerging Technologies in Digital Forensics

Advancements happening in technology also drive the evolution happening within digital forensics. They provide new tools and methodologies to counter cybercrime.

a. Blockchain Technology in Forensics: Applications of blockchain technology in digital forensics are possible. The integrity and credibility of digital evidence in court cases can be improved by using it to create tamper-proof logs.
b. Quantum Cryptography and Computing: The emergence of quantum computing in the field of digital forensics brings with it both possibilities and challenges. Current encryption algorithms may be broken by quantum computers, so developing quantum-resistant cryptography is necessary.

IC3 report year	Total complaints	Total losses
2019	467,361	$ 3,500,000,000
2018	351,937	$ 2,710,000,000
2017	301,580	$ 1,420,000,000
2016	298,728	$ 1,330,000,000
2015	288,012	$ 1,070,711,522
2014	269,422	$ 800,492,073
2013	262,813	$ 781,841,611
2012	289,874	$ 525,441,110
2011	314,246	$ 485,253,871
2010	303,809	
2009	336,655	$ 559,700,000
2008	275,284	$ 264,600,000
2007	206,884	$ 239,100,000
2006	207,492	$ 198,400,000
2005	231,493	$ 183,100,000
2004	207,449	$ 68,100,000
2003	124,515	$ 125,600,000
2002	75,064	$ 54,000,000
2001	50,412	$ 17,800,000

Figure 3.4 The total number of cases of losses tracked by FBI from 2001 to 2019

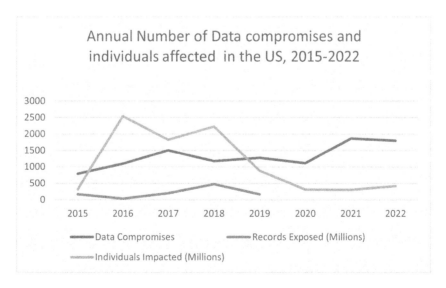

Figure 3.5 Data compromises and the number of individuals affected in the United States, 2015–2022 (Fong & Fong, 2023)

c. AI System Forensic Analysis: The need for forensic analysis of AI systems is growing as these systems become more prevalent. This entails looking into the AI systems that were a part of the incidents or examining the potential applications of AI in cybercrimes.

6. CHALLENGES AND OPPORTUNITIES FOR DIGITAL FORENSICS

While the digital age has undoubtedly revolutionized the lives of many, the major concern raised is that cybercrime has also risen at an alarming rate. Therefore, this is a major concern for cyber specialists as changes in the digital and real world attract a range of cybercrimes. Some of the potential challenges are:

a. Keeping Pace with Technology: Staying ahead of rapid technological advancements seems to be the biggest challenge. Forensic professionals must also update their skills and tools to stay updated on the new types of digital evidence and the cybercrime that arises.
b. Cross-Disciplinary Expertise: In order to effectively combat cybercrime, digital forensics may see increased collaboration between various fields in the future, including cybersecurity, data science and law enforcement.
c. Ethics in Artificial Intelligence and Predictive Policing: Predictive analytics and AI use present ethical challenges, especially when it comes to privacy and potential biases in predictive models. It will be essential to make sure these technologies are used responsibly.

7. ROLE OF LEGISLATION AND POLICY

Along with everything else, the legal and regulatory landscape will have to adapt to the dynamic nature of digital forensics and cybercrime (Flaglien, 2017).

Laws and regulations pertaining to digital evidence and cybercrime will need to be updated to consider the new tools and techniques that cybercriminals are using.

Since cybercrimes frequently occur across national boundaries, it will be crucial to foster greater international cooperation and establish global standards for digital forensics.

7.1 Education and Training in Digital Forensics

In order to make better professionals in the field, it is important to invest in educating and training in digital forensics. There are universities and programs that offer specialized training and programs in digital forensics and cybersecurity that focus on the emerging threats and technologies.

8. FUTURE RESEARCH DIRECTIONS

The challenges presented by emerging technologies and threats will require the focus of research in the fields of digital forensics and cybercrime.

Research on AI and Machine Learning: One of the main areas of focus will be on figuring out how AI and machine learning can be used to fight AI-driven cybercrimes and effectively apply them in digital forensics.

Examining Quantum-Resistant Cryptography: As quantum computing becomes more common, research into creating cryptography that is resistant to attacks using quantum computing will be crucial.

Advancements in technology, the emergence of new threats and the future of digital forensics are intricately tied together. One way to effectively combat cybercrime is by using predictive analysis, which also presents new challenges and allows us to think about the ethics. Together, the field must also begin to adapt to the upcoming threats like AI-powered attacks and IoT vulnerabilities while embracing newer technologies that can improve forensic capabilities.

9. INTEGRATING AI AND MACHINE LEARNING IN FORENSICS

A revolutionary step forward is represented by the integration of machine learning (ML) and artificial intelligence (AI) in forensic science. These technologies have the potential to significantly improve the efficacy, precision and efficiency of forensic investigations—especially in the areas of cybercrime detection and digital forensics.

9.1 AI in Cybercrime Detection

Generative artificial intelligence technology not only threatens human jobs, but also gives rise to various cyberthreats. AI helps cybercriminals generate malware and automate attacks, along with improving effectiveness of scams through tools such as deepfakes and human-sounding AI-powered voice synthesis. AI has a significant role to play in the cyberthreat landscape (Mitchell, 2010). At the same time, cybersecurity experts are making good use of the same AI to improve the defense mechanism, therefore offering preventive solutions (Carlson, 2021). The following are some of the commonly used techniques:

1. Pattern Recognition: AI particularly excels when it comes to identifying patterns in large datasets. This plays an important role in detecting cybercrimes. For example, artificial intelligence (AI) algorithms can analyze network traffic in order to spot odd patterns that point to cyberattacks, like denial-of-service (DDoS) attacks or network intrusions.
2. Anomaly Detection: AI systems are good at spotting behavioral irregularities, which is essential for spotting online dangers. An AI system may, for instance, alert users to unusual activity in their accounts, which may point to a security breach or unauthorized access.
3. Dynamic Risk Assessment: Artificial intelligence (AI) continuously scans data streams for possible threats, enabling dynamic risk assessment. Cyberattacks must be promptly identified and mitigated, which requires real-time analysis.
4. Automated Reactions to Dangers: AI systems are capable of both detecting threats and initiating automated reactions. For example, an AI system can isolate compromised systems to stop malware from spreading after identifying an infection.

Figure 3.6 outlines some of the most prominent benefits of AI in cybercrime and why AI is preferred to combat cybercrimes.

9.2 Machine Learning for Data Analysis

Machine Learning involves automating analytical model building. It is also a branch of artificial intelligence built around the concept that systems also can learn from data, identify any pattern that may exist and make decisions with very minimal human interaction (Al Fahdi et al., 2013). Machine Learning relies on algorithms to analyze data, to identify

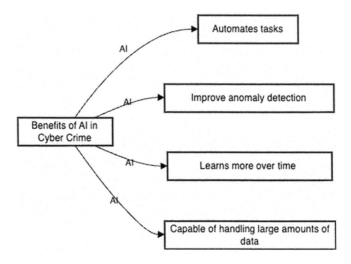

Figure 3.6 Benefits of AI in cybercrime

patterns and build mathematical models based on these identified patterns. Here are some of the ways in which Machine Learning is used for data analysis:

1. Enhanced Data Processing: Handling Large Data Volumes: Given time and resource constraints, one of the main advantages of machine learning (ML) in forensics is its capacity to process and analyze large amounts of data quickly. This is a task that human investigators cannot accomplish.

   Big Data Analytics: ML algorithms are designed to handle big data, which often involves working with matrices and vectors. A simple linear regression model, for instance, can be represented as a matrix equation:

   $$Y = XW + \epsilon$$

   where Y is the response vector, X is the matrix of predictors, W is the weight matrix and ϵ is the error vector.

2. Data Classification and Clustering: Machine learning algorithms are capable of classifying and clustering large datasets, which is essential for forensic investigations as it helps separate pertinent information from irrelevant data.

   Classification: Algorithms like logistic regression model the probability of a binary outcome as a logistic function:

   $$P(Y = 1) = \frac{1}{1 + e^{-(\beta_0 + \beta_1 X)}}$$

   Clustering: K-means clustering, for instance, aims to partition n observations into k clusters in which each observation belongs to the cluster with the nearest mean. The objective function is:

   $$\text{Minimize} \sum_{i=1}^{k} \sum_{x \in S_i} \left\| x - \mu_i \right\|^2$$

   where S_i are the sets of observations in each cluster and μ_i are the means of the clusters.

3. Advanced Analytical Methodologies: Predictive Modeling: Machine learning can be applied to predictive modeling, which makes use of historical data to forecast and anticipate future patterns in cybercrime. This proactive strategy is essential for anticipating and averting future assaults.

Predictive Models: A common predictive model is the decision tree, which can be represented using information gain or Gini impurity. For a set S, Gini impurity is given by:

$$G(S) = 1 - \sum_{i=1}^{n} p_i^2$$

Where p_i is the probability of an item in S belonging to class i.

4. Behavioral Analysis: ML can assist in the profiling of cybercriminals and the comprehension of their strategies, methods and procedures by examining patterns of behavior.

Pattern Recognition: Neural networks are often used in pattern recognition. For example, a basic feedforward neural network can be represented as:

$$Y = f(W_2 \cdot f(W_1 \cdot X + B_1) + B_2)$$

where W_1, W_2 are weight matrices, B_1, B_2 are bias vectors and f is an activation function like the sigmoid or ReLU.

9.3 Automating the Forensic Process

Artificial Intelligence (AI), Machine Learning (ML) and Deep Learning (DL) are some of the methods that have been used to foster automation in forensic science in order to solve crimes (Ahvanooey et al., 2021). Numerous forensic science applications, including image recognition, image and video analysis, gunshot detection, firearm identification, 3D crime scene reconstruction, handwriting identification and large-scale data analysis, have shown AI to be extremely helpful. In addition, this technology has made it possible to determine age, time since death and personal identification using information from dental exams, determine the gender of skeletal remains, reconstruct a person's face in three dimensions from an unknown skull and detect cybercrimes and digital evidence (Garfinkel, 2010). The development of AI technologies has benefited law enforcement and security personnel in detecting, preventing and forecasting crimes. Recently, highly efficient AI algorithms have been created to identify suspicious anomalies, crime patterns and criminal networks. Pattern recognition of crime scene evidence, including bitemarks, shoe prints, bullet marks and lip prints, is made possible by AI. Depending on the kind of learning process, automatic machine recognition performs the function of pattern identification. Based on data analysis, automated AI systems can accurately narrow down a crime's suspects. Neural networks have shown to be the most effective AI algorithm for automatic human face recognition among other algorithms. Neural networks have been used to recognize faces, irises, fingerprints and visual images.

Automated Data Extraction

The extraction of data from numerous digital sources can be automated with the help of AI and ML, greatly accelerating the forensic investigation process.

1. Automated Data Extraction: Term Frequency-Inverse Document Frequency (TF-IDF)

   - Term Frequency (TF) for a word in a document is calculated as:

$$\text{TF}(t,d) = \frac{\text{Number of times term } t \text{ appears in document } d}{\text{Total number of terms in the document}}$$

- Inverse Document Frequency (IDF) is calculated as:

$$\text{IDF}(t,D) = \log\left(\frac{\text{Total number of documents in the corpus } D}{\text{Number of documents with term } t}\right)$$

- Thus, TF-IDF is given by:

$$\text{TF} - \text{IDF}(t,d,D) = \text{TF}(t,d) \times \text{IDF}(t,D)$$

Enhanced Evidence Analysis

Compared to manual techniques, artificial intelligence (AI) can analyze digital evidence—such as photos, videos and documents—more rapidly and precisely. AI systems, for example, are capable of automatically sifting through thousands of files to locate particular kinds of information pertinent to a particular inquiry.

The covariance matrix C of a dataset is given by:

$$C = \frac{1}{N-1}\sum_{i=1}^{N}(x_i - \mu)(x_i - \mu)^T$$

- PCA seeks to find the eigenvalues λ and eigenvectors v of C:

$$Cv = \lambda v$$

Mitigating Human Error

Artificial Intelligence and Machine Learning have the potential to decrease human error in forensic investigations, resulting in more precise and dependable results.

Objective Analysis: By eliminating potential biases that could sway human investigators, machine learning algorithms can offer a certain amount of objectivity in data analysis.

Gini Impurity in Decision Trees

Gini impurity for a dataset is calculated as:

$$G = 1 - \sum_{i=1}^{J} p_i^2$$

where p_i is the probability of an item being classified to class i.

4. Deep Learning for Complex Pattern Recognition: LSTM Networks

- The LSTM cell updates are given by:

$$f_t = \sigma\left(W_f \cdot [h_{t-1}, x_t] + b_f\right)$$
$$i_t = \sigma\left(W_i \cdot [h_{t-1}, x_t] + b_i\right)$$
$$\tilde{C}_t = \tanh\left(W_C \cdot [h_{t-1}, x_t] + b_C\right)$$
$$C_t = f_t * C_{t-1} + i_t * \tilde{C}_t$$
$$o_t = \sigma\left(W_o \cdot [h_{t-1}, x_t] + b_o\right)$$
$$h_t = o_t * \tanh(C_t)$$

where σ is the sigmoid function, and W and b are weights and biases.

Neural Networks for Pattern Recognition:

Fundamentals: Neural networks are systems of interconnected "neurons" that process information using a connectionist approach to computation. In mathematical terms, a simple neuron's output, y, is given by $y = f\left(\sum_{i=1}^{n} w_i x_i + b\right)$, where x_i are inputs, w_i are weights, b is a bias and f is an activation function like the sigmoid or ReLU.

Face Recognition: Convolutional Neural Networks (CNNs), a class of deep neural networks, are widely used for image recognition tasks. In a CNN, the convolution operation is mathematically defined as $S(i,j) = (I * K)(i,j) = \sum_m \sum_n I(m,n) K(i-m, j-n)$, where I is the input image and K is the kernel.

5. Biometric Recognition: Support Vector Machines (SVM)

The optimization problem for SVM is formulated as:

$$\min_{w,b} \frac{1}{2} \| w \|^2$$

subject to $y_i (w \cdot x_i + b) \geq 1$ for each i,

where w is the normal vector to the hyperplane, b is the bias, x_i are the input vectors and y_i are the class labels.

10. INTERNATIONAL COLLABORATION AND POLICIES

Coherent international policies and international collaboration are essential in the face of growing global cyberthreats. Because cyberthreats frequently transcend national boundaries due to the transnational nature of the internet and digital technologies, isolated efforts by individual nations are insufficient (Cisar, Cisar, & Bosnjak, 2014). This section explores the complexities of cross-border data exchange, global cyber laws and the dynamics of international collaboration.

10.1 Global Cyber Laws

The main international treaty that seeks to improve legal instruments, harmonize national laws and fortify international cooperation against cybercrime is the Budapest Convention on Cybercrime, which is a product of the Council of Europe (Edwards, 2023). It covers offenses pertaining to data and computer systems as well as offenses involving content.

Regional Initiatives: Significant efforts have been made by organizations like the European Union to harmonize cybersecurity laws among their member states. The General Data Protection Regulation (GDPR) of the European Union is a groundbreaking legislation that establishes strict guidelines for data protection and has impacted similar laws across the globe.

10.2 Challenges in Global Cyber Law Harmonization

Diverse Legal Frameworks: It is still difficult to harmonize the many legal systems found in various nations. Different national views on state sovereignty, privacy and freedom of speech can make it difficult to create consistent international cyber laws (Praneeth, 2022).

Modernizing Laws to Reflect Technological Advancements: Legislative processes are frequently outpaced by rapid advancements in technology. It's a constant struggle to keep cyber laws current with new technologies like blockchain, AI and IoT.

10.3 International Collaboration in Cybersecurity

Cooperative Initiatives and Information Sharing:

Multilateral Platforms: Through information exchange, best practices, and cooperative operations against cyberthreats, platforms like the Global Cyber Alliance and INTERPOL's Cyber Fusion Centre promote international cooperation (Sabillon et al., 2017).

Joint Cybersecurity Exercises and Training: International cybersecurity drills, such as the Locked Shields exercise conducted by the NATO Cooperative Cyber Defence Centre of Excellence, improve national readiness and collaboration.

Public-Private Partnerships: In order to combat global cyberthreats, cooperation between governments and private organizations, such as tech companies and cybersecurity firms, is essential. These collaborations make use of the advantages and skills of both industries.

10.4 Evolving International Policies

Adapting to New Cyberthreats

Emerging Technology Policies: In response to the challenges presented by these technologies, international policies must change. Regulations concerning, for example, the security of Internet of Things devices and the moral application of AI in cybersecurity are becoming increasingly significant.

Cybersecurity Standards and Best Practices: Creating and implementing global cybersecurity standards and best practices can contribute to the development of a more resilient and safer online community.

Building National Cybersecurity Capabilities: Less developed nations require international assistance to develop their cybersecurity capacities. This entails offering guidance, materials and technical assistance.

Global Cybersecurity Alliances: The United Nations and alliances such as the Five Eyes contribute to international collaboration in the field of cybersecurity.

Because cyberthreats and digital forensics are globally distributed by nature, cooperation and well-coordinated policies are crucial. Even though there have been great advancements in improving cross-border data exchange and harmonizing global cyber laws, there are still difficulties. These include the balancing act between security needs and privacy rights, cultural and legal differences and the rapid evolution of technologies. In order to strengthen international cybersecurity and successfully combat cybercrime, countries must continue to collaborate through multilateral agreements, joint initiatives and cooperative frameworks. The capacity of nations to innovate, cooperate and adapt to a constantly shifting digital threat landscape will determine the direction of international cybersecurity in the future.

10.5 Challenges in International Cooperation

Diverse Capabilities and Resources: There is a huge disparity in the capabilities of cybersecurity and its resources among countries that will obstruct effective collaboration.

Trust and Intelligence Sharing: Having to build trust among nations for intelligence sharing within the realm of cybersecurity is slightly complicated and is often mired in concerns that include national security.

11. THE FUTURE OF DIGITAL FORENSICS AND CYBERCRIME INVESTIGATION

The future of digital forensics and cybercrime investigation offers both formidable challenges and exciting opportunities as we stand at the nexus of technology and law enforcement

(Baggili & Behzadan, 2019). Technological progress has given rise to increasingly complex cybercrimes, which has required a corresponding development in digital forensics (Cvitić, Praneeth, & Peraković, 2021). The future of these fields is examined in this chapter, with particular attention paid to technological developments, the changing nature of cybercrimes, the importance of international cooperation and the moral and legal issues that will influence these fields' courses.

11.1 Technological Advancements and Digital Forensics

Incorporating Cutting-Edge Technologies

a. Artificial Intelligence and Machine Learning: It is anticipated that digital forensics will increasingly use AI and ML in their operations. With the help of these technologies, the investigation process will be able to process massive datasets more efficiently and accurately by identifying patterns and automating certain tasks.

- Linear Regression: A simple linear regression model can be expressed as $y = \beta_0 + \beta_1 x + \epsilon$, where y is the dependent variable, x is the independent variable, β_0 is the y-intercept, β_1 is the slope and ϵ represents the error term.
- Neural Networks: A feedforward neural network with one hidden layer can be mathematically represented as $y = f_2\left(W_2 f_1\left(W_1 x + b_1\right) + b_2\right)$, where W and b are weights and biases, and f represents activation functions like the sigmoid function $\sigma(z) = \dfrac{1}{1 + e^{-z}}$.

b. Quantum Computing: The emergence of quantum computing poses a dual challenge: although it can undermine established cryptographic techniques, it also provides novel instruments for encryption and data processing.

- Qubit Representation: A qubit in a superposition state can be expressed as $|\psi\rangle = \alpha|0\rangle + \beta|1\rangle$, with $|\alpha|^2 + |\beta|^2 = 1$, where α and β are complex probability amplitudes.
- Quantum Entanglement: In an entangled state of two qubits, the state cannot be expressed as a product of the states of individual qubits; for instance, the Bell state $|\Phi^+\rangle = \dfrac{1}{\sqrt{2}}(|00\rangle + |11\rangle)$.

c. Blockchain for Evidence Management: By offering a safe, unhackable way to store and track digital evidence, blockchain technology has the potential to completely transform evidence management in digital forensics.

- Hash Functions: A cryptographic hash function, such as SHA-256 used in Bitcoin, transforms an input (or "message") into a fixed-size string of bytes. The output is typically a 256-bit (32-byte) hash, which is a seemingly random sequence of letters and numbers.
- Proof of Work: Involves solving a computationally difficult problem, which can be represented as finding a number n such that when hashed with the hash function H, the result $H(n)$ begins with a certain number of zero bits.

11.2 Challenges and Opportunities

Keeping Pace with Rapid Technological Change: Keeping forensic techniques and instruments current with quickly advancing technologies will be one of the biggest challenges (Richard & Roussev, 2006).

Skilling and Training: To remain proficient in utilizing new technologies and procedures, forensic professionals will require an ever-increasing amount of ongoing learning and development.

11.3 Evolving Nature of Cybercrime

Cybercrime will continue to evolve with every advancement that happens in technology. The following are some of the possible new forms of cybercrime (Williams, 2023).

Rise of IoT and Smart Device Attacks: IoT devices will probably be the target of more cyberattacks as they become more widespread, posing new difficulties for digital forensics.

Deepfakes and Crimes Produced by AI: Deepfakes and other AI technologies have the potential to be abused, which could lead to fraud and the spread of false information.

Figure 3.7 gives a glimpse of the industries most targeted for cybercrime-related activities. Web-based emails are the most targeted form of phishing, followed by financial institutions, where spam continues to be a dominant force and is often considered to be the easiest way to reach a huge number of victims.

12. ETHICAL AND LEGAL CONSIDERATIONS

Data Security and Personal Freedom

A significant ethical challenge will be striking a balance between the need for security and individual privacy rights in the face of growing surveillance and data analysis capabilities.

Lawful Structures Keeping Up with Technology: In order to safeguard individual rights and facilitate efficient cybercrime investigations, legal frameworks will need to constantly adapt to the complexities brought about by new technologies.

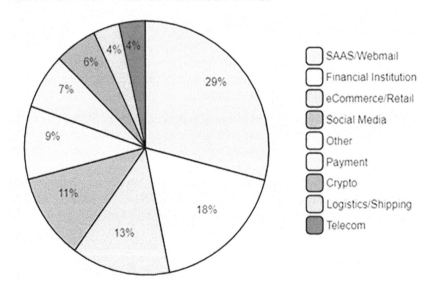

Figure 3.7 Phishing activity trends report in the year 2021 (APWG, 2019)

12.1 AI's Ethical Application in Forensics

Managing Bias in AI: It will be essential to make sure that AI utilized in digital forensics is developed and used ethically, and that it is free of biases (Hefetz, 2023; Sahoo & Gupta, 2021).

Transparency and Accountability: In order to preserve legal requirements and public confidence, it will be crucial to maintain transparency and accountability when using AI and automated systems in forensic investigations.

13. FUTURE RESEARCH AND DEVELOPMENT

13.1 Areas for Future Research

Creating More Complex Forensic Tools: To handle new kinds of digital evidence, ongoing research is required to create more complex and effective forensic tools.

Examining the Societal Impact of Cybercrimes: Creating effective countermeasures will require an understanding of the wider societal impact of cybercrimes, including their psychological and economic ramifications.

Public-Private Collaborations in Research: Collaboration that happens between university, business and law enforcement agencies is one key factor in fostering innovation and research within digital forensics and cybercrime investigation.

14. CONCLUSION

Cybercrime investigation and digital forensics are on the verge of exciting and difficult new frontiers. Technological developments offer improved capabilities in the fight against cybercrimes, but they also introduce new risks and moral dilemmas. There has never been a more pressing need for knowledgeable experts, global cooperation and flexible legal frameworks. To ensure a safe digital future for everybody, it is essential that efforts in digital forensics and cybercrime investigation be comprehensive, inclusive and forward-thinking. It is unlikely that cybercrime in all its manifestations will go away; rather, it will only grow in scope and intensity. It is possible to make inferences from historical events and apply that knowledge to deter crime in the future. Cyberlaw must adapt and advance at the same rate as hackers in order to remain competitive in combating cybercrime. The law must also strike a balance between violating people's rights and shielding them from crime. The internet's freedom and vastness are its advantages.

REFERENCES

Ahvanooey, M. T., Zhu, M. X., Li, Q., Mazurczyk, W., Choo, K. K. R., Gupta, B. B., & Conti, M. (2021). Modern authentication schemes in smartphones and IoT devices: An empirical survey. *IEEE Internet of Things Journal*, 9(10), 7639–7663.

Alawida, M., Omolara, A. E., Abiodun, O. I., & Al-Rajab, M. (2022). A deeper look into cybersecurity issues in the wake of Covid-19: A survey. *Journal of King Saud University – Computer and Information Sciences*, 34(10), 8176–8206. https://doi.org/10.1016/j.jksuci.2022.08.003

Al Fahdi, M., Clarke, N. L., & Furnell, S. M. (2013, August). Challenges to digital forensics: A survey of researchers & practitioners attitudes and opinions. In *2013 Information Security for South Africa* (pp. 1–8). IEEE.

APWG: Phishing Activity Trends Report Q4 2018. (2019). *Computer Fraud & Security*, 2019(3), 4. https://doi.org/10.1016/s1361-3723(19)30025-9

Atlam, H. F., Alenezi, A., Alassafi, M. O., Alshdadi, A. A., & Wills, G. B. (2020). Security, cybercrime and digital forensics for IoT. In *Principles of Internet of Things (IoT) Ecosystem: Insight Paradigm* (pp. 551–577).

Baggili, I., & Behzadan, V. (2019). Founding the domain of AI forensics. *arXiv preprint*, arXiv:1912.06497.

Carlson, B. (2021, May 6). *The Microsoft Exchange Server Hack: A Timeline*. CSO Online. https://www.csoonline.com/article/570653/the-microsoft-exchange-server-hack-a-timeline.html

Chang, Y. T., Chung, M. J., Lee, C. F., Huang, C. T., & Wang, S. J. (2013). Memory forensics for key evidence investigations in case illustrations. *Information Security (Asia JCIS)*, Article 6621658, 96–101.

Cisar, P., Cisar, S., & Bosnjak, S. (2014). Cybercrime and digital forensics-technologies and approaches. In *DAAAM International Scientific Book*. DAAAM International Scientific Book.

Cvitić, I., Praneeth, G., & Peraković, D. (2021). *Digital Forensics Techniques for Social Media Networking* (p. 1). Insights2Techinfo. https://insights2techinfo.com/digital-forensics-techniques-for-social-medianetworking/

Edwards, B. (2023, February 14). *AI-Powered Bing Chat Spills Its Secrets via Prompt Injection Attack* [Updated]. Ars Technica. https://arstechnica.com/information-technology/2023/02/ai-powered-bing-chat-spills-its-secrets-via-prompt-injection-attack/

Flaglien, A. O. (2017). The digital forensics process. In *Digital Forensics* (pp. 13–49). Wiely.

Fong, J., & Fong, J. (2023, May 4). *Global Cybercrime Report: Countries Most at Risk in 2023 | SEON*. SEON. https://seon.io/resources/global-cybercrime-report/

Frąckiewicz, M. (2023, July 16). *The Evolution of Digital Forensics: A Brief History*. TS2 SPACE. https://ts2.space/en/the-evolution-of-digital-forensics-a-brief-history/#gsc.tab=0

Garfinkel, S. L. (2010). Digital forensics research: The next 10 years. *Digital Investigation*, 7, S64–S73.

Gaurav, A., Gupta, B. B., Hsu, C. H., Peraković, D., & Peñalvo, F. J. G. (2021, June). Deep learning based approach for secure web of things (WoT). In *2021 IEEE International Conference on Communications Workshops (ICC Workshops)* (pp. 1–6). IEEE.

Ghazinour, K., Vakharia, D. M., Kannaji, K. C., & Satyakumar, R. (2017, September). A study on digital forensic tools. In *2017 IEEE International Conference on Power, Control, Signals and Instrumentation Engineering (ICPCSI)* (pp. 3136–3142). IEEE.

Gupta, B. B., & Agrawal, D. P. (2021). Security, privacy and forensics in the enterprise information systems. *Enterprise Information Systems*, 15(4), 445–447.

Gupta, B. B., & Quamara, M. (2020). *Internet of Things Security: Principles, Applications, Attacks, and Countermeasures*. CRC Press.

Gupta, B. B., Perez, G. M., Agrawal, D. P., & Gupta, D. (2020). *Handbook of Computer Networks and Cyber Security* (Vol. 10, pp. 3–978). Springer.

Gupta, B. B., Gaurav, A., Chui, K. T., & Hsu, C. H. (2022, January). Identity-based authentication technique for iot devices. In *2022 IEEE International Conference on Consumer Electronics (ICCE)* (pp. 1–4). IEEE.

Harbawi, M., & Varol, A. (2016, April). The role of digital forensics in combating cybercrimes. In *2016 4th International Symposium on Digital Forensic and Security (ISDFS)* (pp. 138–142). IEEE.

Hefetz, I. (2023). Mapping AI-ethics' dilemmas in forensic case work: To trust AI or not?. *Forensic Science International*, 350, 111807.

Hildebrandt, M.; Kiltz, S., & Dittmann, J. (2013). Digitized forensics: Retaining a link between physical and digital crime scene traces using QR-codes. In *Proceedings of SPIE 8667*, Article 86670S.

Jarrett, A., & Choo, K. K. R. (2021). The impact of automation and artificial intelligence on digital forensics. *Wiley Interdisciplinary Reviews: Forensic Science*, 3(6), e1418.

Karie, N. M., & Venter, H. S. (2015). Taxonomy of challenges for digital forensics. *Journal of Forensic Sciences*, 60(4), 885–893. Wiley.

Lillis, D., Becker, B., O'Sullivan, T., & Scanlon, M. (2016). Current challenges and future research areas for digital forensic investigation. *arXiv preprint*, arXiv:1604.03850.

Mishra, A., Gupta, B. B., Peraković, D., Yamaguchi, S., & Hsu, C. H. (2021, January). Entropy based defensive mechanism against DDoS attack in SDN-Cloud enabled online social networks. In *2021 IEEE International Conference on Consumer Electronics (ICCE)* (pp. 1–6). IEEE.

Mitchell, F. (2010). The use of Artificial Intelligence in digital forensics: An introduction. *Digital Evidence & Electronic Signature Law Review*, 7, 35.

Pollitt, M. (2010). A history of digital forensics. In *Advances in Digital Forensics VI: Sixth IFIP WG 11.9 International Conference on Digital Forensics*, Hong Kong, China, January 4–6, 2010, Revised Selected Papers 6 (pp. 3–15). Springer Berlin Heidelberg.

Praneeth. (2022). *Cloud Forensics: Open Issues, Challenges and Future Research Opportunities* (p. 1). Insights2Techinfo. https://insights2techinfo.com/cloud-forensicsopen-issues-challenges-and-future-research-opportunities/

Richard III, G. G., & Roussev, V. (2006). Next-generation digital forensics. *Communications of the ACM*, 49(2), 76–80.

Sabillon, R., Serra-Ruiz, J., Cavaller, V., & Cano, J. J. (2017). Digital forensic analysis of cybercrimes: best practices and methodologies. *International Journal of Information Security and Privacy (IJISP)*, 11(2), 25–37.

Sachdeva, S., Raina, B. L., & Sharma, A. (2020). Analysis of digital forensic tools. *Journal of Computational and Theoretical Nanoscience*, 17(6), 2459–2467.

Sahoo, S. R., & Gupta, B. B. (2021). Multiple features-based approach for automatic fake news detection on social networks using deep learning. *Applied Soft Computing*, 100, 106983.

Vincze, E. A. (2016). Challenges in digital forensics. *Police Practice and Research*, 17(2), 183–194.

What is WannaCry Ransomware? (2023, July 6). www.kaspersky.com. https://www.kaspersky.com/resource-center/threats/ransomware-wannacry

Williams, L. (2023, November 4). *What is Digital Forensics? History, Process, Types, Challenges.* Guru99. https://www.guru99.com/digital-forensics.html

Wong, J. C. (2019). The Cambridge Analytica scandal changed the world–but it didn't change Facebook. *The Guardian*, 18.

Chapter 4

Detailed Evolution Process of CNN-Based Intrusion Detection in the Context of Network Security

Amanpreet Singh, Sunil K. Singh, Amit Chhabra, Gurmehar Singh, Yuvraj, Sudhakar Kumar, and Varsha Arya

INTRODUCTION

In our increasingly interconnected world, where we rely on a multitude of applications and engage in digital activities every day, the dark side of technology has also shown itself—the rise of cybercrimes. As we face a growing number of cyberthreats, the need for effective network intrusion detection systems (IDSs) becomes crucial. While traditional IDSs have been somewhat effective, they struggle to keep up with the complexity of modern cyberattacks. This has led IDSs to embrace artificial intelligence (AI) for a more robust defense. Deep Learning (DL) algorithms, with Convolutional Neural Networks (CNNs) at the forefront, have emerged as powerful tools in this domain.

Interestingly, despite the pivotal role CNNs [1] play in enhancing IDS capabilities, there's a noticeable gap in existing literature. A thorough exploration of CNN-based approaches is lacking. This chapter aims to bridge that gap by diving into the world of CNN-based IDS, offering insights into their different categories based on datasets, data formats, and more. The goal is to provide a clear understanding of CNN-based IDS [2], uncovering their strengths, capabilities, and unique features that make them adept at spotting intrusions and fortifying networks against various cyberthreats.

This chapter is designed to be a user-friendly guide, unraveling the complexities of CNN-based IDS [3] methods and explaining their potential applications in the ever-changing landscape of cybersecurity. By highlighting the significance of CNNs in intrusion detection, this chapter aims to contribute to a broader understanding of how CNNs [4] play a crucial role in securing networks against the evolving challenges posed by cyber threats.

I. INTRUSION DETECTION SYSTEM(S)

An intrusion detection system (IDS) is like a security guard [5] for your computer network, keeping a close eye on all the activities happening within it. Its main job is to spot any signs of trouble, whether it's an unauthorized access attempt, malicious behavior, or any kind of cybercrime. There are two main types of IDS, each specializing in a different aspect of security.

Firstly, we have the Network-Based Intrusion Detection System (NIDS). Think of it as the watchful eye over the entire network. NIDS pays attention to the flow of data packets moving through the network, looking for anything unusual or patterns that might indicate a security threat. It's like having a security camera for the whole neighborhood, ensuring nothing fishy goes unnoticed.

Then, there's the Host-Based Intrusion Detection System (HIDS), which is like having a security guard specifically for each computer or server in your network. It takes a closer look at what's happening on individual devices, checking things like system logs, file changes, and

 DOI: 10.1201/9781003207573-4

user activities [6]. Together, NIDS and HIDS create a solid defense team, watching out for any potential security risks from both the big picture and the finer details. This two-tiered approach helps organizations stay one step ahead, catching and dealing with security issues before they become serious problems.

1.1 Role of IDSs in Network Security

Intrusion detection systems play a crucial role in detecting various security flaws by identifying issues, hence the organizations can respond accordingly to prevent unauthorized activities.

IDS' constantly monitors video display [7], units' community site visitors, gadget logs, or hot spots for styles and behaviors that may imply a security danger or intrusion strive. This consists of identifying various assault sorts and anomalies within the community vicinity. It can distinguish among distinctive styles of attacks. This will help recognize the character of the risk so that suitable techniques can be selected to deal with it [8]. It offers corporations with superior visibility into their community site visitors and sports. This helps in expertise network behavior and identifying modifications which may also suggest a security risk or assault. IDS may be configured to satisfy the unique needs and protection requirements of an agency. Security groups can define custom policies and rules to shield systems from the various assaults [9]. It serves as an early warning system, alerting network administrators or safety personnel to capacity protection incidents in real-time or near-real-time. Early detection permits a speedy response to mitigate ability damage. Figure 4.1 shows how IDS can be used in network security.

1.2 Integrating AI With IDS

This segment discusses how AI empowers IDSs. An IDS allows higher detection and reaction to network security threats. In IDS, AI autonomously uses advanced algorithms to come across and recognize patterns inside the community traffic, identifying recognized and new threats with splendid accuracy. As cyber threats continue to evolve, adaptability is important. AI-powered IDS can shrink high false positive, distinguishing normal conduct from bad conduct.

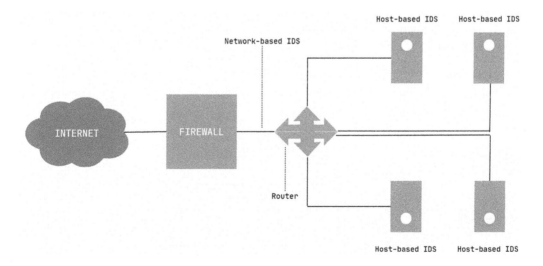

Figure 4.1 IDS in network security

1.2.1 AI in Intrusion Detection

AI in intrusion detection dramatically improves cybersecurity via a robust and flexible technique to figure out and remove protection dangers within the PC community(s). Let's discuss the primary AI additions of intrusion detection.

AI-powered intrusion detection structures regularly consist of the machine learning algorithms, along with choice trees, random forests, or vector support machines, for correlation analysis visitors and safety incidents [10]. These models are skilled on historical statistics to recognize the community behavior, so we can identify adjustments to guard against threats.

AI fashions can adapt to converting community environments and evolving threats. They continuously master new information and might alter their detection competencies over time. This makes them perfectly suited to cope with the changing cyber-risk landscape [11].

AI-based total intrusion detection systems tend to provide fewer fake positives compared to conventional signature-based systems. They can differentiate among benign network hobbies and true safety threats correctly, lowering the alert fatigue regularly related to traditional IDS [12].

Intrusion detection systems [13] that harness the power of artificial intelligence are like the superheroes of network security, able to handle large and complicated networks without breaking a sweat. These AI-based systems are wizards at managing the massive amounts of data networks throw at them, and they do it without sacrificing accuracy [14]. It's like having a super-smart guardian for your network that not only copes with the complexity but also ensures it's on point with the details, making it a robust and reliable defender against potential security threats.

AI models do not just effectively hit upon ongoing assaults but also provide insights into potential future threats via figuring out emerging attack styles and vulnerabilities. Figure 4.2 shows how AI in intrusion detection systems [15] represents community security through offering adaptive, conduct-primarily-based evaluation that reduces false positives, enhances threat detection, and addresses the complexities of the ultra-modern and evolving cyber-risk landscape.

1.2.2 Role of Deep Learning Algorithms

While signature-based Intrusion Detection Systems [16] excel at detecting recognized attacks, offering excessive detection accuracy and fewer false alarms, they falter in relation to figuring out new or unknown threats because of their reliance on predefined guidelines. In evaluation, anomaly-primarily-based IDS [17] is appropriate for uncovering novel assaults but tends to

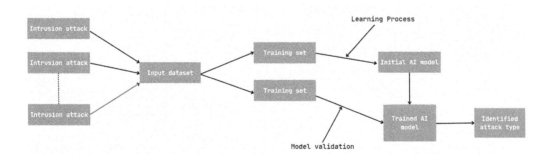

Figure 4.2 AI and IDS

yield multiplied false-nice quotes [18]. First, deciding on appropriate capabilities from community traffic statistics for anomaly detection proves difficult because assault eventualities are ever-changing, and capabilities appropriate for one kind of attack may not apply to others. Second, the absence of categorized visitors' datasets from actual networks hampers NIDS improvement.

Deep learning, a subset of machine learning methods, involves the use of consecutive layers of hierarchical information processing stages to facilitate pattern classification and feature or representation learning. Numerous deep learning methods [19], including Deep Belief Network (DBN), Restricted Boltzman Machine (RBM), Deep Boltzman Machine (DBM), Deep Neural Network (DNN), Auto Encoder, and Deep/stacked Auto Encoder, have been developed. The evolution of learning algorithms holds the promise of enhancing IDS capabilities, potentially achieving higher detection rates and reducing false alarm rates. Deep learning-based approaches are envisaged to address the challenges inherent in building effective NIDS, particularly in the domain of adaptive threat detection.

Such algorithms are also used in Malware Detection [20], User and Entity Behavior Analytics (UEBA), Advanced Persistent Threat (APT) Detection, Security Information and Event Management (SIEM) Enhancement, IoT Security, Cloud Security, Web Application Security, Mobile Device Security, and Zero-Day Vulnerability Detection.

1.3 Convolutional Neural Networks

Now, we shall detail CNNs and their key features.

1.3.1 Defining CNNs

A Convolutional Neural Network (CNN) [21] is a kind of artificial neural network designed for processing and analyzing the grid data, such as snapshots or sequential records. It utilizes convolutional layers to routinely and adaptively study hierarchical representations of input information, making it specifically powerful in obligations involving spatial and sequential styles, such as photo recognition or, in the context of cybersecurity, analyzing network site visitor statistics for intrusion detection.

1.3.2 Key CNN Features for Security

Figure 4.3 represents a CNN [22] architecture along with various design of each stage. CNN is typically designed to regularly and adaptively study the various hierarchies of features in low- to high-stage styles. Minimizing the number of parameters in an ANN is the most important factor of a CNN.

Let's now discuss the major features of CNN for security purposes.

CNNs are robust to variations in images, such as changes in lighting, orientation, and scale. This makes them appropriate for safety packages in which photographs can be captured in one-of-a-kind conditions. As an example, facial reputation systems that use CNNs [23] can recognize faces even if the lighting is dim or the face is partly obscured.

CNNs can routinely extract capabilities from photographs, which can be used for category and detection tasks. That is useful in safety packages where identifying unique features is critical. For instance, CNNs [24] can be used to hit upon guns or different risky gadgets in photos with the aid of figuring out precise shapes or styles. CNNs [25] can utilize snapshots in actual-time, making them suitable for protection packages that require quick response. For example, CNNs can be used to discover intruders in real time by reading video feeds from safety cameras.

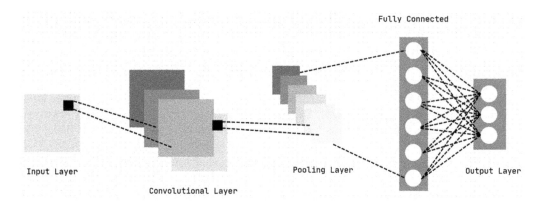

Figure 4.3 CNN architecture

CNNs have shown high accuracy in photograph type and detection responsibilities, making them a dependable device for protection programs. For instance, CNNs may be used to discover people in a crowd with a high degree of accuracy. These are the major CNN [26] features that help in security purposes in real-life applications. The Convolutional layers (The Heart of CNN), Pooling layers (Enhance efficiency and Mitigating Overfitting), and the Fully connected layers are used to extract the features for CNN [27]. The convolutional operation across input feature maps and a convolutional layer within the CNN architecture are provided through the following equation:

$$(n)_j^{(n)} = \sum_{k=1}^{K} \mathbf{h}_k^{(n-1)} * \mathbf{w}_{kj}^{(n)} + b_{k_j}^{(n)} \tag{1}$$

where $*$ is the a 2d convolution, $\mathbf{h}_j^{(n)}$ is the jth feature map's output in the nth hidden layer, $\mathbf{h}_k^{(n-1)}$ is the kth channel in the $(n-1)^{th}$ hidden layer, $w_{kj}^{(n)}$ is the weights of the kth channel in the jth filter in the nth layer, and $b_{kj}^{(n)}$ is its corresponding bias term.

1.3.3 Why CNNS?

Convolutional Neural Networks (CNNs) are specifically beneficial within the context of AI-powered Intrusion Detection Systems (IDS) because they excel at processing and extracting functions from spatial statistics, together with snapshots or sequences. In cybersecurity, community site visitors' information and system logs regularly have a spatial and sequential nature. CNNs, with their hierarchical characteristic mastering and spatial abstraction talents, are able to pick out complicated patterns and anomalies in such facts. Integrating CNNs [28] into AI-based IDS complements the system's potential to correctly recognize and classify diverse and elaborate community behaviors, improving the overall accuracy and performance of chance detection.

2. LITERATURE REVIEW

A series of research studies spanning various domains addresses critical challenges in technology and security. These include advancements in Network Intrusion Detection [29] and Prevention Systems (NIDPSs), the application of deep learning in medical imaging for brain tumor classification, the development of hybrid models for Human Activity Recognition (HAR), and

Table 4.1 Literature review

Authors	Year	Model/approach	Key findings and contributions
Waleed Bul'ajoul et al. [30]	2018	NIDPSs for high-speed and high-load malicious traffic	Identified critical gap in NIDPSs' effectiveness against high-speed and high-load malicious traffic.
Anil Kumar Mandle [31]	2022	VGG-19 CNN for brain tumor classification	Introduced VGG-19 CNN-based model for classifying brain tumors from MRI images.
Sunil K. Singh [32]	2022	Hybrid HAR technique with CNN, Bi-LSTM, and GRU	Addressed challenges in accurate and rapid human activity recognition (HAR) using a limited training set.
Xiaowei Wang [33]	2020	Deep Multi-Scale CNN (DMCNN) for network intrusion detection	Introduced DMCNN to address challenges in network intrusion detection (NID).
Hiren K. Mewada [34]	2017	Adaptive AI-based intrusion detection in e-commerce	Conducted a comprehensive analysis of security algorithms integrating intrusion detection in e-commerce systems.
Leila Mohammadpour [34]	2021	CNN-based IDS survey and empirical experiment	Systematically organized and categorized various CNN-based IDS approaches.
Sinh Ngoc Nguyen [35]	2018	IDS-CNN for Denial-of-Service (DoS) attack detection	Introduced IDS-CNN, a CNN-based platform tailored for detecting DoS attacks.
Minh Tuan Nguyen [36]	2020	Genetic Algorithm and CNN for intrusion detection	Introduced a novel algorithm for NIDS using a feature subset selection through Genetic Algorithm (GA) and Fuzzy C-means clustering (FCM).
Sang-Woong Lee [37]	2021	Review of deep IDS approaches	Systematically reviewed the landscape of deep IDS approaches, emphasizing the utilization of deep learning networks.
Alihossein Aryanfar [38]	2022	CNN-MCL for anomaly detection in IDS	Introduced CNN-MCL, a novel CNN architecture for anomaly detection in IDS.
Hongyu Yang [39]	2019	Improved CNN (ICNN) for wireless network intrusion detection	Introduced ICNN for wireless network intrusion detection, addressing challenges in traditional intrusion detection technologies.

innovative approaches to network intrusion detection using Convolutional Neural Networks (CNNs). Additionally, research explores the security landscape of e-commerce platforms, emphasizing the need for adaptive artificial intelligence-based intrusion detection algorithms.

3. METHODOLOGY AND CLASSIFICATION SYSTEM

Developing an effective methodology and classification system for CNN-based Intrusion Detection Systems (IDS) [40] is like crafting a roadmap for digital security guardians. It involves creating a structured approach to train these intelligent systems, allowing them to recognize and categorize diverse cyberthreats accurately. Think of it as equipping them with a tailored guidebook—clear classifications based on datasets, data formats, and other relevant factors. This systematic approach ensures that CNNs [41], our digital protectors, grasp the nuances of potential intrusions and can proficiently respond to the ever-changing world of cybersecurity challenges.

3.1 Categorization Method for CNN-based IDS

The CNN-primarily-based Intrusion Detection Systems (IDS) category method is a scientific technique to categorize and understand these structures based on numerous key factors that assist researchers and practitioners in studying and comparing the numerous IDS strategies. These classifications consist of schooling facts supply (public, proprietary, or hybrid), convolutional neural community (simple, deep, with transfer getting to know, or custom layers), input statistics layout (with additives inclusive of raw packets, community flows, including logs), and evaluation criteria (accuracy, keep in mind, and many others), key targets [42] (decreasing fake positives, maximizing real positives), overall performance metrics (measuring high-quality accuracy, efficiency, scalability), deployment environments (cloud, on premises, side), and precise use cases (e.g. healthcare, finance, government). Classification based on these features helps inform the skills and suitability of CNN-primarily based IDS structures in numerous community safety eventualities.

3.2 Categorization Based on Dataset Usage

IDS [43] processes can be classified based on the source of their education records. Publicly available datasets, along with the NSL-KDD dataset or the USA-NB15 dataset, are commonly used for research and benchmarking. Proprietary datasets may also consist of network site visitors specific to a business enterprise or enterprise, presenting extra context but probably much less range. Hybrid procedures leverage each type of statistics, imparting a balance between realism and generalizability.

3.3 Categorization Based on Architectural Design

IDS systems [44] vary in the design in their Convolutional Neural Networks. Some appoint notably shallow architectures with a small number of layers to reduce computational complexity. As the architecture becomes more complex, it can extract more information; however, the complexity of the system is also increased. Complexity categorization evaluates the sophistication of the CNN model [45]. Some IDS systems utilize standard CNN architectures without any customization. Others leverage transfer learning, taking pre-trained CNN models (e.g., from ImageNet) and fine-tuning them for intrusion detection. Further complexity can involve the inclusion of custom layers or attention mechanisms to capture specific features.

3.4 Categorization Based on Input Data Format

IDS systems [46] categorize information into formats they can process, inclusive of raw community packet facts, community drift information, or log records. Raw packet records consist of statistics from person community packets, providing a quality-grained element. Network glide records aggregate packet-degree facts into flows for efficiency. Log records derive from log files and offer excessive-level data. Categorization based entirely on pre-processing requirements considers whether the IDS needs significant data preparation before being input to the CNN. For instance, raw packet facts can also require function extraction to convert it into a layout appropriate for CNN evaluation.

3.5 Categorization Based on Evaluation Metrics

IDS approaches measure their effectiveness using various metrics. Precision gauges the accuracy of positive predictions, recall assesses the ability to identify true positives, and the F1-score balances precision and recall. Accuracy provides an overall measure of correctness, while AUC-ROC evaluates the model's ability to discriminate between classes. The choice of performance metrics depends on the primary objective of the IDS. Some systems aim to reduce false positives to minimize unnecessary alerts, making precision a critical metric. Others focus on maximizing true positive detection rates by emphasizing recall.

3.6 Categorization Based on Performance Measures

Performance measures compare the effectiveness of the IDS. Detection accuracy assesses the machine's potential to effectively discover intrusions and anomalies. Computational efficiency considers the rate and aid utilization of the IDS. Scalability examines the device's overall performance as community site visitors and facts extent boom, making sure it may manage larger workloads at the same time as keeping effectiveness.

3.7 Categorization Based on Deployment Environment

IDS methods are categorized based on their deployment environments. Cloud-primarily-based solutions leverage cloud assets for scalability and renovation ease. On-premises deployments can also offer more manipulation but require nearby infrastructure. Edge deployments are optimized for resource-restrained network locations where actual-time processing is essential. The categorization additionally considers the IDS's scalability and adaptableness. Cloud-based totally answers can easily scale by provisioning additional cloud resources. On-premises answers require careful resource control. Edge deployments must be adaptable to varying network scenarios and resource constraints.

3.8 Categorization Based on Use Cases

IDS systems are often designed for specific industries or verticals. Healthcare-focused IDSs may prioritize patient data protection, while financial IDSs may emphasize fraud detection. Government or critical infrastructure IDSs have unique requirements tailored to national security. Categorization with the aid of use cases consists of examples along with corporation community protection, business manipulate systems (ICS/SCADA), IoT networks, healthcare, finance, government, and other verticals. Each use case has requirements that impact IDS design and categorization.

Hence, the categorization technique for CNN-based Intrusion Detection Systems (IDS) gives a scientific method to information and classifying these structures primarily based on key elements, which might be important for comprehending the skills and suitability of CNN-based totally IDS systems in various community safety contexts. This approach encompasses aspects like the supply of education statistics, architectural design of Convolutional Neural Networks (CNNs), enter records layout, assessment metrics, primary objectives, overall performance measures, deployment environments, and particular use cases.

4. CLASSIFICATION SYSTEM WITH DATASET, DESIGN, AND METRIC

In this section, we will direct our interest toward the complicated interaction among datasets, Convolutional Neural Network (CNN) architecture design, and the selection of appropriate assessment metrics within the domain of CNN-based Intrusion Detection Systems (IDS) [47]. We shall explore in depth the vital factors to recollect while classifying and comprehending IDS systems. Furthermore, it is crucial to highlight the importance of selecting applicable assessment metrics that align with the primary objectives of IDS; these may include precision, considering F1-rating accuracy and AUC-ROC.

4.1 Dataset Considerations

Dataset concerns are paramount in the domain of CNN-based totally Intrusion Detection Systems (IDSs) [48]. However, publicly available datasets, which includes NSL-KDD and UNSW-NB15 offer researchers baseline gear for benchmarking and comparing exclusive IDS models. Therefore, those information sets need to be critically examined in terms of their composition, length, sample distribution, and so forth to decide their appropriateness. On the other hand, a few agencies or industries have proprietary datasets that provide a more sensible attitude toward threats they face. Hybrid techniques that mix both aforementioned dataset sorts improve upon deficiencies of every kind. As such, this technique creates a stability among realism and generalizability allowing IDS models to be taught on real-international records while being evaluated against standardized datasets.

4.2 Design of CNN Architectures

Considering intrusion detection, the design of Convolutional Neural Networks (CNNs) plays a vital role. The intensity of these networks, denoting the range of layers they own, exerts a terrific impact on their ability to understand changes within network traffic. Architectures with an increased layer count have the ability to capture more sophisticated features; however, this regularly necessitates larger datasets and computational assets. Diverse categories of layers hired in CNNs [49] contribute significantly to how efficaciously fashions represent network site visitors' facts: convolutional layers facilitate characteristic extraction, while recurrent layers aid in sequence modeling. Moreover, integrating specialized components like interest mechanisms into the structure complements the version's focus on certain segments of statistics—hence bolstering its ability to locate anomalies or intrusions.

The depth of a CNN in terms of the range of layers can notably impact its capacity to capture tricky patterns in community traffic. Deeper networks can constitute greater complex functions but may also require more facts and computational sources.

Specialized components, such as attention mechanisms, enhance model awareness by focusing on specific data elements, thereby bolstering its ability to effectively identify anomalies within the network's intricate patterns. This targeted attention contributes to a more refined understanding, making the model adept at discerning subtle irregularities and strengthening its overall anomaly detection capabilities.

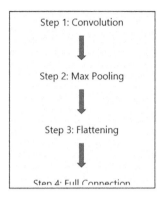

Step 1: Convolution

Step 2: Max Pooling

Step 3: Flattening

Step 4: Full Connection

Figure 4.4 Data flow between pooling layers of CNN

4.3 Choice of Evaluation Metrics

The selection of suitable evaluation metrics is a vital factor of assessing the performance of IDS fashions [51]. Figure 4.4 shows examples of performance matrices for CNN accelerators. This metric performs an essential position in comparing the device's potential to decrease false alarms.

Precision refers to the accuracy of a good prediction made by the IDS. It helps evaluate the ability of the system to reduce positive false alarms, which can be critical in reducing the workload of security analysts. It can be formulated as:

$$\text{Precision} = TP/(TP + FP); \qquad (2)$$

{Here TP, FP, TN, FN are confusion matrix values}.

Recall: Recall, also known as the true positive rate, examines the system's ability to identify actual admissions. High recall indicates a low rate of missed intrusions, which is crucial for comprehensive security. It can be formulated as:

$$\text{Recall} = TP/(TP + FN) \qquad (3)$$

F1-Score: The F1-score is the harmonic means of precision and recall. It balances the trade-off between minimizing false positives and maximizing true positives. It can be formulated as:

$$\text{F1-Score} = 2*(\text{Precision}*\text{Recall})/(\text{Precision} + \text{Recall}) \qquad (4)$$

Accuracy: Accuracy provides a general measure of the system's correctness. It can be formulated as [52]:

$$\text{Accuracy} = TN + TP/(TN + TP + FN + FP) \qquad (5)$$

AUC-ROC: The area below the receiver working function curve (AUC-ROC) evaluates the model's ability to distinguish between ordinary and anomalous network site visitors. It gives a comprehensive assessment of the model's universal overall performance.

4.4 Objective Alignment

The alignment of selected assessment metrics with the unique objectives of the IDS [53] system is a vital consideration. Precision emphasis is critical while the primary objective is to reduce fake effective signals, correctly lowering the variety of false alarms. It measures the proportion of true predictions among all high-quality predictions. Conversely, structures that prioritize the detection of as many genuine intrusions as possible generally tend to empha-size recall. An excessive don't-forget rate signifies a decreased rate of neglected intrusions, improving comprehensive safety.

If the primary objective of the IDS is to limit false positive signals (i.e., reducing the quan-tity of false alarms), precision is a vital metric. It measures the fraction of genuine predictions among all high-quality predictions. Systems that prioritize detecting as many proper intru-sions as possible may emphasize don't-forget.

4.5 Real-World Relevance

This element underscores the paramount significance of making sure that dataset choice, CNN structure [54], and evaluation metrics align harmoniously with the community protec-tion environment. Dataset realism is of primary importance, necessitating that the datasets selected accurately mirror the unique threats and community traits of the deployed network. This is critical to educate a version that performs optimally in actual-international scenarios. Customization of the CNN architecture ought to consider the specific traits of the network, in addition to the generic intrusions in the environment.

4.6 Practical Implications

In this part, we delve into how knowledge of the interaction between these factors can guide the selection and first-class-tuning of CNN-based IDS within real-international network pro-tection scenarios. Model selection, guided with the aid of sensible concerns, entails discus-sions on how businesses need to select or customize existing IDS fashions to high-quality in shape their specific community environment.

Based on practical issues, this segment would possibly indicate how organizations have to pick or customize existing IDS fashions to optimize their network environment. Fine-tuning the selected IDS version is often required to adapt it to the particular characteristics and threats in a specific network. Therefore, those factors are very critical for classifying IDS structures. The preliminary dialogue targets recorded issues, highlighting the importance of publicly available proof and innovative facts applicable to the enterprise context. The advent of composites strikes a balance between precision and generality, adding a layer of nuance to the dataset choice process.

Returning to CNN architectural design, this chapter will look more deeply at the combi-nation of special features, such as deep, layered, and supervised processes, and demonstrate the important role of these options in modeling the traffic network information. The choice of evaluation metrics is addressed in detail, emphasizing their importance in assessing IDS model performance. Precision, recall, F1-Score, accuracy, and AUC-ROC are examined in the context of their relevance to specific IDS objectives, whether minimizing false positives or maximizing intrusion detection rates. Real-world relevance is underlined as a core considera-tion, urging alignment between datasets, CNN architecture, and metrics with the practical network security environment.

5. APPLICATIONS AND CASE STUDIES

CNN is capable of self-studying complex patterns from statistics and has many packages in many fields. The following sections offer an in-depth look at distinct CNN use instances, highlighting their potential programs and demonstrating their overall performance.

5.1 Diverse CNN Use Cases

Convolutional Neural Networks (CNNs) are a type of artificial neural network that can process and analyze images and different types of visual data. CNNs have many use instances in several domains and industries, including search engines like Google, social media, and recommender systems.

CNNs can designate photo type, which is the challenge of assigning labels to photos based on their content material fabric. As an example, a CNN can select whether or not an image includes a cat, a canine, a vehicle, or a person [55, 56]. This can help search engines like Google index and retrieve images based totally on key phrases, social media platforms clear out and tag photos based on person options, and recommender systems to suggest relevant products or content based on individual behavior.

CNNs can carry out object detection, which is the mission of finding and figuring out objects inside an image. For example, a CNN can come across and understand pedestrians, vacationers' signs, vehicles, and road markings in a scene. This will help motors to navigate correctly and effectively in complicated and dynamic environments. CNNs can perform clinical photograph evaluation, which is the task of extracting useful statistics from scientific pictures, including x-rays, MRI scans, CT scans, and ultrasound photographs. For instance, a CNN can discover and classify anomalies, lesions, tumors, and diseases in medical pictures with better accuracy than the human eye. CNN can classify the feelings and opinions of the speaker or writer from textual content or speech. For example, customer service and advertising packages use CNN to investigate remarks and opinions from users and clients.

CNNs had been used for facial reputation in protection applications. For example, the Chinese authorities use facial reputation technology to reveal China's residents and track their movements. Similarly, American Customs and Border Protection uses facial popularity technology to identify vacationers at airports. CNNs can be used to pick out features in snapshots and movies, making them suitable for protection functions including intrusion detection. For instance, in the U.S., the Department of Homeland Security uses a CNN to identify attackers in real time via reading video feeds from security cameras.

CNNs can be used to detect weapons or other suspicious objects in images by tracking a particular shape or pattern. The New York Police Department uses CNN to detect bullets in surveillance images. By leveraging advanced CNN technology, these systems redefine safety by enabling real-time traffic monitoring, playing a pivotal role in accident investigations. With their capacity for swift and efficient responses, CNNs contribute significantly to enhancing the overall resilience of public safety infrastructure. CNNs can also be used for biometric recognition, such as fingerprint and iris recognition. For example, the Government of India implements this concept in Aadhaar cards.

5.2 Demonstrating Practical Application and Performance

A convolutional neural community (CNN) is a deep-knowledge model that can process pictures and different records with spatial or temporal styles. CNN offers picture type, goal detection, face recognition, semantic segmentation, and so forth. The convolution layer is the center element of CNNs, because it applies a hard and fast set of filters to the entered statistics to extract functions. The pooling layer reduces the scale and complexity of the feature maps, while the activation layer introduces non-linearity to the model. The normalization layer improves the steadiness and generalization of the model, and the completely related layer produces the very last output or prediction.

Figure 4.4 shows the control flow of data in the CNN models, and one of the principal benefits of CNNs is that they can analyze abilities robotically from the data, without needing manual engineering or area expertise. This makes them extra adaptable to specific responsibilities and information sources. Another advantage of CNNs is that they can make the most of the spatial or temporal shape of the statistics via the use of community connectivity and weight sharing. This reduces the parameters and computations and improves the performance and robustness of the model.

CNNs do, however, have some barriers and disadvantages. Certainly, one among them is that they require a huge quantity of records and computational assets to teach and optimize. This can be mitigated via using data augmentation, switch studying, or disbursed computing strategies. Another assignment is that CNNs [57] can be troubled by way of overfitting, specifically if facts are noisy, imbalanced, or scarce. This may be addressed via the use of regularization, dropout, or information synthesis strategies. A disadvantage is that CNNs may be tough to interpret and explain, as they regularly act as black-box. This can be progressed by the usage of visualization, attribution, or negative strategies.

CNNs are powerful and versatile options that can contend with diverse sorts of records and obligations. They have high-quality overall performance and outcomes in lots of packages; however, they also have some barriers and challenges that need to be considered and conquered. CNNs are a lively and evolving research area, and there are numerous opportunities and commands for additional development and innovation [58, 59].

6.KEY FINDINGS

6.1 Summary of Critical Findings

Let's discuss the growing call for cybersecurity—it's just like the superhero the virtual world desires right now. With the internet spreading like wildfire, the need for protection has ended up louder than ever. And on this virtual battleground, our trusty sidekicks, Intrusion Detection Systems (IDS), protects our precious digital turf. They're the guardians of our digital domain, making sure we navigate the online universe with a shield against threats.

To be more powerful than cyberthreats, IDS has turned to artificial intelligence (AI) and deep studying (DL) algorithms.

Harnessing the Strength of Deep Learning: Picture deep studying as a powerful ally within the quest to amplify intrusion detection—it is like giving our digital defenses a serious improvement. Now, meet the hero: Convolutional Neural Networks (CNNs). These are the rock stars at gaining deep knowledge of algorithms in the global Intrusion Detection Systems (IDS).

But here's the exciting twist: in spite of CNNs stealing the show inside the deep learning area, it seems they have been somewhat unnoticed inside the existing literature on IDS schemes. It's like they are waiting for their moment in the spotlight. This little gap in research is a bit like an untold tale—it's time to dive deep and find the secrets. Let's shine a light on CNNs in IDS, because a better look isn't simply necessary; it's like finding a treasure trove of opportunities.

This segment targets bridging the distance with the aid of providing insights into the various applications of CNN-based IDS. These classifications are primarily based on fundamental ideas together with records utilization, design standards, information input methods, overall performance metrics, and assessment techniques. Drawing from extensive research, this section aims to shed light on the potential of CNN-based IDS in detecting network intrusions, anomalies, and a wide variety of cyber threats.

For details, this section focuses on the growing need for cybersecurity and the roles of artificial intelligence and deep learning in search penetration, especially CNNs. There is little research in this area. Their objectives are as follows: Various CNN-based IDS applications are classified and described to better understand their resources and capabilities.

6.2 Significance of Research in CNN

Considering convolutional neural networks (CNN) is important in lots of fields and has led to many advances in production. CNNs can modify photo and video. They are typically utilized in applications such as Project Reputation, Image Category, and Video Rating to growth accuracy and efficiency. The regions covered by using the task encompass self-reliant cars, surveillance, and healthcare.

CNNs have been used in language processing obligations to create higher models of text popularity, sentiment evaluation, and speech know-how. This is vital for applications which include chatbots, translation, and commercial enterprise intelligence checking. CNNs have performed an essential role in medication. They can provide resources for early prognosis, interpretation of medical photographs such as x-rays and MRIs, and help lifestyles with appropriate studies. For independent vehicles along with self-driving motors and drones, CNNs are critical for reliable and instant decision-making. They help these utilities recognize their environment, face demanding situations, and determine the way to navigate. CNNs are used in security applications from getting right of entry to detection and facial popularity. They additionally play a key role in detecting suspicious facts and improving community safety features.

Recommendation structures that show applicable statistics to users are typically used to enhance consumers' enjoyment and extend productiveness. Many people have used CNN research areas inclusive of version reliability, fact checking, and simulation. They are assisting with complicated information and have programs in astronomy, particle physics, meteorology modeling, and so forth.

Research on CNNs has improved human-PC interfaces, along with hands-on experience reputation, emotion popularity, and language recognition. This could be very crucial to us within the age of intuitive interfaces. CNNs may be used in environmental monitoring and conservation. They assist in surveying and monitoring satellite TV for PC pictures. They also look for risky issues including animals, fire, or deforestation.

The availability of CNN-primarily-based technologies has had a vast effect. They encourage innovation and create career opportunities in areas including journalism generation and intelligence, contributing to financial increase. Research on CNNs regularly calls for interdisciplinary collaboration with specialists in fields such as computer science, neuroscience, and engineering. This collaboration enables the exchange of records and allows increases in various fields. CNNs have increased our know-how of the ways neural networks can mimic statistical information similarly to the human mind. This fact has implications for each cognitive science and neuroscience.

As an end result, CNN's studies have had a profound effect on fields from medicine to self-control and keeps forcing innovation, technology improvement output, and developing our know-how. The efficiency and effectiveness of CNNs have made them a cornerstone of modern synthetic intelligence research.

7. CONCLUSION AND FUTURE SCOPE

This acknowledgment of the escalating need for robust cybersecurity measures aligns with the rapid expansion of internet usage and the proliferation of digital activities, both of which have become integral aspects of contemporary life. The imperative for a strong defense against cyberthreats becomes evident as online interactions, transactions, and data sharing continue to surge. Within this digital landscape, Intrusion Detection Systems (IDS) emerge as frontline defenders, crucial for preserving the integrity and security of online infrastructure. The evolution of these systems is not merely a response to current threats but a proactive stance in anticipation of increasingly sophisticated and dynamic cyber adversaries. In recognizing the pivotal role of IDS, it becomes clear that traditional approaches face limitations in effectively combating the evolving threat landscape. The sheer complexity and variety of cyberthreats necessitate innovative solutions that can adapt and learn in real-time. The introduction and evolution of Convolutional Neural Networks (CNNs) in the domain of intrusion detection marks a transformative step. CNNs, with their capacity for hierarchical feature extraction and pattern recognition, address the challenges posed by intricate cyberthreats that often employ deceptive tactics.

Moreover, the journey of CNN-based intrusion detection signifies a paradigm shift toward intelligent, data-driven security. The amalgamation of deep learning techniques with intrusion detection not only enhances the accuracy of threat detection but also provides a scalable and adaptable solution. The capability of CNNs to autonomously learn and discern patterns from vast datasets ensures that the IDS can keep pace with the dynamic nature of cyberthreats, including those yet to be identified. As organizations grapple with the complexities of securing their networks, the evolution of CNN-based intrusion detection serves as a beacon for the future of cybersecurity. It emphasizes the need for continuous research, development, and integration of advanced technologies to stay ahead of malicious actors. This proactive stance is vital in the face of emerging technologies, such as the Internet of Things (IoT) and 5G, which bring both opportunities and new security challenges. In conclusion, the evolution of CNN-based intrusion detection is not merely a chapter in the ongoing narrative of cybersecurity but a strategic imperative for organizations aiming to fortify their digital defenses in an era of escalating cyberthreats.

Future CNN-based intrusion detection systems (IDS) aim to enhance network security, particularly against physical fraud attacks. Ongoing research focuses on strengthening CNNs, ensuring transparency, and integrating them into federated networks. With a focus on remote deployment and efficiency, CNN-based IDS adapts to IoT proliferation. The work aims to make CNN-based IDS more flexible by fine-tuning pre-trained models and prioritizing immediate action. Key areas include dynamic behavior analysis, response management integration, and privacy assurance. By collecting diverse data types, CNN-based IDS contributes to comprehensive cybersecurity views, addressing scalability through decentralized architectures. In summary, future CNN-based IDS features include enhanced flexibility and real-time functionality, crucial for safeguarding digital infrastructure from evolving threats.

REFERENCES

[1] Naseer, S.; Saleem, Y.; Khalid, S.; Bashir, M.K.; Han, J.; Iqbal, M.M.; Han, K. (2018) Enhanced network anomaly detection based on deep neural networks. *IEEE Access*, 6, 48231–48246. [CrossRef].

[2] Denning, D.E. (1987) An intrusion-detection model. *IEEE Trans. Softw. Eng.*, 222–232. [CrossRef].

[3] Najafabadi, M.M.; Villanustre, F.; Khoshgoftaar, T.M.; Seliya, N.; Wald, R.; Muharemagic, E. (2015) Deep learning applications and challenges in big data analytics. *J. Big Data*, 2, 1–21. [CrossRef].

[4] LeCun, Y.; Bottou, L.; Bengio, Y.; Haffner, P. (1998) Gradient-based learning applied to document recognition. *Proc. IEEE*, 86, 2278–2323. [CrossRef].

[5] Hochreiter, S.; Schmidhuber, J. (1997) Long short-term memory. *Neural Comput.*, 9, 1735–1780. [CrossRef].

[6] Vincent, P.; Larochelle, H.; Lajoie, I.; Bengio, Y.; Manzagol, P.A. (2010) Stacked denoising autoencoders: Learning useful representations in a deep network with a local denoising criterion. *J. Mach. Learn. Res.*, 11, 3371–3408.

[7]   Rifai, S.; Vincent, P.; Muller, X.; Glorot, X.; Bengio, Y. (2011) Contractive auto-encoders: Explicit invariance during feature extraction. In *Proceedings of the 28th International Conference on Machine Learning, ICML 2011*, Bellevue, WA, USA, 28 June–2 July 2011; pp. 833–840.

[8]   Aldweesh, A.; Derhab, A.; Emam, A.Z. (2020) Deep learning approaches for anomaly-based intrusion detection systems: A survey, taxonomy, and open issues. *Knowl. Based Syst.*, 189, 105124. [CrossRef].

[9]   Chalapathy, R.; Chawla, S. (2019) Deep learning for anomaly detection: A survey. *arXiv*, arXiv:1901.03407.

[10] Zhang, H.; Huang, L.; Wu, C.Q.; Li, Z. (2020) An effective convolutional neural network based on SMOTE and Gaussian mixture model for intrusion detection in imbalanced dataset. *Comput. Netw.*, 177, 107315. [CrossRef].

[11] Potluri, S.; Ahmed, S.; Diedrich, C. (2018) Convolutional neural networks for multi-class intrusion detection system. In *Proceedings of the International Conference on Mining Intelligence and Knowledge Exploration 2018*, Cluj-Napoca, Romania, 20–22 December 2018; pp. 225–238.

[12] Liu, P. (2019) An intrusion detection system based on convolutional neural network. In *Proceedings of the 2019 11th International Conference on Computer and Automation Engineering*, Perth, Australia, 23–25 February 2019; pp. 62–67.

[13] Mohammadpour, L.; Ling, T.C.; Liew, C.S.; Aryanfar, A. (2020) A mean convolutional layer for intrusion detection system. *Secur. Commun. Netw.*, 2020, 8891185.[CrossRef].

[14] Liu, G.; Zhang, J. (2019) CNID: Research of network intrusion detection based on convolutional neural network. *Discret. Dyn. Nat. Soc.*, 2020, 4705982. [CrossRef].

[15] Al-Turaiki, I.; Altwaijry, N. (2021) A convolutional neural network for improved anomaly-based network intrusion detection. *Big Data*, 9, 233–252. [CrossRef].

[16] Lam, N.T. (2021) Detecting unauthorized network intrusion based on network traffic using behavior analysis techniques. *Int. J. Adv. Comput. Sci. Appl.*, 12, 407. [CrossRef].

[17] Jo, W.; Kim, S.; Lee, C.; Shon, T. (2020) Packet preprocessing in CNN-based network intrusion detection system. *Electronics*, 9, 1151. [CrossRef].

[18] Kim, J.; Kim, J.; Kim, H.; Shim, M.; Choi, E. (2020) CNN-based network intrusion detection against denial-of-service attacks. *Electronics*, 9, 916. [CrossRef].

[19] Naseer, S.; Saleem, Y. (2018) Enhanced network intrusion detection using deep convolutional neural networks. *KSII Trans. Internet Inf. Syst.*, 12, 5159–5178. [CrossRef].

[20] Li, Y.; Xu, Y.; Liu, Z.; Hou, H.; Zheng, Y.; Xin, Y.; Zhao, Y.; Cui, L. (2020) Robust detection for network intrusion of industrial IoT based on multi-CNN fusion. *Measurement*, 154, 107450. [CrossRef].

[21] Lin, W.-H.H.; Lin, H.-C.C.; Wang, P.; Wu, B.-H.H.; Tsai, J.-Y.Y. (2018) Using convolutional neural networks to network intrusion detection for cyber threats. In *Proceedings of the 4th IEEE International Conference on Applied System Innovation 2018, ICASI 2018*, Tokyo, Japan, 13–17 April 2018; pp. 1107–1110. [CrossRef].

[22] Zhang, X.; Ran, J.; Mi, J. (2019) An intrusion detection system based on convolutional neural network for imbalanced network traffic. In *Proceedings of the 2019 IEEE 7th International Conference on Computer Science and Network Technology (ICCSNT)*, Dalian, China, 9–20 October 2019; pp. 456–460.

[23] Wang, H.; Cao, Z.; Hong, B. (2020) A network intrusion detection system based on convolutional neural network. *J. Intell. Fuzzy Syst.*, 38, 7623–7637. [CrossRef].

[24] Khan, R.U.; Zhang, X.; Alazab, M.; Kumar, R. (2019) An improved convolutional neural network model for intrusion detection in networks. In *Proceedings of the 2019 Cybersecurity and Cyberforensics Conference*, Melbourne, Australia, 8–9 May 2019; pp. 74–77. [CrossRef].

[25] Mohammadpour, L.; Ling, T.C.; Liew, C.S.; Chong, C.Y. (2018) A convolutional neural network for network intrusion detection system. *Proc. Asia Pacific Adv. Netw.*, 46, 50–55.

[26] Aljumah, A. (2021) IoT-based intrusion detection system using convolution neural networks. *PeerJ Comput. Sci.*, 7, e721. [CrossRef].

[27] Akhtar, M.S.; Feng, T. (2021) Deep learning-based framework for the detection of cyberattack using feature engineering. *Secur. Commun. Netw.*, 2021, 6129210. [CrossRef].

[28] Bouarara, H.A. (2022). N-gram-codon and recurrent neural network (RNN) to update Pfizer-BioNTech mRNA vaccine. *Int. J. Softw. Sci. Comput. Intell.*, 14(1), 1–24. [CrossRef].

[29] Bouarara, H.A. (2021). Recurrent neural network (RNN) to analyse mental behaviour in social media. *Int. J. Softw. Sci. Comput. Intell.*, 13(3), 1–11. [CrossRef].

[30] Bul'ajoul, W.; James, A.; Shaikh, S.A. (2018) New architecture for network intrusion detection and prevention. *IEEE Access*, 7, 18558–18573. [CrossRef]

[31] Thakur, N.; Singh, S.K.; Gupta, A.; Jain, K.; Jain, R.; Peraković, D.; Nedjah, N.; Rafsanjani, M.K. (2022) A novel CNN, bidirectional long-short term memory, and gated recurrent unit-based hybrid approach for human activity recognition. *Int. J. Softw. Sci. Comput. Intell.*, 14(1), 1–19. [CrossRef].

[32] Zhan, Z.; Liao, G.; Ren, X.; Xiong, G.; Zhou, W.; Jiang, W.; Xiao, H. (2022) RA-CNN: A semantic-enhanced method in a multi-semantic environment. *Int. J. Softw. Sci. Comput. Intell.*, 14(1), 1–14. [CrossRef].

[33] Wang, X.; Yin, S.; Li, H.; Wang, J.; Teng, L. (2020) A network intrusion detection method based on deep multi-scale convolutional neural network. *Int. J. Wirel. Inf. Netw.*, 27, 503–517. [CrossRef].

[34] Mewada, H.K.; Patel, S. (2017) Advances in intrusion detection algorithms for secure E-business using artificial intelligence. *Res. J. Inf. Technol.*, 9, 1–6.[CrossRef].

[35] Nguyen, S.-N.; Nguyen, V.-Q.; Choi, J.; Kim, K. (2018) Design and implementation of intrusion detection system using convolutional neural network for DoS detection. In *Proceedings of the 2nd International Conference on Machine Learning and Soft Computing (ICMLSC 2018)*, Phu Quoc Island, Vietnam, 2–4 February 2018; pp. 34–38. [CrossRef].

[36] Nguyen, M.T.; Kim, K. (2020) Genetic convolutional neural network for intrusion detection systems. *Future Gener. Comput. Syst.*, 113, 418–427. [CrossRef].

[37] Lee, S.-W.; Mohammadi, M.; Rashidi, S.; Rahmani, A.M.; Masdari, M.; Hosseinzadeh, M. (2021) Towards secure intrusion detection systems using deep learning techniques: Comprehensive analysis and review. *J. Netw. Comput. Appl.*, 187, 103111. [CrossRef].

[38] Mohammadpour, L.; Ling, T.C.; Liew, C.S.; Aryanfar, A (2022). A Survey of CNN-Based Network Intrusion Detection. Applied Sciences, 12(16), 8162.

[39] Yang, H.; Wang, F. (2019) Wireless network intrusion detection based on improved convolutional neural network. *IEEE Access*, 7, 64366–64374. [CrossRef].

[40] Tripathi, A.; Singh, A.K.; Singh, A.; Choudhary, A.; Pareek, K.; Mishra, K.K. (2022) Analyzing skin disease using XCNN (eXtended convolutional neural network). *Int. J. Softw. Sci. Comput. Intell.*, 14(1), 1–30. [CrossRef].

[41] Chiang, T.; Che, Z.H.; Huang, Y.; Tsai, C. (2022) Using an ontology-based neural network and DEA to discover deficiencies of hotel services. *Int. J. Semantic Web Inf. Syst.*, 18(1), 1–19. [CrossRef].

[42] Tembhurne, J.V.; Almin, M.M.; Diwan, T. (2022) Mc-DNN: Fake news detection using multi-channel deep neural networks. *Int. J. Semantic Web Inf. Syst.*, 18(1), 1–20. [CrossRef].

[43] Ling, Z.; Hao, Z.J. (2022) Intrusion detection using normalized mutual information feature selection and parallel quantum genetic algorithm. *Int. J. Semantic Web Inf. Syst.*, 18(1), 1–24. [CrossRef].

[44] Ling, Z.; Hao, Z.J. (2022) An intrusion detection system based on normalized mutual information antibodies feature selection and adaptive quantum artificial immune system. *Int. J. Semantic Web Inf. Syst.*, 18(1), 1–25. [CrossRef].

[45] Kadri, O.; Benyahia, A.; Abdelhadi, A. (2022) Tifinagh handwriting character recognition using a CNN provided as a web service. *Int. J. Cloud Appl. Comput.*, 12(1), 1–17. [CrossRef].

[46] Mandle, A.K.; Sahu, S.P.; Gupta, G.P. (2022) CNN-based deep learning technique for the brain tumor identification and classification in MRI images. *Int. J. Softw. Sci. Comput. Intell.*, 14(1), 1–20. [CrossRef].

[47] Kwon, D.; Kim, H.; Kim, J.; Suh, S.C.; Kim, I.; Kim, K.J. (2019) A survey of deep learning-based network anomaly detection. *Cluster Comput.*, 22, 949–961. [CrossRef].

[48] Martín, J.M.; Salinas Fernández, J.A. (2022) The effects of technological improvements in the train network on tourism sustainability. An approach focused on seasonality. *Sustain. Technol. Entrepreneurship*, 1(1), 100005. [CrossRef].

[49] Sahoo, L.; Panda, S.K.; Das, K.K. (2022) A review on integration of vehicular ad-hoc networks and cloud computing. *Int. J. Cloud Appl. Comput.*, 12(1), 1–23. [CrossRef].

[50] Srivastava, D.; Kumar, A.; Mishra, A.; Arya, V.; Almomani, A.; Hsu, C.H.; Santaniello, D. (2022) Performance optimization of multi-hop routing protocols with clustering-based hybrid networking architecture in mobile adhoc cloud networks. *Int. J. Cloud Appl. Comput.*, 12(1), 1–15. [CrossRef].

[51] Asare, S.; Yaokumah, W.; Gyebi, E.B.; Abdulai, J. (2022) Evaluating the impact of cryptographic algorithms on network performance. *Int. J. Cloud Appl. Comput.*, 12(1), 1–15. [CrossRef].

[52] Sriram, S.; Simran, K.; Vinayakumar, R.; Akarsh, S.; Soman, K.P. (2019) Towards evaluating the robustness of deep intrusion detection models in adversarial environment. In *International Symposium on Security in Computing and Communication*, Singapore, pp. 111–120. [CrossRef].

[53] Kumar, R.; Singh, S.K.; Lobiyal, D.K.; Chui, K.T.; Santaniello, D.; Rafsanjani, M.K. (2022) A novel decentralized group key management scheme for cloud-based vehicular IoT networks. *Int. J. Cloud Appl. Comput.*, 12(1), 1–34. [CrossRef].

[54] Zhang, L.; Zhang, Z.; Zhao, T. (2021) A novel spatio-temporal access control model for online social networks and visual verification. *Int. J. Cloud Appl. Comput.*, 11(2), 17–31. [CrossRef].

[55] Yen, S.; Moh, M.; Moh, T. (2021) Detecting compromised social network accounts using deep learning for behavior and text analyses. *Int. J. Cloud Appl. Comput.*, 11(2), 97–109. [CrossRef].

[56] Sharma, A.; Singh, S.K.; Kumar, S.; Chhabra, A.; Gupta, S. (2021, September) Security of android banking mobile apps: Challenges and opportunities. In *International Conference on Cyber Security, Privacy and Networking* (pp. 406–416). Springer International Publishing.

[57] https://www.tutorialexample.com/an-introduction-to-accuracy-precision-recall-f1-score-in-machine-learning-machine-learning-tutorial/

[58] Zhang, X.; Chen, J.; Zhou, Y.; Han, L.; Lin, J. (2019) A multiple-layer representation learning model for network-based attack detection. *IEEE Access*, 7, 91992–92008. [CrossRef].

[59] Kaur, P.; Singh, S.K.; Singh, I.; Kumar, S. (2021, December) Exploring convolutional neural network in computer vision-based image classification. In *International Conference on Smart Systems and Advanced Computing (Syscom-2021)*.

Chapter 5

Crime Scene Investigations through Augmented Reality

Recent Advances and Future Directions

*Varsha Arya, Akshat Gaurav, Ritika Bansal,
and Kwok Tai Chui*

INTRODUCTION

Augmented Reality (AR) is a cutting-edge technology that has recently gained significant attention. This deals with overlays of the interaction of users [1–4]. This technology helps create a virtual environment where users can interact [4]. Due to these characteristics, AR has been recognised as a leading technology of the 21st century and a pillar of the new industrial revolution.

The application of AR is not limited to virtual gaming; it has been used for innovative teaching and learning purposes [5–7]. It has been applied to various educational projects, including Sharia financial literacy systems and teaching social studies, to enhance student learning experiences [8, 9]. Also, researchers are exploring AR to train future engineers [10, 11]. AR has shown promising applications in the healthcare sector, such as in surgical planning and perioperative navigation [12]. Furthermore, AR has been applied in surgical simulation, such as Circumcision Augmented Reality Simulation (CARS), providing a novel approach to medical innovation and training applications [13]. The retail industry has also utilised AR technology to provide superior customer experiences and enable new digital services that improve customer interactions [14]. Overall, AR has the potential to revolutionise various domains by enhancing the real-world environment with virtual information.

Due to the wide applications of AR, researchers are also advocating the use of AR in crime scene investigations (CSIs). According to the researchers, AR can potentially revolutionise 3D crime scene reconstruction and forensic investigation [15]. This technology provides a new perspective on crime scene analysis, allowing CSIs to visualise and interact with virtual crime scenes.

Moreover, AR will allow CSIs to analyse the traces at the crime scene and receive rapid identification information while still conducting the investigation [16]. This real-time information can significantly enhance the efficiency and accuracy of crime scene investigations. Furthermore, the use of AR can reduce the CSI period [17].

Integrating AR with other cutting-edge technology can also increase the efficiency of CSIs. In this context, the integration of nanotechnologies with AR could potentially lead to the development of advanced forensic tools for the collection and analysis of evidence at crime scenes [18].

Furthermore, the development of tools for rapid visualisation and extraction of information demonstrates the ongoing efforts to improve the portability, speed, and simplicity of forensic analysis [19]. Infrared-based technologies have also ushered in a new era in crime scene investigations and the identification of evidence obtained from crime scenes [20]. Integrating infrared technology with AR could provide CSIs with additional evidence detection and visualisation tools, further enhancing their capabilities.

DOI: 10.1201/9781003207573-5

Additionally, the use of VR as a tool for teaching and learning in crime scene investigation has been explored, demonstrating its potential to improve forensic science education and practical training for CSI [21]. Studies have shown that VR is helpful for learning and practising problem-solving skills in forensic science and crime scene investigation [22]. Integrating AR with VR could provide a comprehensive training platform for CSIs, allowing them to simulate and practice crime scene investigations in a controlled virtual environment. DNA fingerprinting has revolutionised the forensic sciences, greatly contributing to police investigations and court proceedings [23]. Integrating DNA analysis technologies with AR could provide CSIs with on-site DNA analysis capabilities, allowing them to collect and analyse DNA evidence directly at the crime scene. In this context, we analysis the different research directions related to the application of AR in crime science investigation.

LITERATURE REVIEW

The investigation of the crime scene is a crucial aspect of the evidence collection process, as it determines the selection of elements of the crime scene as evidence. This process involves various scientific disciplines, such as forensic botany, which has been used to analyse small vegetation found on a corpse in a criminal case. Additionally, crime scene investigation has evolved into a discipline known as crime reconstruction, which utilises deductive and inductive reasoning, physical evidence, and scientific methods to gain explicit knowledge of the series of events surrounding the commission of a crime. Furthermore, the evidence system in forensic science emphasises the importance of the link between the victim, the evidence, and the perpetrator at the crime scene.

Geoforensic search, which integrates remote sensing, geophysics, and dogs, has emerged as a subdiscipline within crime scene investigation, with applications in search, crime scene, and sample (trace evidence). In addition, technological advancements have led to the development of interactive and immersive virtual reality crime scenes, providing a platform for learning forensic science and crime scene reconstruction. Additionally, the identification of blood-contaminated fingerprints at crime scenes has been highlighted as crucial evidence for crime scene investigation units.

In the context of a criminal investigation, the analysis and interpretation of hammer transfer stains at a crime scene have been emphasised, demonstrating the effective use of bloodstain evidence with other circumstantial evidence for sequencing events. Furthermore, investigative DNA analysis has been demonstrated in a murder case, showcasing the feasibility of predicting the appearance of an unknown suspect from a mixed crime scene trace. However, challenges arise when biological fluid evidence obtained from crime scenes is contaminated or collected without scientific knowledge, emphasising the importance of proper handling and preservation by forensic scientists.

Developing and implementing scientific and methodological approaches in criminalistics have been identified as crucial for addressing modern problems in countering certain criminal offenses. Additionally, criminal analysis has been categorised into various types, including forensic cartography, intelligence analysis, and geographic profiling, providing valuable insights during pre-trial investigations in criminal proceedings. Moreover, the structure of forensic techniques has been presented, encompassing physical traces of crimes, technical and forensic means, and organisational and legal foundations of forensic support for offense investigation.

The detection of criminal communities based on isomorphic subgraph analytics has been highlighted to recognise traits shared by highly centralised enterprises run by criminals, aiding in the criminal investigative process. Furthermore, the application of nanotechnology in forensic investigation has been instrumental in various areas, such as latent fingerprint development, explosives detection, and nerve gas detection, contributing to time-bound investigations and accurate results. Additionally, the current situation presents significant opportunities to reinvent trace evidence and forensic science, paving the way for redefining the field.

In conclusion, crime scene investigation has evolved significantly, incorporating diverse scientific disciplines and technological advancements to enhance evidence collection, crime reconstruction, and forensic analysis. Integrating various forensic techniques and methodologies has contributed to developing a comprehensive approach to understanding criminal problems and solving cases.

The advancement of augmented reality (AR) technology has significantly impacted forensic science, particularly in crime scene investigation. Immersive technologies, such as AR, have revolutionised 3D crime scene reconstruction and forensic investigation, providing new perspectives and tools for analyzing crime scenes [15]. Additionally, nanotechnology has been crucial in addressing current forensic investigation issues, including collecting and analysing evidence from crime scenes contributing to preventive forensic and security measures. Furthermore, the integration of forensic search, which involves remote sensing, geophysics, and dogs, has provided valuable advancements in the search, crime scene investigation, and trace evidence analysis [24]. Moreover, identifying blood-contaminated fingerprints at crime scenes has been highlighted as crucial evidence for crime scene investigation units, showcasing the significance of technological advancements in forensic science [25].

These advancements in AR technology have not only improved the efficiency and accuracy of crime scene investigations but have also expanded the capabilities of forensic scientists in collecting and analysing evidence. Integrating immersive technologies, nanotechnology, and forensic search has significantly enhanced forensic investigation, providing new tools and methodologies for analysing crime scenes and gathering crucial evidence. As technology continues to advance, it is expected that AR will play an increasingly vital role in forensic science, further improving the accuracy and depth of crime scene investigations.

METHODOLOGY

In this study, we employed a systematic methodology to analyse data from Scopus, focusing on publications in the realm of Crime Scene Investigations (CSI) augmented by Augmented Reality (AR) from 2008 to 2023. The Scopus data collection ensured access to a comprehensive and authoritative dataset. The analysis encompassed several dimensions: geographical distribution of research to understand the global contributions, keyword frequency to identify prevalent research themes, and temporal trends in authors' productivity and citation impact. For each dimension, data was meticulously categorised, evaluated, and synthesised to draw meaningful insights. The findings were then visualised using various graphs and charts, facilitating a clear understanding of the trends, patterns, and dynamics within the field. This methodological approach allowed for a thorough and detailed exploration of the evolving landscape of AR applications in CSI.

The analysis aimed to address the following research questions:

1. **What are the trends in geographical distribution of research in AR applied to CSI?**
   - This question explores which countries are leading in this field and how the global research landscape is shaped.

2. Which keywords are most prevalent in the recent literature on AR in CSI?

   • By identifying key terms, we aim to understand the focus areas and thematic evolution within the field.

3. How has authors' production in this domain evolved over time, and what is its impact?

   • This question seeks to analyse the temporal trends in research output and the citation impact of these contributions.

RESULTS AND DISCUSSION

In this comprehensive analysis, data collected from Scopus spanning from 2008 to 2023 reveals significant insights into the realm of Crime Scene Investigations (CSI) through Augmented Reality (AR). The dataset encompasses a broad range of 30 documents derived from 24 varied sources, including journals and books. These documents, on average 6.1 years from publication, have each garnered an average of 8.1 citations, with a yearly citation rate of approximately 0.9865 per document, cumulatively citing 704 references. The types of documents are diverse, consisting of 4 articles, 5 book chapters, 14 conference papers, 4 conference reviews, and 3 reviews. Additionally, the dataset is rich in keywords, featuring 186 'Keywords Plus (ID)' and 66 'Author's Keywords (DE)', indicating a wide spectrum of research themes and topics within the scope of CSI and AR. The authorship data is equally noteworthy, with contributions from 70 authors who made 80 appearances, highlighting a mix of 3 single-authored and 67 multi-authored documents. This mix underlines the collaborative nature of this field, as reflected by the average of 0.429 documents per author, 2.33 authors per document, and 2.67 co-authors per document, leading to a collaboration index of 3.19. This in-depth data analysis, visually represented in Figure 5.1, not only quantifies the research output but also sheds light on the evolving dynamics of collaboration and thematic diversity at the intersection of CSI and AR.

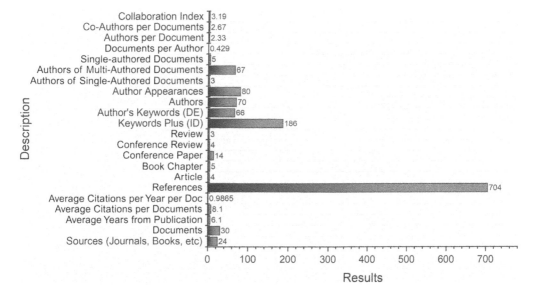

Figure 5.1 Main information

This section delves into the geographical distribution of scientific production in the specified domain, as extracted from the gathered data. The distribution, as illustrated in Figure 5.2, highlights the varying levels of contribution from different countries, spanning from 2008 to 2023. Leading the list in terms of frequency is the Netherlands, with a notable 14 publications, underscoring its significant role in this research area. Following closely are Switzerland and the United Kingdom, each contributing 10 publications, which reflects their active participation in this field. Italy's contribution stands at 9 publications, indicating its substantial involvement. The data also shows meaningful contributions from countries like Indonesia (5 publications), Brazil, Israel, South Africa, and the United States, each with 4 publications. These figures not only exhibit the global interest in the domain but also highlight the diverse geographical perspectives incorporated in the research. Furthermore, India's contribution of 3 publications, along with China and Pakistan's 2 publications each, and the individual contributions from Denmark, Mexico, and Sweden, each with 1 publication, collectively contribute to a more comprehensive understanding of the global scientific effort in this field. This geographical distribution of scientific production, as clearly represented in Figure 5.2 offers critical insights into the global research landscape, showcasing both the leading and emerging contributors in the domain.

This section provides a detailed analysis of the most prevalent keywords in the recent literature on Crime Scene Investigations (CSI) augmented by technological advances, specifically Augmented Reality (AR). The data, as visually summarised in Figure 5.3 showcases the frequency of specific terms, underlining their relevance and prominence in current research.

The term "augmented reality" emerges as the most frequently cited keyword, appearing in 16 instances. This highlights its central role in contemporary CSI methodologies, where AR technology is increasingly being integrated. Following this, the term "crime" appears with a frequency of 14, reflecting the broad scope of the research area. The more specific phrase "crime scene investigations" is mentioned in 8 publications, indicating its significance as a focal point in this field.

Additionally, "forensic science" is another key term with 7 mentions, signifying its foundational role in crime scene analysis. The keywords "crime scenes" and "virtual reality" each appear 6 times, suggesting a growing interest in the application of VR technologies in crime scene reconstruction and analysis.

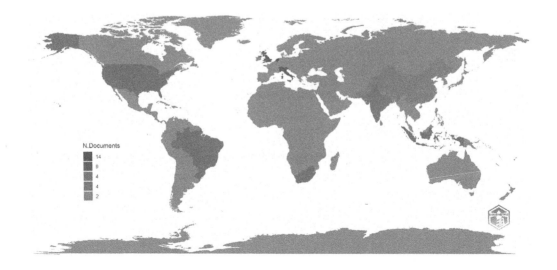

Figure 5.2 Country scientific production

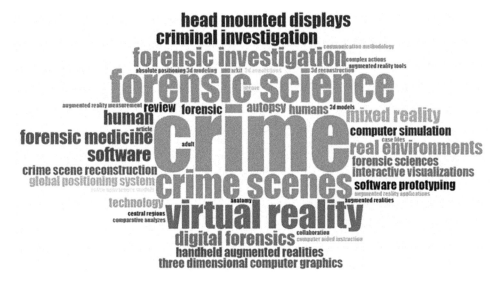

Figure 5.3 Keyword distribution

The data also highlights terms such as "forensic investigation" (4 occurrences), "criminal investigation" (3 occurrences), "digital forensics" (3 occurrences), and "forensic medicine" (3 occurrences). These terms underscore the multi-disciplinary nature of the field, encompassing aspects of technological advancement, legal procedures, and medical examination within the forensic context.

The frequency and distribution of these keywords, as detailed in Figure 5.3, provide a clear indication of the current research trends and focal areas within the domain of CSI and AR. This keyword analysis not only reflects the thematic concentration of the existing literature but also suggests potential avenues for future research in this rapidly evolving field.

This section presents an analysis of authors' scientific production in the field of Augmented Reality (AR) applied to Crime Scene Investigations (CSI) over time, focusing on publication frequency and citation impact. The data, as represented in Figure 5.4 showcases the contributions of various authors across different years, along with their respective total citations (TC) and average citations per year (TCpY).

A noteworthy trend is observed in the frequency of publications per author over time. For instance, ABATE AF published once in 2008 with a TC of 2, averaging 0.125 citations per year. In contrast, AKMAN O's single publication in 2012 has garnered significant attention, with a TC of 76 and an impressive average of 6.333 citations per year. Similarly, ALBEEDAN M's recent contribution in 2022, though yet to be cited, reflects the ongoing research in this area.

The data also highlights several authors with multiple publications across different years. For instance, DATCU D's publications in 2013 and 2016 have respective TCs of 24 and 25, with yearly citation averages of 2.182 and 3.125. Likewise, LUKOSCH S made contributions in both 2012 and 2013, each time receiving substantial citations, indicating the enduring relevance of their work.

Furthermore, the recent contributions from authors like DECKER S and FRANCKEN-BERG S in 2021, each with a TC of 15 and an average of 5.000 citations per year, as well as ISAFIADE OE with 2 publications in 2022 accumulating a total of 9 citations, point towards an increasing interest and recognition in the field.

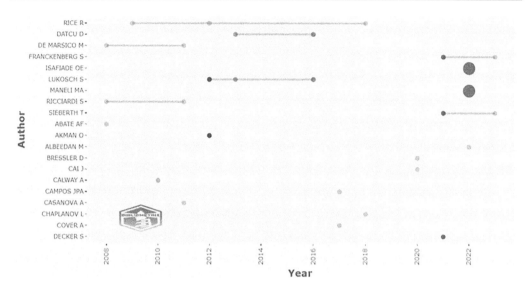

Figure 5.4 Authors' production over time

This detailed analysis of authors' production over time, as illustrated in Figure 5.4, not only sheds light on the individual contributions and their impact through citations but also provides insights into the evolving research trends and the growing interest in AR applications in CSI. It underscores the dynamic nature of the field and the significance of continuous scholarly contributions over the years.

RECENT ADVANCES

Recent technological advancements in crime scene investigations have seen the adoption and testing of various frameworks utilising augmented reality (AR) and virtual reality (VR) technologies. These frameworks have been proposed to enhance the accuracy and efficiency of crime scene reconstructions and forensic investigations. Immersive technologies, including AR, VR, mixed reality (MR), and a combination of VR and AR, have been implemented in crime scene reconstruction, accounting for 15.3% of the articles analysed [15]. This indicates a significant utilisation of AR in crime scene investigations.

Furthermore, crime scene investigators and specialist examiners highlighted the active attempts to incorporate 3D scanning techniques, closely related to AR and VR technologies, into scene preservation and recording [26]. This demonstrates the practical application of AR and VR in preserving and reconstructing crime scenes.

Moreover, identified potential applications of VR technology in crime scene investigation, including data analysis, witness statement evaluation, route visualisation, training, and security planning [27]. This suggests that VR technology is being explored for various aspects of crime scene investigations, indicating its potential for enhancing investigative processes.

Additionally, it aimed to implement modern learning strategies and activities using VR for teaching crime scene investigation, further emphasising the potential of VR in forensic science education and training [22]. Its work also emphasised the use of AR and VR for creating accurate and immersive virtual environments in forensic science, further underlining the relevance of these technologies in crime scene management and investigations [28].

In conclusion, the most recent technological advancements in AR that are being used or tested in crime scene investigations primarily revolve around using AR and VR technologies for crime scene reconstruction, preservation, training, and education. These technologies offer promising prospects for enhancing crime scene investigations' accuracy, efficiency, and immersive nature.

CHALLENGES AND LIMITATIONS

Integrating Augmented Reality (AR) into crime scene investigations faces several technical limitations and challenges. While immersive technologies, including AR, have been implemented in crime scene reconstruction, the current literature indicates that AR accounts for only 15.3% of the articles, with Virtual Reality (VR) being more prevalent at 75% [15]. This suggests a disparity in the adoption and implementation of AR compared to VR in crime scene investigations. Additionally, challenges such as poor training, inadequate funding, and interference from various quarters have been identified as factors that limit the effective use of forensic investigation in criminal investigations [29]. These challenges may hinder AR technology's widespread adoption and seamless integration into crime scene investigations.

Moreover, the potential of Unmanned Aircraft System (UAS) technology in accurately reconstructing crime scenes for forensic investigation purposes has been underscored, indicating a potential alternative or complementary approach to AR integration [30] (Jalal, 2023). This suggests that while AR holds promise, other emerging technologies offer potential solutions for crime scene reconstruction and forensic investigations.

Furthermore, the narrative review on the forensic applications of the hyperspectral imaging technique highlights its potential in detecting and analysing various types of evidence, indicating that alternative technological approaches are being explored in forensic investigations [31]. This suggests integrating AR into crime scene investigations may compete with other advanced imaging and analytical techniques.

Additionally, the potential invasion or revolution of Artificial Intelligence in forensic science, as discussed in a recent article, raises questions about the role of AI in crime scene investigations and its potential impact on the integration of AR technology [32]. The limitless applications of AI in crime scene investigations may pose opportunities and challenges for the seamless integration of AR.

Moreover, the need to address modifications in crime scene data that may change evidence and lead to different investigation results, as highlighted in a study on cybercrime forensics, underscores the importance of ensuring the integrity and reliability of data in crime scene investigations, which is also relevant to the integration of AR technology [33].

In conclusion, while integrating AR into crime scene investigations holds promise for enhancing the efficacy of forensic investigations, it faces technical limitations and challenges, such as disparities in adoption compared to VR, poor training, inadequate funding, competition from alternative technologies, and potential implications of AI. Addressing these challenges is crucial for realising the full potential of AR in crime scene investigations.

LEGAL AND ETHICAL CONCERNS

Augmented Reality (AR) has gained significant attention in forensic contexts due to its potential applications in crime scene investigation, forensic psychiatry, and forensic medicine. However, using AR in these contexts raises legal and ethical concerns, particularly regarding privacy issues and potential misuse.

The ethical considerations associated with AR systems in forensic contexts encompass various aspects such as privacy, property rights, ownership, trust, and informed consent [34]. These concerns are further compounded by the developers' ethical considerations in designing AR products, especially in virtual learning environments, where accountability for ethical design and use of AR products is paramount [35] (Steele et al., 2020). Moreover, the introduction of Extended Reality (XR) in forensic psychiatry has sparked a broader ethical and legal debate, focusing on recognising criminal offenders and forensic patients highlighting the relevance of ethics and human rights in this domain [36].

In forensic medicine, the comparative study of AR software development kits suitable for forensic medicine education underscores the potential for AR to enhance educational practices in this field [37]. Additionally, the impact of mobile augmented reality on learners, particularly in subjects of ethical sensitivity, such as forensic medicine, has been a subject of study, indicating the potential for AR to influence knowledge acquisition and retention in forensic education [38].

However, the potential for misuse of AR technology in forensic contexts cannot be overlooked. The misuse of AR for personal benefit, as evidenced in the case of digital forensics in a virtual world, raises concerns about the ethical implications and potential misuse of AR in virtual environments.

Furthermore, the visualisation of post-mortem computed tomography data using AR techniques has the potential to provide forensic experts with additional information during autopsy, thereby influencing forensic death investigations [39]. Similarly, the influence of AR on forensic fire investigations and its spatiotemporal mapping of evacuee response underscores the far-reaching impact of AR technologies in forensic science [40].

AR, virtual reality, and other 21st-century educational technologies have been identified as critical tools for learning engagement, information delivery, collaboration, and communication, thereby highlighting their potential in forensic science education and training [41]. Moreover, VR for teaching and learning in crime scene investigation has been recognised as an essential component of forensic science education, albeit with challenges related to cost, accessibility, and breadth of experience [21].

In conclusion, integrating AR in forensic contexts presents many legal and ethical concerns, including privacy issues, potential misuse, and the need for ethical design and use of AR products. However, the potential benefits of AR in enhancing forensic education and investigations cannot be overlooked. Therefore, a balanced approach that addresses these concerns while leveraging the potential of AR in forensic contexts is essential.

FUTURE DIRECTIONS

Emerging Trends

The field of crime scene investigation is constantly evolving, and emerging trends in augmented reality (AR) technology are poised to influence future practices in this area significantly. One such trend is using immersive technology, including virtual reality (VR) and augmented reality, for crime scene reconstruction and investigation [15]. This technology allows for the recreation of crime scenes realistically and interactively, providing valuable insights for investigators and potentially enhancing the accuracy of reconstructions. Additionally, AR is being explored as a tool for annotating crime scenes and facilitating collaboration between remote experts and on-site investigators, thereby improving the efficiency and accuracy of investigations [42].

Furthermore, the integration of advanced technologies such as thermal cameras and heat trace tracking techniques presents new opportunities for estimating departure times and tracking heat traces at crime scenes, enhancing the capabilities of law enforcement in high-tech crime investigations [43]. The use of innovations during crime scene investigations, including incorporating the latest technologies, is also emphasised as a crucial aspect of modern investigative processes [44]. These innovations have the potential to streamline investigative actions and improve the overall efficiency of crime scene investigations.

In forensic education and training, virtual reality is being leveraged to support the learning process of forensic scenarios, offering modern and immersive learning strategies and activities for teaching crime scene investigation [22]. Similarly, immersive VR experiences are being utilised to enhance forensic science education, allowing students to engage with realistic crime scenes and gain practical insights into investigative processes [45]. However, implementing simulated crime scene investigation through virtual reality poses challenges related to cost, accessibility, and the breadth of experience, highlighting the need for further advancements in this area [21].

Moreover, the rapid evolution of technology, particularly in the digital realm, presents challenges for investigators and forensic examiners in identifying and interpreting various forms of digital evidence, such as mobile phone evidence, within criminal proceedings [46]. This underscores the importance of staying abreast of technological advancements and developing specialised knowledge and skills to navigate digital evidence in modern crime investigations effectively.

Additionally, advancements in biological and medical fields have implications for legal medicine and forensic science. For instance, distinguishing fly artifacts resulting from insect activity from human bloodstains using DNA-based methods is a notable development in forensic biology, addressing potential confounding factors at crime scenes [47]. Furthermore, the implications of vascularised composite allotransplantation in plastic surgery on legal medicine raise considerations regarding chimerism and its impact on collecting and identifying biological samples from crime scenes, highlighting the intersection of medical advancements and forensic practices [48].

In computer vision systems, reconstructing scenes from imperfect depth data in real-time has broad applications, including in interactive mediums such as virtual reality games and simulations, augmented reality applications, and extended reality technologies [49]. These advancements in computer vision have the potential to enhance the visualisation and analysis of crime scenes, offering new avenues for leveraging AR technology in forensic investigations.

In conclusion, the emerging trends in AR technology are poised to significantly influence future crime scene investigations by offering innovative tools for crime scene reconstruction, enhancing forensic education and training, addressing challenges in digital evidence interpretation, and integrating advancements in biological and medical fields into forensic practices.

CONCLUSION

Our analysis of Scopus data from 2008 to 2023 has provided a thorough understanding of the developments in Augmented Reality (AR) applications within Crime Scene Investigations (CSI). The study highlights the significant contributions from various countries, with the Netherlands leading in research output. Key terms such as "augmented reality", "forensic science", and "crime scene investigations" dominate the research landscape, reflecting the field's evolving focus. Authors' production over time indicates a growing academic interest and an increasing citation impact, signaling the rising importance of AR in forensic investigations. This study not only maps the current state of AR in CSI but also sets the groundwork for future research, emphasising the need for continued innovation and interdisciplinary collaboration in this dynamic field.

REFERENCES

[1] V. Dua, A. Sikri, A. Kaur, and M. Sachdeva, "Augmented reality in orthodontics: The way ahead," *Int. J. Oral Health Dent.*, 2021, doi: 10.18231/j.ijohd.2021.038.

[2] G. M. Santi, A. Ceruti, A. Liverani, and F. Osti, "Augmented reality in industry 4.0 and future innovation programs," *Technologies*, 2021, doi: 10.3390/technologies9020033.

[3] M. Billinghurst, A. Clark, and G. Lee, "*A survey of augmented reality*," 2015, doi: 10.1561/9781601989215.

[4] L. T. Pereira, W. C. Roberti Júnior, and M. F. Moreno, "Photorealism in mixed reality: A systematic literature review," *Int. J. Virtual Real.*, 2021, doi: 10.20870/ijvr.2021.21.1.3166.

[5] S. S. Jamali, M. F. Shiratuddin, K. W. Wong, and C. L. Oskam, "Utilising mobile-augmented reality for learning human anatomy," *Procedia Soc. Behav. Sci.*, 2015, doi: 10.1016/j.sbspro.2015.07.054.

[6] C. Costa, A. Manso, and J. Patrício, "Design of a mobile augmented reality platform with game-based learning purposes," *Inf. Int. Interdiscip. J.*, 2020, doi: 10.3390/info11030127.

[7] N. I. Md Enzai, N. A. Ahmad, M. A. Hamzah Ghani, S. S. Rais, and S. Mohamed, "Development of augmented reality (AR) for innovative teaching and learning in engineering education," *Asian J. Univ. Educ.*, 2021, doi: 10.24191/ajue.v16i4.11954.

[8] R. Sari, P. L. R. Fatimah, S. Ilyana, and H. D. Hermawan, "Augmented reality (AR)-based sharia financial literacy system (AR-SFLS): A new approach to virtual sharia financial socialization for young learners," *Int. J. Islam. Middle East. Finance Manag.*, 2021, doi: 10.1108/imefm-11-2019-0484.

[9] Y. Gümbür and M. Avaroğullari, "Artirilmiş gerçeklik uygulamalarinin sosyal bilgiler eğitimine etkisi," *Araşt. Ve Deneyim Derg.*, 2020, doi: 10.47214/adeder.835927.

[10] С. О. Зелінська, А. А. Азарян, and В. А. Азарян, "Investigation of opportunities of the practical application of the augmented reality technologies in the information and educative environment for mining engineers training in the higher education establishment," *Освітній Вимір*, 2018, doi: 10.31812/pedag.v51i0.3674.

[11] І. С. Мінтій and В. М. Соловйов, "Augmented reality: Ukrainian present business and future education," *Освітній Вимір*, 2018, doi: 10.31812/pedag.v51i0.3676.

[12] K. Wong, H. M. Yee, B. A. Xavier, and G. A. Grillone, "Applications of augmented reality in otolaryngology: A systematic review," *Otolaryngology*, 2018, doi: 10.1177/0194599818796476.

[13] M. S. Maulana, H. Winarto, and G. Amalia, "Augmented reality application for surgery simulation: Circumcision augmented reality simulation (CARS)," *Med. Tek. J. Tek. Elektromedik Indones.*, 2020, doi: 10.18196/mt.020111.

[14] N. Vaidyanathan and S. Henningsson, "Designing augmented reality services for enhanced customer experiences in retail," *J. Serv. Manag.*, 2022, doi: 10.1108/josm-01-2022-0004.

[15] M. A. Maneli and O. E. Isafiade, "3D forensic crime scene reconstruction involving immersive technology: A systematic literature review," *IEEE Access Pract. Innov. Open Solut.*, 2022, doi: 10.1109/access.2022.3199437.

[16] M. de Gruijter, C. Nee, and C. J. de Poot, "Identification at the crime scene: The sooner, the better? The interpretation of rapid identification information by CSIs at the crime scene," *Sci. Justice*, 2017, doi: 10.1016/j.scijus.2017.03.006.

[17] M. de Gruijter, C. J. de Poot, and H. Elffers, "The influence of new technologies on the visual attention of CSIs performing a crime scene investigation," *J. Forensic Sci.*, 2015, doi: 10.1111/1556-4029.12904.

[18] A. Pandya and R. K. Shukla, "New perspective of nanotechnology: Role in preventive forensic," *Egypt. J. Forensic Sci.*, 2018, doi: 10.1186/s41935-018-0088-0.

[19] X. Zhao, N. Cai, X. Huang, W. Liu, F. Gao, and C. Wang, "One-click device for rapid visualization and extraction of latent evidence through multi-moding light source integration and light-guiding technology," *Sci. Rep.*, 2022, doi: 10.1038/s41598-022-21136-0.

[20] M. Asirdizer, Y. Hekimoğlu, and O. Gümüş, "*Usage of infrared-based technologies in forensic sciences*," in *Forensic Analysis from Death to Justice*, 2016, InTech, doi: 10.5772/62773.

[21] R. Mayne and H. Green, "Virtual reality for teaching and learning in crime scene investigation," *Sci. Justice*, 2020, doi: 10.20944/preprints202004.0434.v1.

[22] W. Khalilia, M. Gombár, Z. Palkova, M. Palko, J. Valíček, and M. Harničárová, "Using virtual reality as support to the learning process of forensic scenarios," *IEEE Access Pract. Innov. Open Solut.*, 2022, doi: 10.1109/access.2022.3196471.

[23] G. Chemale, et al., "DNA evidence in property crimes: An analysis of more than 4200 samples processed by the Brazilian federal police forensic genetics laboratory," *Braz. J. Forensic Sci. Med. Law Bioeth.*, 2016, doi: 10.17063/bjfs6(1)y2016108a.

[24] A. Ruffell, B. Rocke, and N. A. Powell, "Geoforensic search to crime scene: Remote sensing, geo-physics, and dogs," *J. Forensic Sci.*, 2023, doi: 10.1111/1556-4029.15293.

[25] Y. Harush-Brosh et al., "Back to *Amido Black*: Uncovering touch DNA in Blood-contaminated fingermarks," *J. Forensic Sci.*, 2021, doi: 10.1111/1556-4029.14783.

[26] S. Yu, G. H. Thomson, V. Rinaldi, C. Rowland, and N. N. Daeid, "Development of a Dundee ground truth imaging protocol for recording indoor crime scenes to facilitate virtual reality reconstruction," *Sci. Justice*, 2023, doi: 10.1016/j.scijus.2023.01.001.

[27] P. Engström, B. J. Jankiewicz, R. Chirico, J. Peltola, and G. Iacobellis, "*Virtual reality for CSI training*," 2023, doi: 10.1117/12.2664217.

[28] V. Sharma, "A new approach to crime scene management: AR-VR applications in forensic science," in *Reinventing Technological Innovations with Artificial Intelligence*, 2023, Bentham Books, doi: 10.2174/9789815165791123010008.

[29] D. Etin-Osa, "Analysis of the application of forensic tools in crime scene investigation in Nigeria; a case study of Benin metropolis," *Cauc. J. Sci.*, 2023, doi: 10.48138/cjo.1179082.

[30] A. J. Jalal, "Assessing precision and dependability of reconstructed three-dimensional modeling for vehicles at crash scenes using unmanned aircraft system," *Jagst*, 2023, doi: 10.11113/jagst. v3n2.76.

[31] M. Pallocci et al., "Forensic applications of hyperspectral imaging technique: A narrative review," *Med. Leg. J.*, 2022, doi: 10.1177/00258172221105381.

[32] E. A. Alaa El-Din, "Artificial intelligence in forensic science: Invasion or revolution?," *Egypt. Soc. Clin. Toxicol. J.*, 2022, doi: 10.21608/esctj.2022.158178.1012.

[33] S. Subair, D. Yosif, A. Ahmed, and C. Thron, "Cyber crime forensics," *Int. J. Emerg. Multidiscip. Comput. Sci. Artif. Intell.*, 2022, doi: 10.54938/ijemdcsai.2022.01.1.37.

[34] C. Turner, "Augmented reality, augmented epistemology, and the real-world web," *Philos. Technol.*, 2022, doi: 10.1007/s13347-022-00496-5.

[35] P. Steele, C. Burleigh, M. Kroposki, M. Magabo, and L. Bailey, "Ethical considerations in designing virtual and augmented reality products—virtual and augmented reality design with students in mind: Designers' perceptions," *J. Educ. Technol. Syst.*, 2020, doi: 10.1177/0047239520933858.

[36] S. Ligthart, G. Meynen, N. Biller-Andorno, T. Kooijmans, and P. Kellmeyer, "Is virtually everything possible? The relevance of ethics and human rights for introducing extended reality in forensic psychiatry," *Ajob Neurosci.*, 2021, doi: 10.1080/21507740.2021.1898489.

[37] K. Tongprasom, W. Boongsood, W. Boongsood, and T. Pipatchotitham, "Comparative study of an augmented reality software development kit suitable for forensic medicine education," *Int. J. Inf. Educ. Technol.*, 2021, doi: 10.18178/ijiet.2021.11.1.1482.

[38] B. R. Alhamad and S. Agha, "Comparing knowledge acquisition and retention between mobile learning and traditional learning in teaching respiratory therapy students: A randomized control trial," *Adv. Med. Educ. Pract.*, 2023, doi: 10.2147/amep.s390794.

[39] L. C. Ebert et al., "A review of post-mortem computed tomography data visualization techniques for forensic death investigations," *Int. J. Legal Med.*, 2021, doi: 10.1007/s00414-021-02581-4.

[40] J. Ouellette, S. Gwynne, R. Brown, and M. Kinateder, "Spatiotemporal mapping of evacuee response," *Fire Mater.*, 2020, doi: 10.1002/fam.2842.

[41] I. Gupta, S. Dangi, and S. Sharma, "Augmented reality based human-machine interfaces in healthcare environment: Benefits, challenges, and future trends," in *2022 International Conference on Wireless Communications Signal Processing and Networking (WiSPNET)*, Chennai, India, March 2022, pp. 251–257, IEEE, doi: 10.1109/WiSPNET54241.2022.9767119.

[42] H. Engelbrecht and S. Lukosch, "Dangerous or desirable: Utilizing augmented content for field policing," *Int. J. Hum. Comput. Interact.*, 2020, doi: 10.1080/10447318.2020.1752473.

[43] J. Xu, B. S. Glicksberg, C. Su, P. Walker, J. Bian, and F. Wang, "Federated learning for healthcare informatics," *J. Healthc. Inform. Res.*, November 2020, doi: 10.1007/s41666-020-00082-4.

[44] V. Lisohor, "The use of innovations during the crime scene investigation," *Econ. Financ. Law*, 2020, doi: 10.37634/efp.2020.5.5.

[45] S. N. Kader, W. B. Ng, S. Tan, and F. M. Fung, "Building an interactive immersive virtual reality crime scene for future chemists to learn forensic science chemistry," *J. Chem. Educ.*, 2020, doi: 10.1021/acs.jchemed.0c00817.

[46] A. Zhang, B. Bradford, R. M. Morgan, and S. Nakhaeizadeh, "Investigating the uses of mobile phone evidence in China criminal proceedings," *Sci. Justice*, 2022, doi: 10.1016/j.scijus.2022.03.011.

[47] C. Bini et al., "A DNA-based method for distinction of fly artifacts from human bloodstains," *Int. J. Legal Med.*, 2021, doi: 10.1007/s00414-021-02643-7.

[48] V. Haug et al., "Implications of vascularized composite allotransplantation in plastic surgery on legal medicine," *J. Clin. Med.*, 2023, doi: 10.3390/jcm12062308.

[49] A. Kulikajevas, R. Maskeliūnas, R. Damaševičius, and E. S. L. Ho, "3D object reconstruction from imperfect depth data using extended YOLOv3 network," *Sensors*, 2020, doi: 10.3390/s20072025.

Chapter 6

Chaotic Watermarking for Tamper Detection
Enhancing Robustness and Security in Digital Multimedia

Harkiran Kaur, Sunil K. Singh, Amit Chhabra, Vanshika Bhardwaj, Ritika Saini, Sudhakar Kumar, and Varsha Arya

1. INTRODUCTION TO CHAOTIC WATERMARKING

The prevalence of digital material in today's world poses serious questions about its integrity and authenticity because of the ongoing risk of tampering [1]. Unauthorized reproduction and dissemination of digital content are ongoing difficulties that people face daily. Digital watermarking has become an essential tool in the fight against these issues, providing a tactical solution to protect the integrity of digital assets. Among the innovative and promising technologies ready to tackle problems and get past barriers in this dynamic ecosystem is chaotic watermarking [2]. Systems that use concepts from chaos theory have significantly improved their security and reliability within this framework.

Information watermarking is a broad term that includes many techniques, each with a distinct function. It is a useful method for proving who owns or authenticating digital content, and it is frequently used with audio, video, and image files. There are many different types of watermarking techniques, such as obvious, visible watermarks and invisible ones that require sophisticated software or detection techniques to identify. Depending on the intended result, including the required level of security and the complexity of the material, several watermarking techniques—whether wavelet-based, spatial domain, or frequency domain—should be used. It is imperative to acknowledge, however, that despite its extensive usage, watermarking is not perfect and can be eliminated or modified.

The suggested Chaotic Watermarking technique presents a strong answer to the problems brought on by the digital era. It offers a fresh method of problem-solving by utilizing the special qualities of chaos theory to greatly improve reliability and safety procedures. When we examine the complexities of Chaotic Watermarking, we find that its incorporation into digital information protection has important consequences regarding the authenticity and integrity issues raised by tampering. This chapter delves into the many facets of Chaotic Watermarking with the goal of offering an understanding of how it may be applied practically and how it might improve content security in the digital world.

1.1 Motivation for Tamper Detection

The primary concern of creators and owners of digital assets is to maintain the originality and integrity of their work. Digital content integrity is ensured by the vital process of tamper detection. Artists, filmmakers, and photographers are among the content producers who depend on their works for income and fame. By preventing unauthorized copying, alteration, or dissemination, tamper detection serves as a protective measure for content providers' intellectual property rights. In a time of false information and fake news, it is critical to verify the authenticity of digital material. By enabling users to confirm whether digital material—such as images, movies, and documents—has been changed or fabricated, tamper detection

DOI: 10.1201/9781003207573-6

preserves the credibility of the content. Tamper-evident material is required by standards and regulations in several businesses. The identification of tampering is of utmost importance in guaranteeing conformity to these guidelines, thereby promoting legal and regulatory conformance for digital material. In security-related applications like forensics and surveillance, the accuracy of captured video footage is crucial. In such cases, tamper detection becomes essential, guaranteeing that recorded video has not been altered and preserving the dependability of security programs.

The significance of tamper detection in safeguarding the authenticity, reliability, and legal conformance of digital material is highlighted by these diverse incentives. It is clear from reading the next section on Chaotic-Based Watermarking that tamper detection techniques must be included to handle the intricate problems that arise from illegal changes made to the digital environment.

1.2 Chaotic-Based Watermarking Overview

As a state-of-the-art technology in digital watermarking, chaotic watermarking employs a unique methodology. Using this cutting-edge method, watermarks may be embedded into digital media by using the complex patterns of chaos. Digital content can contain hidden data called watermarks thanks to a variety of embedding techniques. Above all, there is no way for the original information to be altered because these implanted signals or data are undetectable. Watermarks can be used for a variety of purposes; they can be used as visual cues about the look or quality of material, as well as markers of copyright ownership [3].

The three main roles that watermarks play in chaotic watermarking are authentication, tamper detection, and protection. Interestingly, tamper detection becomes the main priority, with the goal of bolstering digital media security overall. This is a painstaking procedure in which digital assets actively seek any unauthorized changes or additions that may have occurred. Unauthorized editing, unauthorized dissemination, and unauthorized material copying are a few examples of these kinds of alterations.

The integrity and validity of digital assets are mostly protected by the strong tamper detection measures included in chaotic watermarking. By making use of the natural unpredictable nature of chaotic systems, these methods of tamper detection are incredibly effective [2]. Because chaotic dynamics may be used to detect any unlawful changes made to the watermarked information, chaotic watermarking is the best option for protecting digital data against tampering.

These watermarks are essential for content security in general, authentication, and tamper detection. They serve several functions, such as denoting quality and copyright. The chapter emphasizes how important tamper detection is and goes into detail about how chaotic systems' unpredictable properties make it more effective. As we proceed to the following section, the complex function of chaotic watermarking in supporting content security is still apparent, opening the door to a more thorough examination of its core components.

2. FUNDAMENTALS OF CHAOTIC SYSTEMS

After examining the use and importance of chaotic watermarking, we will now examine the fundamental ideas that support this strategy. In this section, we explain the basic characteristics of chaotic systems, with a focus on chaotic maps and their significant uses in watermarking. A key factor in the context of watermarking is the susceptibility of chaotic systems to beginning circumstances, topological mixing, and ergodicity. The unpredictable and random nature required for safe watermark implantation and successful tamper detection is facilitated by these characteristics.

2.1 Basics of Chaotic Maps

Chaotic maps are intriguing mathematical models that are renowned for their unpredictable nature in the field of digital watermarking. They are the foundation of sophisticated methods for protecting digital material. Mathematical functions exhibiting deterministic chaos are called chaotic maps. Due to its nonlinearity and sensitivity to initial circumstances, even minor modifications to the initial state can have a significant impact on the outcome. This characteristic, referred to as the "butterfly effect," emphasizes how chaotic systems are inherently unpredictable.

The logistic map is one of the most basic and common chaotic maps, represented by the deceptively simple equation [4]

$$x_{n+1} = rx_n (1 - x_n) \tag{1}$$

Here, the parameter r acts as a control parameter, and x_n represents the chaotic sequence at time step n. [5] These chaotic sequences exhibit properties like ergodicity, which is highly valuable in tamper detection scenarios.

This one-dimensional dynamical system becomes a cornerstone in watermarking, inducing chaos with sensitivity to initial conditions and bifurcation phenomena.

Expanding the horizons to two dimensions, the Hénon map joins the chaotic dance governed by the equation:

$$x_{n+1} = 1 - ax_n^2 + y_n \tag{2}$$

$$y_{n+1} = bx_n$$

Parameters a and b govern the map's behavior, making Hénon maps suitable for applications requiring enhanced security in tamper detection [6]. It adds an extra layer of complexity to pseudorandom sequences, enriching the security landscape of watermarking.

The tent map, on the other hand, is known for its simplicity and can be represented as:

$$x_{n+1} = r * x_n, \text{ if } 0 \leq x_n < 0.5$$

$$X_{n+1} = r * (1 - x_n), \text{ if } 0.5 \leq x_n < 1 \tag{3}$$

Here r is a parameter between 0 and 2.

In the discrete-time realm, the Arnold cat map emerges as a valuable ally. With equations

$$x_{n+1} = (2x_n + y_n) \bmod m$$

$$y_{n+1} = (x_n + y_n) \bmod m \tag{4}$$

it lends itself to permutations and scrambling tasks, adding diversity to chaotic watermarking.

The different chaotic maps discussed here can be summarized as shown in Fig ure 6.1, which represents a classification of the chaotic maps.

These chaotic maps share defining properties that make them indispensable in the watermarking saga. Sensitivity to initial conditions, a hallmark of chaos, ensures that tiny changes lead to dramatically different outcomes, forming the crux for generating pseudorandom sequences essential for watermark security [7]. The interplay between periodic and aperiodic behaviors in chaotic maps contributes to the adaptability and complexity essential in watermarking. Bifurcation phenomena, observed across various maps, enhance the dynamics, providing fertile ground for secure watermarking.

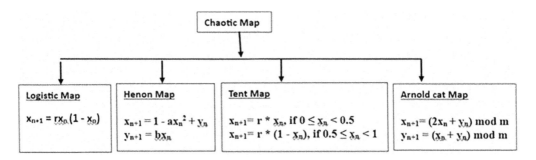

Figure 6.1 Classification of chaotic maps

While the logistic map is a prominent player in this chaotic symphony, it's crucial to recognize the diversity brought in by maps like Hénon and Arnold cat. The logistic map, with its simple yet potent equation, establishes chaos as the foundation. However, it's in the collaborative dance of various chaotic maps that watermarking finds its true strength. Each map adds a unique brushstroke to the canvas of unpredictability, creating a comprehensive security architecture. In the broader context of watermarking, the unpredictability and complexity derived from these chaotic maps become the pillars of security. Watermarking systems, fortified by the diverse dynamics of chaotic maps, exhibit adaptability and robustness [8]. This inherent chaos ensures the evolution of watermarking techniques to effectively withstand tampering attempts. Traversing the fundamentals of chaotic maps and their relevance to watermarking, the collective impact of their properties forms the bedrock of secure digital content protection.

2.2 Dynamics of Chaotic Systems and Pseudorandomness

Moving on from the basics of chaotic maps, we now explore the dynamics of chaotic systems and how they directly relate to chaotic watermarking. Chaotic systems also include topological mixing and starting condition sensitivity, but an additional important property is ergodicity. Trajectories are forced to explore the whole phase space over time by this feature, which lays the groundwork for comprehending how pseudorandom sequences are created.

The concept of pseudorandom sequences and ergodicity posits that chaotic systems eventually delve into every potential state found in their phase space. The creation of pseudorandom sequences, a key component of watermarking, is based on this investigation. Pseudorandom sequences possess unpredictability characteristics that are essential for safe watermark embedding and interception detection.

The role of chaotic dynamics in the generation of pseudorandom sequences has been thoroughly studied by researchers who have realized the potential of chaotic dynamics in producing pseudorandom sequences that are suitable for watermark embedding. Pseudorandom number generators based on chaos, which originate from the dynamics of chaotic systems, provide a unique way to generate random numbers [9]. Chaos dynamics are investigated here and shown to be effective in generating sequences that are secure against assaults and easily conform to the specifications of watermarking applications.

Importance for Watermark Embedding: An essential component of watermark embedding is the special characteristics of pseudorandom sequences produced by chaotic dynamics. These sequences are a reliable option for hiding undetectable signals in digital files because of their unpredictable nature and resistance to patterns. It is clear from delving more into the dynamics of chaotic systems that the security architecture of watermarking benefits greatly from their intrinsic complexity.

Understanding the relationship between pseudorandom sequence creation and chaotic dynamics helps us better understand the mechanics underlying safe watermark embedding. As we move further, the emphasis will be on comprehending the real-world consequences and practical uses of these dynamics, thus establishing chaotic watermarking's position as a highly effective instrument for content protection in the digital sphere.

3. DIGITAL WATERMARKING BASICS

Digital watermarking relies on watermark extraction and embedding techniques. Using material from numerous research articles and academic sources, we will go over the fundamentals shown in Figure 6.2 of these approaches.

3.1 Essentials of Watermark Embedding and Extraction Techniques

Using spatial domain techniques, the watermark is embedded by directly modifying pixel values. This can be accomplished using methods like LSB embedding, in which the watermark bits are substituted for the LSB of the cover picture. Although they're simple to use, spatial domain approaches are open to assault [10].

The watermark is embedded using transform domain techniques, which employ different image transformations such as Discrete Wavelet Transform or Discrete Cosine Transform. By preserving the visual quality of the images, these transforms aid in their compression. To improve resilience against attacks, the watermark is integrated into the transform coefficients.

Spread spectrum techniques embed the watermark by spreading the message signal across the entire frequency bandwidth, making it robust against various attacks. These techniques add a pseudorandom noise-like pattern (referred to as the spreading sequence) to the cover image to carry the watermark. One popular spread spectrum technique is the Direct Sequence Spread Spectrum (DSSS), which modulates the spreading sequence by adding it to each pixel value of the cover image [11]. In order to extract the embedded watermark, correlation-based techniques calculate the correlation between the watermarked image and the original watermark [12]. The correlation between the watermark and the watermarked signal enables the extraction process through the application of these techniques. The location and strength

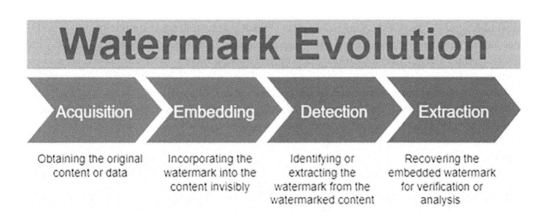

Figure. 6.2 Overview watermarking concept

of the watermark are estimated using a range of correlation algorithms, such as correlation filters and normalized correlation.

Statistical analysis of the image's statistical properties is used in watermark estimation techniques. These techniques typically capitalize on the statistical differences between the cover image and the embedded watermark. For example, the Difference Expansion (DE) technique compares the differences between the original and watermarked image to estimate the watermark.

The embedded watermark is extracted from the watermarked image through the use of transformation techniques, such as DCT or DWT. The inverse transform can be used to extract the watermark from the transformed coefficients. These techniques make use of the transformed domain's watermark embedding, which makes extraction dependable [13].

It should be noted that the choice of embedding and extraction techniques depends on the requirements of the application, such as computational complexity, robustness, and imperceptibility. Academics continue to develop approaches to improve the security and effectiveness of watermarking schemes.

3.2 Principles of Robustness, Imperceptibility, and Data Hiding

Robustness is the capacity of a data-hiding method to tolerate different kinds of attacks as well as inadvertent changes or distortions. When it comes to data hiding, the concealed information needs to be able to be recovered even when common signal processing techniques like noise addition, cropping, rotation, and filtering are present. Robust algorithms ensure that the embedded data can resist these alterations and still be reliably extracted with minimal errors. In many applications, robustness, imperceptibility, and data hiding are critical concepts that intelligent systems help to implement [14]. To achieve robustness, researchers have developed a range of methods, such as spread spectrum approaches, error-correcting codes, and adaptive embedding strategies.

By strengthening the embedded data's resistance to possible attacks and distortions, these techniques guarantee successful retrieval of the data in a variety of scenarios.

A crucial requirement for data-hiding strategies is imperceptibility, especially in situations where the existence of hidden data is meant to remain undetectable to the human eye. Imperceptible embedding ensures that even after the data is hidden, the cover image or signal looks and sounds just like the original. It seeks to maintain the quality and usefulness of the cover signal to the greatest extent possible while reducing any perceptual artifacts or degradation brought about by the embedding process [15].

Imperceptibility is measured using a variety of metrics, including just-noticeable difference thresholds (JNDs), peak signal-to-noise ratio (PSNR), and structural similarity index (SSIM). In an effort to reduce the visual or aural impact caused by the hidden data, researchers have created complex algorithms, including perceptual models based on human visual or auditory systems.

The act of hiding information, such as a picture, audio, or video file, within a carrier signal is known as data hiding. Many uses for it exist, such as data integrity verification, watermarking, steganography (covert communication), authentication, and copyright protection. Any type of digital content, including text, photos, audio, video, and so on, can contain hidden data [16].

Various data-hiding strategies have been developed according to the application's goals and the carrier signal's characteristics. A tradeoff between the three concepts can be seen in Figure 6.3. Spatial domain, frequency domain, transform domain, and reversible data hiding techniques are examples of common hiding techniques.

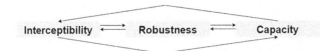

Figure. 6.3 Tradeoff-between-robustness capacity and Imperceptibility constraints

4. CHAOTIC ALGORITHMS FOR WATERMARKING

The digital age and continuous advancements in computer information technology have led to the widespread integration of digital multimedia products into daily life, resulting in a surge in demand for digital goods. Protecting the copyright of these products is a primary concern, leading to focused research on digital watermarking. This technology involves securely embedding copyright information directly into the material, ensuring anonymity and protection [17].

Digital watermarking has evolved, enabling discrete identification of digital products by embedding specific details, such as copyright owner identity or a serial code, within the data. Extraction of the digital watermark can be done using algorithms relevant to copyright disputes, maintaining security and copyright while preserving data value.

There are two main types of digital watermarking technology: frequency domain and spatial domain techniques. Frequency domain methods embed watermark information in frequency coefficients, while spatial domain techniques alter pixel positions. Frequency domain watermarking, known for its resilience and inconspicuous nature, is preferred.

The comprehensive overview of digital watermarking techniques is shown in Figure 6.4, which highlights the contributions of researchers like Fazli and Jing Liu in advancing the field. Techniques such as Discrete Wavelet Transform (DWT), Discrete Cosine Transform (DCT), Singular Value Decomposition (SVD), and Arnold transform have been introduced to enhance the robustness and invisibility of watermarks, facilitating blind extraction. However, some algorithms may focus solely on robustness, potentially overlooking simulated attack scenarios and the strength of watermark embedding.

Jing Liu and colleagues propose a digital watermarking solution combining Dual-Tree Complex Wavelet Transform (DTCWT), DCT, and a Hénon Map. This approach utilizes chaotic scrambling and zero watermarking to enhance security against geometric attacks and identify a region of interest (ROI), though it can be computationally demanding [18].

Various image processing techniques, including Fourier Transform (FFT) and DWT, have gained popularity, with FFT showing promise in digital watermarking. Researchers have successfully embedded watermark data into Fourier coefficients for grayscale images and explored the FFT [17].

The presented book chapter introduces a methodology for assessing image degradation before watermark embedding, selecting a circular region in Fourier frequency domain coefficients for optimal image radius. In the Fourier transform domain, issues in singular value decomposition watermarking are addressed by a method that normalizes the image's quality matrix.

Other methods include creating a distortion model for printed and scanned images, and embedding watermark information in the Fourier-Mellin domain. A technique identifies FFT coefficients corresponding to Log-Polar Mapping coefficients, avoiding polar coordinate inversion to solve vulnerabilities to attacks. Synchronous template embedding based on extracted template data is presented to determine scale adjustments, thwarting attacks like print scanning.

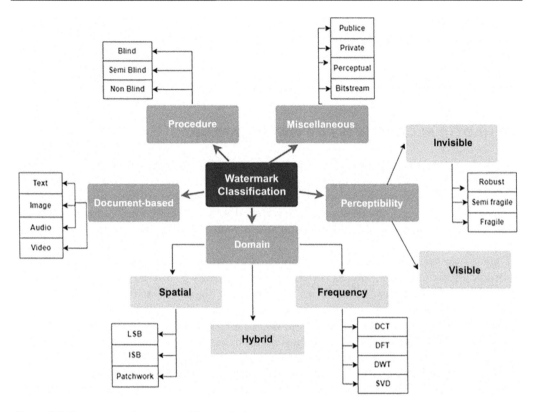

Figure 6.4 Taxonomy of watermarking techniques

While successful in grayscale watermarking, techniques combining FFT and quaternion theory gained popularity for color image watermarking due to alignment with color channels. However, some techniques applied to color images may lead to issues like gradient flipping, halo artifacts, color distortion, and over-enhancement, compromising the final product's quality.

A new quaternion-based method introduces watermark embedding primarily in a parallel direction. Researchers address vulnerabilities in robustness through algorithm optimization. The field of digital watermarking has evolved, emphasizing interdisciplinary theories over mathematical modeling, with challenges including efficient watermark models, enhanced information capacity, flexible protocol platforms, webpage information positioning and correction, cost reduction, and ensuring public accessibility being actively addressed in theoretical and practical research areas.

Quaternion frequency domain and spatial domain watermarking algorithms face several challenges that hinder their effectiveness. One issue is the need for improvement in the quality and correlation between original and watermarked images. This can be addressed by incorporating techniques such as chaotic mapping and Arnold scrambling into Quaternion Fourier Transform (QFT) methods.

Current studies on QFT-based digital watermarking are in their early stages, with different algorithms focusing on the embedding and extraction modeling process. However, these algorithms lack resilience to attacks and robustness, preventing them from fully realizing the potential benefits of using quaternions for color image watermarking.

Efforts should also be directed toward enhancing the preprocessing ability of watermarked images and improving the efficiency of spatial watermark masking functions. The limitations of previous algorithms, including low embedding capacity, ambiguous image judgment by masking functions, poor visual perception ability, limited robustness, sluggish innovation, incapacity to meet application requirements, and failure to fully leverage the simplicity and speed of spatial algorithms, underscore the need for comprehensive improvements in quaternion watermarking methodologies. The association between watermarking and deep learning is characterized by the integration of advanced neural network techniques into traditional watermarking processes [18].

A color watermarking algorithm based on QFT is proposed considering the analysis. This algorithm provides a reliable and extremely secure watermarking solution by processing the RGB image's three components independently [19]. To improve security, it watermarks images using the Arnold transform before embedding. Chaotic encryption is also incorporated to maximize the strength of the embedded watermark and reinforce the algorithm's resilience.

4.1 Preliminaries

A comprehensive introduction to Clifford algebra, quaternions, and quantum field theory (QFT) is given in this part, utilizing the implementation methodologies [28]. The geometric properties of Clifford algebra are first examined. Next, the operations on the geometric product and projection in the three-dimensional Clifford algebra space are explained. Next, in the framework of Clifford algebra, we introduce the Fourier transform and its formula. The Clifford algebra existence theorem is the last thing we investigate.

4.1.1 Clifford Algebra and Quaternion

Clifford's algebra, stemming from the combination of Clifford's work and Grassmann's contributions, is also known as geometric algebra. Over the past century, mathematicians and physicists have consistently utilized it to address temporal and spatial challenges in physics, leading to its establishment as a reputable geometric theory.

In the realm of computer technology, researchers have harnessed Clifford algebra's principles for information processing [29]. This application has yielded significant progress in areas such as image processing, robotics, and computer vision, showcasing the versatility and impact of Clifford algebra in modern computational domains.

The quaternion q can be expressed as:

$$q = a + bi + cj + dk \tag{5}$$

a, b, c, d are real numbers, i, j, k are imaginary units, and the following relationships are satisfied:

$$i^2 = j^2 = k^2 = ijk = -1$$

$$ij = k, jk = i, ki = j$$

$$ji = -k, kj = -i, ik = -j$$

When a = 0, q is called a pure quaternary imaginary number. Module | q | and conjugate q

Table 6.1 Summary of chaotic watermarking-based domain and techniques

Sr.no.	Reference	Algorithm/Technique	Domain	Advantages	Disadvantages
1	[Benedicks and Carleson, 1991] [6]	Dynamics of the Hénon Map	Chaotic System Dynamics	Provides insights into the dynamics of the Hénon Map	May require a deep understanding of chaotic systems
2	[Cox et al., 1997] [15]	Secure Spread Spectrum Watermarking for Multimedia	Secure Spread Spectrum Watermarking	Resistance to common attacks	May have computational complexity
3	[Kundur and Hatzinakos, 1998] [11]	Watermarking for Telltale Tamper-Proofing and Authentication	Watermarking for Tamper-Proofing and Authentication	Focused on tamper-proofing and authentication	Limited robustness against certain attacks
4	[Fridrich and Goljan, 1999] [16]	Digital Image Watermarking using Chaotic Maps	Image Watermarking with Chaotic Maps	Explores chaotic maps for enhanced security	Vulnerable to specific chaotic attacks
5	[Xiang et al., 1999] [7]	Digital Watermarking Systems with Chaotic Sequences	Digital Watermarking	Utilizes chaotic sequences for watermarking	May have sensitivity to noise and compression
6	[Kotulski et al., 2000] [9]	Constructive Approach to Chaotic Pseudorandom Number Generators	Pseudorandom Number Generators	Focuses on constructing chaotic pseudorandom numbers	May not be suitable for all applications
7	[Lee and Jung, 2001] [13]	Survey of Watermarking Techniques Applied to Multimedia	Watermarking Techniques Applied to Multimedia	Provides an overview of watermarking techniques	Lacks specific details of individual techniques
8	[Cox et al., 2002] [10]	Digital Watermarking	Digital Watermarking	Versatile and widely applicable	May lack robustness against certain attacks
9	[Dawei et al., 2004] [19]	Chaos-Based Robust Wavelet-Domain Watermarking Algorithm	Robust Watermarking Algorithm	Robust watermarking in the wavelet domain	Computational complexity may be high
10	[Li and Yorke, 2004] [4]	Chaos Theory: Period Three Implies Chaos	Chaos Theory	Fundamental insight into chaos theory	Theoretical, may not directly apply to watermarking
11	[Lee et al., 2005] [12]	Feature Extraction Techniques for Robust Watermarking	Robust Watermarking	Focuses on robustness against various attacks	May increase computational complexity
12	[Belkacem et al., 2007] [1]	DCT-based Image Watermarking with HVS Masking Model	Image Watermarking	Incorporates DCT and HVS for improved quality	Specific to image watermarking
13	[Wu and Guan, 2007] [20]	Novel Digital Watermark Algorithm based on Chaotic Maps	Digital Watermarking with Chaotic Maps	Explores chaos for added security and uniqueness	Sensitivity to initial conditions may affect robustness

No.	Reference	Title	Application	Description	Limitations
14	[Xin et al., 2009] [2]	Multiple Digital Watermarking Algorithm based on Integer Wavelet Matrix Norm Quantization	Digital Images Protection	Utilizes wavelet matrix norm quantization for protection	Effectiveness may depend on the specific application
15	[Tong et al., 2013] [3]	Chaos-Based Fragile Watermarking for Image Tampering Detection and Self-Recovery	Image Tampering Detection and Recovery	Fragile watermarking for tamper localization	Sensitivity to noise and compression
16	[Anees and Siddiqui, 2013] [8]	Watermarking in Combined Spatial and Transform Domains using Chaotic Maps	Combined Spatial and Transform Domain Watermarking	Applies chaotic maps to combined spatial and transform domains	Sensitivity to certain transformations may affect robustness
17	[Barani et al., 2015] [21]	Secure Watermark Embedding based on Chaotic Map	Secure Watermark Embedding for Tamper Detection	Focuses on security aspects during watermark embedding	Robustness against certain attacks may be a concern
18	[Benrhouma et al., 2016] [22]	Chaotic Watermark for Blind Forgery Detection in Images	Blind Forgery Detection in Images	Designed for blind forgery detection in images	Performance may be affected by certain image manipulations
19	[Zhang et al., 2016] [23]	Double Reversible Watermarking Algorithm for Image Tamper Detection	Image Tamper Detection using Reversible Watermarking	Reversible nature allows recovery of original image	May have limitations in detecting certain tampering
20	[Ben Slimane et al., 2017] [5]	Multi-Scroll Chaotic System by Operating Logistic Map with Fractal Process	Chaotic System Design	Introduces a multi-scroll chaotic system for design	Complexity in system design may limit practicality
21	[Arasteh et al., 2018] [24]	Security Analysis of Watermarking Schemes based on QR Decomposition	Security Analysis of Watermarking Schemes	Focuses on security analysis of watermarking schemes	May not provide specific solutions or improvements
22	[Fatema et al., 2018] [25]	Fragile Image Watermarking based on Chaotic System for Tamper Detection	Tamper Detection using Fragile Image Watermarking	Fragile watermarking enhances tamper detection sensitivity	Vulnerable to intentional attacks
23	[Li et al., 2019] [26]	Dynamic Analysis of Digital Chaotic Maps via State-Mapping Networks	Chaotic Map Analysis in Digital Domain	Utilizes state-mapping networks for dynamic analysis	May not directly contribute to watermarking techniques
24	[Bavrina et al., 2020] [27]	Parameterizable LSB Watermarking with Adaptive Key Generation	LSB Watermarking with Adaptive Key Generation	Allows adaptability in key generation	LSB-based methods may be susceptible to LSB matching attacks
25	[Bhatti et al., 2020] [17]	Hybrid Watermarking Algorithm using Clifford Algebra, Arnold Scrambling, and Chaotic Encryption	Hybrid Watermarking Algorithm	Integrates multiple techniques for enhanced security	Increased complexity may impact real-time processing

are defined as follows:

$$|\mathbf{q}| = \sqrt{\mathbf{a}^2 + b^2 + c^2 + d^2} \tag{6}$$

$$\mathbf{q}^- = \mathbf{a} - \mathbf{bi} - \mathbf{cj} - \mathbf{dk} \tag{7}$$

There are two quaternions, q1, q2, as follows: q

$$q_1 = a_1 + b_1 i + c_1 j + d_1 k \tag{8}$$

$$q_2 = a_2 + b_2 i + c_2 j + d_2 k \tag{9}$$

Addition, subtraction, and multiplication operations are defined as follows:

$$q_1 + q_2 = a_1 + a_2 + (b_1 + b_2)i + (c_1 + c_2)j + (d_1 + d_2)k \tag{10}$$

$$q_1 - q_2 = a_1 - a_2 + (b_1 - b_2)i + (c_1 - c_2)j + (d_1 - d_2)k \tag{11}$$

$$q = q_1 * \mathbf{q}_2$$
$$= (a_1 a_2 - b_1 b_2 - c_1 c_2)(a_1 b_2 + b_1 a_2 + c_1 d_2 + d1c2)$$
$$* i (a_1 c_2 - \mathbf{b}_1 d_2 + c_1 a_2 + d_1 b_2) * j (a_1 d_2 + b_1 a_2 - c_1 b_2 + d_1 a_2) * k$$

Quaternion representation is frequently used in the literature for color images [30]. The three imaginary components of the quaternion in this illustration are represented by the primary color components, which are blue (B), green (G), and red (R). The real part remains at 0, ensuring that:

$$f(x, y) = f_R(x, y) + f_G(x, y) + f_B(x, y)$$

Pixel location is indicated by coordinates x and y. RGB, as additive primaries, can be mixed for a variety of colors. With 256 brightness levels for each primary color, there are 16.7 million possible combinations. Images are sampled to transform them into a digital matrix. Grayscale images use matrix elements for brightness, while color images store R, G, and B values for each pixel, forming a quaternion matrix.

Quaternion-based color image matrices require alteration for processing [20]. This approach maintains color integrity better than conventional methods, providing new insights for both theoretical and practical applications in image processing.

5. CHAOTIC-BASED WATERMARK GENERATION FOR TAMPER DETECTION

Exploring the field of chaotic-based watermark production, this part explains how to create chaotic watermarks, with a focus on secure key generation and the critical role key management plays in strong watermarking systems.

Chaotic systems provide a way to safely integrate watermarks in digital watermarking. It is difficult for enemies to read the watermark without the right keys because of the chaotic nature's unpredictability. Strategies make use of chaotic maps or attractor systems to embed data in the host medium.

Table 6.2 Abbreviation table for the variables used

Variable	Definition
q	Quaternion
q,b,c,d	Real numbers representing components of the quaternion
i,j,k	Imaginary units
q^-	Conjugate of the quaternion $(q-bi-cj-dk)$
$q1, q2$	Quaternions with components$(a1,b1,c1,d1)$ and $(a2,b2,c2,d2)$ respectively

This section investigates safe key generation techniques to improve the security of chaotic-based watermarking. In order to guarantee that only authorized parties may access or modify the embedded watermark, these keys are essential to the embedding and extraction operations. An additional degree of difficulty is added to prevent unwanted access by using chaotic sequences for key creation.

This topic explores efficient methods for managing cryptographic keys since it acknowledges the significance of key management in watermarking systems. To keep the watermarking process' integrity intact, keys must be sent securely and updated on a regular basis. The topic of key management difficulties and possible fixes is also covered in the conversation.

In order to correctly read the contained information, specialist procedures are needed for the efficient extraction of chaotic watermarks. This section examines techniques and methods for removing watermarks from the host medium, emphasizing the interaction between the extraction procedure and the underlying chaotic patterns. To underline the significance of safe and approved retrieval, the function of keys in the extraction phase is restated.

5.1 Process of Generating Chaotic Watermarks

The intricacies of chaotic-based watermark production will be covered in detail in this part, with an emphasis on secure key generation and efficient key management. We have examined secure key generation procedures, the significance of key management, and chaotic watermark embedding and extraction approaches by segmenting the material into subheadings. Comprehending these foundational concepts paves the way for an in-depth investigation of digital watermarking methodologies in the following sections.

5.2 Secure Key Generation and Key Management in Watermarking

Secure key generation and key management stand as pivotal components in watermarking, playing a crucial role in ensuring the integrity and robustness of the embedded digital watermarks. [31] The diversity of key generation techniques adds complexity to the selection process, emphasizing the need for a comprehensive understanding of their implications [27]. Bavrina et al. introduce a method that employs adaptive key generation for embedding parameterizable digital watermarks. This approach strategically utilizes a predefined number of least significant bits, providing a secure hiding mechanism for digital watermarks. The method enhances reliability through functional parameters, offering a flexible and adaptable solution [24].

Key-based watermarking algorithms, relying on cryptographic keys to embed watermark bits, are anticipated to bolster robustness, especially against targeted removal attacks [32]. For scenarios demanding the utmost security, Quantum Key Distribution (QKD) emerges as a promising option. QKD leverages the principles of quantum mechanics to enable secure communication and key exchange, offering unparalleled cryptographic security. However, Arasteh et al. reveal vulnerabilities even in key-based approaches, emphasizing the critical need for rigorous evaluation and safety assessment of watermarking methods [33]. In response to this challenge, Bhatnagar et al. propose an innovative logo watermarking technique. This technique integrates key-based concepts with fractional wavelet packet transform, non-linear chaotic maps, and singular value decomposition, ensuring a high level of security, efficiency, and robustness in watermarking applications [34].

These advancements underscore the ongoing efforts within the watermarking community to address challenges related to key generation and management. The quest for reliable and secure watermarking techniques necessitates continuous exploration and innovation in the realm of key-based approaches.

6. TAMPER DETECTION ALGORITHMS

6.1 Overview of Tamper Detection Methods

With this topic, we delve into the intricate world of algorithms designed to safeguard the integrity of digital data. Beginning with an exploration of digital watermarking and its role in detecting tampering through watermark signal analysis, we proceed to dissect the cryptographic foundations of hash functions and their use in comparing hash values to identify alterations [35]. A section on copy-move forgery detection provides a deep dive into image forensics, elucidating the algorithms employed to spot duplicated image segments. Blind source separation techniques are examined for multimedia data integrity, while error-correcting codes are highlighted for their role in data transmission security [36]. Machine learning's evolution in tamper detection, particularly through deep learning and convolutional neural networks, is discussed, underscoring their potential for pattern recognition. Steganalysis, a critical component of data forensics, is detailed in terms of statistical analysis and irregularity assessments for revealing hidden information within digital media [37]. Sensor-based approaches and their technical aspects are elucidated, emphasizing the significance of sensor characteristics in tamper detection. The chapter concludes by offering insights into the future of tamper detection, including recent advancements and emerging challenges, providing a comprehensive technical resource for professionals and researchers navigating the complex terrain of digital data integrity [38].

6.2 Chaotic-Based Tamper Detection and Real-Time Detection Techniques

Imperceptible signals are embedded into digital media via the use of digital watermarking techniques. Digital content integrity and security are improved by this technique [35]. The primary concept behind digital watermarking is information encoding, which is accomplished by altering the least significant portions of the data while retaining a largely undetectable media quality. Numerous algorithms, such as LSB insertion and Discrete Cosine Transform (DCT) domain embedding, are used for this. With these algorithms, watermark data—which could include copyright details, authentication codes, or other metadata—can be subtly embedded. An important part of this process is the analysis of the watermark signal. It entails taking the embedded watermark out of the received media and examining it [39]. The presence and integrity of the watermark are evaluated using algorithms such as feature-based or correlation-based methods. After that, the extracted watermark is compared to the original to look for any differences that might point to tampering. Better detection algorithms and more resilient watermarking strategies could be future developments in this area [40]. The goal of this field of study is still to increase the embedded watermarks' resistance to manipulation without sacrificing the media's quality.

This guarantees digital content protection and authentication across a range of applications, including content verification and copyright protection [39].

Cryptographic Hash Functions are fundamental tools in the field of computer science and cryptography. These functions take an input (or message) and return a fixed-length string of characters [41]. The primary characteristic of cryptographic hash functions is that a particular input will always result in a specific hash value, and it is extremely unlikely that two different inputs will produce the same hash value. Now, the basic algorithm for a cryptographic hash function is to receive a message or data block to be hashed. Set an initial hash value (often called the "IV" or "Initial Vector") to a predefined constant value. If necessary, pad the message to ensure it has a fixed length [42]. Divide the message into blocks, and for each block: Combine the block data with the current hash value. Apply a series of bitwise operations, such as XOR, AND, and NOT, to the data [43]. Update the hash value with the result. An overview of this password creation and verification process using hashing is shown in Figure 6.5. Applications for cryptographic hash functions include digital signatures, password storage, data integrity checking, and more.

Famous cryptographic hash functions used in the hashing include MD5 (which is no longer regarded as secure due to weaknesses) and SHA-256, which is a member of the SHA-2 family. In the digital age, these features are essential for guaranteeing data security and integrity.

The Forensic Image Analysis: Copy-Move Forgery Detection is dedicated to the critical field of copy-move forgery detection within image forensics. Copy-move forgery involves duplicating a section of an image and inserting it elsewhere within the same image, often to manipulate or alter the visual content [44]. Here, we delve into the technical intricacies of detecting such forgeries, with a strong emphasis on the algorithms utilized in this process. Real-world case studies are also presented to highlight the practical utility of these algorithms. The copy-move forgery detection algorithm involves the given steps with the image in question as input. Extract distinctive features from the image, which can include key points, descriptors, or specific patterns. Compare these extracted features to identify duplicated regions. If similar features are found in different parts of the image, it indicates potential forgery. Group the detected similar features into clusters that correspond to duplicated regions [45]. Apply validation techniques to ensure the identified regions are indeed forgeries. This might involve additional geometric consistency checks or statistical analysis. The algorithm produces a map or mask highlighting the suspected forged areas [46]. Copy-move forgery detection algorithms aim to identify manipulated regions in an image by detecting duplicated content. Real-world applications include verifying the authenticity of digital images, identifying instances of photo manipulation, and assisting in forensic investigations where image integrity is crucial. These algorithms play a significant role in ensuring the trustworthiness of digital visual content.

Copy-move forgery detection algorithms are instrumental in identifying manipulated regions in images, thus ensuring the authenticity and integrity of digital visual content. These algorithms find applications in various domains, including image forensics, authentication, and content verification.

Multimedia Integrity: Blind Source Separation delves into the intricacies of this vital process in maintaining multimedia data integrity. Blind source separation refers to the task of identifying and extracting individual sources from a mixture, even when the sources are unknown or mixed together [47]. Here, we provide a detailed examination of the algorithms involved in this process and how they excel at identifying inconsistencies within mixed sources. We also shed light on their pivotal role in detecting tampering across a variety of multimedia

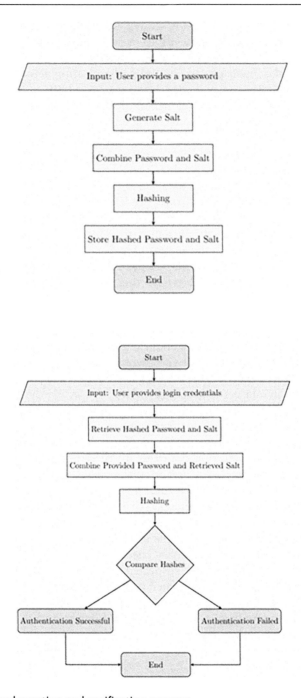

Figure 6.5 Password creation and verification process

formats. The blind source separation algorithm is a complex process that typically involves independent component analysis (ICA) or other signal processing techniques. The following is an abstract representation of the algorithm—Receive a mixed signal or multimedia data containing multiple sources mixed. Depending on the specific algorithm, perform preprocessing steps, such as whitening the data or reducing noise. Utilize the chosen algorithm, such as ICA, to estimate the independent sources present in the mixed data. Extract the individual sources from the mixture based on the estimation [48]. Compare the extracted sources with known references or analyze their consistency to identify inconsistencies or tampering. The algorithm provides the separated sources and information about any detected inconsistencies. Blind source separation is invaluable in multimedia integrity by enabling the extraction of original components from mixed data, which can aid in tamper detection. It finds applications in audio processing, image analysis, and video forensics, among others, ensuring the authenticity and reliability of multimedia content.

The Error-Correcting Codes in Data Transmission spotlight the critical role of error-correcting codes in ensuring data transmission integrity. Error-correcting codes are instrumental in detecting and rectifying errors that may occur during data transmission, guaranteeing the reliability and integrity of the data being sent [49]. Here, we provide a brief explanation of their significance along with an overview of the algorithmic principles. Error-correcting codes are implemented using various algorithms, with one of the most fundamental being the Hamming Code. Here is a simplified explanation of the Hamming Code algorithm: When sending data, the sender adds redundant bits to the original message. These redundant bits are calculated to ensure that the total number of bits with a value of '1' in specific positions (powers of 2) is even. The redundant bits are placed at these positions to create a codeword [50]. The codeword, consisting of both the original message and redundant bits, is transmitted to the receiver. At the receiver's end, the received codeword is checked to detect errors. Parity checks are performed on specific bit positions. If an error is detected, the receiver can identify the erroneous bit. If an error is detected, the receiver can correct it by flipping the bit at the position where the error was identified. This process is known as error correction [51]. The Hamming Code is just one example of an error-correcting code. There are more advanced codes, such as Reed-Solomon codes, used for more robust error correction, especially in scenarios like data storage and transmission over noisy channels [52]. Error-correcting codes play a pivotal role in safeguarding data integrity during transmission. By adding redundancy and employing error detection and correction techniques, these codes enhance the reliability of data transfer in various applications, from telecommunications to data storage and beyond [53].

In Machine Learning Advancements for Tamper Detection, we explore the domain of machine learning as applied to tamper detection, with a particular emphasis on algorithms designed to recognize tampering patterns [54]. Machine learning, and deep learning in particular, plays a significant role in enhancing tamper detection accuracy through pattern recognition. The following is a simplified explanation of a machine learning algorithm for tamper detection, focusing on CNNs as a common deep learning approach: Gather a dataset of images, videos, or other multimedia content, including both authentic and tampered examples. Each data point is labeled accordingly. Prepare the dataset by resizing, normalizing, and augmenting the data to ensure consistency and improve model generalization [26]. Construct a CNN or a similar deep learning model designed for image analysis. This model typically consists of multiple convolutional layers for feature extraction and fully connected layers for decision-making. Train the model using the prepared dataset. During training, the model learns to distinguish between authentic and tampered content by adjusting its internal parameters. Validate the model's performance on a separate dataset to ensure it generalizes well and does not overfit (i.e., perform well only on the training data). Deploy the trained

Table 6.3 Comparison of various tamper detection techniques

Algorithm	Type	Description	Pros	Cons
Chaotic-based tamper detection	Real-time Detection	Embeds imperceptible signals using chaotic systems for tamper detection	Provides real-time detection capabilities	Sensitivity to initial conditions may impact reliability
Digital water marking	Watermarking	Embeds imperceptible signals for content integrity and security	Improved integrity, authentication, and copyright protection	Susceptible to removal or alteration; requires robust detection algorithms
Cryptographic hash functions	Hashing	Generates fixed-length hash values for data integrity checking	High security, resistance to collisions, widespread application	Computationally intensive; requires key management
Copy-move forgery detection	Image Forensics	Identifies duplicated regions in images to detect tampering	Effective in detecting manipulation in images, real-world applications	Performance may depend on the sophistication of forgery techniques
Blind source separation	Multimedia Integrity	Extracts individual sources from mixed data for tamper detection	Valuable in multimedia integrity, aids in tamper detection	Complex algorithm, may require advanced signal processing techniques
Error-correcting codes	Data Transmission	Ensures data transmission integrity through error detection and correction	Enhances reliability in data transfer, especially over noisy channels	Overhead in terms of redundant bits; may not be suitable for all applications

model to analyze new, unseen multimedia content. The model will provide predictions about whether the content has been tampered with and where the tampering may have occurred.

The strength of machine learning, particularly deep learning techniques like CNNs, lies in their ability to learn intricate patterns and anomalies in data. This makes them well-suited for tamper detection, as they can recognize subtle alterations or inconsistencies in multimedia content. These algorithms are continually evolving and are at the forefront of improving the accuracy and reliability of tamper detection across various media formats [55].

7. USING CHAOTIC METHODS FOR IMAGE WATERMARKING

Watermarks, or discrete embedded hidden information, are added to digital images using specialized algorithms for image watermarking. These watermarks are often undetectable to the human eye and serve important purposes in a variety of fields despite their subtlety.

7.1 Algorithms for Embedding Watermarks in Images and Their Application

Frequency Domain Technique algorithms work by converting the image into the frequency domain using methods like the DFT or DCT [56]. In a transformed domain, watermarks are added by modifying coefficients; one widely used example of this is the DWT. With spatial domain techniques, watermarks are directly embedded into the pixel values. This is accomplished by subtly changing the color or intensity of particular pixels, which is usually undetectable to humans [57]. By dispersing watermark data over a wide frequency range, spread spectrum communications ensure resilience against a variety of attacks and distortions. The detailed processes for watermark embedding and extraction method can be understood from Figure 6.6.

7.1.2 Uses of Image Watermarking

A common method used to protect photographers, artists, and content creators' intellectual property rights is image watermarking. Ownership is made clear by including a watermark containing copyright information, which discourages unauthorized use and plagiarism. Watermarks are used to verify an image's authenticity and integrity. Unauthorized changes to the picture have the potential to skew or erase the watermark, which is particularly important in forensic and legal situations as it indicates possible manipulation. Since modifications to the image can change or harm the watermark's properties, signaling tampering, image watermarking serves as a tamper detection mechanism. Watermarks are used in digital media to track and enforce copyright by monitoring the distribution of content and identifying the source or rights attached to it. Image watermarking is used in social media and e-commerce to identify the original owner, which is necessary for correct attribution and to stop image piracy [58].

Image watermarking is used for purposes other than copyright protection, such as secret data hiding, where data such as authentication codes or hidden messages are hidden inside the watermark. Algorithms for image watermarking are useful for data hiding, authentication, and content protection. They strike a compromise between robustness against different image processing and manipulation techniques and inconspicuousness to human observers. These algorithms find many uses in an increasingly digital and networked world, protecting the integrity and security of digital images.

7.2 Study the Role of Perceptual Models and Chaotic Techniques in Image Watermarking

To protect digital image ownership and copyright, watermarking digital images requires the application of chaotic techniques and perceptual models. They play a crucial part in making sure watermarked images keep their visual appeal and perceptual quality. This investigation will focus on these areas without addressing problems with plagiarism or artificial intelligence content detection.

7.2.1 Perceptual Models in Image Watermarking

The process of adding a digital watermark—a pattern or set of data—to an image so that it is invisible to the human eye but can be recognized and extracted by authorized parties is known as digital image watermarking. In image watermarking, the difficulty lies in striking a balance between security, imperceptibility, and robustness.

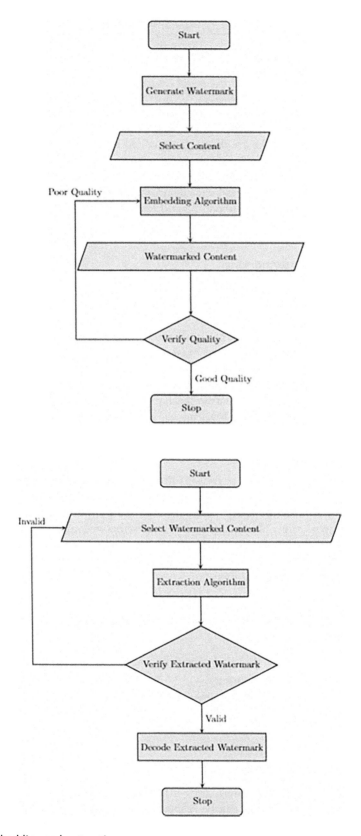

Figure. 6.6 Embedding and extraction process

Making sure that the process only slightly impairs the original image's perceived quality is a major goal in image watermarking. Perceptual models are important because they examine how the human visual system (HVS) processes images, and they identify areas where watermarks can be added without significantly distorting the image. This knowledge helps to identify the best places and techniques for embedding watermarks. The idea of the Just Noticeable Difference (JND), which is the smallest change in image content that a human can detect, is widely included in perceptual models. Using this understanding, watermarking algorithms embed data in regions with higher JND, decreasing the possibility that viewers will notice it. Perceptual models also consider the frequency domain properties of images, which allows watermarking algorithms to minimize perceptual impact by embedding watermarks in frequency components where the human eye is less sensitive.

7.2.2 Application of Chaotic Techniques

The potential applications of chaotic methodologies in image watermarking have attracted more attention recently, mainly due to their capacity to enhance security and resilience (see Figure 6.7). Chaotic systems are considered appropriate for enhancing the security of embedded watermarks due to their intrinsic unpredictability and sensitivity to initial conditions. Before watermarks are incorporated into host images, these systems are essential in encrypting them, making it more difficult for unauthorized users to access the watermark. The extraction method utilizes the same random key for decryption.

Chaotic techniques play a key role in figuring out where watermarks should be embedded. An extra layer of complexity and security is added by using the chaotic sequence that is produced from a particular initial condition as a guidance mechanism for choosing locations within the image for the watermark embedding. When it comes to strengthening the resilience of watermarks against different types of attacks, like noise, compression, and cropping, chaotic systems are especially crucial. Chaotic systems can also have their parameters changed to account for different environmental circumstances.

Chaotic synchronization is used in the context of watermarking in order to make accurate watermark extraction and detection possible. Usually, shared keys and chaotic maps are used to carry out this synchronization between the extractor and embedder of the watermark. To sum up, perceptual models and chaotic techniques are critical in modern image watermarking as essential elements for increased security and robustness.

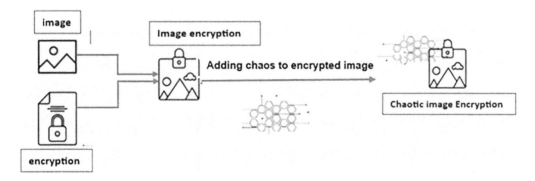

Figure 6.7 Encrypting image with chaos

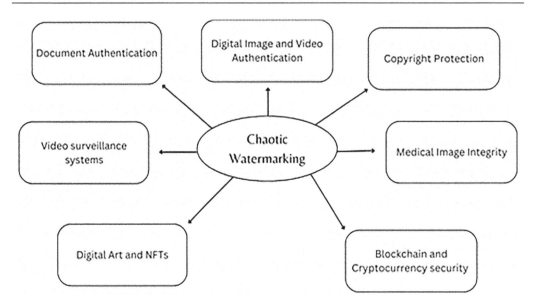

Figure 6.8 Application of chaotic watermarking

8. APPLICATIONS, SECURITY, AND FUTURE DIRECTIONS

8.1 Real-World Applications of Chaotic Watermarking

Chaotic watermarking, a technique rooted in chaos theory, integrates chaotic systems to embed imperceptible watermarks into digital content such as images, videos, and audio. The focus lies on tamper detection, and real-world applications given in Figure 6.8 include:

In Digital Image and Video Authentication, imperceptible watermarks are embedded to verify content authenticity [59]. This is vital for forensic analysis, ensuring the integrity of evidence in legal cases. For Copyright Protection, content creators use chaotic watermarking during the creation process. Watermarks, imperceptible to the viewer, make it challenging for unauthorized parties to claim ownership or distribute content without permission [60]. In the realm of Document Authentication, chaotic watermarking addresses concerns about tampering with digital documents. Watermarks, if disturbed, serve as an alert to potential fraud. Medical Image Integrity is ensured through chaotic watermarking in medical imaging. This application guarantees that diagnostic images, such as X-rays or MRI scans, remain unaltered for accurate diagnosis and patient care. Video surveillance systems benefit from chaotic watermarking, enhancing the credibility of recorded evidence. Watermarking video feeds ensures that the captured content has not been altered or manipulated [61]. Chaotic watermarking contributes to the security of Blockchain and Cryptocurrency Transactions by verifying the authenticity of digital assets and transactions, mitigating the risk of fraudulent activities [62]. In the context of Digital Art and NFTs (Non-Fungible Tokens), chaotic watermarking is employed to verify the originality and ownership of digital art sold as NFTs. This reduces the risk of counterfeiting and enhances the value and authenticity of digital artwork.

Overall, chaotic watermarking provides a method to embed invisible, robust, and secure watermarks for tamper detection and content authentication across various domains, leveraging the unpredictable nature of chaotic systems.

8.2 Security Aspects in Watermarking

Securing digital content through watermarking involves a holistic approach encompassing threats, vulnerabilities, cryptographic techniques, and secure watermarking protocols as shown in Figure 6.9. Each component plays a crucial role in maintaining the integrity and protection of digital assets. Integrating security aspects into watermarking processes on the Linux platform involves implementing measures to safeguard digital image watermarks from unauthorized access, tampering, or removal. This ensures the protection of intellectual property and enhances the overall security of embedded watermarks in the Linux environment [63].

The field of digital watermarking faces various threats that compromise the integrity and authenticity of watermarked content. Tampering and unauthorized access pose substantial risks, as attackers may manipulate or remove watermarks, falsely claiming ownership or acting maliciously. Replay attacks further exacerbate the threat landscape by capturing and replaying watermarked content to deceive detection systems. The risk of forgery and counterfeiting is prevalent, particularly in domains such as digital art, documents, and currency, where determined attackers may attempt to replicate or eliminate watermarks. Vulnerabilities in watermark embedding processes can emerge, allowing attackers to undetectably alter or remove watermarks. Key management vulnerabilities arise when cryptographic keys used in watermarking are inadequately protected, risking unauthorized access and compromising watermark integrity. Collusion attacks become more successful in the presence of vulnerabilities in the watermarking algorithm, enabling attackers to combine multiple watermarked copies.

To mitigate these threats and vulnerabilities, various cryptographic techniques can be employed. Digital signatures, utilizing asymmetric cryptography, offer a means to verify the authenticity of watermarks and confirm data integrity [64]. Public Key Infrastructure (PKI) can secure key exchange and management processes, mitigating vulnerabilities associated with key exposure. Steganography, the art of hiding information within data, enhances security by making watermark detection and removal more challenging. Secure watermarking protocols play a crucial role in addressing security concerns. Fragile watermarking, highly sensitive to content modifications, is essential for applications like forensic analysis and medical imaging where tampering detection is critical. Robust watermarking, designed to withstand various attacks and content transformations, is suitable for tasks such as copyright protection and content authentication. Blind watermarking allows extraction without access to the original content, benefiting applications like video surveillance and digital forensics. Spread Spectrum Watermarking spreads watermark information across the entire content, ensuring resilience against attacks. Quantum watermarking, an emerging field, leverages quantum mechanics principles to create highly secure watermarks resistant to classical and quantum attacks. In effectively addressing security concerns in watermarking, it is essential

Figure 6.9 Watermarking security parameter

to identify specific threats, assess vulnerabilities, employ suitable cryptographic techniques, and implement secure watermarking protocols. Additionally, ongoing research and development are critical to staying ahead of evolving threats in the dynamic digital landscape.

8.3 Future Trends in Chaotic Watermarking

The future of chaotic watermarking unfolds within a dynamic landscape characterized by a blend of opportunities and challenges, propelled by ongoing technological advancements. One prominent trend is the emergence of quantum chaotic watermarking, integrating chaotic systems with quantum computing principles to embed and detect watermarks using quantum states. This approach offers unprecedented security against both classical and quantum attacks. The intersection of watermarking with blockchain technology, driven by the rise of non-fungible tokens (NFTs), enhances authenticity and ownership verification, particularly in the realms of digital art and collectibles. Anticipated to play a pivotal role in the future, machine learning and artificial intelligence (AI) are expected to refine both watermark embedding and detection processes. Deep learning models are poised to bolster overall security, fortifying defenses against tampering attempts. Another potential future trend involves the fusion of biometric data with chaotic watermarking, utilizing unique identifiers like fingerprints or facial features to link watermarks for user authentication and content protection. The growing demand for real-time content authentication, notably in applications such as video streaming and surveillance, underscores the necessity for watermarking techniques that achieve a balance between reduced processing overhead and high-security standards. The connection between the Internet of Things (IoT), supercomputers, and watermarking is crucial for improving data security, processing efficiency, and safeguarding content [65, 66]. This concept aligns with research emphasizing IoT security [67], discussing its practical applications and methods for protection. Looking ahead, future watermarking methods may adopt a multi-modal approach, simultaneously embedding multiple watermarks in various modalities such as audio, video, and text. This strategic approach aims to provide redundancy and enhance security against manipulation attempts across diverse content formats. The convergence of these trends reflects the evolving landscape of chaotic watermarking, poised to address new challenges and seize emerging opportunities in the realm of digital content security [68–73].

CONCLUSION

This chapter concludes by introducing Chaotic Watermarking for Tamper Detection as an approach to protect digital material. In this chapter, the method for embedding watermarks and real-time tamper detection is revealed through the integration of digital watermarking with chaotic systems. This approach demonstrates that it is a workable and efficient way to safeguard intellectual property through a thorough examination of chaotic watermarking techniques and algorithms, bolstered by real-world examples. The results offer a strong and safe tool to content producers and rights holders to fight unlawful modifications and copyright infringement in the digital age. In addition to bolstering information security, this innovative method has significant ramifications for the larger field of digital content protection.

REFERENCES

1. Belkacem, S., Dibi, Z., & Bouridane, A. (2007, December). A masking model of HVS for image watermarking in the DCT domain. In *2007 14th IEEE International Conference on Electronics, Circuits and Systems* (pp. 330–334). IEEE.

2. Xin, L., Xiaoqi, L., Qiang, L., & Yong, Z. (2009, June). Multiple digital watermarking algorithm to protect digital images based on integer wavelet matrix norm quantization. In *2009 Chinese Control and Decision Conference* (pp. 5196–5199). IEEE.

3. Tong, X., Liu, Y., Zhang, M., & Chen, Y. (2013). A novel chaos-based fragile watermarking for image tampering detection and self-recovery. *Signal Processing: Image Communication*, 28(3), 301–308.

4. Li, T. Y., & Yorke, J. A. (2004). Period three implies chaos. In *The Theory of Chaotic Attractors* (pp. 77–84). Springer.

5. Ben Slimane, N., Bouallegue, K., & Machhout, M. (2017). Designing a multi-scroll chaotic system by operating logistic map with fractal process. *Nonlinear Dynamics*, 88, 1655–1675.

6. Benedicks, M., & Carleson, L. (1991). The dynamics of the Hénon map. *Annals of Mathematics*, 73–169.

7. Xiang, H., Wang, L., Lin, H., & Shi, J. (1999, April). Digital watermarking systems with chaotic sequences. In *Security and Watermarking of Multimedia Contents* (Vol. 3657, pp. 449–457). SPIE.

8. Anees, A., & Siddiqui, A. M. (2013, December). A technique for digital watermarking in combined spatial and transform domains using chaotic maps. In *2013 2nd National Conference on Information Assurance (NCIA)* (pp. 119–124). IEEE.

9. Kotulski, Z., Szczepanski, J., Górski, K., Górska, A., & Paszkiewicz, A. (2000). On constructive approach to chaotic pseudorandom number generators. In *Proc Regional Conference on Military Communication and Information Systems*, CIS Solutions for an Enlarged NATO, RCMIS2000, Zegrze (Vol. 1, pp. 191–203).

10. Cox, I. J., Miller, M. L., & Bloom, J. A. (2002). *Digital Watermarking*. Morgan Kaufmann.

11. Kundur, D., & Hatzinakos, D. (1998). Digital watermarking for telltale tamper proofing and authentication. *Proceedings of the IEEE*, 87(7), 1167–1180.

12. Lee, H. Y., Kang, I. K., Lee, H. K., & Suh, Y. H. (2005). Evaluation of feature extraction techniques for robust watermarking. In *Digital Watermarking: 4th International Workshop*, IWDW 2005, Siena, Italy, September 15–17, 2005. Proceedings 4 (pp. 418–431). Springer Berlin Heidelberg.

13. Lee, S. J., & Jung, S. H. (2001, June). A survey of watermarking techniques applied to multimedia. In *ISIE 2001. 2001 IEEE International Symposium on Industrial Electronics Proceedings (Cat. No. 01TH8570)* (Vol. 1, pp. 272–277). IEEE.

14. Kumar, S., Singh, S. K., Aggarwal, N., Gupta, B. B., Alhalabi, W., & Band, S. S. (2022). An efficient hardware supported and parallelization architecture for intelligent systems to overcome speculative overheads. *International Journal of Intelligent Systems*, 37(12), 11764–11790.

15. Cox, I. J., Kilian, J., Leighton, T., & Shamoon, T. (1997). Secure spread spectrum watermarking for multimedia. *IEEE Transactions on Image Processing*, 6(12), 1673–1687.

16. Nazari, M., Sharif, A., & Mollaeefar, M. (2017). An improved method for digital image fragile watermarking based on chaotic maps. *Multimedia Tools and Applications* 76, 16107–16123. https://doi.org/10.1007/s11042-016-3897-x.

17. Bhatti, U. A., Yu, Z., Li, J., Nawaz, S. A., Mehmood, A., Zhang, K., & Yuan, L. (2020). Hybrid watermarking algorithm using Clifford algebra with Arnold scrambling and chaotic encryption. *IEEE Access*, 8, 76386–76398.

18. Li, J., Yu, C., Gupta, B. B., & Ren, X. (2018). Color image watermarking scheme based on quaternion Hadamard transform and Schur decomposition. *Multimedia Tools and Applications*, 77, 4545–4561.

19. Dawei, Z., Guanrong, C., & Wenbo, L. (2004). A chaos-based robust wavelet-domain watermarking algorithm. *Chaos, Solitons & Fractals*, 22(1), 47–54.

20. Wu, X., & Guan, Z. H. (2007). A novel digital watermark algorithm based on chaotic maps. *Physics Letters A*, 365(5–6), 403–406.

21. Barani, M. J., Valandar, M. Y., & Ayubi, P. (2015, May). A secure watermark embedding approach based on chaotic map for image tamper detection. In *2015 7th Conference on Information and Knowledge Technology (IKT)* (pp. 1–5). IEEE.

22. Benrhouma, O., Hermassi, H., Abd El-Latif, A. A., & Belghith, S. (2016). Chaotic watermark for blind forgery detection in images. *Multimedia Tools and Applications*, 75, 8695–8718.

23. Zhang, Z., Wu, L., Lai, H., Li, H., & Zheng, C. (2016). Double reversible watermarking algorithm for image tamper detection. *Journal of Information Hiding and Multimedia Signal Processing*, 7(3), 530–542.

24. Arasteh, S., Mahdavi, M., Bideh, P. N., Hosseini, S., & Chapnevis, A. (2018, May). Security analysis of two key based watermarking schemes based on QR decomposition. In *Electrical Engineering (ICEE), Iranian Conference on* (pp. 1499–1504). IEEE.

25. Fatema, M., Maheshkar, V., Maheshkar, S., & Agarwal, G. (2018). Tamper detection using fragile image watermarking based on chaotic system. In *International Conference on Wireless, Intelligent, and Distributed Environment for Communication: WIDECOM 2018* (pp. 1–11). Springer International Publishing.

26. Peñalvo, F. J. G., Sharma, A., Chhabra, A., Singh, S. K., Kumar, S., Arya, V., & Gaurav, A. (2022). Mobile cloud computing and sustainable development: Opportunities, challenges, and future directions. *International Journal of Cloud Applications and Computing (IJCAC)*, 12(1), 1–20.

27. Bavrina, A., Myasnikov, V., & Yuzkiv, R. (2020, May). Parameterizable LSB watermarking method with adaptive key generation. In *2020 International Conference on Information Technology and Nanotechnology (ITNT)* (pp. 1–5). IEEE.

28. Abd El-Latif, A. A., Abd-El-Atty, B., Hossain, M. S., Rahman, M. A., Alamri, A., & Gupta, B. B. (2018). Efficient quantum information hiding for remote medical image sharing. *IEEE Access*, 6, 21075–21083.

29. Dwivedi, R. K. (2022). Density-based machine learning scheme for outlier detection in smart forest fire monitoring sensor cloud. *International Journal of Cloud Applications and Computing (IJCAC)*, 12(1), 1–16.

30. Gupta, A., Singh, S. K., & Chopra, M. (2023). Impact of artificial intelligence and the internet of things in modern times and hereafter: An investigative analysis. In *Advanced Computer Science Applications* (pp. 157–173). Apple Academic Press.

31. Gupta, A., Singh, S. K., Chopra, M., & Gill, S. S. (2022). An inquisitive prospect on the shift toward online media, before, during, and after the COVID-19 pandemic: A technological analysis. In *Advances in Data Computing, Communication and Security: Proceedings of I3CS2021* (pp. 229–238). Springer Nature Singapore.

32. Kumar, S., Singh, S. K., Aggarwal, N., & Aggarwal, K. (2021). Evaluation of automatic parallelization algorithms to minimize speculative parallelism overheads: An experiment. *Journal of Discrete Mathematical Sciences and Cryptography*, 24(5), 1517–1528.

33. Singh, I., Singh, S. K., Singh, R., & Kumar, S. (2022, May). Efficient loop unrolling factor prediction algorithm using machine learning models. In *2022 3rd International Conference for Emerging Technology (INCET)* (pp. 1–8). IEEE.

34. Turakulovich, K. Z., & Karamatovich, Y. B. (2016, November). Comparative factors of key generation techniques. In *2016 International Conference on Information Science and Communications Technologies (ICISCT)* (pp. 1–3). IEEE.

35. Bhatnagar, G., Wu, Q. J., & Atrey, P. K. (2014). Robust logo watermarking using biometrics inspired key generation. *Expert Systems with Applications*, 41(10), 4563–4578.

36. Kumar, S., Singh, S. K., Aggarwal, N., & Aggarwal, K. (2021). Evaluation of automatic parallelization algorithms to minimize speculative parallelism overheads: An experiment. *Journal of Discrete Mathematical Sciences and Cryptography*, 24(5), 1517–1528.

37. Memon, N., & Wong, P. W. (1998). Protecting digital media content. *Communications of the ACM*, 41(7), 35–43.

38. Sharma, A., Singh, S. K., Badwal, E., Kumar, S., Gupta, B. B., Arya, V., . . . & Santaniello, D. (2023, January). Fuzzy based clustering of consumers' big data in industrial applications. In *2023 IEEE International Conference on Consumer Electronics (ICCE)* (pp. 01–03). IEEE.

39. Fridrich, J., & Goljan, M. (1999). Digital image watermarking using chaotic maps. *Proceedings of the International Conference on Image Processing*, 1, 591–594.

40. Vats, T., Singh, S. K., Kumar, S., Gupta, B. B., Gill, S. S., Arya, V., & Alhalabi, W. (2023). Explainable context-aware IoT framework using human digital twin for healthcare. *Multimedia Tools and Applications*, 1–25.

41. Galiautdinov, R. (2021). Digitally-signed video/audio streams as prevention of AI-based attacks. *International Journal of Software Science and Computational Intelligence (IJSSCI)*, 13(4), 54–63.

42. Cox, I. J., Kilian, J., Leighton, T., & Shamoon, T. (1997). Secure spread spectrum watermarking for multimedia. *IEEE Transactions on Image Processing*, 6(12), 1673–1687.

43. Fridrich, J. (1998, October). Image watermarking for tamper detection. In *Proceedings 1998 International Conference on Image Processing. ICIP98 (Cat. No. 98CB36269)* (Vol. 2, pp. 404–408). IEEE.

44. Singh, R., Singh, S. K., Kumar, S., & Gill, S. S. (2022). SDN-aided edge computing-enabled AI for IoT and smart cities. In *SDN-Supported Edge-Cloud Interplay for Next Generation Internet of Things* (pp. 41–70). Chapman and Hall/CRC.

45. Gupta, S., Agrawal, S., Singh, S. K., & Kumar, S. (2023). A novel transfer learning-based model for ultrasound breast cancer image classification. In *Computational Vision and Bio-Inspired Computing: Proceedings of ICCVBIC 2022* (pp. 511–523). Springer Nature Singapore.

46. Chopra, M., Singh, S. K., Sharma, A., & Gill, S. S. (2022). A comparative study of generative adversarial networks for text-to-image synthesis. *International Journal of Software Science and Computational Intelligence (IJSSCI)*, 14(1), 1–12.

47. Kaur, P., Singh, S. K., Singh, I., & Kumar, S. (2021, December). Exploring convolutional neural network in computer vision-based image classification. In *International Conference on Smart Systems and Advanced Computing (Syscom-2021)*. Springer.

48. Kaur, P., Singh, S. K., Singh, I., & Kumar, S. (2021, December). Exploring convolutional neural network in computer vision-based image classification. In *International Conference on Smart Systems and Advanced Computing (Syscom-2021)*.

49. Barni, M., Podilchuk, C. I., Bartolini, F., & Delp, E. J. (2001). Watermark embedding: Hiding a signal within a cover image. *IEEE Communications Magazine*, 39(8), 102–108.

50. Singh, S. K., Kaur, K., Aggarwal, A., & Verma, D. (2015). Achieving high performance distributed system: Using grid cluster and cloud computing. *International Journal of Engineering Research and Applications*, 5(2), 59–67.

51. Singh, S. K., Madaan, A., Aggarwal, A., & Dewan, A. (2014). Computing power utilization of distributed systems using distributed compilation: A clustered HPC approach. *British Journal of Mathematics & Computer Science*, 4(20), 2884–2900.

52. Uchida, Y., Nagai, Y., Sakazawa, S., & Satoh, S. I. (2017, June). Embedding watermarks into deep neural networks. In *Proceedings of the 2017 ACM on International Conference on Multimedia Retrieval* (pp. 269–277). Association for Computing Machinery.

53. Mengi, G., Singh, S. K., Kumar, S., Mahto, D., & Sharma, A. (2021, September). Automated machine learning (AutoML): The future of computational intelligence. In *International Conference on Cyber Security, Privacy and Networking* (pp. 309–317). Springer International Publishing.

54. Kumar, S., Singh, S. K., Aggarwal, N., Gupta, B. B., Alhalabi, W., & Band, S. S. (2022). An efficient hardware supported and parallelization architecture for intelligent systems to overcome speculative overheads. *International Journal of Intelligent Systems*, 37(12), 11764–11790.

55. Li, D., Deng, L., Gupta, B. B., Wang, H., & Choi, C. (2019). A novel CNN based security guaranteed image watermarking generation scenario for smart city applications. *Information Sciences*, 479, 432–447.

56. Mishra, A., Gupta, B. B., Peraković, D., Yamaguchi, S., & Hsu, C. H. (2021, January). Entropy based defensive mechanism against DDoS attack in SDN-cloud enabled online social networks. In *2021 IEEE International Conference on Consumer Electronics (ICCE)* (pp. 1–6). IEEE.

57. Solikhin, M., Pratama, Y., Pasaribu, P., Rumahorbo, J., & Simanullang, B. (2022). Analisis watermarking Menggunakan metode discrete cosine transform (DCT) dan discrete fourier transform (DFT). *Jurnal Sistem Cerdas*, 5(3), 155–170.

58. Singh, S. K., Singh, R. K., & BHATIA, M. S. (2010). System level architectural synthesis & compilation technique in reconfigurable computing system. In *ESA 2010: Proceedings of the 2010 International Conference on Embedded Systems & Applications*, Las Vegas, NV, July 12–15, 2010 (pp. 109–115). CSREA Press.

59. Ding, F., Jin, J., Meng, L., & Lin, W. (2023). JND-based perceptual optimization for learned image compression. *arXiv preprint*, arXiv:2302.13092.

60. Gupta, S., Singh, S. K., & Jain, R. (2010). Analysis and optimisation of various transmission issues in video streaming over Bluetooth. *International Journal of Computer Applications*, 11(7), 44–48.

61. Kumari, K. (2021). *Online Social Media Threat and It's Solution* (p. 1). Insights2Techinfo.
62. Zhang, Y., Liu, M., Guo, J., Wang, Z., Wang, Y., Liang, T., & Singh, S. K. (2022, December). Optimal revenue analysis of the stubborn mining based on Markov decision process. In *International Conference on Machine Learning for Cyber Security* (pp. 299–308). Springer Nature Switzerland.
63. Singh, S. K., Sharma, S. K., Singla, D., & Gill, S. S. (2022). Evolving requirements and application of SDN and IoT in the context of industry 4.0, blockchain and artificial intelligence. *Software Defined Networks: Architecture and Applications*, 427–496.
64. Singh, S. K. (2021). *Linux Yourself: Concept and Programming*. CRC Press.
65. Aggarwal, K., Singh, S. K., Chopra, M., Kumar, S., & Colace, F. (2022). Deep learning in robotics for strengthening industry 4.0.: Opportunities, challenges and future directions. *Robotics and AI for Cybersecurity and Critical Infrastructure in Smart Cities*, 1–19.
66. Arora, M., & Khurana, M. (2020). Secure image encryption technique based on jigsaw transform and chaotic scrambling using digital image watermarking. *Optical and Quantum Electronics*, 52, 1–30.
67. Gupta, B. B., & Quamara, M. (2020). *Internet of Things Security: Principles, Applications, Attacks, and Countermeasures*. CRC Press.
68. Gaurav, A., Gupta, B. B., & Panigrahi, P. K. (2023). A comprehensive survey on machine learning approaches for malware detection in IoT-based enterprise information system. *Enterprise Information Systems*, 17(3), 2023764.
69. Gupta, B. B., Perez, G. M., Agrawal, D. P., & Gupta, D. (2020). *Handbook of Computer Networks and Cyber Security* (Vol. 10, pp. 3–978). Springer.
70. Khan, A., & Peraković, D. (2021). *Top 50 Cyber Security Tools for IT and Business Professionals in 2022* (p. 1). Insights2Techinfo. https://insights2techinfo.com/top-50-cyber-security-tools-for-it-and-business-professionals-in-2022/
71. Mengi, G., Singh, S. K., Kumar, S., Mahto, D., & Sharma, A. (2021, September). Automated machine learning (AutoML): The future of computational intelligence. In *International Conference on Cyber Security, Privacy and Networking* (pp. 309–317). Springer International Publishing.
72. Peñalvo, F. J. G., Sharma, A., Chhabra, A., Singh, S. K., Kumar, S., Arya, V., & Gaurav, A. (2022). Mobile cloud computing and sustainable development: Opportunities, challenges, and future directions. *International Journal of Cloud Applications and Computing (IJCAC)*, 12(1), 1–20.
73. Kumar, R., Singh, S. K., & Lobiyal, D. K. (2023). UPSRVNet: Ultralightweight, privacy preserved, and Secure RFID-based authentication protocol for VIoT Networks. *The Journal of Supercomputing*, 1–28.

Chapter 7

Secure Health Features

Implementing Hyperledger Fabric in Blockchain-Driven Healthcare Management Systems

Mosiur Rahaman, Chun Yuan Lin, Ikbal Rachmat, Ritika Bansal, and Prayitno

I. INTRODUCTION

1.1 Blockchain in Healthcare Management

Blockchain is a new technology that is being used to develop creative solutions in several industries, including healthcare. In order to store and share patient data among hospitals, labs, pharmacies, and doctors, the healthcare system uses a blockchain network (Tagde et al., 2021). Blockchain-based software can reliably detect serious errors, including potentially harmful ones, in the medical domain. As a result, it can enhance the efficiency, security, and openness of medical data exchange within the healthcare system. Medical facilities can improve the analysis of medical information and obtain new insights with the use of this technology (Haleem et al., 2021).

Blockchain is a public, decentralized digital ledger that keeps track of transactions across multiple devices. This ensures that no record may be changed backward without changing any subsequent blocks. Blockchain creates a lengthy chain by verifying and connecting to the previous "Block." Blockchain is the name of the record (Gad et al., 2022). Blockchain offers a high degree of accountability because every transaction is recorded and verified publicly. Data entered into the blockchain cannot be changed by anyone (Politou et al., 2021). It does this by proving that the data is real and unaltered. Blockchain improves reliability by keeping data on networks, rather than in a single database that could expose its vulnerability to attack (Jadhav & Deshmukh, 2022).

Blockchain aids marketers in keeping track of medical consumption of goods. Blockchain technology will be used by the health and pharmaceutical industries to eradicate counterfeit drugs, making it possible to track down all of these treatments (Munasinghe & Halgamuge, 2023). It aids in identifying the source of fabrication. Patient medical records can be kept confidential in blockchain technology, which can also preserve medical histories in an unalterable format (Nishi et al., 2022).

1.2 The Exposure of Hyperledger Fabric

The integration of Hyperledger Fabric into healthcare administration marks a significant advancement in the sharing, managing, and safeguarding of healthcare data. Its complete potential has not yet been reached, but its influence is already apparent in many healthcare fields. In the future of healthcare, Hyperledger Fabric is expected to be crucial as the technology develops and more providers use it (Rejeb et al., 2024).

The manner in which health data is stored, accessible, and secured has significantly advanced with the introduction of Hyperledger Fabric into healthcare management systems. With the expanding digitization of medical information and the growing worries about data security and privacy, this discovery is especially noteworthy (Manikandan et al., 2022).

Prior to analyzing Hyperledger Fabric's application in healthcare, it is critical to comprehend what it is. It is an open-source permissioned blockchain platform suitable for enterprise use. Its capacity to build a network of networks—where several independent blockchain networks can communicate with one another without threatening security and privacy—is one of its primary characteristics. In the healthcare industry, where data sensitivity is critical, this is especially important (Mohan M & Sujihelen, 2023).

Patient data is extremely sensitive and highly personal. The architecture of Hyperledger Fabric enables a degree of privacy and data control that is difficult to achieve with conventional databases or even other blockchain systems. Because data is permissioned, its use is strictly regulated, guaranteeing that only those with permission can access sensitive information (Elghoul et al., 2023).

1.3 Chapter Objectives

These four chapter objectives could serve as a guide for the discussion's content and the following form. Each of these goals looks at existing applications and envisions future developments in order to provide a thorough understanding of Hyperledger Fabric's role in healthcare.

1. Describe the fundamental ideas behind blockchain technology and go into detail about what Hyperledger Fabric is, what makes it special, and how it differs from other blockchain solutions.
2. Describe how the permissioned blockchain structure of Hyperledger Fabric addresses important issues like patient confidentiality and data integrity to ensure the safe and private management of health data.
3. Examine how Hyperledger Fabric improves patient record accuracy and reduces errors in data management procedures in the healthcare industry.
4. Forecast the use of Hyperledger Fabric in the healthcare industry going forward, considering possible integrations with AI, IoT, and other cutting-edge technologies.

2. LITERATURE REVIEW

Data management and security could undergo a transformation with the application of blockchain technology in the healthcare industry, which has been the subject of much research. Research highlights the obstacles to preserving data privacy and integrity, where the immutable, transparent, and decentralized character of blockchain technology becomes especially important (Taherdoost, 2023a). One blockchain framework that stands out is Hyperledger Fabric; it is perfect for healthcare applications because of its flexible and modular architecture. A layer of trust and control is added by its permissioned network, which addresses the sensitive nature of patient data (Hasnain et al., 2023). Compared to conventional blockchain systems, this architecture offers better performance, scalability, and anonymity, as demonstrated by Gupta et al. (2022).

The scalability, privacy, and performance benefits of Hyperledger Fabric over alternative blockchain technology are noteworthy. For enterprise applications, Thakur et al. (2023) note that its pluggable consensus method and effective transaction processing make it better than Proof of Work (PoW) systems. In the healthcare industry, where efficiently and securely processing large amounts of data is paramount, this is especially important. Furthermore, the manuscript highlights the significance of Hyperledger Fabric's superior encryption algorithms and the need to adhere to rules such as GDPR and HIPAA in order to improve the security of healthcare data (Islam et al., 2023).

However, there are a number of difficulties in putting Hyperledger Fabric into practice in the healthcare industry. These include the requirement for system integration, privacy problems, and scalability issues. Promising case studies, such as Guardtime and the Estonian Healthcare Foundation, illustrate its use in safe patient record systems. However, to overcome these obstacles, cooperation and ongoing innovation in the industry are required (Jain & Maltoni, 2003).

The prospects for Hyperledger Fabric in the healthcare industry appear bright, as it may be integrated with AI, IoT, and other cutting-edge technologies to improve patient care, lower data management errors, and increase the accuracy of patient records ("Digital Forensics Techniques for Social Media Networking," 2021) (*Computer Networks, Cyber Security – Principles & Paradigms*, 2021). However, for successful implementation and broad adoption, negotiating the intricacies and regulations of the healthcare industry is essential. Despite some difficulties, the literature indicates that Hyperledger Fabric adoption might greatly improve healthcare data management systems and establish it as a useful tool for upcoming breakthroughs in healthcare (Zhou et al., 2023).

3. CONCEPTION OF BLOCKCHAIN TECHNOLOGY

The healthcare sector is always looking for new and creative ways to boost operational effectiveness, safeguard sensitive patient data, and improve patient care. Originally developed for the digital asset Bitcoin, the use of blockchain technology has shown promise in addressing these issues. With its secure, transparent, and decentralized framework for managing health records, supply chains, and other aspects, it has the potential to significantly transform the healthcare industry (Khezr et al., 2019).

3.1 Basic Blockchain

Understanding blockchain's underlying principles is crucial to comprehending its application in the healthcare industry. A distributed database known as a blockchain keeps an ever-expanding list of organized data, or "blocks," on hand. Every block in the chain has a timestamp and a link to the block before it (Ghosh et al., 2023).

Significant Blockchain Aspects: Decentralized governance: Blockchain splits information over a network of computers, as opposed to conventional databases that are controlled by a single entity. The possibility of data manipulation and cyberattacks is decreased by this decentralization (M. A. Uddin et al., 2021).

The term immutability: Data cannot be easily changed once it is added to the blockchain. The integrity of transactions and medical records is protected by this feature.

The concept of transparency: Blockchain enables a transparent audit of data transactions while preserving privacy. Building trust and adhering to regulations both depend on this quality (Javaid et al., 2021).

Blockchain technology structures: To validate transactions, blockchain uses consensus algorithms such as Proof of Work or Proof of Stake. This guarantees that everyone in the network is in agreement regarding the authenticity of the data (Hussein et al., 2023).

Proof of Work (PoW): The first consensus algorithm applied to a blockchain network was Proof of Work (PoW). It's employed in the generation of new blocks for the chain and transaction confirmation. PoW sets participants against one another to finish network operations and earn the benefits (Lasla et al., 2022).

Basis in Mathematics

PoW is based on the fundamental mathematical idea of cryptographic hashing. A hash function accepts an input and outputs a random-looking fixed-length string of bytes.

A particular kind of hash function known as $SHA-256$ (Secure Hash Algorithm 256 bit) is used by the blockchain.

The aim of extraction is to find a hash that is less than a target value. This process is called cracking a cryptographic enigma.

For example:

> Let's say that participants need to locate a nonce N such that hash $(D + N)$ yields a value less than the target. The block contains data D.
> Both D and N are concatenated and run through $SHA-256$ if the hash is $SHA-256$.
> The nonce value is just an arbitrary number that participants experiment with until they find one that produces a hash output that satisfies the requirements.
> Proof of Stake (PoS): PoS is a kind of consensus algorithm that chooses validators based on how much of the corresponding cryptocurrency they own.

The Foundation in Mathematical Thinking

PoS uses algorithms that choose validators based on the quantity of coins they possess and are willing to "stake" as collateral, as opposed to utilizing computing power to mine blocks. The user's stake (S) may have a proportionate effect on the probability P of being selected as a validator.

For instance:

> A user's probability of being selected to validate a block could be computed as follows if they have staked 100 coins out of the 10,000 coins that have been staked on the network, so chosen validate block could be calculated as $P = \dfrac{S}{Total\ Staked} = \dfrac{100}{10000} = 0.01\ or\ 1\%$
> When using Proof of Stake (PoS), the selected validator verifies the transactions, approves the block, and broadcasts it to the network. The validator gets paid if the block is included in the blockchain; this payment is frequently made up of transaction fees.

3.2 Blockchain Supremacy in Healthcare

Confidentiality and Data Security: Breach of healthcare data is becoming more common. Over 21 million records were impacted by more than 600 documented breaches in 2020 (Source: U.S. Department of Health & Human Services). Every patient record is added to the blockchain as an encrypted block. Based on 2020 data, a blockchain system may be able to protect over 2 million patient records yearly if data breaches are reduced by even 10% (Rowe, 2023).

Traceability of Drugs: Drug counterfeiting is a serious worldwide issue. 10% of medications in developing nations, according to WHO estimates, are fake or of poor quality. Blockchain establishes an open ledger system to monitor a drug's whole life, from production to delivery. Potentially, a supply chain enabled by blockchain technology could improve traceability (M. Uddin, Salah, et al., 2021).

Patient-Centric Data Management: Because patients frequently do not have control over their medical records, privacy and consent issues arise. Blockchain offers patients the ability to authorize or deny access to their medical information through a shared platform.

Blockchain technology has the potential to greatly improve patient involvement and data confidentiality if 80% of patients manage their health data through it (Taherdoost, 2023b).

i. Security and Confidentiality

Blockchain secures data with cryptographic algorithms (SHA-256). A chain is created by each data block having a cryptographic hash of the one before it.

Consider a simple hash function H applied to a block B, where $H(B)$ generates a unique ID. If an attacker changes any information in B, $H(B)$, changes drastically, easily indicating tampering.

There is a very small chance that data can be successfully changed without being discovered, typically around $\frac{1}{2^{256}}$ for SHA-256, which is practically impossible to achieve.

ii. Trace Drug in Immutable Ledger

On the blockchain, every transaction that occurs in the supply chain is documented as a block. Assume each block B_n in the blockchain contains its hash $H(B_n)$ and the hash of the previous block $H(B_{n-1})$. To alter B_n, an attacker must also alter $H(B_{n-1})$ and all subsequent blocks, which is computationally infeasible due to the Proof of Work required for each block. Also, assume that a block takes ten minutes to mine: it would take six blocks to change a block that was created an hour ago. Given current computational capabilities, this is practically impossible to accomplish in a reasonable amount of time.

iii. Data Organization in Patient Side

Patients have cryptographic keys that control access to their information. In that case, if a patient information D is encrypted using the private key $K_p, E\left(D, K_p\right)$, then only the owner can access it.

3.3 Challenges in Healthcare Data Management

Even though blockchain technology holds great promise for enhancing health care information governance, there are still a few implementation issues. Scalability issues, integration challenges with legacy systems, regulatory obstacles, and privacy concerns are some of these challenges.

Because the healthcare sector produces enormous volumes of information every single day, reliable and scalable blockchain solutions are required. Processing massive amounts of information rapidly and affordably is a problem for current blockchain platforms, especially those that employ traditional Proof of Work consensus mechanisms (Javaid et al., 2021). Blockchain's intrinsic design causes scalability problems because every transaction needs to be confirmed and stored on every node in the network, which could result in bottlenecks (Makhdoom et al., 2020).

Another difficulty is integrating blockchain with the current healthcare infrastructure. According to Dehghani et al. (2022), many healthcare providers employ antiquated legacy systems that are incompatible with blockchain technology. To guarantee smooth communication between blockchain solutions and legacy systems, the integration process necessitates a substantial time expenditure in addition to technical know-how (Hang et al., 2022).

Although blockchain's immutability promotes safety and openness, it also raises concerns regarding privacy, particularly when handling sensitive personal health information. There are situations in the healthcare industry where data needs to be changed or removed, such as to fix errors to the GDPR's "right to be forgotten." It is a difficult task to address these privacy issues while protecting the benefits and authenticity of blockchain technology (Zarchi et al., 2023).

4. HYPERLEDGER FABRIC TECHNOLOGY

The modular architecture of Hyperledger Fabric, an open-source platform for creating distributed ledger systems, offers high levels of secrecy, flexibility, resilience, and scalability. This makes it possible to modify solutions created using fabric for use in any industry. The Linux Foundation is in charge of this framework, which is private and confidential (Pelekoudas-Oikonomou et al., 2023, Gupta et al., 2022).

4.1 Basics of Hyperledger Fabric

It functions on a permissioned network, which is different from public blockchains in that users are acquainted with one another. This adds a layer of control and trust that blockchains with no permission lack. Because of Fabric's highly modular architecture, a network can be customized with plug-and-play components for identity management, ledger storage, and consensus to meet the demands of specific sectors. A broader spectrum of developers can access smart contracts in Fabric, as they are referred to as chain code and can be written in universal programming languages like Java (Munasinghe & Halgamuge, 2023).

4.2 Advantages and Key Features

The improved privacy and confidentiality capabilities of Hyperledger Fabric are among its main benefits for the healthcare industry. Fabric functions on a permissioned network basis, as opposed to public blockchains, allowing for strict control and management of data access and guaranteeing the confidentiality of patient information (Sutradhar et al., 2024).

Healthcare systems that handle massive amounts of information require better scalability and performance, which is made possible by Hyperledger Fabric's modular architecture. Healthcare applications, where speed and efficiency are critical, can benefit greatly from the platform's ability to handle a higher transaction throughput with lower latency than traditional blockchain systems (Swathi & Venkatesan, 2021).

The integrity and confidence model can be customized by healthcare entities to meet their unique needs, thanks to the freedom in selecting consensus-building mechanisms. This is especially crucial in the healthcare industry because various parties have different requirements and degrees of trust (Siala & Wang, 2022; Swathi & Venkatesan, 2021).

Increased interconnection between various healthcare systems and entities is made possible by Hyperledger Fabric. Research collaborations, medical information analytics, and coordinated patient care all depend on this interoperability (Shinde et al., n.d.). Rich inquiries about functionality against ledger data are supported by Fabric. This feature is especially helpful in the healthcare industry, as managing and analyzing patient data requires complicated searches (Dash et al., 2019).

4.3 Hyperledger Fabric vs Other Blockchain Technologies

Compared to conventional public blockchains, Hyperledger Fabric is a better option for enterprise applications because of its permissioned, modular, and flexible blockchain architecture. Because of its focus on scalability, privacy, and performance as well as its compatibility with various languages of programming for smart contracts, it can better benefit companies and organizations with particular blockchain requirements (Guggenberger et al., 2022).

Hyperledger Fabric runs on a permissioned network, in contrast to the digital currency and its permissionless nature. Because participants are known and thoroughly screened, a safe and reliable environment is created, which is crucial for companies and organizations where privacy and identity verification are important (Zhong et al., 2023). This controlled access model is better suited for businesses that are prohibited from using public networks because of privacy or legal constraints.

Because of its reusable architecture, Fabric processes transactions more quickly than Ethereum and Bitcoin, which rely on Proof of Work (PoW)-based systems. Its pluggable consensus mechanism, which can be customized to a network's unique requirements and avoid the resource-intensive PoW process, is the reason for its efficiency (De Angelis et al., 2023). Fabric can therefore handle higher transaction rates with lower latency, which is essential for enterprises that need quick and effective execution of transactions.

Fabric's design offers a unique way to protect information confidentiality and privacy. Data privacy and confidentiality are ensured by features like networks and secret information collections, which allow transactions to be visible to a subset of participants only (Antwi et al., 2021). In open-source blockchains like Bitcoin and Ethereum, where every transaction is transparent and visible to each user of the network, this level of privacy is not possible.

5. ROLES OF HYPERLEDGER FABRIC IN HEALTHCARE

By granting patients control over their medical records and fostering systemic openness, Hyperledger Fabric empowers patients. Patients can access their medical files from any healthcare provider and share them with other providers when required through the Hyperledger Fabric. This confirms that medical personnel have access to the latest information and eliminates the need for patients to carry tangible copies of their documents (Mohan & Sujihelen, 2023).

Additionally, Hyperledger Fabric enables medical innovation and research. Scholars can do studies and create new treatments by secretly accessing anonymous patient information that is kept on the blockchain with the consent of the patient. This accelerates the search for medical breakthroughs and creates novel possibilities for research.

Many healthcare organizations worldwide have already started using Hyperledger Fabric to solve connectivity and information confidentiality problems. The "Guardtime" and the Estonian Healthcare Foundation's collaboration are noteworthy instances. Along with the Estonian Healthcare Foundation, "Guardtime," which was a top supplier of blockchain solutions, put in place a blockchain-based patient health record security system. The Hyperledger Fabric-based system facilitates safe access to and exchange of medical records between healthcare providers by guaranteeing the privacy and security of information about patients (Omar et al., 2020; Dharan et al., 2022).

5.1 Data Security Enhancement

By using its permissioned network structure and cutting-edge encryption techniques, Hyperledger Fabric improves data security in the medical field. Uddin, Memon, et al. (2021) assert that maintaining compliance with healthcare regulations such as HIPAA and GDPR and safeguarding sensitive patient information depend heavily on this sensitive ecosystem.

One of the key components of Hyperledger Fabric's structure is its security approach, specifically its utilization of cutting-edge encryption techniques. To fully understand these techniques mathematically, one has to investigate the cryptographic algorithms and methods that are used by the system (Ma et al., 2019).

Cryptographic Hash Functions

Cryptographic hash functions are widely used in Hyperledger Fabric to ensure information safety and authenticity.

H is a Hash function which helps to convert any input with a fixed size random string of bytes.

i. x is an input value with a hash function H and generates fixed size strings, $H(x)$.
ii. For the input x to find y is computationally infeasible so that $H(y) = H(x)$, guaranteed the data security.
iii. Digital signature in Hyperledger Fabric ensures based on public-key cryptography, where a private key is used for signing, and a public key is used for verification.
iv. If $Sign(m, k_{private})$ is the signature of message m with private key $k_{private}$, then $Verify(m, Sign(m, k_{private}), k_{public} = true$.

Where k_{public} is corresponding public key.

v. A public key infrastructure is used by Hyperledger Fabric to regulate, share, and verify public keys, particularly in environments that require permission. Entails the use of key pairs $(k_{public}, k_{private})$ generated in asymmetric cryptography.
vi. Encrypted with public key $E(m, k_{public})$ can only be decrypted with their corresponding private key $D(E(m, k_{public}), k_{private}) = m$.
vii. For the security and preservation of information, Hyperledger Fabric can encrypt information using cryptographic algorithms.
Encrypted message $C = E(m, k)$ where C is ciphertext and m is plain text, encryption key is k.
Decrypted message $m = D(C, k)$ where D is the decryption algorithm.

All these elements seem essential to preserving a reliable and safe blockchain environment, which is critical in fields like healthcare where data sensitivity is vital. The real application of these cryptographic techniques in Fabric entails intricate algorithms and protocols created to satisfy the unique security requirements of a permissioned blockchain, even though these explanations only offer an in-depth computational summary.

5.2 Data Management in Healthcare

Managing enormous amounts of information accurately and efficiently is a major challenge in the healthcare sector. In order to improve the general standard of health care information management, Hyperledger Fabric offers a simplified framework for data storage and retrieval. It is the perfect platform for managing healthcare data because of its capacity to manage intricate transactions and interface with current healthcare systems (Antwi et al., 2021).

i. The world state and the transaction log are the two components of the ledger that Hyperledger Fabric uses to keep the information.
World State: Shows the ledger's current state. All keys have the most recent values stored in this the database.

Transaction Log: An exhaustive record of every transaction leading to the current state of the world. Let's represent it mathematically:

$L = \{S, T\}$, Where S-World State and T-Transaction logs

'tx' is for the transaction and world state is updated to $S' = f(S, tx)$ with the state transition function f.

ii. Like smart contracts, chain-code is used in Hyperledger Fabric to manage the ledger. A chain-code function C for a transaction tx can be represented as $C(tx) \rightarrow \{true, false\}$ where *true* indicates valid transaction.

iii. The utilization of channels and confidential information collections by Hyperledger Fabric guarantees data confidentiality and privacy, which is an essential aspect in the healthcare industry.

   Distinct ledgers for various participant subsets. Mathematically, each channel i has its own ledger L_i and a subset of participants P_i if there are m channels and n participants. Assuring that sensitive information is not accessible to the entire network permits data sharing among a subset of participants.

5.3 Implementations of Hyperledger Fabric

For the healthcare sector, Hyperledger Fabric provides a strong framework that addresses important issues with data security, privacy, and traceability. Its applications in healthcare are expanding, with the potential to enhance patient care, efficiency, and transparency. In terms of management of healthcare, Figure 7.1 illustrates the several advantages that Hyperledger Fabric can offer and the range of applications that it has seen.

How different participants engage with the system and its internal elements. This is a quick description of the diagram:

Participants:

   i. Patient: Supports for individuals whose data is handled by the system and who are the recipients of care.
   ii. A healthcare Provider: A healthcare provider is a hospital, clinic, or other medical facility that treats patients and communicates with their medical information.
   iii. Pharmacy Company: Produces and distributes medicines; accountable for medicine traceability.
   iv. Medical Scholar: Engaged in research and clinical trials and needs access to patient information and trial information.
   v. Regulatory Authority: Oversees and controls the healthcare sector, guaranteeing adherence to regulations and precision in provider data.

Hyperledger Fabric Structure

This is the main package in the figure, and it stands for the essential parts of the distributed ledger system for the Hyperledger Fabric.

   i. Smart Contracts: Hyperledger Fabric's business logic and rules are encoded in chaincode, also known as smart contracts. Chaincode is used by each use case, such as medication traceability or patient record management, to carry out its unique procedures reliably and securely (Mohan & Sujihelen, 2023).
   ii. Ledger: The ledger is a crucial element that serves as an inventory of all transactions and states. It is made up of a transaction log, which is the history of every transaction,

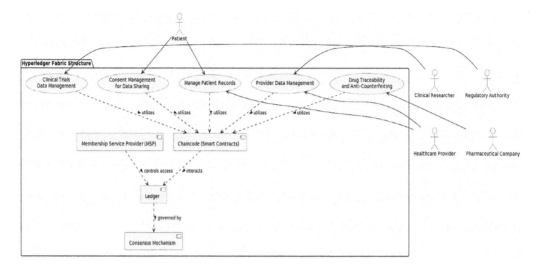

Figure 7.1 Framework and Implementations of Hyperledger Fabric in Healthcare Management

and a world state, which is the ledger's current state (*Ledger—Hyperledger-Fabricdocs Main Documentation*, n.d.).

iii. Consensus Mechanism: This part is in charge of validating transactions and keeping the distributed ledger network in a consistent state. It guarantees that everyone involved agrees on the ledger's current state.

iv. Membership Service Provider (MSP): MSP is responsible for maintaining login credentials and verifying network members. A permissioned blockchain such as Hyperledger Fabric needs to make sure that only authorized parties are able to interact with the network (Yawalkar et al., 2023).

v. Interactions: Different use cases are interacted with by each actor, such as the patient and the healthcare provider. Patients engage with systems such as "Manage Patient Records" and "Consent Management for Data Sharing," for instance. "Chaincode" is then used by the use cases to carry out their operations. This demonstrates how each unique application's business logic is implemented using smart contracts in Hyperledger Fabric (Majeed et al., 2021).

Chaincode in Hyperledger Fabric is usually written in either Go or Node.js. In the following instance, provide a basic Go framework for a fictitious smart contract that could handle patient records in accordance with one of the use cases shown in the figure.

A straightforward Hyperledger Fabric smart contract for patient record management is described in this 'Go' code. It outlines fundamental procedures such as establishing, reading, and revising consent for sharing information in the records of patients. To save and retrieve information, the chaincode communicates with the ledger via the Hyperledger Fabric API.

To create the patient record function in the chaincode, this operation defines mathematically how the parameter and different function working principle in the following:

Function $- f_{create}$
Definition of Function $- f_{create}(S, p) \rightarrow S'$

S-ledger current state

```go
package main

import (
  "bytes"
  "encoding/json"
  "fmt"

  "github.com/hyperledger/fabric-contract-api-go/contractapi"
)

// PatientRecord struct defines the patient record
type PatientRecord struct {
  ID      string `json:"id"`
  Name    string `json:"name"`
  Records string `json:"records"`
  Consent bool   `json:"consent"`
}

// PatientContract for handling patient records
type PatientContract struct {
  contractapi.Contract
}

// CreatePatientRecord adds a new patient record to the ledger
func (c *PatientContract) CreatePatientRecord(ctx contractapi.TransactionContextInterface, id string, name string, records string) error {
  patient := PatientRecord{
    ID:      id,
    Name:    name,
    Records: records,
    Consent: false,
  }

  patientJSON, err := json.Marshal(patient)
```

```go
  if err != nil {
    return err
  }

  return ctx.GetStub().PutState(id, patientJSON)
}

// ReadPatientRecord returns the patient record stored in the ledger
func (c *PatientContract) ReadPatientRecord(ctx contractapi.TransactionContextInterface, id string) (*PatientRecord, error) {
  patientJSON, err := ctx.GetStub().GetState(id)
  if err != nil {
    return nil, err
  } else if patientJSON == nil {
    return nil, fmt.Errorf("the patient %s does not exist", id)
  }

  var patient PatientRecord
  err = json.Unmarshal(patientJSON, &patient)
  if err != nil {
    return nil, err
  }

  return &patient, nil
}

// UpdateConsent updates the patient's consent for data sharing
func (c *PatientContract) UpdateConsent(ctx contractapi.TransactionContextInterface, id string, consent bool) error {
  patient, err := c.ReadPatientRecord(ctx, id)
  if err != nil {
    return err
  }

  patient.Consent = consent

  patientJSON, err := json.Marshal(patient)
  if err != nil {
    return err
```

```
    }
    return ctx.GetStub().PutState(id, patientJSON)
}

func main() {
    chaincode, err := contractapi.NewChaincode(&PatientContract{})
    if err != nil {
        fmt.Printf("Error creating chaincode: %s", err)
        return
    }

    if err := chaincode.Start(); err != nil {
        fmt.Printf("Error starting chaincode: %s", err)
    }
}
```

p-Patient information needs to be added, where $p = \{id, name, records, consent\}$

- Operation
  i. Check if the patient id $p.id$ already exists in S. If not in record, then add p to S, with a new state S'.
  ii. Initially, $S = \{p_1, p_2, \ldots \ldots, p_n\}$ and then execute $S' = \{p_1, p_2, \ldots \ldots, p_n\}$.

- Patient's record retrieve function

  $f_{read}(S, id) \rightarrow p$ where parameters are S-Ledger current state.
  id-Unique identifier and the process for search record S where records match with id and return value p.

- Update record function

  Update patient's record function which is represent as f_{update}.
  Define function like $f_{update}(S, id, consent) \rightarrow S'$, where parameters are S-ledger current state,
  id-patient's unique id and $consent$-Value true or false.

      i. Find the Patient's record id in S
      ii. And represent records with p_i in S, $p_i. consent = c$. Where, after execution, the resulting new states S $pi. consent = consent$.

6. IMPLEMENTING PROCESS OF HYPERLEDGER FABRIC

Healthcare Hyperledger Fabric implementation is a challenging but rewarding process that calls for meticulous planning, cooperation from a range of stakeholders, and in-depth knowledge of the technology and healthcare industry. Addressing the difficulties associated with managing healthcare data, such as privacy, security, interoperability, and regulatory compliance, is necessary for the implementation to be successful.

This mind map diagram illustrates the way Hyperledger Fabric is being implemented in healthcare management, covering a range of phases from planning and assessment to reporting and regulatory compliance in Figure 7.2.

   i. Evaluation and Organization:
      Determine and examine the particular healthcare domains where blockchain technology can be advantageous. For both technical and financial viability, do a thorough feasibility study. Engage stakeholders in conversation to learn about their needs and concerns.

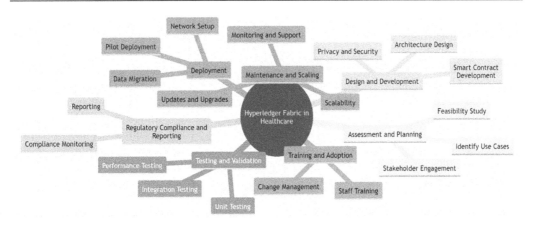

Figure 7.2 Hyperledger fabric implementation in healthcare management

ii. Development and Design

Construct the network architecture, considering membership services and node con-figuration. Create chaincodes to ensure solid data management for specific healthcare applications. Pay attention to security and privacy while making sure that all healthcare laws are followed.

iii. Verification and Testing

Test chaincodes and component parts thoroughly at the unit level. To guarantee a smooth interface with the current healthcare systems, conduct integration testing. Conduct performance evaluations to verify the system's capability in practical situations.

iv. Utilization

Launch a pilot programmed to assess performance and obtain input. If integrating current information, put an information relocation strategy into action. Establish the distributed ledger network, making sure that permissions and nodes are set up properly.

v. Education and Acceptance

Offer thorough system usage training to IT teams and healthcare personnel. Use change management techniques to make adoption go more smoothly. To ensure ongoing improvement, welcome user input and involvement.

vi. Upkeep and Extension

Keep an eye on the system at all times, responding quickly to problems and offering assistance. Update and improve the system frequently to improve functionality. Consider scalability in order to meet changing needs and increasing usage.

vii. Reporting and Regulatory Compliance

Verify that the system complies with healthcare laws and guidelines. Establish efficient reporting systems to foster stakeholder communication and transparency.

6.1 Technical and Management Readiness

Technical Readiness for Hyperledger Fabric in Healthcare: With an emphasis on hardware, network, and storage capabilities, healthcare organizations must assess how well their IT infrastructure supports the use of blockchain technology. It's imperative for assessing how well the system integrates with current healthcare apps, like EHRs. Having or gaining technical know-how in blockchain development, implementation, and continuous maintenance is crucial. It's important to comprehend the unique specifications of Hyperledger Fabric, such as its permissioned network and modular design. To safeguard private health information, it's also essential to make sure strong cybersecurity safeguards are in place.

Healthcare Industry Management Readiness for Hyperledger Fabric:

The implementation process ought to be in line with the strategic goals of the healthcare organization, including improving patient care and supply chain efficiency. To make the switch to a blockchain-based system easier, a thorough change management strategy is essential. To guarantee the new technology is adopted and used smoothly, staff training and stakeholder engagement are crucial. To effectively manage roles, permissions, and policies in the blockchain network, a clear governance model must be established. Top priority should be given to adhering to healthcare standards and regulations, including data privacy laws like GDPR and HIPAA.

6.2 Existing Healthcare Infrastructure and Integration

The detailed and fragile nature of healthcare information and processes necessitates meticulous planning and implementation when integrating Hyperledger Fabric into the current infrastructure. The basic structure for an activity diagram representing the steps is seen in Figure 7.3.

Compatibility Assessment: Determine whether the current healthcare IT system is compatible with Hyperledger Fabric. This entails determining the hardware specifications, network capacity, and possibility of supplementary resource requirements.

Data Integration: Integrating Hyperledger Fabric with current medical information systems, such as Health Information Exchanges (HIEs) and Electronic Health Records (EHRs), is one of the major challenges. Data fields must be mapped, consistent data formats must be maintained, and secure data transfer protocols must be established.

Interoperability Standards: It is imperative to follow interoperability standards such as HL7, FHIR, or DICOM. These standards guarantee that the integration permits smooth communication and data exchange between various healthcare applications and systems.

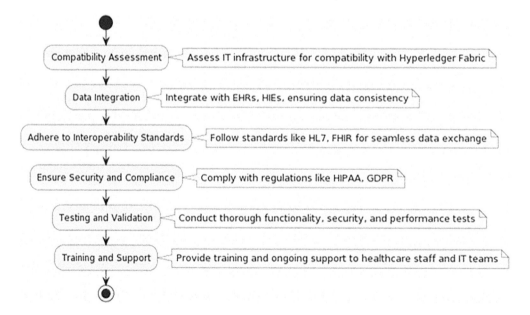

Figure 7.3 Sequential steps in integrating hyperledger fabric into existing healthcare systems

Security and Compliance: Verify that the Hyperledger Fabric integration complies with US and European healthcare laws, such as HIPAA. This entails controlling consent, protecting patient data privacy, and guaranteeing safe access to medical information.

Testing and Validation: Make sure the integrated system has undergone extensive testing prior to full deployment. Functionality, data integrity, performance, and security are all tested in this way. In a controlled setting, issues can be identified and mitigated with the aid of pilot studies or phased rollouts.

Training and Support: To help healthcare personnel and IT teams adjust to the new blockchain-integrated system, provide them with sufficient training. Sustained technical assistance is essential for resolving issues that might occur both during and after integration.

7. SECURITY AND PRIVACY CONCERNS IN HEALTHCARE INFRASTRUCTURE

Because medical information is sensitive, security and privacy issues are critical to the electronic health care infrastructure. Key areas of concern are emphasized by the following aspects:

i. Cyberattacks and Data Breaches: The sensitive and valuable nature of health data makes healthcare systems attractive targets for cyberattacks. Unauthorized access to financial data, patient records, and other sensitive data can result from breaches.

ii. Privacy of Patient Data: A primary concern is making sure that patient data is kept private and accessible only to authorized individuals.

iii. Insider Threats: Insiders pose a serious risk due to their potential for harm or incompetence. Serious privacy breaches may result from staff members' unintentional exposure, misuse of data, or unauthorized access.

iv. Device and Endpoint Security: Protecting these endpoints from vulnerabilities is essential given the growing use of mobile devices and the Internet of Things (IoT) in the healthcare industry. If not adequately secured, these devices may serve as entry points for cyberattacks.

v. Authentication and Access Control: Robust authentication protocols are imperative to guarantee that solely authorized personnel possess entry to confidential health information. This entails putting strict access controls and multi-factor authentication into place.

vi. Data Integrity: It's critical to guarantee the precision and coherence of health data across systems. Data corruption or manipulation can result in inaccurate medical diagnoses and treatments.

vii. Data Storage and Elimination: In order to preserve patient privacy, health data must be securely stored and disposed of in accordance with legal requirements and industry best practices.

viii. Training and Awareness: To reduce the risks of human error and to keep healthcare personnel up to date on the most recent security procedures and threats, regular training and awareness programs are essential.

7.1 Regulations of Data Protection

Following data protection laws is essential in the field of e-healthcare management to guarantee patient confidentiality and security. These laws, which differ from place to place, establish strict guidelines for the handling, storage, and disclosure of patient data. The Health

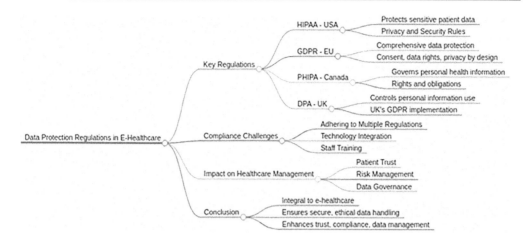

Figure 7.4 Illustrating the regulations of data Protection in e-healthcare infrastructure

Insurance Portability and Accountability Act (HIPAA) in the US establishes requirements for the security and privacy of medical records and requires the protection of sensitive patient data. Comparably, the General Data Protection Regulation (GDPR) of the European Union, which affects any organization handling the data of EU citizens, places a strong emphasis on consent, data rights, and privacy. The Personal Health Information Protection Act (PHIPA) in Canada and the Data Protection Act (DPA) in the UK are two other noteworthy regulations that guarantee the protection of personal health information within their respective jurisdictions. The regulations of data protection in e-healthcare infrastructure are shown in Figure 7.4.

Because they must sort through a complex web of different regulatory requirements, these regulations present serious compliance challenges for healthcare organizations, especially those that operate internationally. Key components of sustaining regulatory adherence include integrating compliant technologies into current healthcare systems and requiring ongoing staff training on best practices and legal requirements. Beyond merely ensuring legal compliance, these regulations have a significant impact on patient trust, which is essential to the provision of healthcare services. Good data protection and governance ensure that patient data is handled with the highest care and confidentiality, which not only reduces the risks associated with data breaches but also improves the general quality of healthcare management.

7.2 Ensuring Hyperledger Fabric Conformation

Given the importance and sensitivity of healthcare data, ensuring Hyperledger Fabric complies with e-healthcare infrastructure and security requires a number of crucial steps. If these steps are taken, the authorized networks and improved confidentiality characteristics made possible by Hyperledger Fabric's architecture can be successfully applied in the healthcare industry (Antwi et al., 2021). Figure 7.5 shows how in Hyperledger Fabric CA node and node manager work for security improvements.

Ensuring strong access control is a crucial aspect of incorporating Hyperledger Fabric into the healthcare industry. Membership Service Providers (MSPs) are essential in authorizing and authenticating participants on the network. Compliance is guaranteed and security is improved by putting role-based access controls into place and auditing access logs. Moreover, by utilizing Hyperledger Fabric's capabilities, such as confidential information collections,

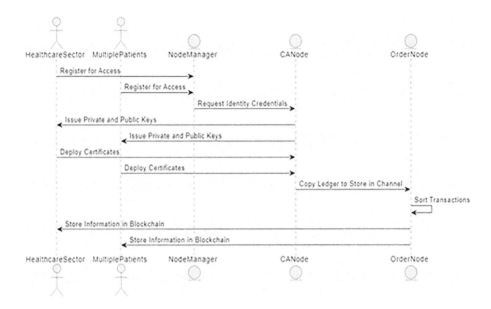

Figure 7.5 **Hyperledger fabric node manager and CA node security sequence transaction with all the nodes**

which allow the selective sharing of sensitive information, patient data privacy and confidentiality can be maintained. To protect against changing cybersecurity threats, regular security audits, applying the most recent security patches to the Hyperledger Fabric framework, and ongoing monitoring are essential. Moreover, reducing operational risks and improving the overall efficiency of the Hyperledger Fabric implementation in the healthcare industry are achieved by educating healthcare professionals about data security and providing training on blockchain technology.

Healthcare Sector and Multiple Patients have a transaction in the Network. If the Healthcare Sector and Multiple Patients want to communicate to get information about any Patient information and medical instruments or drugs, they need to register through node manager in CA node. It will issue private and public keys as identity credentials. Each node deploys its certificates and copies the ledger to store in the channel. Now in Hyperledger Fabric, order node sorted out the transactions created in the channel stored that information in the Blockchain network (Antwi et al., 2021).

7.3 Secure Data Transmission Process

Ensuring safe communication of information in Hyperledger Fabric requires several processes and protections intended to protect information throughout its journey, particularly in a delicate area like health care administration. An outline of the standard procedure for handling secure data transmission in this situation is illustrated in Figure 7.6.

The secure transmission of data is critical in a healthcare system built on the Hyperledger Fabric. Encrypting sensitive health information while it's in transit and at rest to maintain confidentiality and integrity makes patients and healthcare providers the main actors in this network. When it comes to sharing patient information in a private, confidential way that is only available to authorized parties, healthcare providers must make use of private channels and collections. To maintain identity and verify network users, Membership Service

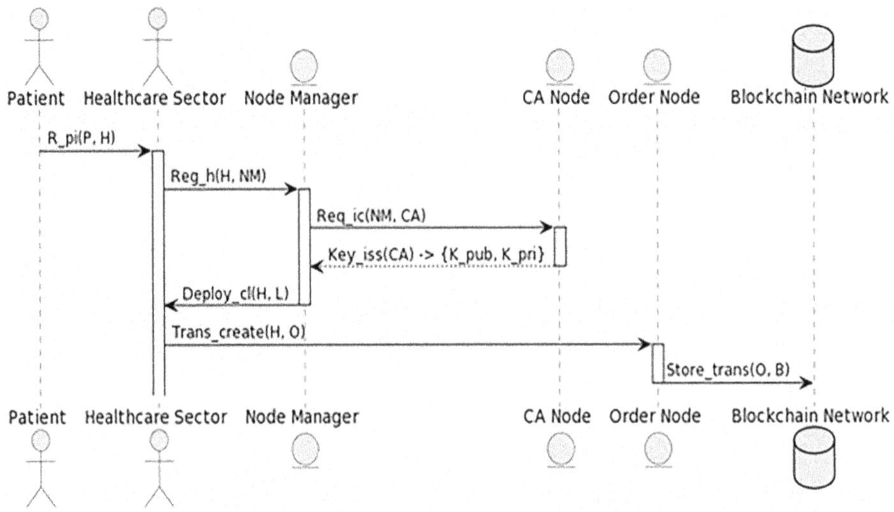

Figure 7.6 Secure data transmission process in hyperledger fabric

Providers (MSP) are essential. With the help of Public Key Infrastructure (PKI), they can issue digital certificates that guarantee network access is restricted to valid users.

In charge of client authentication and network activity monitoring, network administrators keep an eye on the security of the system. Healthcare providers and other clients are authenticated using certificates that are issued by reputable Certificate Authorities (CAs). This procedure secures access and authenticates users on the network. Chaincode, or smart contracts, are executed and validated in isolated environments, with access managed by endorsement policies. Maintaining the network's dependability and credibility depends on the consensus mechanism, which guarantees the integrity and ordering of transactions.

Regulatory agencies conduct routine audits and compliance checks to make sure the network complies with HIPAA and other healthcare regulations. Network administrators keep a close eye on the system to identify and address any security risks, and they control access and permissions to keep the network safe. Hyperledger Fabric offers a safe and effective framework for handling private medical data, guaranteeing privacy and legal compliance, and building e-healthcare system trust by integrating these safeguards.

1. Patients Request Information

   Mathematical representation: $R_{pi}(P,H)$
   Where R_{pi}-Request patient information
   P-Patients and H-Healthcare Sector.

2. Healthcare Sector Registers for Transaction

   Mathematical representation: $R_{eg_h}(H,NM)$
   H-Healthcare Sector and NM-Node Manager

3. Node Manager Requests Identity Credentials

   Mathematical representation: $Req_{ic}(NM,CA)$
   Where, Req_{ic}-Request for credential identity
   NM-Node Manager
   CA-Certificate Authority

4. CA Node Issues Keys

Mathematical representation $Key_{iss}(CA) \rightarrow \{K_{pub}, K_{pri}\}$
Where, Key_{iss}-Function for key issuance
K_{pup} and K_{pri}-Public and Private key.

5. Deployment of Certificates and Ledger Copy

Mathematical representation: $Deploy_{cl}(H, L)$
Where, $Deploy_{cl}$-Ledger copy and Deployment certificate. L represents Ledger.

6. Creation of Transactions in Channel

Mathematical representation: $Trans_{create}(H, O)$
Where, $Trans_{create}$-Function for transaction creation.
O-Node order

7. Order Node Stores Transactions

Mathematical representation: $Store_{trans}(O, B)$
$Store_{trans}$-Storing transaction in the blockchain
B-Blockchain Network.

Since the main purpose of a sequence diagram is to show how various actors interact with the system, these mathematical representations would normally be included in the extensive documentation that goes with the diagram. The data flow and transactions in a healthcare setting within the Hyperledger Fabric network are conceptually represented by the mathematical functions presented here.

8. THE FUTURE OF HEALTHCARE

Advances in technology, especially in the fields of telemedicine, blockchain, and artificial intelligence (AI), have the potential to completely transform the future of electronic healthcare. Healthcare will likely change significantly as a result of the integration of these technologies, becoming more individualized, accessible, and efficient. By removing geographical restrictions and offering remote consultations, diagnostics, and treatment options, telemedicine will only grow in the future, improving access to healthcare, particularly in underserved or rural areas. Because of its capacity to process enormous volumes of data for personalized treatment plans, disease prevention through predictive analytics, and diagnostics, AI is expected to play an increasingly larger role in e-healthcare. Furthermore, by facilitating the safe and easy exchange of patient data amongst different healthcare providers and guaranteeing data integrity, blockchain technology is expected to improve the security and privacy of electronic health records (EHRs).

Furthermore, in the future of e-healthcare, the emphasis on patient-centered care will grow stronger. Patients will be able to track their health in real time with wearable health technology and Internet of Things (IoT) devices, which will provide important data for managing chronic diseases and preventive healthcare. With people taking an active role in managing their health, this change will promote a more proactive approach to wellness and health. By optimizing processes, cutting down on redundancies, and averting unfavorable health events through early intervention, these technological advancements will also help lower healthcare costs. E-healthcare's future holds the promise of improving care quality while also strengthening healthcare systems' resilience, sustainability, and ability to adapt to changing population needs.

8.1 Recent Trends and Hypothesis

A visual overview of the user and the emerging technologies in the healthcare sector are shown in Figure 7.7.

The healthcare industry is undergoing a transformation due to notable advancements in technology. Due in large part to the COVID-19 pandemic, telehealth is rapidly growing and becoming more widely available by standardizing remote consultations, diagnostics, and treatment. Simultaneously, there has been an increase in the application of machine learning and artificial intelligence (AI) in the healthcare industry, which has improved diagnostic accuracy and allowed for predictive analytics for disease trends and patient care management. Furthermore, wearable health technology is becoming more commonplace. It offers real-time monitoring of important health metrics and helps with the proactive management of chronic illnesses. As for the safe administration of electronic health records (EHRs), which guarantee patient privacy and data integrity, blockchain technology is being embraced more and more.

In the future, several theories call for increased technological integration in the medical field. It is projected that telehealth will play a central role in healthcare delivery as a standard practice. It is anticipated that artificial intelligence (AI) will play a major role in preventive healthcare by creating complex models for disease prevention and patient monitoring. It is predicted that wearable health data will be easily incorporated with EHRs, improving medical record accuracy and helping healthcare professionals make well-informed decisions. A universal health record system that is accessible to all authorized providers could be supported by blockchain technology in the future, enhancing the continuity and caliber of care. Lastly, it is expected that the use of IoT devices in remote patient monitoring will increase, greatly improving post-operative care and chronic condition management and creating a more effective and patient-centered healthcare system.

9. CONCLUSION

A major technological advancement in the management, sharing, and security of healthcare data is represented by the integration of Hyperledger Fabric into the clinical environment.

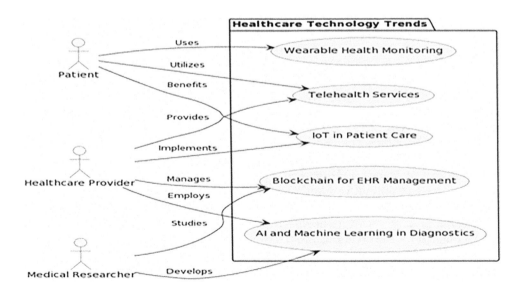

Figure 7.7 A visual overview of users and the emerging technologies in the healthcare sector

Compared to conventional databases or other blockchain systems, its permissioned blockchain architecture provides a noticeably higher degree of privacy, data control, and security. Because patient data is extremely sensitive and needs to be kept strictly confidential and intact, this is especially important in the healthcare industry.

With possible integrations with AI, IoT, and other cutting-edge technologies, Hyperledger Fabric's future in the healthcare industry appears bright. It is anticipated that this integration will increase patient record accuracy, lower data management errors, and enhance overall patient care.

Although Hyperledger Fabric has many benefits, there are drawbacks as well, such as issues with privacy, legal hurdles, scalability, and integration with legacy systems. Effectively addressing these drawbacks is essential to the technology's successful deployment and broad adoption in the healthcare industry. But because of the opportunities it offers, like enhanced information management, increased security, and patient empowerment, it's an excellent asset for healthcare's future.

In simple terms, because Hyperledger Fabric can transform patient care and information management while negotiating the complexities and laws that are specific to the healthcare sector, its role in the field is growing and changing. The effective deployment of this technology will necessitate cooperative efforts, continuous innovation, and a dedication to conquering the inherent difficulties in incorporating modern technology into healthcare organizations.

REFERENCES

Antwi, M., Adnane, A., Ahmad, F., Hussain, R., Habib ur Rehman, M., & Kerrache, C. A. (2021). The case of HyperLedger Fabric as a blockchain solution for healthcare applications. *Blockchain: Research and Applications*, 2(1), 100012. https://doi.org/10.1016/j.bcra.2021.100012

Computer Networks, Cyber Security—Principles & Paradigms. (2021, November 8). Meet the Tech Entrepreneur, Cybersecurity Author, and Researcher. https://guptadeepak.com/handbook-of-computer-networks-and-cyber-security/

Dash, S., Shakyawar, S. K., Sharma, M., & Kaushik, S. (2019). Big data in healthcare: Management, analysis and future prospects. *Journal of Big Data*, 6(1), 54. https://doi.org/10.1186/s40537-019-0217-0

De Angelis, S., Lombardi, F., Zanfino, G., Aniello, L., & Sassone, V. (2023). Security and dependability analysis of blockchain systems in partially synchronous networks with Byzantine faults. *International Journal of Parallel, Emergent and Distributed Systems*, 0(0), 1–21. https://doi.org/10.1080/17445760.2023.2272777

Dehghani, M., William Kennedy, R., Mashatan, A., Rese, A., & Karavidas, D. (2022). High interest, low adoption. A mixed-method investigation into the factors influencing organisational adoption of blockchain technology. *Journal of Business Research*, 149, 393–411. https://doi.org/10.1016/j.jbusres.2022.05.015

Digital Forensics Techniques for Social Media Networking. (2021, September 1). Insights2Techinfo. https://insights2techinfo.com/digital-forensics-techniques-for-social-media-networking/

Elghoul, M. K., Bahgat, S. F., Hussein, A. S., & Hamad, S. H. (2023). Management of medical record data with multi-level security on Amazon Web Services. *SN Applied Sciences*, 5(11), 282. https://doi.org/10.1007/s42452-023-05502-9

Gad, A. G., Mosa, D. T., Abualigah, L., & Abohany, A. A. (2022). Emerging trends in blockchain technology and applications: A review and outlook. *Journal of King Saud University – Computer and Information Sciences*, 34(9), 6719–6742. https://doi.org/10.1016/j.jksuci.2022.03.007

Ghosh, P. K., Chakraborty, A., Hasan, M., Rashid, K., & Siddique, A. H. (2023). Blockchain application in healthcare systems: A review. *Systems*, 11(1), Article 1. https://doi.org/10.3390/systems11010038

Guggenberger, T., Sedlmeir, J., Fridgen, G., & Luckow, A. (2022). An in-depth investigation of the performance characteristics of Hyperledger Fabric. *Computers & Industrial Engineering*, 173, 108716. https://doi.org/10.1016/j.cie.2022.108716

Gupta, B. B., Mamta, Mehla, R., Alhalabi, W., & Alsharif, H. (2022). Blockchain technology with its application in medical and healthcare systems: A survey. *International Journal of Intelligent Systems*, 37(11), 9798–9832. https://doi.org/10.1002/int.23014

Haleem, A., Javaid, M., Singh, R. P., Suman, R., & Rab, S. (2021). Blockchain technology applications in healthcare: An overview. *International Journal of Intelligent Networks*, 2, 130–139. https://doi.org/10.1016/j.ijin.2021.09.005

Hang, L., Chen, C., Zhang, L., & Yang, J. (2022). Blockchain for applications of clinical trials: Taxonomy, challenges, and future directions. *IET Communications*, 16(20), 2371–2393. https://doi.org/10.1049/cmu2.12488

Hasnain, M., Albogamy, F. R., Alamri, S. S., Ghani, I., & Mehboob, B. (2023). The Hyperledger fabric as a blockchain framework preserves the security of electronic health records. *Frontiers in Public Health*, 11. https://www.frontiersin.org/articles/10.3389/fpubh.2023.1272787

Hussein, Z., Salama, M. A., & El-Rahman, S. A. (2023). Evolution of blockchain consensus algorithms: A review on the latest milestones of blockchain consensus algorithms. *Cybersecurity*, 6(1), 30. https://doi.org/10.1186/s42400-023-00163-y

Islam, Md. A., Islam, Md. A., Jacky, Md. A. H., Al-Amin, Md., Miah, Md. S. U., Khan, Md. M. I., & Hossain, Md. I. (2023). Distributed ledger technology based integrated healthcare solution for Bangladesh. *IEEE Access*, 11, 51527–51556. https://doi.org/10.1109/ACCESS.2023.3279724

Dharani, J., Sundarakantham, K., & Singh, K. (2022). A privacy-preserving framework for endorsement process in Hyperledger Fabric. *Computers & Security*, 116, 102637. https://doi.org/10.1016/j.cose.2022.102637

Jadhav, J. S., & Deshmukh, J. (2022). A review study of the blockchain-based healthcare supply chain. *Social Sciences & Humanities Open*, 6(1), 100328. https://doi.org/10.1016/j.ssaho.2022.100328

Jain, A. K., & Maltoni, D. (2003). *Handbook of Fingerprint Recognition*. Springer-Verlag.

Javaid, M., Haleem, A., Pratap Singh, R., Khan, S., & Suman, R. (2021). Blockchain technology applications for Industry 4.0: A literature-based review. *Blockchain: Research and Applications*, 2(4), 100027. https://doi.org/10.1016/j.bcra.2021.100027

Khezr, S., Moniruzzaman, M., Yassine, A., & Benlamri, R. (2019). Blockchain technology in healthcare: A comprehensive review and directions for future research. *Applied Sciences*, 9(9), Article 9. https://doi.org/10.3390/app9091736

Lasla, N., Al-Sahan, L., Abdallah, M., & Younis, M. (2022). Green-PoW: An energy-efficient blockchain proof-of-work consensus algorithm. *Computer Networks*, 214, 109118. https://doi.org/10.1016/j.comnet.2022.109118

Ledger—Hyperledger-Fabric Docs Main Documentation. (n.d.). Retrieved November 20, 2023, from https://hyperledger-fabric.readthedocs.io/en/release-2.2/ledger/ledger.html

Ma, C., Kong, X., Lan, Q., & Zhou, Z. (2019). The privacy protection mechanism of Hyperledger fabric and its application in supply chain finance. *Cybersecurity*, 2(1), 5. https://doi.org/10.1186/s42400-019-0022-2

Majeed, U., Khan, L. U., Yaqoob, I., Kazmi, S. M. A., Salah, K., & Hong, C. S. (2021). Blockchain for IoT-based smart cities: Recent advances, requirements, and future challenges. *Journal of Network and Computer Applications*, 181, 103007. https://doi.org/10.1016/j.jnca.2021.103007

Makhdoom, I., Zhou, I., Abolhasan, M., Lipman, J., & Ni, W. (2020). PrivySharing: A blockchain-based framework for privacy-preserving and secure data sharing in smart cities. *Computers & Security*, 88, 101653. https://doi.org/10.1016/j.cose.2019.101653

Manikandan, S., Rahaman, M., & Song, Y.-L. (2022). Active authentication protocol for IoV environment with distributed servers. *Computers, Materials & Continua*, 73(3), 5789–5808. https://doi.org/10.32604/cmc.2022.031490

Mohan M, S., & Sujihelen, L. (2023). An efficient chain code for access control in hyper ledger fabric healthcare system. *E-Prime – Advances in Electrical Engineering, Electronics and Energy*, 5, 100204. https://doi.org/10.1016/j.prime.2023.100204

Munasinghe, U. J., & Halgamuge, M. N. (2023). Supply chain traceability and counterfeit detection of COVID-19 vaccines using novel blockchain-based Vacledger system. *Expert Systems with Applications*, 228, 120293. https://doi.org/10.1016/j.eswa.2023.120293

Nishi, F. K., Shams-E-Mofiz, M., Khan, M. M., Alsufyani, A., Bourouis, S., Gupta, P., & Saini, D. K. (2022). Electronic healthcare data record security using blockchain and smart contract. *Journal of Sensors*, 2022, e7299185. https://doi.org/10.1155/2022/7299185

Omar, I., Jayaraman, R., Salah, K., Yaqoob, I., & Ellahham, S. (2020). Applications of Blockchain technology in clinical trials: Review and open challenges. *Arabian Journal for Science and Engineering*. https://doi.org/10.36227/techrxiv.12635783.v1

Pelekoudas-Oikonomou, F., Ribeiro, J. C., Mantas, G., Sakellari, G., & Gonzalez, J. (2023). Prototyping a Hyperledger Fabric-based security architecture for IoMT-based health monitoring systems. *Future Internet*, 15(9), Article 9. https://doi.org/10.3390/fi15090308

Politou, E., Casino, F., Alepis, E., & Patsakis, C. (2021). Blockchain mutability: Challenges and proposed solutions. *IEEE Transactions on Emerging Topics in Computing*, 9(4), 1972–1986. https://doi.org/10.1109/TETC.2019.2949510

Rejeb, A., Rejeb, K., Appolloni, A., Jagtap, S., Iranmanesh, M., Alghamdi, S., Alhasawi, Y., & Kayikci, Y. (2024). Unleashing the power of internet of things and blockchain: A comprehensive analysis and future directions. *Internet of Things and Cyber-Physical Systems*, 4, 1–18. https://doi.org/10.1016/j.iotcps.2023.06.003

Rowe, A. (2023, October 20). *Healthcare Data Breaches Impacted 25% of Americans in 2023*. Tech. Co. https://tech.co/news/healthcare-data-breaches-impact-americans

Shinde, R., Patil, S., Kotecha, K., Potdar, V., Selvachandran, G., & Abraham, A. (n.d.). Securing AI-based healthcare systems using blockchain technology: A state-of-the-art systematic literature review and future research directions. *Transactions on Emerging Telecommunications Technologies*, n/a(n/a), e4884. https://doi.org/10.1002/ett.4884

Siala, H., & Wang, Y. (2022). SHIFTing artificial intelligence to be responsible in healthcare: A systematic review. *Social Science & Medicine*, 296, 114782. https://doi.org/10.1016/j.socscimed.2022.114782

Sutradhar, S., Karforma, S., Bose, R., Roy, S., Djebali, S., & Bhattacharyya, D. (2024). Enhancing identity and access management using Hyperledger Fabric and OAuth 2.0: A block-chain-based approach for security and scalability for healthcare industry. *Internet of Things and Cyber-Physical Systems*, 4, 49–67. https://doi.org/10.1016/j.iotcps.2023.07.004

Swathi, P., & Venkatesan, M. (2021). Scalability improvement and analysis of permissioned-blockchain. *ICT Express*, 7(3), 283–289. https://doi.org/10.1016/j.icte.2021.08.015

Tagde, P., Tagde, S., Bhattacharya, T., Tagde, P., Chopra, H., Akter, R., Kaushik, D., & Rahman, Md. H. (2021). Blockchain and artificial intelligence technology in e-Health. *Environmental Science and Pollution Research*, 28(38), 52810–52831. https://doi.org/10.1007/s11356-021-16223-0

Taherdoost, H. (2023a). Privacy and security of blockchain in healthcare: Applications, challenges, and future perspectives. *Sci*, 5(4), Article 4. https://doi.org/10.3390/sci5040041

Taherdoost, H. (2023b). The role of blockchain in medical data sharing. *Cryptography*, 7(3), 36. https://doi.org/10.3390/cryptography7030036

Thakur, A., Ranga, D. V., & Agarwal, R. (2023). *Performance Benchmarking and Analysis of Blockchain Platforms* (SSRN Scholarly Paper 4385643). https://doi.org/10.2139/ssrn.4385643

Uddin, M. A., Stranieri, A., Gondal, I., & Balasubramanian, V. (2021). A survey on the adoption of blockchain in IoT: Challenges and solutions. *Blockchain: Research and Applications*, 2(2), 100006. https://doi.org/10.1016/j.bcra.2021.100006

Uddin, M., Memon, M., Memon, I., Ali, I., Memon, J., Abdelhaq, M., & Alsaqour, R. (2021). Hyperledger fabric blockchain: Secure and efficient solution for electronic health records. *Computers, Materials & Continua*, 68(2), Article 2. https://doi.org/10.32604/cmc.2021.015354

Uddin, M., Salah, K., Jayaraman, R., Pesic, S., & Ellahham, S. (2021). Blockchain for drug traceability: Architectures and open challenges. *Health Informatics Journal*, 27(2), 14604582211011228. https://doi.org/10.1177/14604582211011228

Yawalkar, P. M., Paithankar, D. N., Pabale, A. R., Kolhe, R. V., & William, P. (2023). Integrated identity and auditing management using blockchain mechanism. *Measurement: Sensors*, 27, 100732. https://doi.org/10.1016/j.measen.2023.100732

Zarchi, G., Sherman, M., Gady, O., Herzig, T., Idan, Z., & Greenbaum, D. (2023). Blockchains as a means to promote privacy protecting, access availing, incentive increasing, ELSI lessening

DNA databases. *Frontiers in Digital Health*, 4. https://www.frontiersin.org/articles/10.3389/fdgth.2022.1028249

Zhong, B., Gao, H., Ding, L., & Wang, Y. (2023). A blockchain-based life-cycle environmental management framework for hospitals in the COVID-19 context. *Engineering (Beijing, China)*, 20, 208–221. https://doi.org/10.1016/j.eng.2022.06.024

Zhou, Y., Song, L., Liu, Y., Vijayakumar, P., Gupta, B. B., Alhalabi, W., & Alsharif, H. (2023). A privacy-preserving logistic regression-based diagnosis scheme for digital healthcare. *Future Generation Computer Systems*, 144. https://doi.org/10.1016/j.future.2023.02.022

Chapter 8

Security Threats and Countermeasures for Digital Images in Smart Systems

Anupama Mishra, Brij B. Gupta, and Kshitij Mishra

1. INTRODUCTION

Smart systems, also known as intelligent systems or smart technologies, refer to integrated and interconnected systems that leverage advanced computing, sensors, and communication technologies to enhance efficiency, automation, and decision-making. These systems often incorporate artificial intelligence (AI) and the Internet of Things (IoT) to collect and analyze data, respond to changes in the environment, and adapt their behavior accordingly (Guebli et al., 2021). The Internet of Things (IoT) is a significant development in the field of information communications that makes it possible for devices to communicate with one another in a direct, ongoing, and automatic manner (this includes M2M and CPS communication). It has been shown to have a great amount of utility in several practical applications. Drones and/or virtual reality provide an additional layer by acting as a superimposed element. Industrial automation (Industrial IoT) and process control systems of any kind have been serving as the foundation for IoT implementations up until this point (Madhu et al., 2022). This includes the management of the power grid, traffic tracking, smart cities, video surveillance, crowd sensing, and body area networks/e-health. The term "smart" implies an ability to learn, adapt, and optimize performance over time (Raj & Prakash, 2022). The incorporation of digital images is becoming more commonplace as the use of intelligent systems continues to spread into more and more areas of our everyday lives. The usage of digital images is fundamental to the operation of a variety of technologies, including security cameras and the image recognition software found in autonomous vehicles, among others. However, as more technologies become networked, the safety of digital pictures stored in intelligent systems has become an issue of the utmost importance. This chapter takes an extensive look into the variety of security risks that are inherent to digital images and investigates the different preventative steps that may be taken to keep these images safe. As per Figure 8.1, one out of every five people who use the internet had their email account compromised as a result of a breach that occurred over the course of a single year (Jelušić et al., 2022). The average cost to enterprises of a data breach in 2022 is estimated to be $4.35 million dollars. During the first six months of 2022, there were 236.1 million ransomware attacks around the world. In the first half of 2022, 53.35 million people living in the United States were victims of cybercrime.

The chapter will present issues and challenges in the field of digital images, along with their latest developments to provide solutions including cutting-edge technologies, tools, and other mechanisms.

2. OVERVIEW OF DIGITAL IMAGE SECURITY

Digital images play an important part in a variety of modern technological applications, including communication, entertainment, healthcare, and surveillance, amongst others.

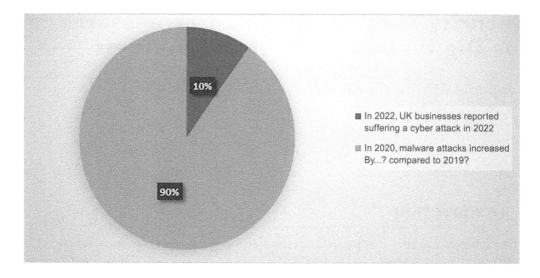

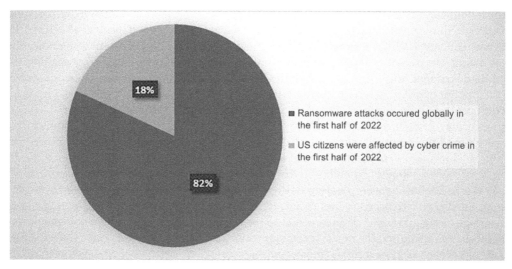

Figure 8.1 Statistics of cyber attacks

The proliferation of high-resolution cameras, various image processing techniques, and the increasing prevalence of internet use have all contributed to an increase in the number of digital photos that are being created, shared, and stored. As a consequence of this, the necessity of protecting these photographs against illegal access, alteration, or misuse has assumed a position of utmost importance (Mansour et al., 2021). For the purpose of making decisions and conducting analysis, intelligent systems, such as artificial intelligence (AI), machine learning, and the Internet of Things (IoT), significantly rely on digital images. Processing enormous amounts of image data is necessary for a variety of applications, including facial recognition, driverless vehicles, medical imaging, and surveillance systems (Tripathi et al., 2022). The dependability and safety of smart systems are directly correlated to the level of protection that is afforded to these images. Any breach in the security of digital photographs might result in erroneous conclusions and potentially disastrous repercussions (Nhi et al., 2022). Digital images play an increasingly important

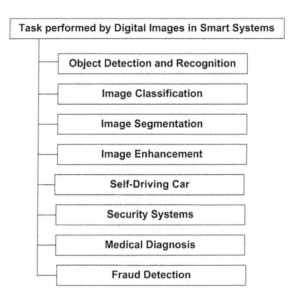

Figure 8.2 Tasks performed by digital images in smart systems

role in smart systems. They are used for a wide variety of tasks, as presented in Figure 8.2, including:

Object Detection and Recognition: It is possible for intelligent systems to recognize items in real life by using digital images. A wide range of applications, including robotics, security systems, and self-driving cars, benefit from the utilization of this technology.

Image Classification: These digital images can be used by intelligent systems to categorize items into a variety of distinct groups. Product recognition, medical diagnosis, and the detection of fraudulent activity are just some of the applications that make use of this technology.

Image Segmentation: The process of turning an image into a collection of sections of pixels that are represented by a mask or a labeled image is referred to as image segmentation. Through the process of breaking a picture into segments, it is possible to process only the segments of the image that are of significant importance, rather than processing the complete image. Digital images can be utilized by intelligent systems to create distinctions between items and the environment in which they are located. This is applied in a broad variety of applications, some of which include medical imaging, satellite images, and autonomous vehicles, among any number of other applications.

Image Enhancement: An image enhancement is a process that involves increasing the quality of the original data as well as the information content of the data before it is processed. Through the utilization of digital images, it is feasible for intelligent systems to realize an improvement in the quality of images. This has a wide variety of applications, some of which include the removal of noise, the sharpening of images, and the enhancement of contrast.

The following is a list of a few applications that are being used to make use of digital images in smart systems:

Self-Driving Cars: A vehicle that is capable of perceiving its surroundings and operating without the intervention of a human driver is referred to as a self-driving vehicle.

A human passenger is not necessary to assume control of the car at any time, nor is a human passenger required to be present in the vehicle at any time. Self-driving cars make use of digital imagery to identify a variety of objects that are present on the road to make decisions regarding safe navigation of the road. These objects include pedestrians, other vehicles, and traffic signs.

Security Systems: Security systems make use of digital images to keep an eye out for activity that may be considered suspicious. There is a possibility that criminal behavior can be stopped, criminals can be detected, and intruders can be recognized through the utilization of technology. A home security system is a network of integrated electronic devices that work together with a central control panel to protect against burglars and other potential intruders who may enter the home. Door and window sensors, motion sensors, glass break sensors, and security cameras are the components that make up a fundamental home security system. A control panel or base station with a separate keyboard is necessary for this system.

Medical Diagnosis: Digital images are utilized by medical practitioners in the process of disease diagnosis. Detecting malignancies, determining fractures, and tracking the evolution of diseases are all possible applications for this as well. From conventional computed tomography to advanced multi-dimensional three-dimensional imaging, medical imaging is continuously undergoing development. In addition to several other technologies, the healthcare industry is dependent on multi-dimensional 3D visualization. Developers of healthcare technology have begun to take advantage of the benefits offered by cloud computing, augmented reality and virtual reality, artificial intelligence, and cinematic rendering. These technologies provide better and more distinct images, which are necessary for the precise diagnosis of patients.

Fraud Detection: To identify fraudulent behavior, financial institutions utilize digital photographs. These can identify signatures that have been forged, detect papers that have been falsified, and prevent identity theft. It is possible to commit image fraud by manipulating digital photos to deceive others. Forgery of documents and the creation of false identities are two examples of unlawful acts that use this resource. Photoshop and other image-editing programs are utilized by con artists to manipulate digital photographs and other digital files. One of the most common types of image fraud is the falsification and manipulation of images of official documents such as driver's licenses and bank statements.

3. SECURITY THREATS TO DIGITAL IMAGES IN SMART SYSTEMS

"Digital Image Security" refers to the collection of safeguards and procedures that are utilized to prevent unauthorized access, alteration, or distribution of digital images (Srivastava et al., 2022). The significance of ensuring the safety of digital images has considerably increased as the world continues to become more computerized. It is essential to ensure the confidentiality, integrity, and authenticity of digital photographs in a variety of contexts, including personal privacy, commercial operations, and national security, among others, because digital photos may contain private or confidential information (Jang et al., 2007). Digital images are susceptible to myriad security threats that can compromise integrity, confidentiality, and availability. Some of the prominent threats include:

Unauthorized Access and Data Breaches: It is possible for data breaches to occur as a result of unauthorized access to digital picture repositories, which could result in the disclosure of sensitive visual information. Malicious actors can exploit weaknesses in

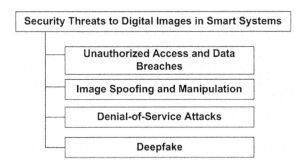

Figure 8.3 Security threats to digital images in smart systems

smart systems in order to gain unauthorized access, which can lead to violations of privacy as well as security breaches (Adhitya et al., 2020).

Image Spoofing and Manipulation: Digital images can be manipulated by their adversaries in a number of ways, including changing (Adhitya et al., 2020) the substance of the image or adding false information. Image spoofing offers a serious risk in contexts such as facial recognition systems because it allows an adversary to acquire unauthorized access by presenting an altered version of a legitimate image.

Denial-of-Service Attacks: Attacks that deny service to users can easily compromise intelligent systems that rely largely on digital images. It is possible to disrupt regular operations and cause service interruptions if the system is overloaded with a large number of picture requests or if image processing pipelines are flooded with too many requests (Dora Pravina et al., 2021; Abd El-Latif et al., 2018).

Deepfake: Deepfake is the name given to a method that makes use of artificial intelligence (AI), and more specifically deep learning algorithms, to generate fake content that appears authentic, most frequently in the form of videos or still photos (Li et al., 2019). Deepfake technology is capable of manipulating a person's facial expressions, lip movements, and even their voice to create the illusion that they are saying or doing something that they have not actually done or said.

4. COUNTERMEASURES AND SECURITY SOLUTIONS

4.1 Encryption and Secure Transmission

The utilization of encryption is of utmost importance in safeguarding digital photos, as it involves the conversion of the initial image data into an unreadable format that necessitates the possession of the correct decryption key for comprehension (Hasan, 2023). This mechanism aids in safeguarding sensitive photographic content from unwanted access, hence guaranteeing the security and integrity of the data. Encryption is a crucial security mechanism employed to protect digital images against unauthorized intrusion. The process entails the utilization of algorithms to transform visual data into an unintelligible structure, necessitating decryption in order to restore it to its initial state. The implementation of encryption techniques effectively thwarts any attempts made by unauthorized parties to access or extract sensitive information included within those photos (APA4, APA11). The application of encryption is utilized to enhance the security of digital photos during their transmission across networks, such as the Internet, as well as while they are kept on different devices, including servers and cloud storage. This measure effectively prevents any potential interception or unauthorized access to the photographs (Rahman et al., 2018).

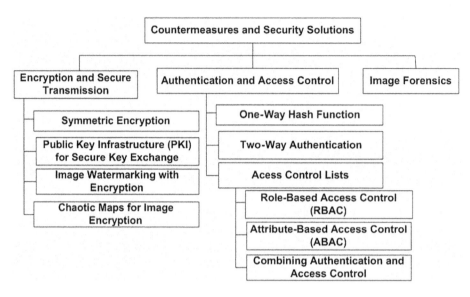

Figure 8.4 Countermeasures and security solutions

4.1.1 Symmetric Encryption

In the area of secure digital communication, symmetric encryption is a cornerstone that plays a critical role in protecting the confidentiality and integrity of information that is communicated. This is because symmetric encryption uses a pair of keys to encrypt and decrypt information. Symmetric encryption relies on the usage of a secret key that is known to both parties involved in the communication (Voronin et al., 2018). This key is kept in a secure location and acts as the pivotal component in this process. Before sending the message, the sender converts the plaintext message into ciphertext using the secret key. Even if someone with malevolent intent manages to intercept the data being communicated, they will be unable to understand the information since they do not have the secret key. Symmetric encryption methods, such as the Advanced Encryption Standard (AES), which is commonly used, or Data Encryption Standard (DES), are chosen for their efficiency, which ensures quick and secure communication (Badue et al., 2021). Both standards were developed by the National Institute of Standards and Technology (NIST). Notably, despite the fact that symmetric encryption performs exceptionally well in point-to-point applications, it is frequently combined with other authentication mechanisms, such as digital signatures or message authentication codes, in order to strengthen authentication and guard against unauthorized tampering. Symmetric encryption is an essential tool for preserving the confidentiality and integrity of digital communication in a wide variety of applications because of its scalability, speed, and practicality (Memos et al., 2018).

Encryption Process: The basic symmetric encryption process for an image involves applying a cryptographic algorithm (Alsmirat et al., 2017) (e.g., Advanced Encryption Standard—AES) with a secret key (K) to transform the image data (P) into ciphertext (C).

$$C = E_K(P)$$

Decryption Process: To decrypt the ciphertext and retrieve the original image, the decryption function (D) is applied with the same secret key.

$$P = D_K(C)$$

4.1.2 Public Key Infrastructure (PKI) for Secure Key Exchange

A dual-key system that handles crucial aspects of confidentiality, authentication, and secure key exchange is introduced in asymmetric encryption, which serves as a cornerstone in the process of ensuring the safety of digital communication by introducing asymmetric encryption. In this configuration, every participant has a one-of-a-kind set of keys (Mansour et al., 2021): a public key that can be freely distributed, as well as a private key that must be kept confidential. With this pair, one can encrypt messages using the recipient's public key so only the private key owner can decipher them. Implementing encryption techniques protects messages from interception and unauthorized access (Tian et al., 2019). Asymmetric encryption generates and verifies digital signatures, making it essential for authentication. The sender's public key lets the recipient verify a message's authenticity. The sender signs with their private key, and the recipient verifies it. This method builds trust and verifies the message's integrity during transmission. Additionally, asymmetric encryption facilitates secure key exchange, allowing parties to agree on a secret key for symmetric encryption (Harirchi et al., 2017; Jakaria et al., 2019). This solves the problem of safely communicating secret keys via channels that may or may not be secure. We can strengthen the foundations of confidentiality, authentication, and the secure transmission of information by integrating asymmetric encryption into the fabric of digital communication. This allows us to navigate the complicated landscape of current communication systems with more ease.

Public key cryptography is often used in digital image encryption, employing a pair of public and private keys for secure key exchange, ensuring that only authorized parties can decrypt the images.

In asymmetric encryption, two keys are used: a public key (K_{public}) for encryption and a private key (K_{private}) for decryption.

$$C = E_{K_{\text{public}}}(P)$$

$$P = D_{K_{\text{private}}}(C)$$

4.1.3 Image Watermarking With Encryption

Combining the benefits of several watermarking and encryption methods is an effective method for guaranteeing that digital communication is kept private (Chen et al., 2020; Ikrissi et al., 2021). This is accomplished by using image watermarking in conjunction with encryption. The imperatives of content authentication and confidentiality can both be addressed by utilizing this dual-layered technique. A digital watermark, which is effectively a one-of-a-kind and undetectable identifier, is inserted into the image utilizing several procedures that are associated with watermarking in this model (Alsmirat et al., 2019). This watermark not only acts as a method for certifying the image, but it also has the ability to communicate other information, such as ownership or usage rights. It is common practice to encrypt the embedded watermark with the use of cryptographic techniques in order to increase the level of security afforded by the watermark and to ensure that the information contained inside the watermark cannot be altered. This combination of picture watermarking and encryption also guarantees that only those who have the correct decryption key will be able to read the information that is stored in the image (Arya, 2023). This approach is useful in contexts where ensuring the integrity of visual content, verifying ownership, and having safe communication are of the utmost importance. Some examples of these contexts include digital rights management, medical imaging, and the transmission of sensitive documents.

Ongoing research explores advanced encryption techniques for digital images, addressing challenges such as computational efficiency, robustness against attacks, and the ability to handle multimedia content.

The basic symmetric encryption process for an image involves applying a cryptographic algorithm (e.g., Advanced Encryption Standard—AES) with a secret key (K) to transform the image data (P) into ciphertext.

4.1.4 Digital Image Watermarking

The confidentiality of the embedded watermark is ensured by the utilization of encryption, which involves encrypting the watermark with a secret key.

Combining encryption with image watermarking involves embedding a watermark (W) into the image (I) using a secret key (K).

$$\text{Watermarked Image} = I + \alpha \cdot E_K(W)$$

Watermark Extraction: To extract the watermark from the watermarked image ($I_{watermarked}$), the decryption function is applied with the same secret key (K).

$$W = D_K(I_{watermarked} - I)$$

4.1.5 Chaotic Maps for Image Encryption

This approach leverages the inherent unpredictability of chaotic systems to create a key stream that significantly enhances the security of the encryption process (Balaji & Rajesh 2017). The sensitivity to initial conditions in chaotic maps ensures that a slight change in the input leads to drastically different outputs, contributing to the robustness of the encryption scheme. This combination of chaos-based key generation and XOR-based encryption adds an additional layer of security to cryptographic systems, making them more resilient against various types of attacks.

Chaotic Maps Transformation: Chaotic maps (e.g., Logistic map) can be used to introduce chaos into the encryption process.

$$x_{n+1} = \mu \cdot x_n \cdot (1 - x_n)$$

Chaotic Key Stream: The chaotic map can generate a key stream ($K_{chaotic}$) for XOR-based encryption.

$$C = P \oplus K_{chaotic}$$

4.2 Authentication and Access Control

Authentication and access control play a crucial role in safeguarding the security of digital picture transmission by validating the identity of anyone engaging with them. This is achieved through various techniques such as usernames, passwords, and multi-factor authentication, which collectively help to prevent illegal entry. Concurrently, access control methods, such as role-based access control (RBAC) and access control lists (ACL), govern the actions that users are authorized to undertake on digital images, contingent upon their designated roles and permissions. The use of this comprehensive methodology provides protection against unauthorized modifications, thus guaranteeing that solely verified and authorized individuals possess the ability to retrieve, transfer, or manipulate digital photos. The integration of authentication and access control is of utmost importance in industries where visual data possesses a high level of sensitivity. This integration serves as a strong safeguard against unauthorized disclosure or modification inside digital picture communication systems.

The authentication process verifies the identity of a user attempting to access image data. It often involves the use of a username (U) and a password (P).

Credentials $= (U, P)$

4.2.1 One-way Hash Function

Data integrity and authenticity depend on one-way hash algorithms in digital picture security. One-way hash functions convert input data, such as a digital image, into a fixed-size string of characters, called the hash value or digest. The one-way nature of this procedure makes it computationally feasible to compute the hash value from the original image, but it is harder to reconstruct the image from its hash value. One-way hash functions are reliable for digital image integrity verification due to this characteristic. One can rapidly detect image tampering by comparing the generated hash value at different times or between parties. As digital picture security grows more important in numerous fields, one-way hash algorithms are essential to visual data dependability. Passwords are often stored as hash values (H) using a one-way hash function ($H = \text{hash}(P)$). This ensures that even if the hash is compromised, the original password is not easily recoverable.

$H = \text{hash}(P)$

4.2.2 Two-Factor Authentication (2FA)

The use of two-way authentication, which is also known as mutual authentication, has emerged as an effective method for boosting the security of digital images. In this scenario, not only does the system verify the user or entity viewing the digital photos, but the user or entity also authenticates the system, thus creating a trust verification that goes in both directions. This is referred to as a bidirectional trust verification (Krundyshev & Kalinin, 2020). This reciprocal verification procedure reduces the likelihood of digital image systems being subjected to unauthorized access or other forms of possible assault, hence improving the systems' overall security posture. For example, when a user accesses a protected image repository, they must supply authentication credentials, and at the same time, the system must present its credentials to the user. In this scenario, the user must submit both sets of credentials. This dual verification helps to reduce the risk of impersonation or fraudulent access by ensuring that both parties are who they say they are.

Two-factor authentication involves using two of the three authentication factors: something you know (password), something you have (security token), and something you are (biometric data).

2FA $=$ (Password, Biometric Data)

4.2.3 Access Control Lists (ACL)

ACLs provide a systematic and adaptable framework for visual data access, which is essential to digital image security. A robust ACL for digital photographs uses RBAC and ABAC to fine-tune permissions based on user responsibilities and image properties (Ferrag et al., 2020). RBAC grants users access rights depending on their organizational or system roles, responsibilities, and privileges. An image editor may have different permissions than a viewer. ABAC uses user attributes, image metadata, and contextual information to take a more dynamic approach (Gupta et al., 2018). This provides complex access decisions, such as barring sensitive image access by department or classification level. RBAC and ABAC in ACLs streamline administrative operations and ensure context-aware, adaptive, and security-aligned digital picture access. In situations where exact access rights control is crucial, this layered method greatly improves digital image repository security and integrity. ACLs define the permissions associated with image data, specifying which users or system processes are granted access and what operations they can perform.

$$ACL = \{(U_1, \text{Read}), (U_2, \text{Write}), ...\}$$

Role-Based Access Control (RBAC): RBAC assigns roles to users based on their job functions, and access permissions are granted based on roles rather than individual user identities.

$$RBAC = \{(U_1, \text{ Admin}), (U_2, \text{ User}),...\}$$

Access Control Matrix: The access control matrix (ACM) represents the permissions for each user and each object in a system.

$$ACM_{ij} = \text{Permission}(U_i, O_j)$$

Attribute-Based Access Control (ABAC): ABAC defines access policies based on attributes associated with users, objects, and environmental conditions.

$$ABAC = \{(U, \text{ Role}, \text{Department}), (O, \text{ Confidentiality})\}$$

Boolean Logic for Policy Evaluation: Access control policies often use Boolean logic to evaluate conditions and determine whether access should be granted or denied.

$$\text{Policy} = (\text{Role} == \text{Admin}) \wedge (\text{Confidentiality} \geq \text{Level})$$

Combining Authentication and Access Control: Access control decisions often depend on successful authentication. A user must authenticate before the access control system determines their permissions.

$$\text{Access} = \text{Authenticate}(\text{Credentials}) \rightarrow \text{Access Control}(\text{Permissions})$$

Authentication Token: An authentication token is often generated upon successful authentication and is used as proof of authentication during subsequent access control decisions.

$$\text{Token} = \text{Generate Token}(\text{Credentials})$$

4.3 Image Forensics

Within the context of digital content, the field of picture forensics has evolved as an indispensable instrument, assuming a pivotal function in the identification and mitigation of occurrences involving image modification. This phenomenon arises from the inherent challenge associated with detecting image modification. Because of the widespread availability of complex image editing tools and the growing prevalence of deepfake technologies, there is an urgent requirement for reliable systems that can guarantee the authenticity of digital images. Image forensics uses a wide variety of methods, ranging from statistical studies to deep learning algorithms, to investigate the authenticity of photographs and identify any possible modifications. Investigators can discover tiny adjustments, concealed watermarks, or evidence left behind throughout the editing process when they make use of these forensic techniques. In addition, picture forensics plays an important role in assigning authorship to digital photographs, which is helpful in legal circumstances where establishing the credibility of visual evidence is of the utmost importance. Image forensics, in its most fundamental sense, performs the function of a sentinel by bolstering the reliability of digital visual content and establishing confidence in the integrity of images utilized across a variety of industries. This is of utmost significance in professions such as journalism, law enforcement, and digital media, which rely heavily on the reliability and precision of visual information.

4.3.1 Significant Techniques in Image Forensics

Fourier Transform for Frequency Analysis: The Fourier Transform is utilized in image forensics to analyze the frequency components of an image (Shankar et al., 2021). The Fourier Transform is an essential tool for performing frequency analysis in image security. It helps in the detection of modifications, the use of watermarking as a means of authenticating digital photos, and the application of cryptographic safeguards to protect digital images. The conduct of this analysis in the frequency domain is essential to ensure the honesty and safety of visual information. This is crucial for identifying anomalies or hidden patterns that may indicate manipulation.

$$F(u,v) = \iint f(x,y)\, e^{-i2\pi(ux+vy)}\, dx\, dy$$

Error Level Analysis (ELA): Error Level Analysis measures the difference in compression levels within an image. Error Level Analysis, often known as ELA, is a critical part of image security since it pinpoints inconsistencies within an image's compression levels. It is a helpful tool for forensic analysis and ensures the integrity of digital photos by identifying potential areas of manipulation or tampering in digital photographs (Gupta et al., 2022; Sri et al., 2021). Because ELA is so good at identifying discrepancies that may be introduced into an image during editing, it is an essential part of both the forensic investigation process and the image authentication procedure (Raj & Pani, 2022). It is based on the premise that manipulated regions often exhibit different error levels compared to the rest of the image.

$$ELA(x, y) = \frac{|I_{\text{original}}(x, y) - I_{\text{manipulated}}(x, y)|}{I_{\text{original}}(x, y)}$$

Principal Component Analysis (PCA): PCA is employed for dimensionality reduction and feature extraction in image forensics. Because it enables dimensionality reduction and the extraction of relevant information from digital images, principal component analysis, also known as PCA, is an essential tool for image security. In the context of security, pattern classification analysis helps discover essential patterns and traits, which is helpful for activities like picture recognition, authentication, and the identification of anomalies (Hildebrand & Koethe, 1993). PCA improves computing efficiency and simplifies the implementation of effective security measures in a variety of image-related applications. This is accomplished by lowering the dimensionality of picture data. It helps identify significant features and patterns within the image data.

$$\text{Covariance Matrix } C = \frac{1}{N-1}\sum_{i=1}^{N}(X_i - \bar{X})(X_i - \bar{X})^T$$

$$\text{Eigenvectors } V, \text{ Eigenvalues } D : CV_i = \lambda_i V_i$$

Benford's Law for Image Forensics: Benford's Law is applied in image forensics to detect anomalies in the distribution of leading digits within image data. Benford's Law, a mathematical principle about dataset digit frequency distribution, is used in picture forensics to discover irregularities (Reddy, 2023). Benford's Law states that some digits are more often the leading digit in real-world datasets. In picture forensics, deviations from this predicted digit distribution may suggest manipulation (Shafie et al., 2014). Forensic analysts can detect tampering by evaluating the leading digit distribution of pixel values, image sizes, or other image attributes. Benford's Law provides a statistical foundation for digital image authenticity and integrity, adding to image forensics' armory. It is particularly useful for identifying inconsistencies in naturally captured images.

$$P(d) = \log_{10}\left(1 + \frac{1}{d}\right)$$

Watermarking Using Discrete Wavelet Transform (DWT): Discrete Wavelet Transform is employed in image forensics for embedding watermarks that can later be used for authentication and detecting unauthorized alterations. The utilization of Discrete Wavelet Transform (DWT) for watermarking in the field of digital forensics refers to a methodology wherein indiscernible data is incorporated into the frequency domain of digital images. The discrete wavelet transform enables the partitioning of images into distinct frequency components, while employing watermarking techniques within this domain guarantees resilience against typical image processing processes. The utilization of this technique holds significant importance in the field of digital forensics, particularly in the areas of authenticity and integrity verification. The presence or absence of watermarks within the examined images can be regarded as a dependable signal of potential tampering or unauthorized alterations.

$$W(a,b) = \sum_{n} s(n)\psi_{a,b}(n)$$

Image Hashing for Duplicate Detection: Image hashing involves generating a hash value that represents the unique characteristics of an image. The process of image hashing in the field of digital forensics pertains to the generation of a distinct hash value that is derived from the content of an image (Wang et al., 2020; Yu et al., 2018). This hash value serves to identify and detect duplicate images. The hash functions as a distinctive identifier that exhibits a high level of sensitivity to even minor alterations within the image. Within the realm of digital forensic investigations, the utilization of picture hashing serves the purpose of discerning the presence of duplicate or similar photographs. This method becomes valuable in aiding the identification process. The utilization of picture hashing is highly advantageous in the optimization of investigations, the mitigation of redundancy, and the detection of probable occurrences of image-based content tampering or duplication.

$$\text{Hash} = \text{Hashing\_Function}(\text{Image})$$

5. CONCLUSION

The chapter discusses various and diverse characteristics of security vulnerabilities that digital images encounter within the domain of smart systems. The growing dependence on visual data calls for a proactive strategy to mitigate vulnerabilities and protect against harmful activity. The countermeasures that have been investigated encompass a range of techniques, including encryption, access control, and authentication. These measures provide a strategic set of tools to strengthen defensive capabilities. Nevertheless, it is imperative to acknowledge the dynamic characteristics of security threats and the necessity for ongoing assessment and adjustment of security tactics. This chapter provides a solid foundation for continued activities with the goal of protecting the resilience and security of digital images against growing dangers, as the prevalence of intelligent systems continues to grow.

REFERENCES

Abd El-Latif, A. A., Abd-El-Atty, B., Hossain, M. S., Rahman, M. A., Alamri, A., & Gupta, B. B. (2018). Efficient quantum information hiding for remote medical image sharing. *IEEE Access*, 6, 21075–21083.

Adhitya, Y., Prakosa, S. W., Köppen, M., & Leu, J. S. (2020). Feature extraction for cocoa bean digital image classification prediction for smart farming application. *Agronomy*, 10(11), 1642.

Alsmirat, M. A., Jararweh, Y., Obaidat, I., & Gupta, B. B. (2017). Internet of surveillance: A cloud supported large-scale wireless surveillance system. *The Journal of Supercomputing*, 73, 973–992.

Alsmirat, M. A., Al-Alem, F., Al-Ayyoub, M., Jararweh, Y., & Gupta, B. (2019). Impact of digital fingerprint image quality on the fingerprint recognition accuracy. *Multimedia Tools and Applications*, 78(3), 3649–3688.

Arya, V. (2023). *Cloud-Driven AI and Blockchain: Innovations and Applications* (p. 1). In-sights2techinfo. https://insights2techinfo.com/cloud-driven-ai-and-blockchain-innovations-and-applications/

Badue, C., Guidolini, R., Carneiro, R. V., Azevedo, P., Cardoso, V. B., Forechi, A., . . . & De Souza, A. F. (2021). Self-driving cars: A survey. *Expert Systems with Applications*, 165, 113816.

Balaji, G. N., & Rajesh, D. (2017). Smart vehicle number plate detection system for different countries using an improved segmentation method. *Imperial Journal of Interdisciplinary Research (IJIR)*, 3(6), 263–268.

Chen, D. J. I. Z. (2020). Smart security system for suspicious activity detection in volatile areas. *Journal of Information Technology and Digital World*, 2(1), 64–72.

Dora Pravina, C. T., Buradkar, M. U., Jamal, M. K., Tiwari, A., Mamodiya, U., & Goyal, D. (2022, December). A sustainable and secure cloud resource provisioning system in industrial internet of things (IIoT) based on image encryption. In *Proceedings of the 4th International Conference on Information Management & Machine Intelligence* (pp. 1–5). Association for Computing Machinery.

Ferrag, M. A., Shu, L., Yang, X., Derhab, A., & Maglaras, L. (2020). Security and privacy for green IoT-based agriculture: Review, blockchain solutions, and challenges. *IEEE Access*, 8, 32031–32053.

Guebli, W., & Belkhir, A. (2021). Inconsistency detection-based LOD in smart homes. *International Journal on Semantic Web and Information Systems (IJSWIS)*, 17(4), 56–75.

Gupta, B. B., Gaurav, A., Marín, E. C., & Alhalabi, W. (2022). Novel graph-based machine learning technique to secure smart vehicles in intelligent transportation systems. *IEEE Transactions on Intelligent Transportation Systems*, 1–9.

Gupta, B. B., Yamaguchi, S., & Agrawal, D. P. (2018). Advances in security and privacy of multimedia big data in mobile and cloud computing. *Multimedia Tools and Applications*, 77, 9203–9208.

Harirchi, F., Yong, S. Z., Jacobsen, E., & Ozay, N. (2017). Active model discrimination with applications to fraud detection in smart buildings. *IFAC-PapersOnLine*, 50(1), 9527–9534.

Hasan, A. (2023). Smart cities and IoT integration. *AICyberInnovate Spectrum Magazine*, 1(1), 7–10. http://aicybersecuritycenter.com/wp-content/uploads/2023/11/Smart-Cities-and-IoT-Integration-2.pdf

Hildebrand, A., & Koethe, U. (1993, October). SMART: System for segmentation matching and reconstruction. In *State-of-the-Art Mapping* (Vol. 1943, pp. 66–78). SPIE.

Ikrissi, G., & Mazri, T. (2021). IOT-based smart environments: State of the art, security threats and solutions. *The International Archives of the Photogrammetry, Remote Sensing and Spatial Information Sciences*, 46, 279–286.

Jakaria, A. H. M., Rahman, M. A., & Hasan, M. G. M. M. (2019, June). Safety analysis of AMI networks through smart fraud detection. In *2019 IEEE Conference on Communications and Network Security (CNS)* (pp. 1–7). IEEE.

Jang, C. J., Lee, J. Y., Lee, J. W., & Cho, H. G. (2007, October). Smart management system for digital photographs using temporal and spatial features with exif metadata. In *2007 2nd International Conference on Digital Information Management* (Vol. 1, pp. 110–115). IEEE.

Jelušić, P. B., Poljičak, A., Donevski, D., & Cigula, T. (2022). Low-frequency data embedding for DFT-based image steganography. *International Journal of Software Science and Computational Intelligence (IJSSCI)*, 14(1), 1–11.

Krundyshev, V., & Kalinin, M. (2020, September). The security risk analysis methodology for smart network environments. In *2020 International Russian Automation Conference (RusAutoCon)* (pp. 437–442). IEEE.

Li, D., Deng, L., Gupta, B. B., Wang, H., & Choi, C. (2019). A novel CNN-based security guaranteed image watermarking generation scenario for smart city applications. *Information Sciences*, 479, 432–447.

Madhu, S., Padunnavalappil, S., Saajlal, P. P., Vasudevan, V. A., & Mathew, J. (2022). Powering up an IoT-enabled smart home: A solar powered smart inverter for sustainable development. *International Journal of Software Science and Computational Intelligence (IJSSCI)*, 14(1), 1–21.

Mansour, R. F., El Amraoui, A., Nouaouri, I., Díaz, V. G., Gupta, D., & Kumar, S. (2021). Artificial intelligence and internet of things enabled disease diagnosis model for smart healthcare systems. *IEEE Access*, 9, 45137–45146.

Memos, V. A., Psannis, K. E., Ishibashi, Y., Kim, B. G., & Gupta, B. B. (2018). An efficient algorithm for media-based surveillance system (EAMSuS) in IoT smart city framework. *Future Generation Computer Systems*, 83, 619–628.

Nhi, N. T. U., & Le, T. M. (2022). A model of semantic-based image retrieval using C-tree and neighbor graph. *International Journal on Semantic Web and Information Systems (IJSWIS)*, 18(1), 1–23.

Rahman, Z., Aamir, M., Pu, Y. F., Ullah, F., & Dai, Q. (2018). A smart system for low-light image enhancement with color constancy and detail manipulation in complex light environments. *Symmetry*, 10(12), 718.

Raj, A., & Prakash, S. (2022). A privacy-preserving authentic healthcare monitoring system using blockchain. *International Journal of Software Science and Computational Intelligence (IJSSCI)*, 14(1), 1–23.

Raj, M. G., & Pani, S. K. (2022). Chaotic whale crow optimization algorithm for secure routing in the IoT environment. *International Journal on Semantic Web and Information Systems (IJSWIS)*, 18(1), 1–25.

Reddy, K. T. (2023). A comprehensive examination of Bluetooth device vulnerabilities and countermeasures. *Next-Gen Tech Insights Magazine*, 1(01), 10–14. https://insights2techinfo.com/wp-content/uploads/2023/11/A-Comprehensive-Examination-of-Bluetooth-Device-Vulnerabilities-and-Countermeasures.pdf

Shafie, A. A., Ibrahim, A. B. M., & Rashid, M. M. (2014). Smart objects identification system for robotic surveillance. *International Journal of Automation and Computing*, 11, 59–71.

Shankar, K., Perumal, E., Elhoseny, M., Taher, F., Gupta, B. B., & El-Latif, A. A. A. (2021). Synergic deep learning for smart health diagnosis of COVID-19 for connected living and smart cities. *ACM Transactions on Internet Technology (TOIT)*, 22(3), 1–14.

Sri, M. R., Prakash, S., and Karuna, T. (2021). *Classification of Fungi Microscopic Images—Leveraging the Use of AI* (p. 1). Insights2Techinfo. https://insights2techinfo.com/classification-of-fungi-microscopic-images-leveraging-the-use-of-ai/

Srivastava, A. M., Rotte, P. A., Jain, A., & Prakash, S. (2022). Handling data scarcity through data augmentation in training of deep neural networks for 3D data processing. *International Journal on Semantic Web and Information Systems (IJSWIS)*, 18(1), 1–16.

Tian, S., Yang, W., Le Grange, J. M., Wang, P., Huang, W., & Ye, Z. (2019). Smart healthcare: Making medical care more intelligent. *Global Health Journal*, 3(3), 62–65.

Tripathi, A., Singh, A. K., Singh, A., Choudhary, A., Pareek, K., & Mishra, K. K. (2022). Analyzing skin disease using XCNN (eXtended convolutional neural network). *International Journal of Software Science and Computational Intelligence (IJSSCI)*, 14(1), 1–30.

Voronin, V., Semenishchev, E., Frants, V., & Agaian, S. (2018, September). Smart cloud system for forensic thermal image enhancement using local and global logarithmic transform histogram matching. In *2018 IEEE International Conference on Smart Cloud (SmartCloud)* (pp. 153–157). IEEE.

Wang, T., Yao, Y., Chen, Y., Zhang, M., Tao, F., & Snoussi, H. (2018). Auto-sorting system toward smart factory based on deep learning for image segmentation. *IEEE Sensors Journal*, 18(20), 8493–8501.

Wang, H., Li, Z., Li, Y., Gupta, B. B., & Choi, C. (2020). Visual saliency guided complex image retrieval. *Pattern Recognition Letters*, 130, 64–72.

Yu, C., Li, J., Li, X., Ren, X., & Gupta, B. B. (2018). Four-image encryption scheme based on quaternion Fresnel transform, chaos and computer generated hologram. *Multimedia Tools and Applications*, 77(4), 4585–4608.

Chapter 9

Deep Learning Model for Digital Forensics Face Sketch Synthesis

Eshita Badwa, Sunil K. Singh, Sudhakar Kumar, Ayushi, Vanshika Chilkoti, Varsha Arya, and Kwok Tai Chui

1. INTRODUCTION

In the realm of digital forensics, face sketch synthesis is a crucial tool for enhancing investigative processes. Acting as a visual bridge between textual descriptions or eyewitness accounts and tangible facial representations, this specialized technique aids law enforcement in the meticulous identification of suspects. The essence of face sketch synthesis lies in its ability to transform textual or verbal details into lifelike facial sketches, a process executed by forensic experts leveraging digital technology and artistic interpretation. This proves particularly valuable in cases where traditional methods face limitations. The accuracy of suspect identification is paramount in criminal investigations, and face sketch synthesis serves as a vital tool when concrete visual leads are imperative. Whether through the expertise of forensic artists or advanced software, law enforcement can generate facial sketches that offer a clearer profile of potential suspects, surpassing the constraints of conventional investigative avenues.

Additionally, deep learning models have surfaced as revolutionary solutions in the field of face sketch synthesis, capitalizing on their ability to extract and understand intricate patterns and representations from extensive datasets[1]. This transformative capacity stems from the fundamental architecture of deep learning, which involves neural networks with multiple layers, allowing them to discern complex features and relationships within the data[2]. In the realm of face sketch synthesis, the nuanced and intricate nature of facial features poses a unique challenge. Traditional methods often struggle to capture the subtleties required for realistic sketches. Deep learning models, however, excel in this domain by autonomously learning and extracting the intricate details that define facial characteristics. In the context of digital forensics, the fusion of deep learning and face sketch synthesis is particularly crucial for reconstructing suspect appearances based on eyewitness testimonies, aiding law enforcement agencies in solving crimes and improving suspect identification accuracy.

This chapter begins by introducing the background and significance of applying deep learning models to face sketch synthesis in digital forensics. The purpose of data augmentation in this context is then explored. The literature review section offers an overview of face sketch synthesis, delving into the role of deep learning and the importance of data augmentation. Existing data augmentation techniques for face sketch synthesis are also discussed. The subsequent section focuses on advanced data augmentation techniques, including geometric transformations, style transfer, image-to-image translation, generative adversarial networks (GANs), and variational autoencoders (VAEs). A dedicated portion of the chapter explores domain-specific data augmentation considerations[2] for forensic face sketch synthesis. This includes discussions on facial attribute modification, age progression and regression, as well as variations in emotion and expression. The chapter then shifts its attention to evaluation metrics and frameworks, outlining objective metrics for face sketch synthesis, subjective

DOI: 10.1201/9781003207573-9

evaluation methods, and cross-validation techniques. Case studies are presented in the following section, highlighting real-world applications of data augmentation in face sketch synthesis. Comparative studies between scenarios with and without data augmentation are also discussed.

Challenges and future directions form the core of the penultimate section, addressing limitations in current data augmentation techniques, ethical and privacy considerations, and potential avenues for future developments.

1.1 Background and Significance

The identification of individuals based on facial sketches poses a difficult endeavor. Footage from security cameras[3], which is frequently of low quality, fails to provide the necessary information desired by law enforcement authorities. Therefore, detectives enlist the aid of forensics artists or computer programs specialized in creating sketches of potential suspects during their investigations. However, the differences between photographs and sketches create even more difficulty for the technology for facial recognition set-up based on the sketches. Despite humans being quick at identifying faces, the process of comparing facial sketches to images of suspects takes considerable time and expertise, turning into mistakes if the process is not scaled accurately.

To address this important issue, there is a need for an automated system that can quickly and accurately compare facial sketches with suspect images. This system will depend on recent advances in information technology[4] and electronic components achieved by various researchers.

Fortunately, significant progress has been made in the field of information technology[5] and electronic components. These developments have contributed to the expansion of 5G IoT[6] systems, significantly enhancing the quality and efficiency of various urban and suburban services provided to the general public.

By capitalizing on these technological advancements[7], it is possible to create an automated facial sketch recognition system. This proposed system aims not only to improve the quality and efficiency of law enforcement and investigative processes but also to reduce the reliance on skilled professionals.

In conclusion, despite notable progress in information technology and electronic components, the domain of facial sketch recognition still necessitates the expertise of skilled professionals. However, with the development of an automated system, the efficiency and accuracy of facial sketch recognition can be greatly improved.

Digital forensics[8] plays a crucial role in the investigation of cybercrimes. Digital forensics involves the scientific collection, examination, and preservation of information stored in electronic devices, which can be presented as evidence in a legal proceeding.

This field, on the whole, encompasses the scientific gathering, analysis, and protection of electronic data stored in devices, which can be utilized as proof in a legal context.

To expand the training set, data augmentation[6] is employed as a method for generating additional copies of a dataset through the manipulation of existing data. This process involves making subtle alterations to the dataset or utilizing deep learning algorithms to produce novel data points.

Augmented data is driven from original data with some minor changes[9]. In the case of image augmentation, we make geometric and color space transformations (flipping, resizing, cropping, brightness, contrast) to increase the size and diversity of the training set.

Privacy concerns regarding data collection and usage are prevalent in today's world. Consequently, numerous researchers and companies are resorting to synthetic data generation methods to construct datasets. Nonetheless, augmented data is typically favored over synthetic data due to its ability to closely resemble the original data, which is a limitation of synthetic data.

Data augmentation techniques have been steadily gaining traction in recent years due to several compelling reasons. One key advantage is their ability to enhance the effectiveness of machine learning models by introducing greater diversity into datasets. These methods are extensively employed in a wide range of cutting-edge applications, including object detection, image classification, image recognition, natural language understanding, and semantic segmentation, among others. By generating fresh and varied instances for training datasets, augmented data is proving instrumental in improving the performance and outcomes of deep learning models.

1.2 Purpose of Data Augmentation in Face Sketch Synthesis

In practical scenarios, we may encounter a collection of images taken under specific circumstances. However, our intended application can take on various forms, including different orientations, positions, sizes, and levels of brightness. To address these variations, we can train deep neural networks using artificially manipulated data. By doing so, we enable these models, such as CNNs, to learn intricate distinguishing characteristics by extensively examining numerous examples. Hence, the performance of deep learning models depends on the type and size of the input dataset.

Data augmentation is a method to deal with the issue of limited data. In data augmentation, we opt to use a few techniques that artificially increase the amount of data from the existing data and address this problem.

The outcome of face-related tasks in deep learning heavily relies on the quality of the training set. The process of gathering and labeling sufficient samples with balanced distributions is a time-consuming effort. In the following, various augmentation techniques will be discussed, with a particular focus on those rooted in deep learning. While these techniques primarily pertain to facial recognition, they can be applied to other domains as well. Given the significant interest in the human face, extensive research has been conducted in this field.

2. LITERATURE REVIEW

2.1 Overview of Face Sketch Synthesis

Face recognition has been receiving a lot of attention lately due to its potential applications in law enforcement. One such application is the ability to assist law enforcement in identifying suspects. By automatically retrieving photos of suspects from police mug-shot databases, potential suspects can be narrowed down quickly[10]. However, there are cases where a photo image of a suspect is not available. In such situations, sketch drawings based on eyewitness recollection are often used as a substitute. The ability to search through photo databases using sketch drawings can be a very useful tool in these circumstances.

Not only does it aid law enforcement in pinpointing potential suspects, but it also facilitates collaboration between witnesses and artists for interactive modifications to sketch drawings based on retrieved similar photos. However, the considerable disparity between sketches and photos, coupled with the elusive psychological processes involved in sketch generation, makes face sketch recognition significantly more challenging than conventional face recognition based on photographic images. Despite three decades of research, there is a scarcity of effective face sketch recognition systems in prior studies. The crux of sketch-based face photo recognition lies in mitigating the disparities between these two modalities.

2.2 Deep Learning in Face Sketch Synthesis

Face sketch synthesis plays a pivotal role in the realm of face recognition, particularly within law enforcement applications. Presently, existing face sketch synthesis approaches generate sketches from photos based on models trained on specific databases, typically collected from individuals of the same ethnicity. Consequently, these sketches inherit distinct facial distributions in terms of shape and texture from the utilized database. This limitation renders such models unsuitable for real-world applications, which inherently involve diverse photo variations, including pose, lighting conditions, skin color, and ethnic origin.

A unified face sketch synthesis model addresses the aforementioned limitations by considering ethnicity issues and accommodating various photo variations. The proposed model employs a novel deep learning scheme designed to handle the generic visual representation and global structure of the face[11]. To achieve this, we leverage the recent success of deep residual blocks and incorporate them into a plain feedforward network, called DResNet. This network is specifically tailored to learn a regression model for face sketch synthesis.

To train the DResNet model, we utilize a heterogeneous database comprising photos with variations in lighting, ethnicity, hair, and skin characteristics. Through extensive subjective and objective evaluations, our results demonstrate the superiority of the proposed DResNet method over state-of-the-art face sketch synthesis methods. This is one such example showing how deep learning models can be used in face sketch synthesis.

Following the limitations of data-driven methods, model-driven approaches were subsequently introduced in the realm of face sketch synthesis to address the associated challenges. These methods establish an end-to-end relationship between the photo and sketch domains by conceptualizing it as a model. This model effectively learns the mapping from the photo domain to the sketch domain.

In contrast to their data-driven counterparts, model-driven methods streamline the process by directly predicting the target sketch based on the learned model. This eliminates the necessity to traverse the training database to obtain optimal candidate patches, thereby considerably reducing the synthesis processing time.

2.3 Role of Data Augmentation in Deep Learning

The role of data augmentation in deep learning is pivotal for enhancing model performance and generalization. In the context of training deep neural networks, having a diverse and extensive dataset is crucial for the model to learn robust features. Data augmentation entails applying various transformations to an existing dataset, including rotations, flips, zooms, and adjustments in brightness or contrast. This process artificially enlarges the dataset, allowing the model to familiarize itself with a broader spectrum of variations present in real-world data. The effectiveness of this approach lies in its capacity to reduce overfitting by encouraging more consistent pattern recognition. Moreover, data augmentation plays a crucial role in constructing a robust and adaptable model, enhancing its performance on new, unseen data by simulating diverse conditions it may encounter during inference. In essence, data augmentation stands as a foundational strategy in deep learning, facilitating model generalization and fortifying its capability to handle the complexities of the real world.

2.4 Existing Data Augmentation Techniques in the Industry for Face Sketch Synthesis

In the domain of synthesizing face sketches, employing data augmentation techniques is crucial in trying to improve the training dataset and bolster the effectiveness of deep learning models. Several data augmentation techniques suited for face sketch synthesis have been devised, including:

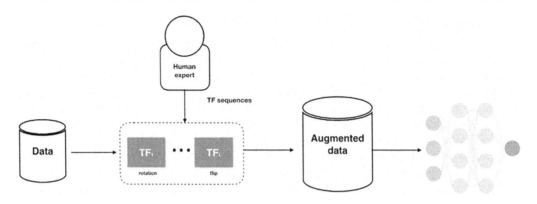

Figure 9.1 Data augmentation-block diagram[9]

2.4.1 Position Augmentation

To make deep learning models more adaptable and robust, data augmentation techniques[12] such as positional augmentation are deployed. Varied positional or locational differences are introduced in the input data, contributing to the enhancement of the model's adaptability[13] and overall flawlessness. In the domain of sketching human faces, positional augmentation can be implemented to add subtle changes to facial expressions' positions, head direction, and general facial outlines. This enhances the model's learning and fine-tuning in face recognition under differing conditions. Here are several specific positional augmentation techniques established for face sketching.

Some of the techniques are:

1. Translation: Move the facial diagram around within the image frame, either horizontally or vertically. By doing this, minor changes in the face's position can be replicated, allowing the model to become immune to these differences.
2. Rotation: Vary the angle that the face is sketched at during rotation. This ensures that the model can recognize and identify faces from various perspectives, which is essential for certain applications.
3. Scaling: Resize the face sketch to different scales. This can simulate variations in the distance of the face from the camera, helping the model generalize to faces of different sizes.
4. Shearing: Apply shearing transformations to the face sketch. Shearing distorts the shape of the image, introducing variations that can be useful for training a model to recognize faces with different facial structures.
5. Zooming: Zoom in or out on the face sketch. This helps the model become invariant to variations in the distance between the camera and the subject.
6. Flipping: Flip the face sketch horizontally or vertically. This introduces mirror images and helps the model become invariant to left-right or up-down orientations.

When introducing positional changes, it's crucial to maintain the facial meaning intact. Simply flipping the face orientation without updating the associated labels accordingly can lead to labeling issues. In application, data augmentation[14] libraries in commonly used deep learning frameworks like PyTorch and TensorFlow make this process simpler. These libraries come with helpful transformations functions that work on image data during the training phase. Figure 9.2 shows an example of positional argumentation.

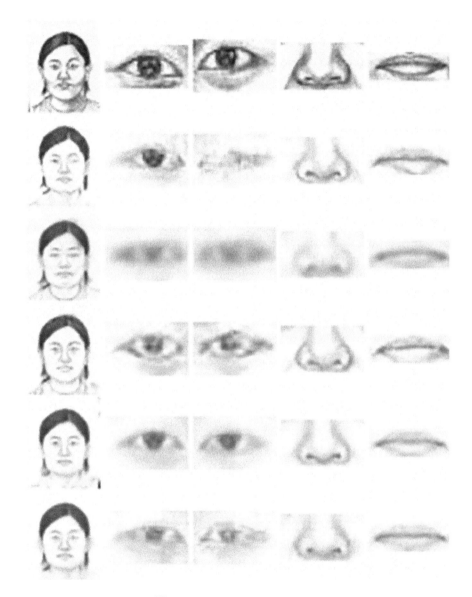

Figure 9.2 Position augmentation[15]

2.4.2 Color Augmentation

Color augmentation is another powerful technique used in deep learning to increase the diversity of training data and improve the robustness of models. In the context of face sketching, applying color augmentations can introduce variations in lighting conditions, skin tones, and other color-related factors. Here are some color augmentation techniques that are considered for face sketching:

1. Brightness Adjustment: Modify the face sketch's overall brightness. This can help the model become invariant to variations in illumination by simulating various lighting conditions.

2. Contrast Adjustment: Adjust the face sketch's contrast. By simulating changes in lighting intensity, this can strengthen the model's resistance to various lighting conditions.
3. Saturation Adjustment: Modify the facial sketch's color saturation. This can mimic variations in the skin tones and overall richness of color in the pictures.
4. Hue Adjustment: Modify the color tones in the face drawing. This can replicate changes in skin tones and lighting.
5. Color Jittering: Make sporadic, tiny changes to the color values. This may result in minute adjustments to the facial sketch's appearance, strengthening the model's capacity for generalization.
6. Grayscale Conversion: Create a grayscale version of the face sketch. In cases where the color of the sketch is not critical to the task, this can help the model become invariant to color information and concentrate on other salient features.

It is crucial to make sure that the semantic content of the face is maintained when implementing color augmentations. For example, you wouldn't want to alter the skin tone in a way that would make the person's underlying identity in the face sketch appear false.

OpenCV and other image augmentation libraries, as well as deep learning frameworks like TensorFlow and PyTorch, can be used to implement color augmentations. During the training phase, these libraries frequently offer functions for modifying saturation, brightness, contrast, and other color-related parameters. To make sure that the augmented data is still representative of the real-world variations the model might encounter, you should also carefully select the range and magnitude of the color augmentations[16]. Figure 9.3 shows how it is implemented.

Cutting-edge methods for augmenting data have become indispensable for improving deep learning models' performance and capacity for generalization. These advanced techniques go beyond conventional augmentations like rotations and flips in an effort to produce training

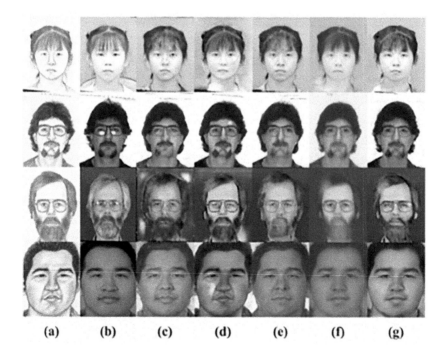

(a)   (b)   (c)   (d)   (e)   (f)   (g)

Figure 9.3 Color augmentations[17]

datasets that are more realistic and diverse. Among these methods is CutMix, which encourages the model to learn from a variety of contextual data by swapping out a portion of one image for another. Another cutting-edge method, called MixUp, combines two images with the labels that go with them to reduce overfitting and encourage smoother decision boundaries. Furthermore, by modifying domain-specific elements like background and lighting, Domain Randomization adds variability and makes it easier to adapt to a variety of real-world scenarios. Furthermore, synthetic data is produced by Generative Adversarial Networks (GANs), which enhances the dataset by adding authentic samples. These advanced techniques collectively contribute to robust model training, enabling deep learning models to excel in tasks that demand adaptability to diverse and complex real-world scenarios. Let us take a closer look at some of these techniques.

3. ADVANCED DATA AUGMENTATION TECHNIQUES

3.1 Geometric Transformations

Geometric transformations[16] play a crucial role in deep learning for tasks such as face sketch synthesis, where generating realistic and diverse samples is essential. Geometric transformations[18] involve changes in the spatial structure and arrangement of elements in an image. Here are some geometric transformations relevant to face sketch synthesis:

1. Affine Transformations:
   - Translation: Move the face sketch horizontally or vertically. This can simulate variations in head position within the image.
   - Rotation: Rotate the face sketch at different angles. This is particularly useful for generating sketches with varying head orientations.
   - Scaling: Resize the face sketch to different scales. This can simulate variations in the size of facial features.

2. Perspective Transformations: Simulate the effect of perspective changes, as if the face sketch is viewed from different distances or angles.
3. Elastic Transformations: Introduce local deformations to simulate small variations in facial structure. Elastic transformations can help generate more realistic and diverse face sketches.[19]
4. Projection Transformations: Simulate changes in the viewpoint of the observer. This is particularly relevant for face sketch synthesis, where variations in lighting conditions and angles are crucial.
5. Shearing: Apply shearing transformations to the face sketch. This can simulate distortions in facial features, contributing to the diversity of synthesized sketches.

Any distortions caused by translations or rotations should not lose important characteristics of facial features that may result in a wrong representation. Several tools can help with implementing these transformations, such as OpenCV or image augmentation libraries provided by deep learning frameworks including TensorFlow and PyTorch. Incorporating these transformations into the data augmentation pipeline that is used in training your facial sketch synthesis model is another consideration to keep in mind. However, it is vital to strike a balance between variability and maintaining coherence of the synthesized face sketches when implementing these techniques. Ultimately, exposing the model to varying inputs while maintaining a resemblance to real-life facial sketches is a crucial goal to aim for.

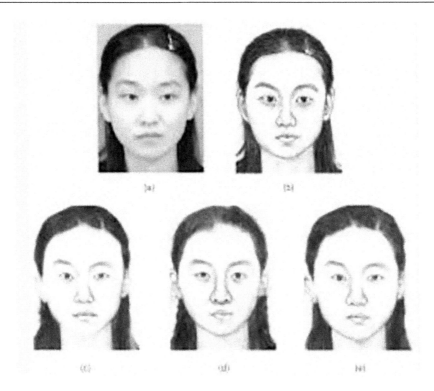

Figure 9.4 Geometric transformations[20]

3.2 Style Transfer and Image-to-Image Translation

Style transfer[21] and image-to-image translation are innovative applications of deep learning that leverage data augmentation techniques to generate visually appealing and contextually relevant outputs.

I. Style Transfer: Style transfer is the transformation of an image's visual style while preserving its content. This process utilizes deep neural networks, specifically convolutional neural networks (CNNs), which are trained to differentiate and recombine content and style features. The resulting adaptations enable an image's style to resemble that of another, yielding visually captivating results. While known for its creative applications, style transfer also serves practical purposes, enhancing images for various uses.

II. Image-to-Image Translation: Image-to-image translation, facilitated by models like conditional GANs and U-Net architectures, entails converting an input image from one domain to another, inducing changes in appearance or style. This process finds application in various scenarios, such as translating satellite images to maps, transforming black and white photos into colored versions, or altering day scenes to night scenes.

III. Data Augmentation in Style Transfer[6] and Image-to-Image Translation: Data augmentation is integral to training models for tasks like style transfer and image-to-image translation. It enhances model robustness by introducing diverse variations in the training data, allowing the models to handle a wide range of input styles and conditions effectively. Augmentation techniques, such as geometric transformations, color manipulations, and the introduction of noise, contribute to the model's ability to generalize beyond the specific characteristics of the training dataset.

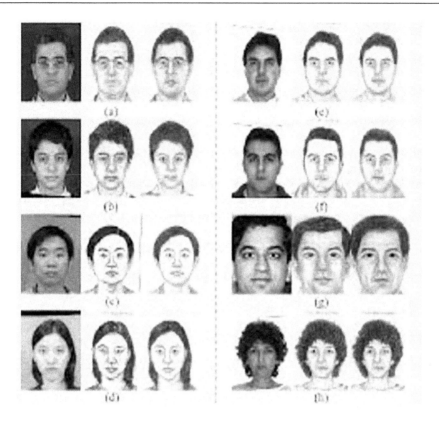

Figure 9.5 Style transfer[22]

Additionally, incorporating domain-specific data augmentation strategies is vital. For instance, in satellite-to-map translation, variations in lighting conditions, weather patterns, and seasonal changes can be simulated to enhance the model's adaptability to real-world scenarios. These techniques collectively contribute to the success of style transfer and image-to-image translation models by enabling them to generate realistic and diverse outputs, even in situations not explicitly encountered during training. As a result, these applications have found utility in creative fields, design, and numerous practical domains where transforming and translating visual content is valuable.

3.3 Generative Adversarial Networks (GANs) for Data Augmentation

Generative Adversarial Networks (GANs) have proven to be a powerful tool for data augmentation in various machine learning tasks, including image generation, style transfer, and image-to-image translation. When applied to data augmentation, GANs create synthetic data samples that are indistinguishable from the original training data, effectively expanding the dataset and improving the model's generalization. Here's how GANs are employed for data augmentation:

I. Training GANs: GANs consist of two neural networks: a generator and a discriminator. The generator creates synthetic samples, and the discriminator evaluates whether a given sample is real or generated. The two networks are simultaneously trained in a competitive manner, resulting in the generator producing increasingly realistic samples.

II. Generating Synthetic Data: Once trained, the generator of a GAN can be used to produce synthetic data that closely resembles the original training samples. This is particularly beneficial when the size of the original dataset is limited or when specific classes or scenarios are underrepresented.

III. Improving Model Robustness: GAN-based data augmentation contributes to the robustness of machine learning models. By exposing the model to a broader range of variations present in both real and synthetic data, GANs help prevent overfitting and improve the model's performance on unseen data.

IV. Domain Adaptation: GANs are valuable for domain adaptation tasks, where the model needs to generalize well to data from a new distribution. By generating synthetic samples that capture the characteristics of the target domain, GANs aid in training models that can adapt more effectively to diverse real-world conditions.

V. Class Imbalance Correction: In datasets with imbalances among classes, GANs can be used to generate additional samples for underrepresented classes, addressing class imbalances and improving the model's ability to recognize minority classes.

VI. Style and Augmentation Consistency: GANs allow for consistent stylization and augmentation of data. For example, in image recognition tasks, GANs can be trained to generate images with varying lighting conditions, poses, or styles, ensuring that the model becomes invariant to these factors during training.

VII. Data Privacy: GANs provide a way to generate synthetic data that preserves the statistical properties of the original dataset without compromising sensitive information. This is particularly relevant in scenarios where privacy concerns limit the sharing of real data.

Where GANs do offer significant benefits for data augmentation, it's important that we carefully validate the quality of the samples generated and monitor for any biases that may have been introduced during the training process. Proper tuning of GAN hyperparameters and regularizing techniques is essential to ensure that the generated data effectively enhances the model's performance without introducing artifacts or biases.[23] Figure 9.6 gives us a representation of the GANs working.

3.4 Variational Autoencoders (VAEs) for Data Augmentation

Variational Autoencoders (VAEs)[21] are another class of generative models that can be effectively used for data augmentation in machine learning tasks. VAEs are designed to learn a probabilistic representation of the input data and generate new samples from that distribution. Here's how VAEs are employed for data augmentation:

I. Probabilistic Representation: VAEs encode input data into a latent space where each point represents a probabilistic distribution rather than a deterministic point. This probabilistic encoding allows for the generation of diverse samples by sampling from the learned distributions.

II. Latent Space Interpolation: One of the strengths of VAEs lies in their ability to smoothly interpolate between points in the latent space. By interpolating between representations of real data samples, VAEs can generate synthetic samples that exhibit gradual transitions in appearance or style, contributing to realistic data augmentation.

III. Sample Generation: VAEs can generate new samples by sampling points from the latent space and decoding them back into the data space. This process leads to the production of novel samples that share similarities with the original data, effectively augmenting the dataset.

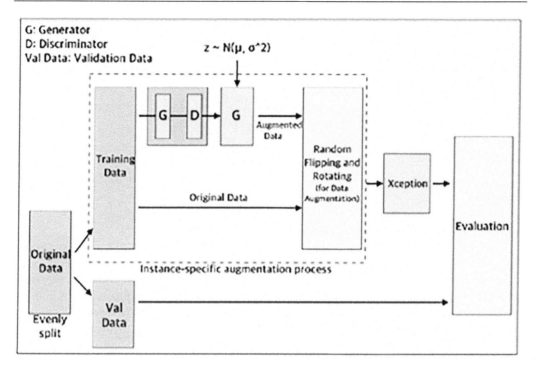

Figure 9.6 Generative adversarial networks (GANs)[23]

IV. Uncertainty Estimation: VAEs tend to naturally capture uncertainty in the data. While generating samples, VAEs provide information about the uncertainty of each generated sample, hence helping in tasks where understanding the model's confidence is crucial.

V. Handling Imbalanced Datasets: VAEs can be particularly beneficial when managing imbalanced datasets. By generating synthetic samples for classes with less representation, VAEs can help in addressing class imbalances and improving the model's ability to recognize minority classes.

VI. Data Generation with Constraints: VAEs can be conditioned to certain attributes or constraints during the process of generation. This allows for the generation of samples that are coherent with the specific characteristics required, and hence suitable for tasks like style-preserving data augmentation.

VII. Semi-Supervised Learning: VAEs can also be extended to semi-supervised learning scenarios, where labeled and unlabeled data are combined. By means of the generative capabilities of VAEs, additional samples can be generated to augment the labeled dataset, ultimately improving the model's performance.

VIII. Domain Adaptation: Quite similar to GANs, these can contribute to domain adaptation by generating samples that can bridge the gap between different domains. This helps in training models that generalize well to data from diverse distributions.

Like GANs, the successful application of VAEs for data augmentation requires careful consideration of hyperparameters and monitoring for potential biases. VAEs offer a probabilistic and smooth generative approach, making them particularly suitable for tasks where a continuous, interpretable latent space and uncertainty estimation are valuable features. Figure 9.7 shows a diagram of VAEs.

In conclusion, advanced data augmentation techniques have emerged as indispensable tools in the realm of machine learning, significantly elevating the robustness and performance

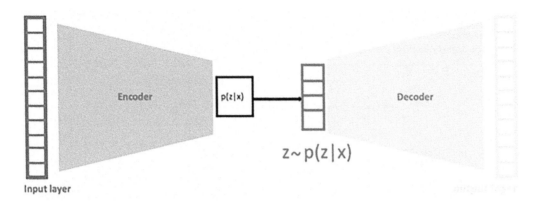

Input layer

Figure 9.7 Variational autoencoders (VAEs)[21]

of models. Geometric transformations, such as rotations, scaling, and flips, lay the foundation by introducing spatial variations to augment datasets, enhancing a model's ability to generalize across different orientations. Concurrently, Generative Adversarial Networks (GANs) stand out as powerful engines for synthetic data generation, creating samples that closely mimic the intricate patterns of the original data. GANs, with their adversarial training paradigm, excel in producing diverse, realistic data, effectively addressing challenges related to dataset size and class imbalance.

On a parallel front, Variational Autoencoders (VAEs) offer a probabilistic approach to data augmentation by capturing uncertainty in the latent space. VAEs enable the generation of diverse samples through latent space interpolation, providing smooth transitions between representations and offering valuable insights into model confidence. Both GANs and VAEs contribute significantly to tasks involving style transfer, image-to-image translation, and domain adaptation, showcasing their versatility in handling complex real-world scenarios.

These advanced techniques, when strategically combined, create a synergy that empowers models with a profound understanding of spatial relationships, intricate patterns, and the generation of synthetic data. As machine learning continues to advance, the incorporation of geometric transformations, GANs, and VAEs in data augmentation becomes increasingly pivotal. These techniques collectively propel the field toward more resilient models capable of navigating the intricacies of diverse datasets and real-world challenges. Ultimately, the fusion of geometric transformations and generative models heralds a new era in data augmentation, providing models with the depth and adaptability needed to excel in an ever-expanding array of applications.

Improving data augmentation is an effective method to increase the broader applicability of deep learning models. However, the underlying augmentation methods primarily rely on manual chores like image data flipping and cropping. These augmentation methods are often developed by human experience or trial and error. Because it treats data augmentation as a learning job and chooses the best method to improve the data, automated data augmentation, or AutoDA, is a promising field for future research. In this survey, we classify the state-of-the-art AutoDA techniques into three categories: generation-, mixing-, and composition-based strategies. After that, we examine each topic in more detail. We discuss the problems and possible fixes in light of the analysis, and we provide suggestions for applying AutoDA techniques by considering the dataset, computational effort, and accessibility to changes that are domain-specific. In the hopes of helping data partitioners when using AutoDA in real-world scenarios, this chapter aims to offer a helpful list of AutoDA techniques

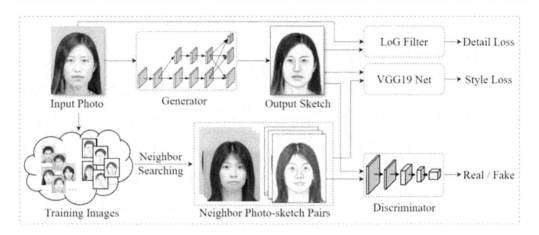

Figure 9.8 Use of the techniques in face sketch synthesis[24]

and recommendations. In this developing field of research, the survey can potentially be used as a reference by researchers.

4. DOMAIN-SPECIFIC DATA AUGMENTATION

Domain-specific data augmentation is a pivotal component in the development of deep learning models for forensic face sketch synthesis[25]. In this specialized field, the availability of comprehensive and diverse training data is essential to enhance the model's accuracy and generalization capabilities. Domain-specific data augmentation techniques are tailored to the unique requirements of the task, considering factors such as variations in lighting conditions, perspectives, and the inherent noise associated with forensic sketches. By intelligently augmenting the training data, these techniques can simulate real-world scenarios that forensic artists encounter, providing the deep learning model with the necessary exposure to the complexities of forensic sketch generation. This approach not only enables the model to generate more reliable and faithful sketches but also enhances its adaptability to the challenging and dynamic nature of digital forensics. Domain-specific data augmentation, therefore, plays a vital role in ensuring that the deep learning model performs optimally in the context of forensic face sketch synthesis.

There are lots of ways to identify people in sketches that people have seen, but they don't always work when you're using real-world sketches and galleries that look like police mugshots. Deep learning has been used for face recognition in a lot of different applications, but it hasn't been used for sketch recognition yet. This is because there aren't enough sketch images to train big networks. This chapter aims to fix this problem by using transfer learning to tune a pre-trained model for face photo recognition, a 3D morphable model to synthesize new images and expand the training data so the network can learn better features, multiple synthetic sketches in the testing stage, and a combination of the proposed method and the best algorithm to make it even better. A broad assessment of a few famous and cutting-edge calculations is likewise performed utilizing freely accessible datasets, in this manner filling in as a benchmark for future calculations. Contrasted with a main strategy, the proposed system is displayed to decrease the blunder rate by 80.7% for viewed sketches and bring down the mean recovery rank by 32.5% for real-world measurable representations.

4.1 Considerations for Forensic Face Sketch Synthesis

In the realm of forensic face sketch synthesis, specialized considerations play a pivotal role in the accuracy and reliability of generated sketches. Unlike generic face generation tasks, forensic applications require a heightened attention to detail and adherence to the subtle cues that can make or break an investigation. Achieving accuracy and precision is paramount in forensic face sketch synthesis, where sketches play a vital role in identifying potential suspects or missing persons. Various factors, including witness descriptions, environmental conditions, and the emotional state of the witness, significantly influence sketch quality. Therefore, a deep learning model for this purpose must be meticulously fine-tuned to consider these unique aspects. The objective is to ensure that the resulting sketches not only exhibit visual accuracy but also align closely with details provided by eyewitness accounts. This meticulous approach is essential in the pursuit of justice and safeguarding innocent individuals from wrongful accusations[26].

4.2 Facial Attribute Modification

The ability to alter facial attributes is one of the intriguing uses of deep learning in the context of forensic face sketch synthesis. Investigators can refine and improve the features that might be most relevant to a particular case with this capability. For example, changing features on a suspect's sketch, like facial hair, scars, or eyeglasses, could make the sketch more consistent with a witness's memory, which would increase the likelihood of identifying the person. Additionally, altering facial features can help create variants for various sketches of a suspect, enabling law enforcement to investigate and consider alternative scenarios. It is an invaluable tool in the toolbox of forensic artists and law enforcement organizations because these attributes are easily adjustable.

4.3 Age Progression and Regression

In forensic face sketch synthesis, age progression and regression play a crucial role in identifying individuals who are missing or fugitives. It is possible to predict and illustrate how a person's face might change over time by using deep learning models with generative capabilities. Age regression helps depict the potential youthful appearance of an older suspect, while age progression helps investigators envision how a missing person might appear years after their disappearance. These methods are very helpful in long-term investigations and cold cases because they give insight into possible changes that a person may have experienced over time. Law enforcement organizations can greatly benefit from the ability to faithfully replicate these changes in their efforts to uphold the law.

Age progression and regression are important aspects in the field of forensic face sketch synthesis that are vital to the resolution of missing persons and runaway identification problems. These methods allow for the prediction and representation of changes in facial features over time by utilizing the sophisticated capabilities of generative architectures in conjunction with deep learning models. The visualization of a missing person's potential facial feature evolution years after their disappearance is made easier by age progression. Simultaneously, age regression contributes by suggesting that an elderly suspect might look younger, which helps investigators compile a detailed timeline of possible changes.

Accurately simulating and visualizing these changes represents a technological advance in forensic techniques. It is an effective tool for law enforcement because it gives important information about possible long-term changes that an individual may have undergone.

Investigators' capacity to reconstruct facial features over time is greatly improved by this tactical use of deep learning in age progression and regression, which eventually advances the quest for justice in intricate and protracted cases.

In this context, the technical strength of deep learning models is their ability to gradually learn complex patterns and correlations within facial structures. These models can produce extremely realistic and contextually relevant facial representations by picking up on minute details in aging trajectories, which improves the precision and dependability of forensic face sketch synthesis. Moreover, the incorporation of sophisticated algorithms facilitates the adjustment of age progression and regression models to a range of datasets, guaranteeing resilient performance in a variety of forensic contexts and augmenting the adaptability of these approaches in practical uses.

To sum up, the forensic toolkit is incomplete without age progression and regression, which are facilitated by deep learning models. The ability to accurately anticipate changes in facial features over time gives law enforcement a significant advantage in solving unsolved cases and clarifying the dynamic nature of facial features, which in turn helps the pursuit of justice more precisely and effectively.

4.4 Emotion and Expression Variations

The complex features of human faces, such as emotions and expressions, add depth to the forensic face sketch synthesis process when they are included. While identifying suspects, investigators can consider a variety of scenarios thanks to the ability of deep learning models to generate sketches that reflect a range of emotions and expressions. These variants offer a broader perspective on a suspect's potential looks and aid in ensuring that the sketches produced correspond with eyewitness accounts, which frequently contain emotional states. The capacity to depict emotions through synthesized sketches, be it intense anger, a furrowed brow, or a subtle smile, is invaluable in forensic investigations. This degree of information can help reduce the number of possible suspects and increase the precision of identifications, which will ultimately help with the resolution of criminal cases.

The subtle integration of expressions and emotions becomes a new technical frontier in the complex field of forensic face sketch synthesis, adding to the process' complexity and depth. With careful training, deep learning models—which are renowned for their amazing ability to recognize intricate patterns—can produce sketches that capture a wide variety of expressions and emotions. This tactical enhancement greatly increases the adaptability and efficiency of the forensic procedure by enabling investigators to investigate a wide range of scenarios while identifying suspects[27].

In practical terms, this advanced capability in emotion and expression synthesis serves as a powerful aid in forensic investigations. The ability to represent a suspect's emotions through synthesized sketches significantly enriches the pool of visual information available to investigators. This heightened level of detail proves invaluable in narrowing down potential suspects, enhancing the accuracy of identifications, and ultimately contributing to the expeditious resolution of criminal cases.

In conclusion, the technical prowess demonstrated in the integration of emotion and expression variations within forensic face sketch synthesis underscores the evolving landscape of deep learning applications in digital forensics. By delving into the intricacies of human emotional expressions, these models extend the boundaries of traditional forensic sketching, presenting a paradigm shift in the field's capabilities and contributing to the continual advancement of forensic methodologies.

5. EVALUATION METRICS AND FRAMEWORKS

Evaluation metrics and frameworks are crucial components in assessing the performance and effectiveness of deep learning models for face sketch synthesis. The aforementioned metrics function as numerical assessments to evaluate the precision, authenticity, and general caliber of the combined illustrations. Structural integrity, pixel-level similarity, and feature correspondence between the synthesized and ground truth sketches are just a few of the aspects that can be measured using objective evaluation metrics, which offer a regular and computational method. Comparatively, subjective evaluation techniques rely on human judgment and perception to assess the generated sketches' level of realism and visual quality. A thorough grasp of the model's capabilities and limitations can be attained by researchers by integrating objective and subjective evaluation techniques. Making sure that the performance of the face sketch synthesis model is robustly and reliably assessed requires careful consideration of evaluation metrics and frameworks.

5.1 Objective Metrics for Face Sketch Synthesis

In order to measure the precision and accuracy of face sketch synthesis models, objective criteria are essential. Through comparison with reference photos or ground truth sketches, these metrics offer a methodical and quantitative assessment of the synthesized sketches. Peak Signal-to-Noise Ratio (PSNR), Mean Squared Error (MSE), and Structural Similarity Index (SSI) are examples of common objective measures. PSNR and MSE quantify the pixel-by-pixel discrepancies between the generated and ground truth images, while SSI evaluates the structural similarity between them. A more thorough evaluation is frequently obtained by combining different objective metrics, the selection of which is contingent upon the particular demands of the face sketch synthesis process. A consistent and repeatable evaluation procedure is ensured using objective measures, which add to the model's dependability.

Comparative Analysis: Measures of Image Quality

Image quality needs to be measured to compare restoration outcomes. The Mean-Squared Error and the Peak Signal-to-Noise Ratio are two frequently used metrics. The mean-squared error (MSE) between two images g(x,y) and g'(x,y) is:

$$e_{MSE} = \frac{1}{MN}\sum_{n=1}^{M}\sum_{m=1}^{N}[\hat{g}\,(n,m) - g(n,m)]^2 \qquad \text{eq(1)}^{[8]}$$

This issue is avoided by Peak Signal-to-Noise Ratio (PSNR), which scales the MSE based on the image range:

$$PSNR = -10log_{10}\frac{e_{MSE}}{S^2} \qquad \text{eq(2)}^{[8]}$$

where S is the maximum pixel value. PSNR is measured in decibels (dB).

5.2 Subjective Evaluation Methods

The visual quality and realism of the synthesized face sketches are evaluated using subjective evaluation techniques, which rely on human vision and judgment. Human evaluators provide qualitative comments on aspects like overall similarity, interpretability, and correctness of face features. These evaluators are frequently forensic art professionals or people

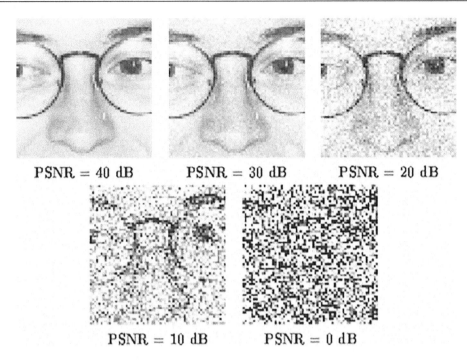

Figure 9.9 Illustration of the PSNR measure[8]

with relevant experience. Subjective evaluations pick up on subtleties that objective measures might miss, providing a window into the created sketches' perceptual elements. The most common methods for conducting these assessments are user studies or surveys, in which the assessors share their thoughts and preferences. This strategy, though more subjective by nature, works in tandem with objective data to provide a more comprehensive picture of the model's performance and its usefulness in actual forensic circumstances.

5.3 Cross-Validation Techniques

Face sketch synthesis models are evaluated for generality and robustness using cross-validation techniques. By dividing the available data into several subsets for testing and training, these strategies ensure that the model's performance is assessed on a variety of samples. Common cross-validation techniques include leave-one-out cross-validation, in which every data point acts as a test set alternately, and k-fold cross-validation, in which the data is split into k subsets and the model is trained and tested k times. In addition to reducing overfitting, cross-validation yields a more precise estimation of the model's performance on hypothetical data. Researchers can learn more about the stability and efficacy of the model in a variety of settings by methodically validating it across diverse subsets. This enhances the model's dependability in real-world forensic applications.

6. CASE STUDIES

Case studies provide compelling examples of the real-world uses and effects of data augmentation in face sketch synthesis. These studies, which explore real-world settings, offer important insights into the ways in which data augmentation techniques, when combined with deep learning models, enhance the area of digital forensics. A notable instance is the identification of a suspect who was identified successfully based on a facial sketch created from a restricted eyewitness account. Domain-specific data augmentation was a crucial component in improving the resulting sketch's realism and accuracy, which helped law enforcement capture the offender. These case studies demonstrate the concrete advantages of using data augmentation in forensic face sketch synthesis, demonstrating how it may transform investigative procedures and improve the credibility of suspect identifications[28].

6.1 Real-World Applications of Data Augmentation in Face Sketch Synthesis

Real-world applications of data augmentation in face sketch synthesis are emblematic of the transformative impact these techniques can have in forensic investigations. Consider a scenario where a surveillance camera captures a blurred image of a potential suspect. Through the integration of data augmentation methods such as image rotation, scaling, and contrast adjustment, the deep learning model can enhance the clarity and fidelity of the suspect's facial features. This augmentation not only aids forensic artists in creating more accurate sketches but also significantly improves the chances of matching the generated sketch to an existing database of known individuals. Moreover, in cases involving incomplete witness descriptions, data augmentation techniques can help extrapolate missing facial details, providing investigators with a more comprehensive and usable sketch. These real-world applications underscore the practical importance of data augmentation in elevating the efficacy of face sketch synthesis within the realm of digital forensics.

The practical instantiation of data augmentation in face sketch synthesis within real-world forensic applications stands as a testament to the transformative potential these techniques wield in the field of digital forensics. Delving into the technical intricacies of these applications illuminates the profound impact of data augmentation methodologies in enhancing the efficacy of forensic investigations.

Consider the scenario wherein a surveillance camera captures a blurred image of a potential suspect, presenting a classic challenge in forensic face sketch synthesis. The integration of advanced data augmentation methods becomes instrumental in surmounting this obstacle. Techniques such as image rotation, scaling, and contrast adjustment are systematically applied by the deep learning model to rectify the blurred features and enhance the clarity and fidelity of the suspect's facial attributes. The technical finesse within these augmentation methods lies in their capacity to introduce variations, mimicking different viewing perspectives and lighting conditions commonly encountered in real-world forensic scenarios.

The augmentation not only serves to refine the accuracy of sketches but also plays a pivotal role in improving the matching accuracy against existing databases of known individuals. By systematically augmenting the data, the model equips itself with a more comprehensive understanding of potential facial variations, thereby bolstering the chances of successfully identifying the suspect. This application becomes particularly potent when faced with challenges posed by blurred or incomplete facial imagery[29].

Furthermore, in instances where witness descriptions are incomplete, data augmentation emerges as a critical tool in extrapolating missing facial details. By intelligently varying facial attributes through augmentation, the model generates sketches that encapsulate a broader spectrum of potential appearances, aiding investigators in creating a more comprehensive and usable sketch. The technical dexterity lies in the model's ability to extrapolate missing information without compromising the fidelity or realism of the synthesized sketch.

In essence, these real-world applications underscore the pragmatic significance of data augmentation in the realm of forensic face sketch synthesis. The technical precision within these methodologies not only elevates the accuracy of individual sketches but also contributes significantly to the overarching goal of matching and identifying suspects in the complex and dynamic landscape of digital forensics. The fusion of advanced data augmentation with deep learning models serves as a cornerstone in the evolution of forensic methodologies, offering unparalleled capabilities to forensic artists and investigators alike[30].

6.2 Comparative Studies: Leveraging Data Augmentation in Forensic Face Sketch Synthesis

In the pursuit of refining the efficacy of forensic face sketch synthesis models, rigorous comparative studies serve as a technical crucible, shedding light on the pivotal role of data augmentation in enhancing performance and adaptability. This nuanced exploration into the comparative landscape dissects the technical intricacies underpinning the integration of data augmentation, unraveling its transformative impact on model robustness[31].

When deep learning models are subjected to training without the augmentation paradigm, a potential compromise in their ability to generalize across diverse and dynamic forensic scenarios becomes evident. The absence of augmentation limits the model's exposure to variations in lighting conditions, perspectives, and facial features, hindering its capacity to navigate the multifaceted challenges inherent in forensic investigations.

In stark contrast, models fortified with data augmentation emerge as stalwarts in the face of these challenges, exhibiting superior performance metrics that underscore heightened robustness and adaptability. The technical underpinning of this phenomenon lies in the model's enriched training dataset, imbued with artificially diversified samples through augmentation techniques. This comprehensive exposure equips the model with a broader understanding of the intricate nuances within forensic scenarios, enabling it to navigate the complexities with finesse.

A poignant illustration of the efficacy of data augmentation unfolds in a comparative study involving the synthesis of facial sketches from particularly challenging witness descriptions. In this arena, the model leveraging data augmentation consistently outshines its unaugmented counterpart in terms of both accuracy and visual fidelity. The augmentation-enhanced model adeptly maneuvers through the intricacies posed by incomplete or ambiguous descriptions, yielding sketches that more faithfully encapsulate the features described by witnesses.

These empirical findings substantiate the foundational claim that data augmentation serves as a catalyst for catapulting the performance of face sketch synthesis models to new heights. The technical narrative woven through these comparative studies underscores the indispensable nature of data augmentation as a standard practice in the development of advanced forensic face sketch synthesis models. The amalgamation of empirical evidence and technical rationale forms a robust argument in favor of embracing data augmentation as an integral facet of the model development process, ensuring that these models not only meet but exceed the demanding standards set by the dynamic landscape of forensic investigations.

Comparative studies that juxtapose the performance of face sketch synthesis models with and without data augmentation yield valuable insights into the tangible benefits of these techniques. When a deep learning model is trained without augmentation, its ability to generalize across diverse and dynamic forensic scenarios may be compromised. In contrast, models enriched with data augmentation exhibit superior performance, demonstrating increased robustness and adaptability. For instance, in a comparative study involving the synthesis of facial sketches from challenging witness descriptions, the model employing data augmentation consistently outperformed its unaugmented counterpart in terms of accuracy and visual fidelity. These findings substantiate the claim that data augmentation serves as a catalyst for improved model performance, ensuring that face sketch synthesis models are better equipped to handle the complexities inherent in forensic investigations. Such comparative studies provide empirical evidence supporting the integration of data augmentation as a standard practice in the development of advanced forensic face sketch synthesis models.

Ethical and Societal Implications: Bridging Digital Forensics Innovations With Sustainable Development Goals

The connection between digital forensics and sustainable development within the context of a Deep Learning Model for Face Sketch Synthesis lies in the broader societal impact and ethical considerations associated with technology development and application[32]. Here are several points of connection:

I. **Ethical Use of Technology:** Sustainable development emphasizes the ethical use of technology for societal benefit. In the realm of digital forensics, the responsible and ethical application of deep learning models ensures that the technology contributes positively to justice and public safety.

II. **Reducing Unjust Accusations and Enhancing Justice:** A well-developed face sketch synthesis model, when applied ethically in digital forensics, can contribute to reducing unjust accusations and enhancing justice. By providing law enforcement with accurate and reliable tools for suspect identification, the technology supports a fair and just legal system, aligning with principles of sustainable development.

III. **Human Rights and Privacy Considerations:** Sustainable development places a strong emphasis on protecting human rights and privacy. In the context of digital forensics, it is crucial to ensure that the use of face sketch synthesis models respects individual privacy rights and is conducted within the bounds of legal and ethical frameworks[33].

IV. **Collaboration and Knowledge Sharing:** Sustainable development encourages collaboration and knowledge sharing for the greater good. In the development and application of deep learning models for digital forensics, collaboration between technologists, legal experts, and policymakers is vital to ensure responsible use, avoiding negative societal impacts.

V. **Environmental Impact of Technology Development:** While not directly related to face sketch synthesis, sustainable development also considers the environmental impact of technology. It is important to approach the development of deep learning models with considerations for energy efficiency and environmental sustainability, promoting the responsible use of computational resources[34].

VI. **Addressing Bias and Inequality:** Sustainable development goals include reducing inequalities. In the context of face sketch synthesis, it's crucial to address potential biases in the model's training data and algorithms to ensure fair and unbiased results, contributing to societal equity.

VII. **Public Trust and Acceptance:** Sustainable development requires technologies that are accepted and trusted by the public. Ensuring transparency in the development and deployment of face sketch synthesis models, along with public education about their ethical use, fosters trust and aligns with sustainable development principles[35].

By aligning the development and application of deep learning models in digital forensics with principles of ethical use, privacy protection, collaboration, and societal well-being, the technology can contribute positively to sustainable development goals. It is essential to approach these advancements with a holistic perspective that considers not only technological innovation but also its broader societal implications.

7. CHALLENGES AND FUTURE DIRECTIONS

7.1 Limitations of Current Data Augmentation Techniques

While data augmentation has been proven to be a pivotal strategy in enhancing the robustness and generalization of face sketch synthesis models, this technique does not come without its limitations. Understanding and addressing these limitations is an essential step for furthering the advancements in the field[36].

A notable challenge is the potential introduction of unrealistic artifacts during the augmentation process. Augmentation techniques, in general, manipulate and generate variations in the training data; hence, there is a risk of synthesizing facial features that may not align with realistic human characteristics. Striking a delicate balance between introducing diversity in the dataset (by means of variations) and preserving the authenticity of facial features is a critical consideration while performing data augmentation of datasets of this particular nature[37,38].

Moreover, there is the question of adaptability of current data augmentation techniques to highly specialized domains, such as forensic face sketch synthesis. This is an area that particularly demands attention due to the fact that forensic applications often require precise and accurate representations of facial features, and the generic nature of some augmentation techniques may fall short in capturing the specific intricacies needed for such applications[39].

Another limitation is the potential and prevalent over-reliance on standard augmentation methods (such as flipping and rotations). As models become more sophisticated, there is a need for augmentation techniques that go beyond simple geometric transformations or color variations[40]. Advanced models can potentially benefit from novel augmentation strategies that can introduce more complex and apt variations, ensuring that the model is exposed to a more diverse and representative range of scenarios on a limited dataset.

One important consideration for researchers looking for more effective data augmentation techniques is the computational cost and complexity for each of these techniques. Some advanced augmentation methods may be computationally expensive, which potentially limits their practicality in resource-constrained environments[41].

Addressing these limitations calls for continuous research and innovation in the realm of data augmentation for face sketch synthesis and in general. In striving for a deeper and better understanding of the interplay between variability and realism, there is a need for tailoring augmentation techniques to specific application domains, and exploring advanced strategies that align with the capabilities of evolving models are key avenues for overcoming current limitations[42]. As the field progresses, a refined understanding of these challenges will contribute to the development of more sophisticated and effective data augmentation techniques in the context of face sketch synthesis.

7.2 Ethical and Privacy Considerations

As face sketch synthesis technologies continue to advance, some ethical and privacy considerations come to the forefront, which necessitate that we carefully examine the implications associated with their deployment.

    a. Informed Consent and Privacy Concerns: The generation of facial sketches, particularly in forensic or law enforcement contexts, raises major concerns about informed consent and privacy of individuals. The use of facial images, even in a synthesized form, has an impact on personal privacy, and individuals may have limited control over the use and potential consequences of their own facial data[42, 43]. Striking a balance between the societal benefits of face sketch synthesis and the protection of individual privacy requires robust frameworks and ethical considerations[44].

b. Risk of Misuse: The likely misuse of generated facial sketches poses a significant ethical dilemma. In forensic applications, there is a risk that synthesized sketches could be used for unintended purposes, leading to the potential misidentification or profiling of individuals. Establishing guidelines for the responsible use of face sketch synthesis technologies and the sketches produced by them is crucial to mitigate these risks and prevent unintended consequences[45].

c. Transparency and Accountability: Ethical deployment of face sketch synthesis technologies necessitates transparency in how these tools are developed, used, and governed. Clear communication about the capabilities and limitations of the technology, as well as the intentions behind its use, is vital. Accountability measures must be in place to address any unintended consequences or ethical breaches that may arise during the application of face sketch synthesis in various domains[46]. This also correlates to the current debate revolving around AI technologies and the onset of concepts like Explainable AI becoming the need of the hour in all domains, not just face sketch synthesis.

d. Bias and Fairness: The potential for bias in synthesized sketches adds another layer of ethical consideration. If the training data used for synthesis is biased, it can lead to the reproduction of existing societal biases in the generated sketches. Ethical deployment requires continuous efforts to identify and mitigate biases in both the training data and the synthesis process, ensuring fairness and impartiality[47].

e. Cross-Cultural Sensitivity: The ethical implications of face sketch synthesis extend to cross-cultural considerations. Facial features and expressions can vary across different ethnicities and cultures, and the synthesis process must be sensitive to these variations. Ensuring that synthesized sketches are respectful and unbiased across diverse cultural contexts is imperative[48].

In navigating the ethical and privacy dimensions of face sketch synthesis, a collaborative approach involving researchers, developers, ethicists, and policymakers is essential.[49] Establishing clear guidelines, promoting transparency, and fostering a dialogue around the responsible use of these technologies are crucial steps toward ensuring that the benefits of face sketch synthesis are realized without compromising individual privacy and ethical standards[50].

7.3 Potential Future Developments

The horizon of face sketch synthesis brims with exciting prospects for future developments, propelled by continuous advancements in technology and research. Anticipating the trajectory of this field provides valuable insights into potential areas of growth and innovation. Future developments are expected to witness the refinement and evolution of deep learning architectures specifically tailored for face sketch synthesis[51]. Enhanced architectures, with an improved capacity for capturing intricate facial details and expressions, will contribute to the ongoing enhancement of accuracy and realism in synthesized sketches[52].

Another promising avenue for future exploration involves the integration of generative models with unsupervised learning techniques[53,54]. This approach holds the potential to empower models to autonomously discover patterns and features within the data, reducing reliance on labeled datasets and fostering a more self-sufficient synthesis process. Another direction could be that of parallelism in deep learning for face sketch synthesis, which refers to the simultaneous execution of multiple computations or tasks, enhancing the efficiency and speed of the synthesis process[55,56]. This concept is particularly relevant in the context of training deep neural networks for face sketch synthesis, where complex models require substantial computational resources. Additionally, future research might delve into cross-modal learning, seamlessly integrating information from various modalities such as photographs and sketches. This holistic understanding could lead to improved synthesis processes by leveraging complementary data sources for a more comprehensive and nuanced representation of facial characteristics[57,58].

Addressing the interpretability of face sketch synthesis models is a significant focus for the future. The integration of explainable AI techniques is envisioned to provide insights into the decision-making processes of these models, offering a deeper understanding of how and why certain features are synthesized[59]. Moreover, tailoring face sketch synthesis techniques to specific domains, such as forensic investigations or medical applications[60], is likely to gain prominence[61]. Future developments may involve the creation of domain-specific augmentation methods and synthesis strategies to meet the unique requirements and challenges of these specialized applications.

Continuing efforts in mitigating biases in synthesized sketches remains a critical area for ongoing development. Future endeavors may focus on refining techniques to identify and mitigate biases, ensuring fairness, impartiality, and equitable representation in the generated sketches across diverse demographic groups. As the field progresses, there is a growing recognition of the need to embed ethical considerations directly into the design and deployment of face sketch synthesis models. Ensuring ethical principles are integral to model development will be a crucial aspect of future advancements[62,63].

Furthermore, the future of face sketch synthesis is likely to involve collaborative efforts across interdisciplinary domains, including computer vision, psychology, and ethics. Collaborative research endeavors are anticipated to contribute to a more holistic understanding of the ethical, societal, and psychological implications of synthesized facial representations. As researchers and practitioners embark on these future directions, the field of face sketch synthesis is poised to witness not only technological advancements but also a deeper integration of ethical considerations and a more nuanced understanding of the societal impact of these technologies.

8. CONCLUSION

In delving into the intricacies of data augmentation for face sketch synthesis, myriad insights surface from our thorough exploration. The synthesis of facial sketches, an intricate task with wide-ranging applications in law enforcement, digital entertainment, and forensic artistry, has witnessed a paradigm shift with the infusion of deep learning methodologies. This comprehensive review underscores the transformative impact of deep learning on conventional approaches to face sketch synthesis. The pivotal role played by data augmentation cannot be overstated in this context. It emerges as a linchpin for fortifying model robustness, facilitating generalization, and enhancing adaptability across diverse datasets. The augmentation of training data introduces a pivotal element of variability, empowering the model to encapsulate a broader spectrum of facial nuances and expressions. The cutting-edge techniques discussed, spanning geometric transformations, style transfer, GANs, and VAEs, not only emphasize the innovation in data augmentation but also underscore the evolving landscape beyond traditional augmentation methodologies. Moreover, the chapter underscores the indispensability of tailoring data augmentation strategies to domain-specific needs, especially in the context of forensic face sketch synthesis. The capacity to manipulate facial attributes, simulate age progression and regression, and accurately encapsulate diverse emotional expressions adds a layer of sophistication to the augmentation process, aligning it seamlessly with the intricacies of real-world scenarios. The detailed exploration of evaluation metrics and frameworks provides a robust toolkit for both objective and subjective assessments of face sketch synthesis models. This encompasses not only quantitative measures but also incorporates considerations for human perceptual nuances and cross-validation techniques, ensuring a thorough and well-rounded evaluation. The showcased case studies serve as examples, illustrating the pragmatic applications of data augmentation in real-world scenarios. Whether amplifying the efficacy of forensic investigations or contributing to the immersive quality of digital entertainment, the integration of advanced augmentation techniques exemplifies their effectiveness in elevating the accuracy and authenticity of synthesized facial sketches.

Yet, despite the remarkable strides achieved, challenges persist. Ethical quandaries and privacy considerations, coupled with the inherent limitations of current techniques, accentuate the dynamic nature of this research domain. As we chart a course into the future, the promise of further advancements in data augmentation techniques looms large, shaping the trajectory of face sketch synthesis and pushing the boundaries of what can be accomplished, marking a continuous evolution in this captivating field. In essence, the fusion of deep learning and data augmentation in face sketch synthesis not only expands the horizons of achievable outcomes but also establishes a foundational framework for prospective breakthroughs. This journey into the realm of creating realistic facial sketches through synthetic means is dynamic, promising avenues of exciting possibilities, and contributes significantly to the broader landscape of computer vision and artificial intelligence.

REFERENCES

[1] Webology. (n.d.-a). *Sketch-Based Face Recognition Using Deep Learning.* https://www.webology. org/data-cms/articles/20220901115620amwebology%2019%20(3)%20-%20267.pdf

[2] Thakur, N., Singh, S. K., Gupta, A., Jain, K., Jain, R., Peraković, D., . . . & Rafsanjani, M. K. (2022). A novel CNN, bidirectional long-short term memory, and gated recurrent unit-based hybrid approach for human activity recognition. *International Journal of Software Science and Computational Intelligence (IJSSCI)*, 14(1), 1–19.

[3] Gupta, B. B., Perez, G. M., Agrawal, D. P., & Gupta, D. (2020). *Handbook of Computer Networks and Cyber Security* (Vol. 10, pp. 3–978). Springer.

[4] Azhar, I., Sharif, M., Raza, M., Khan, M. A., & Yong, H.-S. (2021). A decision support system for face sketch synthesis using deep learning and artificial intelligence. *Sensors*, 21(24), 8178. https://doi.org/10.3390/s21248178

[5] Biswas, A., Nasim, M. A. A., Imran, A., Sejuty, A. T., Fairooz, F., Puppala, S., & Talukder, S. (2023, June 7). *Generative adversarial networks for data augmentation.* arXiv.org. https://arxiv.org/abs/2306.02019.

[6] Radman, A., Sallam, A., & Suandi, A. A. (2022). Deep residual network for face sketch synthesis. *Expert Systems with Applications*, 190, 115980. https://doi.org/10.1016/j.eswa.2021.115980

[7] Gaurav, A., Gupta, B. B., Hsu, C. H., Peraković, D., & Peñalvo, F. J. G. (2021, June). Deep learning-based approach for secure web of things (WoT). In *2021 IEEE International Conference on Communications Workshops (ICC Workshops)* (pp. 1–6). IEEE.

[8] *Measures of Image Quality.* (n.d.). Retrieved from https://homepages.inf.ed.ac.uk/rbf/CVonline/LOCAL_COPIES/VELDHUIZEN/node18.html

[9] V7. (n.d.). *The Essential Guide to data augmentation in Deep Learning.* https://www.v7labs.com/blog/data-augmentation-guide

[10] Sahoo, S. R., & Gupta, B. B. (2021). Multiple features-based approach for automatic fake news detection on social networks using deep learning. *Applied Soft Computing*, 100, 106983.

[11] Mengi, G., Singh, S. K., Kumar, S., Mahto, D., & Sharma, A. (2021, September). Automated machine learning (AutoML): The future of computational intelligence. In *International Conference on Cyber Security, Privacy and Networking* (pp. 309–317). Springer International Publishing.

[12] *Albumentations Documentation – What is Image Augmentation. What is Image Augmentation – Albumentations.* https://albumentations.ai/docs/introduction/image_augmentation/#:~:text=Image% 20augmentation%20is%20a%20process,slightly%20change%20the%20original%20image

[13] Sun, J., Yu, H., Zhang, J. J., Dong, J., Yu, H., & Zhong, G. (2022). Face image-sketch synthesis via generative adversarial fusion. *Neural Networks*, 154, 179–189. https://doi.org/10.1016/j. neunet.2022.07.013

[14] Gupta, B. B., & Agrawal, D. P. (2021). Security, privacy and forensics in the enterprise information systems. *Enterprise Information Systems*, 15(4), 445–447.

[15] Bi, H., Liu, Z., Yang, L., et al. (2021). Face sketch synthesis: A survey. *Multimedia Tools and Applications*, 80, 18007–18026. https://doi.org/10.1007/s11042-020-10301-0

[16] Golan, I., & El-Yaniv, R. (2018). Deep anomaly detection using geometric transformations. *Advances in Neural Information Processing Systems*, 31.

[17] Cao, B., Wang, N., Li, J., Hu, Q., & Gao, X. (2022). Face photo-sketch synthesis via full-scale identity supervision. *Pattern Recognition*, 124, 108446. ISSN: 0031-3203. https://doi.org/10.1016/j. patcog.2021.108446

[18] Golan, I., & El-Yaniv, R. (1970, January 1). Deep anomaly detection using geometric transformations. *Advances in Neural Information Processing Systems*. https://proceedings.neurips.cc/paper_ files/paper/2018/hash/5e62d03aec0d17facfc5355dd90d441c-Abstract.html

[19] Yasmina, D., Karima, R., & Ouahiba, A. (2018). "Traffic signs recognition with deep learning. In *International Conference on Applied Smart Systems (ICASS)*, Medea, Algeria, 2018 (pp. 1–5). doi: 10.1109/ICASS.2018.8652024

[20] Wang, X., & Tang, X. (2009, November). Face photo-sketch synthesis and recognition. *IEEE Transactions on Pattern Analysis and Machine Intelligence*, 31(11), 1955–1967. doi: 10.1109/ TPAMI.2008.222

[21] Kingma, D. P., & Welling, M. (2019, November 27). An introduction to variational autoencoders. In *Foundations and Trends® in Machine Learning*. https://www.nowpublishers.com/article/ Details/MAL-056

[22] Ji, F., Sun, M., Qi, X., Li, Q., & Sun, Z. (2022). MOST-Net: A memory oriented style transfer network for face sketch synthesis. In *26th International Conference on Pattern Recognition (ICPR)* (pp. 733–739). IEEE.

[23] Wang, G., Kang, W., Wu, Q., Wang, Z., & Gao, J. (2018). Generative adversarial network (GAN) based data augmentation for palmprint recognition. In *Digital Image Computing: Techniques and Applications (DICTA)* (pp. 1–7). IEEE.

[24] Wan, W., Yang, Y., & Lee, H. J. (2021). Generative adversarial learning for detail-preserving face sketch synthesis. *Neurocomputing*, 438, 107–121. https://doi.org/10.1016/j.neucom. 2021.01.050.

[25] Eivazi, S., Santini, T., Keshavarzi, A., Kübler, T., & Mazzei, A. (2019). Improving real-time CNN-based pupil detection through domain-specific data augmentation. In *Proceedings of the 11th ACM Symposium on Eye Tracking Research & Applications (ETRA '19)*. Association for Computing Machinery, New York, NY, USA, Article 40, 1–6. https://doi.org/10.1145/ 3314111.3319914

[26] Galea, C., & Farrugia, R. A. (2017). Forensic face photo-sketch recognition using a deep learning-based architecture. *IEEE Signal Processing Letters*, 24(11), 1586–1590. doi: 10.1109/ LSP.2017.2749266

[27] Xiao, Q., Luo, H., & Zhang, C. (2017, October 2). Margin sample mining loss: A deep learning based method for person re-identification. *arXiv preprint*, arXiv:1710.00478v3.

[28] Kaur, P., Singh, S. K., Singh, I., & Kumar, S. (2021, December). Exploring convolutional neural network in computer vision-based image classification. In *International Conference on Smart Systems and Advanced Computing (Syscom-2021)*.

[29] Chopra, M., Singh, S. K., Sharma, A., & Gill, S. S. (2022). A comparative study of generative adversarial networks for text-to-image synthesis. *International Journal of Software Science and Computational Intelligence (IJSSCI)*, 14(1), 1–12.

[30] Peñalvo, F. J. G., Maan, T., Singh, S. K., Kumar, S., Arya, V., Chui, K. T., & Singh, G. P. (2022). Sustainable stock market prediction framework using machine learning models. *International Journal of Software Science and Computational Intelligence (IJSSCI)*, 14(1), 1–15.

[31] Wang, L., Sindagi, V., & Patel, V. (2018). High-quality facial photo-sketch synthesis using multi-adversarial networks. In *2018 13th IEEE International Conference on Automatic Face & Gesture Recognition (FG 2018)*, Xi'an, China (pp. 83–90). doi: 10.1109/FG.2018.00022

[32] Ivan Cvitić, G. Praneeth, D. Peraković (2021). *Digital Forensics Techniques for Social Media Networking* (p. 1). Insights2Techinfo. https://insights2techinfo.com/digital-forensics-techniques-for-social-media-networking/

[33] Aggarwal, K., Singh, S. K., Chopra, M., Kumar, S., & Colace, F. (2022). Deep learning in robotics for strengthening Industry 4.0: Opportunities, Challenges, and Future Directions. In *Robotics and AI for Cybersecurity and Critical Infrastructure in Smart Cities*, 1–19.

[34] Wu, C.-J., Raghavendra, R., Gupta, U., Acun, B., Ardalani, N., Maeng, K., Chang, G., Behram, F. A., Huang, J., Bai, C., Gschwind, M., Gupta, A., Ott, M., Melnikov, A., Candido, S., Brooks, D., Chauhan, G., Lee, B., Lee, H.-H. S., . . . Hazelwood, K. (2022, January 9). *Sustainable AI: Environmental implications, challenges and opportunities*. arXiv.org. https://arxiv.org/abs/2111.00364v2

[35] Perkowitz, S. (n.d.). *The Bias in the Machine: Facial Recognition Technology and Racial Disparities*. Retrieved from https://mit-serc.pubpub.org/pub/bias-in-machine/release/1?readingCollection=34db8026

[36] Maharana, K., Mondal, S., & Nemade, B. (2022). A review: Data pre-processing and data augmentation techniques. *Global Transitions Proceedings*, 3. https://doi.org/10.1016/j.gltp.2022.04.020

[37] Lv, J. J., Shao, X. H., Huang, J. S., Zhou, X. D., & Zhou, X. (2016). Data augmentation for face recognition. *Neurocomputing*, 230. https://doi.org/10.1016/j.neucom.2016.12.025

[38] Singh, N., & Jaiswal, U. C. (2022). Analysis of student study of virtual learning using machine learning techniques. *International Journal of Software Science and Computational Intelligence (IJSSCI)*, 14(1), 1–21. http://doi.org/10.4018/IJSSCI.309995

[39] Hernández-García, A., & König, P. (2018). Further advantages of data augmentation on convolutional neural networks. In V. Kůrková, Y. Manolopoulos, B. Hammer, L. Iliadis, & I. Maglogiannis (Eds.), *Artificial Neural Networks and Machine Learning—ICANN 2018* (p. 11139). Springer. https://doi.org/10.1007/978-3-030-01418-6_10

[40] Gupta, A., Singh, S. K., & Chopra, M. (2023). Impact of artificial intelligence and the internet of things in modern times and hereafter: An investigative analysis. In *Advanced Computer Science Applications* (pp. 157–173). Apple Academic Press.

[41] Summers, C., & Dinneen, M. J. (2019). Improved mixed-example data augmentation. In *2019 IEEE Winter Conference on Applications of Computer Vision (WACV)*, Waikoloa, HI, USA (pp. 1262–1270). doi: 10.1109/WACV.2019.00139

[42] Pickering, B. (2021). Trust, but verify: Informed consent, AI technologies, and public health emergencies. *Future Internet*, 13, 132. https://doi.org/10.3390/fi13050132

[43] Boggaram, A., Boggaram, A., Sharma, A., Srinivasa Ramanujan, A., & Bharathi, R. (2022). Sign language translation systems: A systematic literature review. *International Journal of Software Science and Computational Intelligence (IJSSCI)*, 14(1), 1–33. http://doi.org/10.4018/IJSSCI.311448

[44] Jones, M. L., Kaufman, E., & Edenberg, E. (2018). AI and the ethics of automating consent. *IEEE Security & Privacy*, 16(3), 64–72. doi: 10.1109/MSP.2018.2701155

[45] Javadi, S. A., Cloete, R., Cobbe, J., Lee, M. S. A., & Singh, J. (2020). Monitoring misuse for accountable 'artificial intelligence as a service'. In *Proceedings of the AAAI/ACM Conference on AI, Ethics, and Society (AIES '20)* (pp. 300–306). Association for Computing Machinery. https://doi.org/10.1145/3375627.3375873

[46] von Eschenbach, W. J. (2021). Transparency and the black box problem: Why we do not trust AI. *Philosophy & Technology*, 34, 1607–1622. https://doi.org/10.1007/s13347-021-004770

[47] Lewicki, K., Lee, M. S. A., Cobbe, J., & Singh, J. (2023). Out of context: Investigating the bias and fairness concerns of "artificial intelligence as a service". In *Proceedings of the 2023 CHI*

Conference on Human Factors in Computing Systems (CHI '23). Association for Computing Machinery, New York, NY, USA, Article 135, 1–17. https://doi.org/10.1145/3544548.3581463

[48] Chen, H., Chan-Olmsted, S., & Thai, M. (2023). Culture sensitivity and information access: A qualitative study among ethnic groups. *The Qualitative Report*, 28(8), 2504–2522. https://doi.org/10.46743/2160-3715/2023.5981

[49] Tripathi, T., & Kumar, R. (2022). Performance comparison of machine learning algorithms for dementia progression detection. *International Journal of Software Science and Computational Intelligence (IJSSCI)*, 14(1), 1–18. http://doi.org/10.4018/IJSSCI.312553

[50] Sharma, A., Singh, S. K., Kumar, S., Chhabra, A., & Gupta, S. (2021, September). Security of android banking mobile apps: Challenges and opportunities. In *International Conference on Cyber Security, Privacy and Networking* (pp. 406–416). Springer International Publishing.

[51] Praneeth. (2022). *Cloud Forensics: Open Issues, Challenges and Future Research Opportunities* (p. 1). Insights2Techinfo. Retrieved from https://insights2techinfo.com/cloud-forensics-open-issues-challenges-and-future-research-opportunities/

[52] Akram, A., Wang, N., Li, J., & Gao, X. (2018). A comparative study on face sketch synthesis. *IEEE Access*, 6, 37084–37093. doi: 10.1109/ACCESS.2018.2852709

[53] Kazemi, H., Taherkhani, F., & Nasrabadi, N. M. (2018). Unsupervised facial geometry learning for sketch to photo synthesis. In *2018 International Conference of the Biometrics Special Interest Group (BIOSIG)*, Darmstadt, Germany (pp. 1–5). doi: 10.23919/BIOSIG.2018.8552937

[54] Raj, A., & Minz, S. (2021). A scalable unsupervised classification method using rough set for remote sensing imagery. *International Journal of Software Science and Computational Intelligence (IJSSCI)*, 13(2), 65–88. http://doi.org/10.4018/IJSSCI.2021040104

[55] Kumar, S., Singh, S. K., & Aggarwal, N. (2023). Speculative parallelism on multicore chip architecture strengthen green computing concept: A survey. In *Advanced Computer Science Applications* (pp. 3–16). Apple Academic Press.

[56] Kumar, S., Singh, S. K., Aggarwal, N., & Aggarwal, K. (2021). Evaluation of automatic parallelization algorithms to minimize speculative parallelism overheads: An experiment. *Journal of Discrete Mathematical Sciences and Cryptography*, 24(5), 1517–1528.

[57] Ouyang, S., Hospedales, T., Song, Y. Z., & Li, X. (2015). Cross-modal face matching: Beyond viewed sketches. In D. Cremers, I. Reid, H. Saito, & M. H. Yang (Eds.), *Computer Vision—ACCV 2014* (p. 15). Springer. https://doi.org/10.1007/978-3-319-16808-1_15

[58] Gupta, S., Agrawal, S., Singh, S. K., & Kumar, S. (2023). A novel transfer learning-based model for ultrasound breast cancer image classification. In *Computational Vision and Bio-Inspired Computing: Proceedings of ICCVBIC 2022* (pp. 511–523). Springer Nature Singapore.

[59] Kumar, P. S. (2022). Computationally simple and efficient method for solving real-life mixed intuitionistic fuzzy 3D assignment problems. *International Journal of Software Science and Computational Intelligence (IJSSCI)*, 14(1), 1–42. http://doi.org/10.4018/IJSSCI.291715

[60] Kumar, S., Singh, S. K., Aggarwal, N., Gupta, B. B., Alhalabi, W., & Band, S. S. (2022). An efficient hardware-supported and parallelization architecture for intelligent systems to overcome speculative overheads. *International Journal of Intelligent Systems*, 37(12), 11764–11790.

[61] Ratner, A. J., Ehrenberg, H., Hussain, Z., Dunnmon, J., & Ré, C. (2017). Learning to compose domain-specific transformations for data augmentation. *Advances in Neural Information Processing Systems*, 30.

[62] Gaurav, A., Gupta, B. B., & Panigrahi, P. K. (2023). A comprehensive survey on machine learning approaches for malware detection in IoT-based enterprise information system. *Enterprise Information Systems*, 17(3), 2023764.

[63] Ahvanooey, M. T., Zhu, M. X., Li, Q., Mazurczyk, W., Choo, K. K. R., Gupta, B. B., & Conti, M. (2021). Modern authentication schemes in smartphones and IoT devices: An empirical survey. *IEEE Internet of Things Journal*, 9(10), 7639–7663.

Chapter 10

Forgery Detection Based on Deep Learning for Smart Systems

Recent Advances and Collection of Datasets

Akshat Gaurav, Brij B. Gupta, Shavi Bansal, and Kwok Tai Chui

I. INTRODUCTION

Forgery means an operation performed on digital assets to conceal their original content. For the case of image forgery, it involves manipulating and tampering with digital images to hide or add incorrect information [1]. There are several types of digital image forgeries, including copy-move forgery, splicing forgery, morphing forgery, resampling forgery, retouching forgery, and images composed entirely of computer graphics.

There are many negative effects of image forgery that lead to financial and economic loss in various industries. Moreover, image forgery can also have severe consequences in legal cases, where digital images are often used as evidence. To combat the growing threat of image forgery, forgery detection techniques have been developed.

Recently, with the development of deep learning algorithms, there has been significant progress in forgery detection methods [2, 3]. There are various deep learning models, such as CNN, RNN, GRU, and GAN, available that can be used to identify the forged image. These deep-learning models are trained on large datasets of authentic and forged images to learn patterns and detect inconsistencies in the visual content. In this context, Sari & Fahmi [4] proposed a CNN-based image forgery detection method. Similarly, Celebi & Hsu [5] conclude that deep learning models can effectively identify the forged images if the source file is in JPEG format. Moreover, Doegar et al. [6] proposed a VGG-16 model for a forged image detection model. However, sometimes complex deep learning models are not efficient for the detection of forged images. In this context, Mariappan et al. proposed a lightweight deep learning model for an image forgery detection approach, which achieved high accuracy while being computationally efficient. Additionally, researchers have also focused on developing explainable AI algorithms for image forgery detection. This research shows that there is a wide potential for deep learning models in detecting image forgery [7].

With the recent development of deepfake technologies, the importance of image forgery detection has become even more crucial. Therefore, researchers have started focusing on developing advanced secure forgery detection techniques that can specifically detect image forgery [8]. Also, with different deep learning models, there is a growing need for suitable datasets that accurately represent the various types of image forgeries. In this context, this chapter presents a survey of recent advances in forgery detection based on deep learning techniques. This chapter aims to provide an overview of the latest methods and approaches in forgery detection, specifically focusing on those utilizing deep learning techniques.

DOI: 10.1201/9781003207573-10

2. LITERATURE REVIEW

2.1 Types of Image Forgery

Nowadays, attackers use different types of image forgery techniques such as copy-mode forgery, image splicing, images resembling, and image retouching. In this section of the chapter, we will explain some of these techniques.

1. Copy-move forgery: In this type of image forgery, the attacker duplicates the original imager and creates a forged image. As the forged image is made up of the original image, it is difficult to differentiate the forged image from the original [9]. However, researchers are working to develop an efficient deep learning model that can identity copy-move forgery. In this context, Kohale et al. [10] proposed an integrated feature-based approach that effectively detects copy-move forgery. Also, Abdalla et al. [11] proposed a CNN-based approach that detects copy-move forgery attack.

   In addition, some research has focused on clustering-based techniques for the identification of the forged image [12–14].
2. Image splicing forgery: In this type of forgery, two different images are merged and a new forged image is created. As the new image has the content of old images, it is difficult to identify the forged image.
3. Image resampling forgery: In this type of forgery, the attacker resamples the image with a different sampling rate. The sampling rate is an important factor in this situation. In this context, many researchers developed forgery detection models based on integrating deep learning techniques and image sampling rates [15–17].

2.2 Challenges in Forgery Detection

As more and more advanced tools are developed, it will be difficult to distinguish the forged image from the original image. In most image forgery cases, attackers change the basic features of the image like bit rate, quantization ratio, compression ratio, etc.; this makes the

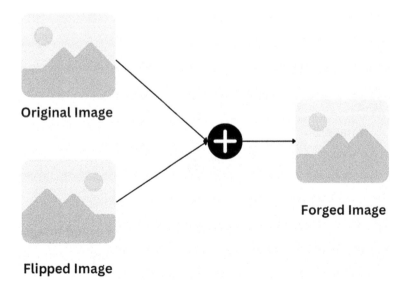

Original Image

Flipped Image

Forged Image

Figure 10.1 Copy-move forgery

detection of the forged image difficult. In the case of video forgery, the attacker manipulates the video encoder features [18].

Recently, with the development of deep learning techniques, the efficiency of forgery detection methods has increased. However, there are many challenges in forgery detection using deep learning; one is that there are not sufficient datasets available to train the deep learning models. In addition to that, most of the deep learning models are highly complex and require high processing resources and long training time [19]. Also, there are block-based forgery detection methods; but they also have high complexity and low efficiency in zero-day attacks. Some researchers proposed keypoint-based forgery detection methods; however, these techniques also lack efficiency and accuracy.

Hence, the main challenge for forgery detection is that each type of forgery attack has a different signature and characteristics, so it is challenging to create a common detection technique [17, 20–27]. The next biggest challenge is a reduction in the complexity of detection algorithms [28–33]. Detection of semantic manipulation of images is also a significant challenge, as semantic image forgery changes the meaning of the original image and non-semantic forgery alters the appearance of the original image [34–36].

With the development of generative adversarial networks (GANs), it is more difficult to detect the forged image [37–39]. Apart from all of the aforementioned challenges, identifying the authentication and integrity of an original image is also a big challenge in the field of image forgery detection [40–42].

2.3 Forgery Detection Methods

In this subsection, we will discuss the latest image forgery detection techniques and frameworks proposed. As data preprocessing is the key point in deep learning models, Baumy et al. [43] advocated the use of advanced data preprocessing techniques, such as histogram equalization and high-pass filtering. Shwetha & Sathyanarayana [44] proposed a novel segmentation technique for image forgery detection. According to the authors, the proposed model is more efficient than block-based detection models. Suresh & Rao [22] modeled a multifaceted

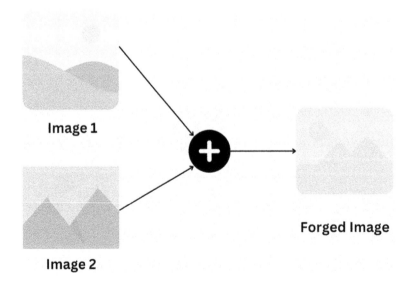

Figure 10.2 Image splicing forgery

approach that focuses on the reduction of the complexity of deep learning models for image forgery detection. Some authors also proposed hybrid models for image forgery detection; Abdalla et al. [11] proposed a hybrid technique of integrating statistical and deep learning principles.

2.4 Current Research in Forgery Detection

Figure 10.3 represents information on papers published in Scopus-indexed sources. The period of study ranges from 2014 to 2024 and presents a comprehensive overview of academic contributions across various fields. This dataset encompasses 377 sources, including journals and books, and comprises 733 documents. A significant aspect of this data is its citation metrics: on average, each document has garnered 11.63 citations, which is notable given that the average publication age is just 1.64 years. This translates to an average of 2.686 citations per year for each document, underscoring the relevance and impact of the research. The total count of references in these documents is 21,453, indicating extensive research and wide-ranging studies.

In terms of document types, the dataset is diverse, consisting of 332 articles, 11 book chapters, 318 conference papers, 50 conference reviews, 21 reviews, and a short survey. Such variety reflects the multidisciplinary nature the research encompasses.

The richness of the dataset is further evidenced by its extensive keyword usage, with 2802 Keywords Plus (ID) and 1481 Author's Keywords (DE), highlighting the broad array of topics and themes explored in these documents.

Regarding authorship, the dataset includes contributions from 1876 authors, with a total of 2629 author appearances. This includes a mix of 17 single-authored documents and 1859 multi-authored documents, indicating a strong inclination toward collaborative research. The collaboration metrics are particularly telling, with an average of 2.56 authors per document and 3.59 co-authors per document. The collaboration index, sitting at 2.8, reflects a healthy level of cooperation and joint efforts among researchers.

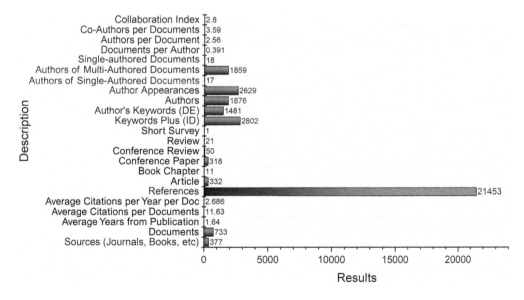

Figure 10.3 Information about research papers published related to forgery detection

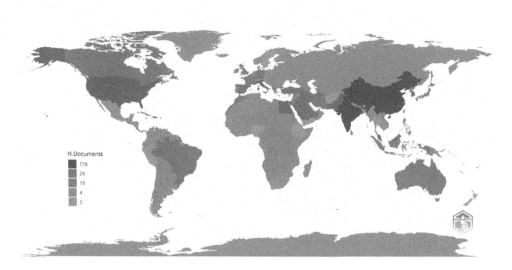

Figure 10.4 Country scientific production

Figure 10.4 indicates that the scientific production across different countries reveals a diverse landscape of research output. China and India are at the forefront, with 779 and 763 contributions respectively, reflecting their massive investment in scientific research. The United States follows with a significant but lower volume of 141. European nations like Italy and emerging research hubs like Pakistan and Egypt also show notable contributions, indicating their growing focus on scientific advancement. South Korea and Malaysia demonstrate their commitment to research and development with substantial contributions, while countries like Saudi Arabia, Iraq, and Spain contribute actively, reflecting their individual research strengths. Other countries like Turkey, Canada, Iran, Brazil, the UK, France, Germany, Indonesia, and Australia, though lower in frequency, play vital roles in the global scientific community, showcasing a wide array of expertise and research interests. This data not only illustrates the quantity of scientific output but also highlights the diverse and dynamic nature of global research efforts, influenced by economic, educational, and policy factors.

3. SMART SYSTEMS AND THEIR VULNERABILITIES

Smart systems, encompassing Internet of Things (IoT) and smart urban frameworks, have catalyzed a transformative shift in urban development and technological innovation. The integration of IoT technologies into the urban fabric marks a significant stride in affecting diverse urban life aspects, heralding the advent of smart cities. These cities employ a nexus of interconnected devices, sensors, and data analytics, focusing on augmenting efficiency, sustainability, and life quality. Central to these IoT applications in smart cities is the deployment of efficient communication networks, pivotal for a range of services from smart grid management to intelligent transportation systems and smart healthcare, all hinging on precise and ubiquitous connectivity, as highlighted by Yaacoub & Alouini [45].

In smart cities, the core aim of IoT is to sculpt an environment that is not only convenient and comfortable but also safe and stable for its inhabitants. IoT stands at the forefront of this endeavor, interlinking smart devices, objects, and individuals, facilitating seamless data exchange across cloud networks without direct human interaction. This network of smart

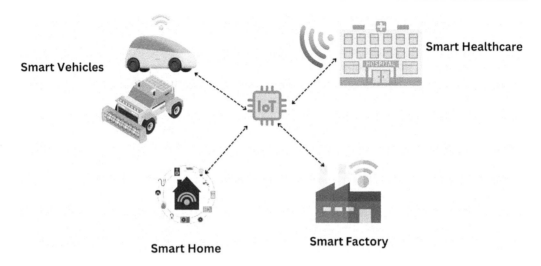

Smart Vehicles

Smart Healthcare

Smart Home

Smart Factory

Figure 10.5 Smart devices' application

devices and sensors lays the groundwork for advanced service delivery, thereby elevating the urban experience in smart cities [46].

Security in the IoT landscape within smart cities is paramount, given the diverse application domains ranging from healthcare to energy management. The security of IoT devices and networks is critical to thwart cyber threats and vulnerabilities, emphasizing the need for secure IoT integration for the successful realization of smart city initiatives and the safeguarding of critical infrastructure and sensitive data [47].

Advancing IoT-based smart city systems necessitates extensive research and ongoing projects focused on conceptualizing and implementing state-of-the-art solutions. These research endeavors aim at harnessing IoT for crafting infrastructures that not only uplift urban living but also promote sustainability and optimize resource utilization, thereby catering to the evolving needs of urban populations [48].

The synergy between smart cities and IoT technologies acts as a catalyst in the evolution of both domains. The integration of IoT within smart city components is essential for creating a seamlessly interconnected urban environment, enhancing various aspects of city life, including energy management and environmental sustainability [49].

Extending beyond traditional urban infrastructure, the deployment of IoT in smart cities covers a broad spectrum of applications, impacting daily life activities. These applications, ranging from smart healthcare to industrial IoT, underscore the transformative potential of IoT in sculpting the future of smart cities [50].

Designing and implementing IoT-based smart city platforms necessitates foresight into future standards and services. As IoT technologies evolve, these platforms must be adaptable and scalable to accommodate emerging innovations and advancements [51].

The role of IoT in urban development and smart city realization is indispensable. IoT infrastructure is crucial for enhancing urban services, optimizing resources, and elevating the efficiency and sustainability of smart cities. This integration is pivotal for driving urban innovation and tackling the complexities of modern urban environments [52].

IoT initiatives create interconnected environments that enhance urban life quality and contribute to the sustainable development of smart cities [53].

The fusion of IoT with systems like AI and 5G is accelerating the activation of various IoT industries. This convergence is rapidly advancing IoT technologies, transforming urban landscapes, and activating smart city initiatives [54].

IoT implementation in smart cities impacts urban governance, planning, and collaborative initiatives significantly. The synergy of smart technology, collaboration, and governance drives transformative changes and enhances life quality in urban environments [55].

IoT utilization on smart campuses aims to enhance infrastructure, optimize resources, and improve efficiency and sustainability. These initiatives foster interconnected environments that elevate the learning experience and promote sustainability [56].

The deployment of IoT in urban surveillance systems leverages automated object detection algorithms, crucial for enhancing security, optimizing operations, and ensuring safety in smart city environments [57].

Integrating IoT in smart cities is vital for optimizing resources, enhancing services, and promoting sustainability. IoT initiatives create interconnected environments, improving urban life quality and contributing to smart city sustainable development [58].

The confluence of IoT with AI and 5G drives the rapid activation of IoT industries. This synergy accelerates IoT technology development, transforming urban landscapes and advancing smart city initiatives [59].

IoT in smart cities has profound implications for urban governance, planning, and collaborative initiatives. The amalgamation of smart technology, collaboration, and governance is essential for transformative urban changes and enhancing life quality in smart cities [60, 63].

4. DEEP LEARNING IN FORGERY DETECTION

The ascendance of deep learning as a formidable methodology in forgery detection realms is undeniable, bestowing superior faculties for discernment and pinpointing diverse forms of image manipulations [64–66]. The adoption of deep neural architectures, especially convolutional neural networks (CNNs), has exponentially augmented the precision and steadfastness in forgery identification practices [67–69]. The comparative analysis by Celebi and Hsu [5] on seam carving forgery in JPEG images, utilizing deep learning paradigms, underlines the burgeoning prowess of these techniques in image forensic investigations. Correspondingly, Fahmi and Sari [4] have highlighted the efficacy of deep learning frameworks in pixel-specific image forgery discernment, demonstrating their unparalleled proficiency in pattern analysis and image categorization. The deployment of advanced neural modalities, inclusive of deep convolutional networks, is pivotal in unraveling the intricacies in forgery detection, as delineated in the studies by Sari and Fahmi [4], Abdalla et al. [11], reinforcing the critical role of deep learning in elevating detection accuracy and operational performance of such systems.

Furthermore, amalgamating deep learning with cutting-edge technological spheres like cloud computing and AI has birthed more potent forgery detection mechanisms [70–71]. The innovative self-consistency learning splicing forgery detection algorithm proposed by Zhang et al. [32], rooted in deep learning methodologies, exemplifies the enhanced efficacy achievable through such synergies. Moreover, the fusion of conventional forgery forensics with deep learning insights, as elucidated by Zhuang et al. [3], has been pivotal in recognizing nuanced textural disparities, contributing to more holistic and precise forgery detection frameworks [72–74].

Additionally, the evolution of deep learning algorithms, notably the Cascaded Deep Sparse Auto Encoder (CDSAE) and CNNs, has played a transformative role in the identification and categorization of counterfeit imagery, as evidenced in the work of Balasubramanian et al. [75] and Kumar et al. [76]. These advancements signify the escalating prominence and effectiveness of deep learning techniques in surmounting the challenges posed in image forgery detection. The extension of deep learning methodologies to encompass copy-move forgery, facial manipulation identification, and image segmentation further broadens the spectrum of deep learning applications within the forgery detection domain.

4.1 Advantages of Deep Learning Over Traditional Methods

The implementation of deep learning paradigms, specifically convolutional neural networks (CNNs), heralds a significant advancement over conventional techniques in the realm of image forgery detection. Deep learning frameworks facilitate autonomous extraction and learning of features from input data, thereby obviating the requirement for manually engineered features, as elucidated by Kuznetsov. This capability of self-driven feature discernment enables these models to intricately identify and analyze nuanced patterns and subtle manipulations in images, thereby heightening the fidelity and resilience of forgery detection mechanisms. Furthermore, deep learning methodologies exhibit adaptability to a spectrum of intricate manipulation techniques, encompassing image splicing, copy-move forgery, and facial alterations, by leveraging extensive datasets and demonstrating effective generalization to novel contexts [84]. The innate ability of these models to discern critical discriminative features for forgery detection, as showcased by [3], significantly amplifies the performance and reliability of these detection systems.

Moreover, deep learning approaches proffer augmented interpretability, facilitating an in-depth analysis and comprehension of the model's internal representations and decision-making processes, which is crucial for ascertaining the veracity of forgery classifications. Such interpretability offers invaluable insights into the detection dynamics, empowering forensic experts to decipher the foundational elements influencing the identification of image manipulations. In addition, the convergence of deep learning with sophisticated optimization algorithms, like deep neuro-fuzzy networks, escalates the adaptability and efficiency of forgery detection methodologies, fostering the development of fortified and optimized detection frameworks.

Contrasting traditional methodologies, deep learning-centric forgery detection techniques exhibit superior prowess in navigating perturbations and distortions prevalent in real-world scenarios, such as JPEG compression and gamma correction [2]. The resilience of these models to such challenges underscores their efficacy in detecting forgeries under diverse and rigorous conditions. Furthermore, the amalgamation of deep learning with domain-specific acumen, as delineated by Rössler et al. [85], significantly bolsters the accuracy and trustworthiness of forgery detection, achieving unprecedented precision even under severe compression and adversarial manipulations.

Table 10.1 Comparison of deep learning-based forgery detection

Source	Techniques used	Detection	Dataset	Accuracy
[77]	CNN and ConvLSTM	Image forgery	MICC-220, MICC-600, MICC 2000	95%, 73%, 94%
[78]	Device fingerprinting model using CNN	Node forgery	UNSW dataset	95%
[79]	CNN	Image forgery	MICC-F220	100%
[80]	SIFT and Keypoint Vector Construction	Image forgery	MICC-F220	96%
[81]	SIFT and Keypoint Removal and Injection	Image forgery	INRIA Holidays data set	97%
[82]	SURF and HAC	Image forgery	MICC-F220	85%
[83]	ROI and Correlation	Image forgery	MICC-F220, MICC-F2000, MICC-F600, and SATS-130	99%

4.2 Key Deep Learning Models Used in Forgery Detection

Contemporary advancements in image forgery detection have witnessed the extensive incorporation of deep learning models, including Convolutional Neural Networks (CNNs), Recurrent Neural Networks (RNNs), and Generative Adversarial Networks (GANs), to tackle the intricacies of digital image manipulation. The efficacy of CNNs in identifying copy-move forgery, as demonstrated by Abdalla et al. [11], exemplifies the pervasive utilization of CNN-centric deep learning approaches in universal image manipulation and forgery detection. Further, Doegar et al. [6] have accentuated the proficiency of deep learning models, such as CNNs, in extracting robust features from images, facilitating tasks like image classification and recognition. Xue et al. [2] have also emphasized the prevalence of deep learning detection methodologies in the forgery detection arena, signifying the extensive adoption of these techniques in countering image manipulation challenges.

The integration of GANs in forgery detection represents a significant research trajectory. For example, Abdalla et al. [11] employed a GAN-based image classifier to devise a sophisticated forgery discriminator, underscoring the potential of GANs in identifying image forgeries. The study by Sharma et al. [86] illuminated the utility of GANs in tackling challenges posed by photo-realistic images, emphasizing the role of deep learning, including GANs, in differentiating manipulated images from genuine ones.

Additionally, the application of RNNs in forgery detection has garnered research interest. Sabeena and Abraham [87] introduced an innovative deep learning framework comprising Inflated 3D (I3D) and Siamese-based RNNs, targeting challenges in video surveillance object forgery detection. This approach signifies the integration of RNNs in addressing the complexities of video forgery detection, highlighting the versatility of deep learning models across various domains.

In summation, the latest image forgery detection methodologies have leveraged the capabilities of deep learning models, such as CNNs, RNNs, and GANs, to confront the multifaceted challenges of digital image manipulation. These advancements underscore the extensive adoption of deep learning technologies in crafting robust and effective forgery detection systems.

4.3 Advantage of Deep Learning in Forgery Detection

Deep learning models have risen to prominence as pivotal instruments in image forgery detection, offering a multitude of advantages in navigating the intricacies of digital image manipulation. The deployment of deep learning algorithms, notably Convolutional Neural Networks (CNNs), significantly benefits forgery detection by enabling the extraction of complex statistical features from high-dimensional data [4]. This attribute permits deep learning models to autonomously learn representations and undertake image classification and recognition tasks, thereby diminishing the reliance on manual feature engineering or traditional

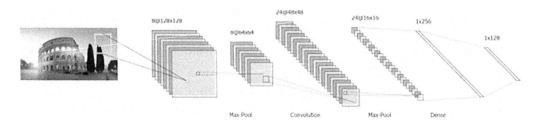

Figure 10.6 CNN-based image analysis method

feature approaches [88]. Furthermore, the incorporation of deep learning architectures, including CNNs, has evidenced promising outcomes in various image classification challenges, equipping these systems to extract pertinent and robust features from images, thus enhancing the accuracy of forgery detection [6].

Moreover, the application of deep learning algorithms simplifies learning complexities and augments detection precision, as manifested by novel deep learning frameworks employing advanced techniques to address forgery detection challenges [87]. The utilization of deep learning models, such as CNNs, RNNs, and GANs, has been instrumental in amplifying the precision and resilience of forgery detection systems, offering enhanced capabilities in pinpointing, localizing, and combating digital image manipulations. Furthermore, deep learning classifiers and models, when amalgamated with additional domain-specific knowledge, have demonstrated unparalleled accuracy in forgery detection, outshining human evaluators even under conditions of intense compression [85].

Additionally, deep learning approaches have proven efficacious in detecting a wide array of image manipulations, including seam carving forgery, patch-based image inpainting, and GAN-generated fake images, showcasing the adaptability and versatility of deep learning models in addressing diverse forgery detection challenges [84, 89, 90]. The use of deep learning algorithms has also been pivotal in automating the forgery detection processes, alleviating the burden of manual detection, and enabling inspectors to concentrate on other critical tasks, such as welding defect inspection [91].

5. DATASETS FOR FORGERY DETECTION

The evaluation and progression of forgery detection methodologies hinge critically on the examination of existing datasets tailored for this purpose. The necessity of having a variety of comprehensive datasets for training and testing these algorithms is paramount. To this end, multiple datasets have been curated, targeting the complexities of forgery detection across different mediums such as images and videos. A notable example is the DeeperForensics-1.0 dataset, a specialized large-scale collection designed for detecting real-world face forgeries, known for its high-quality manipulated videos that surpass other datasets in performance, thus marking a significant leap in forgery detection research. Additionally, datasets like MICC-F220, SATs-130, and MICC-F600, referenced by Zainal et al., are instrumental in the application of forgery detection methods, underscoring the value of publicly available benchmark datasets in technique evaluation.

Furthermore, the FaceForensics++ dataset, encompassing videos manipulated through advanced methods such as Face2Face, FaceSwap, DeepFakes, and NeuralTextures, has been pivotal in propelling face forgery detection research. Another critical contribution is the DeepFakes Detection dataset, which fulfills the demand for high-quality resources in detecting deepfake videos, thereby aiding in the fortification of forgery detection methodologies. These datasets are vital in the evolution of forgery detection research and in benchmarking cutting-edge detection methods.

Moreover, datasets like the Illumination Inconsistency Sleuthing discussed by Carvalho et al., and the Tampered and Inconsistent Image Detection Techniques mentioned by Tiwari et al., are instrumental in tackling the intricacies of inconsistency and tampering detection in digital images. They provide invaluable insights and resources for the development of techniques capable of identifying manipulated features within digital imagery. Additionally, the Digital Image Forgery Detection Schemes dataset, introduced by Kim and Lee, plays a significant role in the practical analysis of various forgery detection methods, offering a deeper understanding of their strengths and weaknesses.

Table 10.2 Image dataset analysis

Dataset	Number of images	Type of images	Purpose/usage	Additional notes
MICC-F220	220	Forensic analysis	To test forgery detection algorithms	Contains real and forged images
MICC-F2000	2000	Forensic analysis	Larger set for robustness testing	Includes a diverse range of manipulation types
MICC-F600	600	Forensic analysis	Intermediate dataset for testing	Mix of real and forged with varying complexities
SATS-130	130 (approx.)	Unknown	Likely used for specific analysis	Details might be less publicly available

In summary, the accessibility of diverse, high-quality datasets is fundamental to the advancement of forgery detection research. These datasets are crucial in fostering the development and evaluation of innovative detection techniques, thereby contributing significantly to the ongoing endeavors in combating image and video manipulation challenges across various domains.

6. ETHICAL CONSIDERATIONS AND FUTURE DIRECTIONS

The field of forgery detection is grappling with several imminent challenges that require innovative solutions. These highly realistic forgeries are increasingly challenging to detect, necessitating more robust detection methods to combat this threat. The emergence of new face forgery techniques further complicates this issue, demanding innovative approaches for their identification and mitigation.

Another challenge is the limitations of available datasets. Current datasets often fail to represent the complexity of real-world forgeries, indicating a need for more comprehensive datasets to enhance the accuracy of detection methods.

Moreover, the growing automated tools and techniques present a challenge for the detection models. Therefore, there is a need for the development of new models that can detect the forged images generated by automated tools.

7. CONCLUSION

This chapter presents a comprehensive analysis of the advancements in deep learning-based forgery detection in the context of smart systems. This chapter explores the latest developments in deep learning models combat forgeries. The study critically evaluates existing datasets, underscoring their importance and the need for expansion. This chapter aims to provide valuable insights and serve as a guiding framework for future research and development in the field of forgery detection in smart systems.

REFERENCES

[1] M. A. Elaskily, M. M. Dessouky, O. S. Faragallah, and A. Sedik, "A survey on traditional and deep learning copy move forgery detection (CMFD) techniques," *Multimed. Tools Appl.*, 82(22), 34409–34435, September 2023, doi: 10.1007/s11042-023-14424-y.

[2] Z. Xue, X. Jiang, Q. Liu, and Z. Wei, "Global–local facial fusion based GAN generated fake face detection," *Sensors*, 2023, doi: 10.3390/s23020616.

[3] M. Zhuang, G. Li, and K. Ding, "Design and simulation analysis of trajectory planning algorithm for 6-DoF manipulator based on deep learning," *Mob. Inf. Syst.*, 2022, 1–9, June 2022, doi: 10.1155/2022/8715036.

[4] W. P. Sari and H. Fahmi, "Effect of error level analysis on the image forgery detection using deep learning," *Kinet. Game Technol. Inf. Syst. Comput. Netw. Comput. Electron. Control*, 2021, doi: 10.22219/kinetik.v6i3.1272.

[5] N. H. Celebi and T.-L. Hsu, "A comparison study to detect seam carving forgery in JPEG images with deep learning models," *J. Surveill. Secur. Saf.*, 2022, doi: 10.20517/jsss.2022.02.

[6] A. Doegar, S. Hiriyannaiah, S. G. Matt, S. K. Gopaliyengar, and M. Dutta, "Image forgery detection based on fusion of lightweight deep learning models," *Turk. J. Electr. Eng. Comput. Sci.*, 2021, doi: 10.3906/elk-2005-37.

[7] S. Walia, K. Kumar, M. Kumar, and X. Gao, "Fusion of handcrafted and deep features for forgery detection in digital images," *IEEE Access Pract. Innov. Open Solut.*, 2021, doi: 10.1109/access.2021.3096240.

[8] W. Zhao, P. Yang, R. Ni, Y. Zhao, and H. Wu, "Security consideration for deep learning-based image forensics," *IEICE Trans. Inf. Syst.*, 2018, doi: 10.1587/transinf.2018edl8091.

[9] Y. Wang and S. Kamata, "Copy move image forgery detection based on polar fourier representation," *Int. J. Mach. Learn. Comput.*, 2018, doi: 10.18178/ijmlc.2018.8.2.680.

[10] T. A. Kohale, S. D. Chede, and P. R. Lakhe, "Forgery of copy move image detection technique by integrating block and feature based method," *IJARCCE*, 2015, doi: 10.17148/ijarcce.2015.4129.

[11] Y. E. Abdalla, M. T. Iqbal, and M. Shehata, "Convolutional neural network for copy-move forgery detection," *Symmetry*, 2019, doi: 10.3390/sym11101280.

[12] H. Chen, X. Yang, and Y. Lyu, "Copy-move forgery detection based on keypoint clustering and similar neighborhood search algorithm," *IEEE Access Pract. Innov. Open Solut.*, 2020, doi: 10.1109/access.2020.2974804.

[13] Ch. S. Rao and S. Babu, "Image authentication using local binary pattern on the low frequency components," in *Microelectronics, Electromagnetics and Telecommunications. Lecture Notes in Electrical Engineering*, Springer, 2015, doi: 10.1007/978-81-322-2728-1_49.

[14] G. Gani and F. Qadir, "A robust copy-move forgery detection technique based on discrete cosine transform and cellular automata," *J. Inf. Secur. Appl.*, 2020, doi: 10.1016/j.jisa.2020.102510.

[15] J. Bunk et al., "Detection and localization of image forgeries using resampling features and deep learning," *Presented at the 2017 IEEE Conference on Computer Vision and Pattern Recognition Workshops (CVPRW)*, pp. 1881–1889, IEEE, 2017.

[16] J. A. Cortés Osorio, J. A. Chaves Osorio, and C. D. López Robayo, "Hybrid algorithm for the detection of pixel-based digital image forgery using markov and SIFT descriptors," *Rev. Fac. Ing. Univ. Antioquia*, 2021, doi: 10.17533/udea.redin.20211165.

[17] A. Flenner, L. Peterson, J. Bunk, T. M. Mohammed, L. Nataraj, and B. S. Manjunath, "*Resampling forgery detection using deep learning and a-contrario analysis*," ArXiv Prepr. ArXiv180301711, 2018.

[18] W. El-Shafai, M. A. Fouda, E.-S. M. El-Rabaie, and N. A. El-Salam, "A comprehensive taxonomy on multimedia video forgery detection techniques: Challenges and novel trends," *Multimed. Tools Appl.*, May 2023, doi: 10.1007/s11042-023-15609-1.

[19] F. Z. Mehrjardi, A. M. Latif, M. S. Zarchi, and R. Sheikhpour, "A survey on deep learning-based image forgery detection," *Pattern Recognit.*, 144, 109778, December 2023, doi: 10.1016/j.patcog.2023.109778.

[20] G. C. Shanthi and V. Raj, "A novel approach for efficient forgery image detection using hybrid feature extraction and classification," *Int. J. Eng. Technol.*, 2018, doi: 10.14419/ijet.v7i3.27.17879.

[21] H. G. Kim, J. S. Park, D. G. Kim, and H.-K. Lee, "Two-stream neural networks to detect manipulation of JPEG compressed images," *Electron. Lett.*, 2018, doi: 10.1049/el.2017.4444.

[22] G. Suresh and C. S. Rao, "Localization of copy-move forgery in digital images through differential excitation texture features," *Int. J. Intell. Eng. Syst.*, 2019, doi: 10.22266/ijies2019.0430.05.

[23] R. Kaur, "Image forgery and detection of copy move forgery in digital images: A survey of recent forgery detection techniques," *Int. J. Comput. Appl.*, 2016, doi: 10.5120/ijca2016909164.

[24] A. K. Gupta, "A new copy move forgery detection technique using adaptive over-segmentation and feature point matching," *Bull. Electr. Eng. Inform.*, 2018, doi: 10.11591/eei.v7i3.754.

[25] S. G. Upase and S. V. Kuntawar, "Copy-move detection of image forgery by using DWT and SIFT methodologies," *Int. J. Comput. Appl.*, 2016, doi: 10.5120/ijca2016911220.

[26] O. Mayer, "*Exposing fake images with forensic similarity graphs*," 2019, doi: 10.48550/arxiv.1912.02861.

[27] P. Selvaraj and K. Muneeswaran, "Inter-frame forgery detection and localisation in videos using earth mover's distance metric," *IET Image Process.*, 2020, doi: 10.1049/iet-ipr.2020.0287.

[28] C. Zhang, G. Hu, J. Hu, Y. Zhang, and Y. Xie, "Design and implementation of image forgery detection system based on cloud computing," *Destech Trans. Eng. Technol. Res.*, 2020, doi: 10.12783/dtetr/mcaee2020/35024.

[29] K. Sharma and P. Abrol, "Non-overlapping block-based parametric forgery detection model," *Int. J. Comput. Appl.*, 2016, doi: 10.5120/ijca2016907773.

[30] Z. Xue, X. Jiang, and Q. Liu, "Semantic modeling and pixel discrimination for image manipulation detection," *Secur. Commun. Netw.*, 2022, doi: 10.1155/2022/9755509.

[31] H.-S. Kim and J. Lee, "An implementation and pragmatic analysis of the digital image forgery detection schemes," *Int. J. Future Comput. Commun.*, 2015, doi: 10.18178/ijfcc.2015.4.5.410.

[32] L. Li et al., "*Face X-ray for more general face forgery detection*," 2020, doi: 10.1109/cvpr42600.2020.00505.

[33] A. Dixit and R. Gupta, "Copy-move image forgery detection using frequency-based techniques: A review," *Int. J. Signal Process. Image Process. Pattern Recognit.*, 2016, doi: 10.14257/ijsip.2016.9.3.07.

[34] Y. Obara, Y. Niwa, and S. Wada, "Detection and identification of image manipulation based on reversible histogram shift," *Electron. Commun. Jpn.*, 2017, doi: 10.1002/ecj.11973.

[35] T. Osakabe, T. Miki, Y. Kinoshita, and H. Kiya, "*CycleGAN without checkerboard artifacts for counter-forensics of fake-image detection*," 2021, doi: 10.1117/12.2590977.

[36] A. Kumar, A. Bhavsar, and R. Verma, "*Syn2Real: Forgery classification via unsupervised domain adaptatio*n," 2020, doi: 10.1109/wacvw50321.2020.9096921.

[37] Q. Chen, J. Zhang, and P. Luo, "*Emerging concern of scientific fraud: Deep learning and image manipulation*," 2020, doi: 10.1101/2020.11.24.395319.

[38] K. Akash, K. Ahalya, N. Dhinesh, and K. Diya Shereef, "Detecting fake images using machine learning," *Int. J. Res. Publ. Rev.*, 2023, doi: 10.55248/gengpi.2023.4.4.35702.

[39] E. Ardizzone and G. Mazzola, "*A tool to support the creation of datasets of tampered videos*," 2015, doi: 10.1007/978-3-319-23234-8_61.

[40] S. J. Jacob, G. Krishnalal, and V. P. Jagathy Raj, "Revealing image forgery on digital images by applying contrast enhancement," *Int. J. Comput. Appl.*, 2015, doi: 10.5120/ijca2015906675.

[41] N. Evdokimova, A. Kuznetsov, and R. Samara, "*Copy-move detection algorithm based on local derivative patterns*," 2016, doi: 10.18287/1613-0073-2016-1638-304-312.

[42] B. Jiang, J. Xia, B. Wu, and Z. Wei, "*SGCN: Spatially gradient convolution network for certificate document image manipulation localization*," 2022, doi: 10.1117/12.2653519.

[43] A. Baumy, A. D. Algarni, M. I. Abdalla, W. El-Shafai, F. E. Abd El-Samie, and N. F. Soliman, "Efficient forgery detection approaches for digital color images," *Comput. Mater. Contin.*, 2022, doi: 10.32604/cmc.2022.021047.

[44] B. Shwetha and S. V. Sathyanarayana, "Application of superpixels segmentation in digital image forgery detection," *JNNCE J. Eng. Manag.*, 2022, doi: 10.37314/jjem.2022.060116.

[45] E. Yaacoub and M.-S. Alouini, "Efficient fronthaul and backhaul connectivity for IoT traffic in rural areas," *IEEE Internet Things Mag.*, 2021, doi: 10.1109/iotm.0001.1900061.

[46] C. Jung, J. Awad, and A. H. Chohan, "The planning of smart elderly housing in Dubai with IoT technologies," *Open House Int.*, 2021, doi: 10.1108/ohi-08-2020-0121.

[47] A. S. Cvetković, S. Jokić, S. Adamović, N. Ristić, and N. Pavlović, "Internet of things security aspects," *Zb. Rad. Univ. Sinergija*, 2020, doi: 10.7251/zrsng2001027c.

[48] M. Bouzidi, Y. Dalveren, F. A. Cheikh, and M. Derawi, "Use of the IQRF technology in internet-of-things-based smart cities," *IEEE Access Pract. Innov. Open Solut.*, 2020, doi: 10.1109/access.2020.2982558.

[49] B. Hammi, R. Khatoun, S. Zeadally, A. Fayad, and L. Khoukhi, "IoT technologies for smart cities," *IET Netw.*, 2018, doi: 10.1049/iet-net.2017.0163.

[50] M. Mohseni, M. Joorabian, and A. L. Ara, "Distribution system reconfiguration in presence of internet of things," *IET Gener. Transm. Distrib.*, 2020, doi: 10.1049/gtd2.12102.

[51] A. Krylovskiy, M. Jahn, and E. Patti, "*Designing a smart city internet of things platform with microservice architecture*," 2015, doi: 10.1109/ficloud.2015.55.

[52] W. H. N. Evertzen, R. Effing, and E. Constantinides, "*The internet of things as smart city enabler: The cases of palo alto, nice and Stockholm*," 2019, doi: 10.1007/978-3-030-29374-1_24.

[53] G. Ptichnikova and A. V. Antyufeev, "'Smart city', man and architecture," *E3s Web Conf.*, 2020, doi: 10.1051/e3sconf/202016405027.

[54] A. K. M. Al-Qurabat and A. K. Idrees, "Data gathering and aggregation with selective transmission technique to optimize the lifetime of internet of things networks," *Int. J. Commun. Syst.*, 2020, doi: 10.1002/dac.4408.

[55] V. Baltac, "Smart cities—a view of societal aspects," *Smart Cities*, 2019, doi: 10.3390/smartcities2040033.

[56] L. Anthopoulos, M. Janssen, and V. Weerakkody, "*A unified smart city model (USCM) for smart city conceptualization and benchmarking*," 2018, doi: 10.4018/978-1-5225-5646-6.ch025.

[57] S. M. Riazul Islam, D. Kwak, Md. H. Kabir, M. Hossain, and K. Kwak, "The internet of things for health care: A comprehensive survey," *IEEE Access Pract. Innov. Open Solut.*, 2015, doi: 10.1109/access.2015.2437951.

[58] D. Jadhav, V. Muddebhalkar, and L. Khandare, "Utilization of resource's in IoT," *Int. J. Comput. Appl.*, 2017, doi: 10.5120/ijca2017914206.

[59] P. Shinde Sayali and N. Phalle Vaibhavi, "A survey paper on internet of things-based healthcare system," *IARJSET*, 2017, doi: 10.17148/iarjset/nciarcse.2017.38.

[60] R. Kusumastuti and J. Rouli, "Smart city implementation and citizen engagement in Indonesia," *IOP Conf. Ser. Earth Environ. Sci.*, 2021, doi: 10.1088/1755-1315/940/1/012076.

[61] I. Permana, M. T. Hidayat, and M. Siswoyo, "The implementation of a local wisdom-based smart city system in Cirebon," *Hong Kong J. Soc. Sci.*, 2023, doi: 10.55463/hkjss.issn.1021-3619.60.27.

[62] A. Lepekhin, A. Borremans, and O. Iliashenko, "Design and implementation of IT services as part of the 'smart city' concept," *MATEC Web Conf.*, 2018, doi: 10.1051/matecconf/201817001029.

[63] C. Yin, X. Zhang, H. Chen, J. Wang, D. Cooper, and B. David, "A literature survey on smart cities," *Sci. China Inf. Sci.*, 2015, doi: 10.1007/s11432-015-5397-4.

[64] A. Meijer and M. P. Rodríguez Bolívar, "Governing the smart city: A review of the literature on smart urban governance," *Int. Rev. Adm. Sci.*, 2015, doi: 10.1177/0020852314564308.

[65] A. V. Twist, M. Melenhorst, M. Veenstra, E. Ruijer, M. Kolk, and A. Meijer, "*Designing guidelines for smart city collaboration tools*," 2022, doi: 10.24251/hicss.2022.334.

[66] N. Cavus, S. E. Mrwebi, I. M. Ibrahim, T. Modupeola, and A. Y. Reeves, "Internet of things and its applications to smart campus: A systematic literature review," *Int. J. Interact. Mob. Technol.*, 2022, doi: 10.3991/ijim.v16i23.36215.

[67] M. A. Alharbe, "Cyber security, forensics and its impact on future challenges in Saudi Arabia smart cities case study on the modern, urban planning and design," *Int. J. Adv. Trends Comput. Sci. Eng.*, 2020, doi: 10.30534/ijatcse/2020/235922020.

[68] G. A. Naidu, S. Kodati, and J. Selvaraj, "A smart health care applications and benefits using IoT," *Int. J. Recent Technol. Eng.*, 2019, doi: 10.35940/ijrte.c5916.098319.

[69] S. Gupta, "Smart city paradigm in India: Gwalior a case study," *Humanit. Soc. Sci. Rev.*, 2019, doi: 10.18510/hssr.2019.7444.

[70] E. D. Madyatmadja, T. R. Yulia, D. J. Malem Sembiring, and S. M. Br Angin, "IoT usage on smart campus: A systematic literature review," *Int. J. Emerg. Technol. Adv. Eng.*, 2021, doi: 10.46338/ijetae0521_06.

[71] M. Prauzek, T. Paterova, M. Stankus, M. Mikus, and J. Konecny, "Analysis of LoRaWAN transactions for TEG-powered environment-monitoring devices," *Elektron. Ir Elektrotechnika*, 2022, doi: 10.5755/j02.eie.31265.

[72] S. Khan and A. Ali, "CLIFD: A novel image forgery detection technique using digital signatures," *J. Eng. Res.*, 2021, doi: 10.36909/jer.v9i1.8379.

[73] E. Mahesh, M. Suman, and D. S. Rao, "A novel method of scale-invariant feature transform-based image forgery detection," *Int. J. Intell. Eng. Syst.*, 2018, doi: 10.22266/ijies2018.0430.15.

[74] M. E. Azol, N. M. Ramli, Y. S. Lee, and S. A. Abuzar, "A coarse-to-fine copy-move image forgery detection method based on discrete cosine transform," *Indones. J. Electr. Eng. Comput. Sci.*, 2019, doi: 10.11591/ijeecs.v14.i2.pp843-851.

[75] K. Nanath, S. Balasubramanian, V. Shukla, N. Islam, and S. Kaitheri, "Developing a mental health index using a machine learning approach: Assessing the impact of mobility and lockdown during the COVID-19 pandemic," *Technol. Forecast. Soc. Change*, 178, 2022, doi: 10.1016/j.techfore.2022.121560.

[76] S. Ha, J. Ryu, H. Kim, D. Won, and Y. Lee, "Cryptanalysis of Kumar et al.'s authentication protocol for wireless sensor networks," in K. J. Kim and H.-Y. Kim (Eds.), *Information Science and Applications*, vol. 621, *Lecture Notes in Electrical Engineering*, pp. 329–340, Springer Singapore, 2020, doi: 10.1007/978-981-15-1465-4_34.

[77] A. Sedik *et al.*, "AI-enabled digital forgery analysis and crucial interactions monitoring in smart communities," *Technol. Forecast. Soc. Change*, 177, 121555, 2022.

[78] R. R. Chowdhury, A. C. Idris, and P. E. Abas, "A deep learning approach for classifying network connected IoT devices using communication traffic characteristics," *J. Netw. Syst. Manag.*, 31(1), 26, 2023.

[79] F. M. Al-Azrak *et al.*, "An efficient method for image forgery detection based on trigonometric transforms and deep learning," *Multimed. Tools Appl.*, 79, 18221–18243, 2020.

[80] I. Amerini, L. Ballan, R. Caldelli, A. Del Bimbo, and G. Serra, "A sift-based forensic method for copy–move attack detection and transformation recovery," *IEEE Trans. Inf. Forensics Secur.*, 6(3), 1099–1110, 2011.

[81] A. Costanzo, I. Amerini, R. Caldelli, and M. Barni, "Forensic analysis of SIFT keypoint removal and injection," *IEEE Trans. Inf. Forensics Secur.*, 9(9), 1450–1464, 2014.

[82] P. Mishra, N. Mishra, S. Sharma, and R. Patel, "Region duplication forgery detection technique based on SURF and HAC," *Sci. World J.*, 2013, 2013.

[83] M. A. Elaskily, H. A. Elnemr, M. M. Dessouky, and O. S. Faragallah, "Two stages object recognition-based copy-move forgery detection algorithm," *Multimed. Tools Appl.*, 78, 15353–15373, 2019.

[84] L. Nataraj *et al.*, "Detecting GAN generated fake images using co-occurrence matrices," *Electron. Imaging*, 2019, doi: 10.2352/issn.2470-1173.2019.5.mwsf-532.

[85] A. Rössler, D. Cozzolino, L. Verdoliva, C. Rieß, J. Thies, and M. Nießner, "*FaceForensics++: Learning to detect manipulated facial images,*" 2019, doi: 10.1109/iccv.2019.00009.

[86] P. Sharma, M. Kumar, and H. K. Sharma, "Comprehensive analyses of image forgery detection methods from traditional to deep learning approaches: An evaluation," *Multimed. Tools Appl.*, 2022, doi: 10.1007/s11042-022-13808-w.

[87] M. Sabeena and L. Abraham, "Digital image forensic using deep flower pollination with adaptive Harris hawk optimization," *Multimed. Tools Appl.*, 2021, doi: 10.1007/s11042-021-10925-w.

[88] A. Doegar, M. Dutta, and G. Kumar, "Image forgery detection using google net and random forest machine learning algorithm," *J. Univ. Shanghai Sci. Technol.*, 2020, doi: 10.51201/jusst12508.

[89] Q. Liu, "An approach to detecting JPEG down-recompression and seam carving forgery under recompression anti-forensics," *Pattern Recognit.*, 2017, doi: 10.1016/j.patcog.2016.12.010.

[90] M. M. Wang, J. Zhang, and X. You, "Machine-type communication for maritime internet of things: A design," *IEEE Commun. Surv. Tutor.*, 22(4), 2550–2585, 2020, doi: 10.1109/COMST.2020.3015694.

[91] F. Zhang, B. Zhang, and X. Zhang, "Automatic forgery detection for X-ray non-destructive testing of welding," *Weld. World*, 2021, doi: 10.1007/s40194-021-01211-2.

Chapter 11

Deep Learning-Based Forensics and Anti-Forensics

Princy Pappachan, Novi Susatediyo Adi, Gerry Firmansyah, and Mosiur Rahaman

1. INTRODUCTION

In today's digital age, the new era of technological growth and exponential increase in the number of digital devices has forced an unparalleled surge in the need for digital forensics. The advent of deep-learning, a subset of Artificial Intelligence (AI), has significantly transformed how crime is perceived and investigated through advanced analytical capabilities (Dwivedi et al., 2023). In the past, forensic analysis heavily relied on manual investigations and basic computer techniques. However, the emergence of deep learning, a subset of artificial intelligence that focuses on training neural networks to mimic the working of the human brain, has enhanced forensic techniques with its interconnected layers of algorithms that can recognise and analyse complex patterns, extract valuable information, and make intelligent decisions based on vast amounts of data (Jenis et al., 2023). Utilising this ability to learn from large datasets, forensic experts can now identify patterns, detect anomalies, and extract relevant information. This advent of deep learning has also simultaneously opened the doors to developing techniques for manipulating and concealing digital evidence, known as anti-forensics (El-Shafai et al., 2023).

The initial section of the chapter discusses the technological revolution in forensics, emphasising the transformative impact of deep learning in areas such as biometrics, digital forensics, and predictive policing and highlighting the enhanced accuracy and efficiency in criminal investigations. Following this, the chapter addresses the challenges and obstacles in integrating deep learning into forensic science, including issues like data availability, quality, ethical and legal constraints, and the potential for biases. The subsequent section discusses the emergence of anti-forensics, particularly deep learning-based methods like data poisoning and adversarial attacks, highlighting the need for advanced detection strategies. Future advancements in forensic science are also explored, focusing on the potential impacts of technologies like blockchain, sophisticated biometrics, virtual/augmented reality, and IoT. Additionally, the chapter delves into the ethical and legal implications of these advancements, particularly emphasising the role of Explainable Artificial Intelligence (XAI) in addressing privacy and data governance challenges. The chapter concludes by summarising the importance of incorporating deep learning into forensic science, stressing the need to balance technological innovation with ethical, legal, and privacy considerations, thereby influencing the future direction of forensic research.

2. LITERATURE REVIEW

In the evolving domain of deep learning-based forensics and anti-forensics, AI-driven technologies have revolutionised traditional forensic methods, mainly digital forensics, predictive

DOI: 10.1201/9781003207573-11

policing, and biometric analysis. Its efficacy in sifting through electronic evidence across social media, email, and other online platforms has significantly improved digital investigations. A key area of influence is biometric analysis, where AI enhances identification and verification processes with advanced recognition algorithms. These AI-driven biometric systems have expanded beyond classical fingerprint recognition to include facial, iris, voice, and even gait analysis, offering unparalleled precision and efficiency in identity verification. The use of AI in image and video analysis, mainly through facial recognition algorithms and computer vision, has also seen remarkable advancements. These technologies assist in organising and scrutinising vast amounts of surveillance data, locating missing persons, and constructing detailed 3D crime scene models. Furthermore, deep learning also influences forensic toxicology and serology, allowing for more precise chemical identification and insights into how compounds respond under different circumstances. However, this technological shift also introduces challenges, including privacy and ethical concerns, the opaque nature of AI models, and the need for explainable AI to ensure transparency and comprehensibility in forensic procedures.

In present-day forensic research, significant emphasis is placed on enhancing security and privacy within enterprise information systems through deep learning technologies (Gupta and Agrawal, 2021). One important area of interest is the significance of real-time analysis in actual forensic scenarios, especially for cyber-physical systems. With a more comprehensive and advanced approach to digital investigations, this is especially helpful when looking at digital traces found in emails, social media, and other digital platforms (Bansal, 2023). But this change also brings new difficulties, such as privacy and ethical issues, the "black box" nature of deep learning models, and the requirement for explainable artificial intelligence. Transparency in AI algorithms is emphasised to overcome these obstacles in applying AI in forensic science. Such systems will ensure that the methods and decisions are transparent and comprehensible, as these algorithms can be opaque and complex.

1.1 Understanding the Basics of Deep Learning

Deep learning is founded on the principles of neural networks, which are modelled after the human brain and consist of interconnected nodes or neurons arranged in layers. Each layer in this network, with its respective weights, performs specific transformations on the input it receives, gradually extracting higher-level characteristics. The depth of these layers is the source of its high analytical capabilities and what gives it its name (LeCun, Bengio, and Hinton, 2015). Accordingly, the neural networks are trained with vast volumes of data for the system to learn how to recognise patterns and make decisions. To direct the learning process and improve prediction accuracy, a process known as backpropagation is used alongside optimisation algorithms like gradient descent (Ruder, 2016).

On the data input, deep learning can be categorised into 'supervised learning', where it learns from labelled data, 'unsupervised learning', where it learns from unlabelled data, and 'semi-supervised learning', which combines both approaches (M. Yang et al., 2023; Schmidhuber, 2015). There is also 'reinforcement learning', where models learn by trial and error, receiving feedback from the environment (Barto, 1997; Li, 2017). Depending on the problem that needs to be addressed, the different learning models are applied to deep learning applications in forensic science. For example, forensic science tasks such as facial recognition, fingerprint analysis, and DNA sequence classification will require training on a large dataset labelled with correct identification. Conversely, analysing large volumes of data for anomaly detection would require the application of unsupervised learning (Kute et al., 2021). On the other hand, the semi-supervised learning approach is useful when only a limited amount of labelled data and a more extensive set of unlabelled data are available. However, although the application of reinforcement learning was less common in traditional forensic science, it is now adopted in areas like predictive policing, where feedback is required to teach the system how to make decisions (G. Yang et al., 2022).

Deep learning applications in forensic science thus include traditional biometric identification (facial or fingerprint) to more sophisticated tasks, like crime scene digital analysis and predictive policing. Deep learning models are now significantly more accurate and faster than traditional methods in processing and analysing large datasets (Gibb and Riemen, 2023).

1.2 The Evolution of Forensic Science With AI

Incorporating artificial intelligence and deep learning in forensic science marks a significant departure from traditional, manual methods to sophisticated, automated techniques. This transition can be seen in several important domains, as shown in Figure 11.1:

Biometric analysis: Biometrics involves identifying individuals by their unique physiological or behavioural characteristics. In forensics, biometric analysis primarily only involved fingerprint analysis. However, with the evolution of artificial intelligence algorithms based on deep learning, the scope of biometric analysis has expanded to include facial recognition,

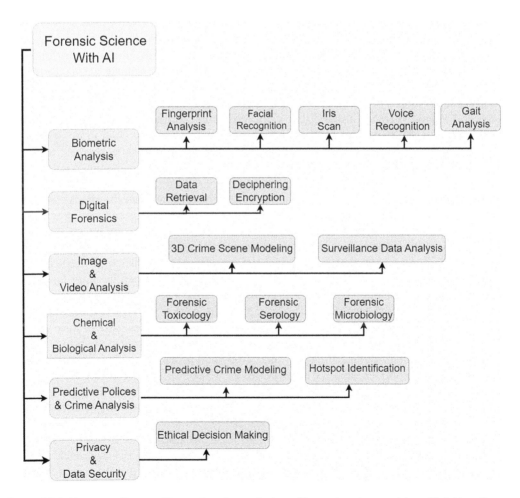

Figure 11.1 Use-case diagram illustrating the evolution of forensic science with artificial intelligence

iris scan, voice recognition, and even gait analysis. Artificial intelligence-enhanced biometric systems have thus revolutionised identity verification with deep learning algorithms' power to analyse facial features, iris patterns, fingerprints, voice, and gait with high accuracy and efficiency (Zhang et al., 2022).

Minaee et al. (2023) provide an in-depth overview of biometric recognition from the traditional biometric recognition system that used handcrafted features (Zhang et al., 2009) to the present-day biometric recognition system equipped with an end-to-end learning framework that concurrently learns feature representation while conducting classification and regression.

Digital Forensics: With the widespread use of digital technology in every part of life and the proliferation of digital devices, digital forensics, which deals with recovering and examining content found on these devices, have been significantly essential (Gulshan et al., 2018). In the early days of digital forensics, data analysis was manually performed, which was time-consuming and bound by human constraints. Garfinkel (2010) explains the history of digital forensics as belonging to three time periods: the early days (1980s and 1990s), the golden age (1999–2007), and the coming digital forensics crisis (current scenario), which is aptly accurate (Humphries et al., 2021). With artificial intelligence, deep learning assists with large-scale dataset analysis, data retrieval, and deciphering complex encryption. It also works accurately and effectively to examine emails, social media accounts, and other digital traces that suspects may have left behind (Ivan Cvitić et al., 2021). However, this tremendous transformation in digital forensics has also given rise to new challenges and questions on ethics, privacy, and legal admissibility (Najafabadi et al., 2015; Casino et al., 2022).

Image and Video Analysis: Artificial intelligence-driven facial recognition algorithms have made it very feasible to sort through several hours of surveillance footage to identify people quickly, a previously laborious and error-prone operation (Sreenu and Durai, 2019). These algorithms and computer vision can also produce detailed 3D models of crime scenes from photos and videos, offering insights that were impossible to obtain from static 2D images (Abbas et al., 2018). Furthermore, these advancements have been crucial in analysing and cross-referencing vast amounts of surveillance data to look for missing persons (Şengönül et al., 2023; Al-Waisy et al., 2018).

Chemical and Biological Analysis: In forensic science, chemical analysis constitutes forensic toxicology, the study of the science of poisons (chemicals that cause harm). Although the onset of forensic toxicology resulted from the growth of chemistry and biology approximately 200 years ago (Lappas and Lappas, 2021), the present advancement in forensic toxicology owes itself to technological advancements. These advancements are in the form of sophisticated equipment that uses specialised algorithms to gather and store data that enables comparison with mass spectrum libraries (Soria, 2023). Deep learning has further boosted forensic toxicology with its ability to detect New Psychoactive Substances (NPS) by utilising complex analytical methods that aid in the complex interpretation of data for precise substance identification (Malaca et al., 2020). In biological analysis, forensic serology (DNA typing) and forensic microbiology (application of microorganisms) are other domains that have incorporated deep learning into their analytical process (Busia et al., 2018; Zhang et al., 2021; Bosco and Di Gangi, 2017; McCord et al., 2018). Furthermore, deep learning's predictive modelling capabilities are instrumental in understanding how a substance might react under different conditions or predicting how a biological sample might have changed over time (Chung and Choe, 2017; Vidaki et al., 2017).

Predictive Policing and Crime Analysis: This analysis goes beyond reactive strategies and marks a significant shift in enforcement methodologies. A proactive approach to crime prevention is taken by predicting criminal activity and identifying possible crime hotspots from vast datasets, including past crime reports and demographic and social media trends (Hardyns and Rummens, 2018). Accordingly, law enforcement can allocate their resources more strategically and efficiently, focusing on locations and times when crimes are most likely to happen (Meijer and Wessels, 2019). This proactive strategy, powered by artificial intelligence and fueled by deep learning, can stop crimes before they occur and respond to them when they do (Brayne, 2017).

Even though integrating artificial intelligence in forensic science has become increasingly important, new challenges with privacy, data security, and ethical implications of artificial intelligence decisions have risen.

2. APPLICATIONS OF DEEP LEARNING

Deep learning applications in forensics are paramount in domains like image and video analysis, audio and voice recognition, and network forensics and anomaly detection.

2.1 Image and Video Analysis

This forensic science domain has seen a significant transition with the advent of deep learning, particularly the application of Convolutional Neural Networks (CNNs). This particular deep learning algorithm is designed to automatically learn hierarchical representations from input data, enabling them to extract valuable features directly from raw pixels (Chai et al., 2021).

In the context of forensics, this is highly effective in image and video processing tasks since it can be used for various applications like tampering detection, forgery identification, content authentication, and image/video classification. This process typically involves training the CNN model on labelled datasets using supervised learning techniques. Accordingly, the network learns to recognise particular features or artefacts linked with manipulations through multiple layers of convolutional filters followed by pooling operations. As a result, the network can capture both low-level details (e.g. edges, textures) and high-level semantic information (e.g. object shapes). Once the training is completed, unseen images and videos can be applied to the model for forensic analysis, which compares the extracted features from the new images and videos with those learned during training to make predictions (Diallo et al., 2020).

Furthermore, CNNs are highly proficient in deciphering and evaluating intricate patterns present in visual data at the pixel level. This feature is crucial when details such as a suspect's face or a vehicle's license plate might be obscured or so faint that the naked eye cannot discern it. Forensic experts can utilise CNNs by applying deep learning techniques to enhance the quality of such surveillance footage or even extract features from low-lighting or motion blur images and videos. In the identification of suspects, CNNs can be trained to recognise and compare facial features against databases, even if the face is partially obscured or presented from different angles. Also, in cases of missing people or unidentified persons, CNNs can be trained to estimate the age and gender of individuals from visual data. New directions in this domain include analysing body movements or gait from video footage when facial recognition is impossible (Zou et al., 2018).

Additionally, video footage can be used to reconstruct crime scenes by analysing the spatial and temporal information in the video data, granting crime investigators a sequence of events. This is also very beneficial in cases where the physical crime scene is not fully accessible or preserved (Dwivedi et al., 2022).

As demonstrated, deep learning and CNNs have enormous potential to revolutionise the field of digital forensics and provide law enforcement and investigative agencies with new capabilities and tools to use in the pursuit of truth and justice (Khan et al., 2021).

2.2 Audio Forensics and Voice Recognition

Audio forensics involves detailed analysis and evaluation of sound recordings, often used in legal and law enforcement contexts. CNNs, known for their effectiveness in processing and analysing visual data, also play a critical role in audio forensics, with their success in extracting voice recognition and audio classification features. This is done by handling the spectrogram representation of audio signals where sound waves are converted into visual formats. However, CNNs struggle to capture long-term temporal dependencies essential in audio analysis, such as speech understanding. Also problematic is the varying audio length, as CNNs are more accustomed to fixed-size units (Fayyad-Kazan et al., 2021).

So instead of a straightforward neural network, RNNs or Recurrent Neural Networks with a single hidden layer and a self-loop that allows it to retain information from previous steps are designed to recognise patterns in sequential data. RNNs can analyse the time-dependent features in audio recordings and capture the nuances in speech recognition, rhythm, and intonation, making it essential for accurate speech recognition. Also, on account of RNNs' capacity to remember previous input "memory" networks, it can be employed in scenarios that require an understanding of temporal dynamics and how elements in a sequence are related. In this neural network paradigm, the output from the previous step is fed back into the network as output for the next step (Dvornek and Li, 2023).

RNNs can additionally be utilised in scenarios where it is essential to understand changes over time to make predictions. Unlike the CNNs, RNNs are used in various types of learning paradigms: supervised learning for speech recognition, language translation and time-series prediction; unsupervised learning for anomaly detection in time-series data; semi-supervised learning to find patterns; and reinforcement learning for environments where understanding temporal dynamics is crucial. However, RNNs fail to perform efficiently with tasks involving long sequences where understanding long-range dependencies is crucial (Ahmed et al., 2023).

To address these limitations, the Long Short-Term Memory (LSTM) and Gated Recurrent Units (GRUs) were designed as advanced variants of RNNs. The LSTM features a set of gates (input, forget, and output) and maintains a cell state for long-term memory and a hidden state for short-term memory, thereby effectively managing memory by controlling what information to retain, discard, or output at each time step. The LSTM architecture is simplified to form the GRUs by merging the cell and hidden states into one state and the input and output gates into a single update gate. This makes the GRUs a much less complex and efficient structure with quicker training and greater computational efficiency (Nabi et al., 2021).

Accordingly, the best comprehensive approach to audio forensics is the integration of CNNs and RNNs with LSTM and GRUs, depending on the tasks at hand and the available data. This is particularly significant in audio authentication, where CNNs can handle the spectral aspects of the sound, while RNNs, LSTM, and GRUs can deal with temporal dynamics to detect and analyse any form of manipulation, from simple edits to complex alterations (Sánchez-Hevia et al., 2022).

As shown in Figure 11.2, a CNN for image analysis, an RNN for time-series data analysis, and a GNN for graph structure analysis are used by the data analyst. While multidimensional social network analysis is aided by GNN, integrated sensor network analysis is facilitated by both CNN and RNN.

2.3 Network Forensics and Anomaly Detection

Network forensics involves meticulously monitoring and analysing computer network traffic to identify and thwart unauthorised access or malicious activities. Deep learning with

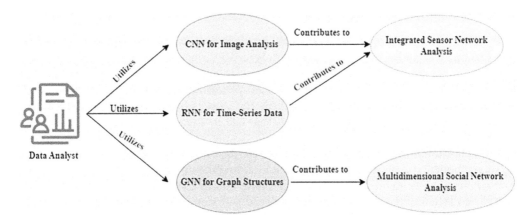

Figure 11.2 Use-case diagram illustrating the utilisation of different neural network models by a data analyst

different learning paradigms and neural networks enhances this field to analyse network traffic in real-time, detect intrusions, detect and identify malware, and detect phishing attempts and fraudulent activities (Shrivastava et al., 2018).

With supervised learning, models are trained to categorise traffic data as normal or malicious, enabling them to identify patterns and recognise threats in real-time traffic. On the other hand, unsupervised learning is crucial to detect novel or evolving cyber threats by identifying anomalies based on deviations from established normal patterns. Combining these two learning paradigms enhances the model to learn from a limited amount of labelled data while adapting to new, unseen network behaviours.

In terms of neural network architecture in network forensics, CNNs and RNNs with their advanced variants LSTM and GRUs are employed to monitor, analyse, and secure computer networks. However, they are severely limited in addressing all the nuances of data analysis because of the relationships between data points. Graph Neural Networks (GNNs) are specifically designed for this purpose as they can process and analyse data with relationships and interconnections between them. GNNs differ from CNNs and RNNs that use a more traditional tabular format in their analysis. By presenting network traffic as a graph with nodes like servers, routers, endpoints, and edges corresponding to connections between these entities, GNNs can analyse the graph structures to identify patterns indicative of cyber-attacks.

Hybrid approaches combining the different architectures, GNNs with CNNs and RNNs, are instrumental for various applications. Applications requiring temporal dynamics and complex relationship analysis can benefit from a combined RNNs and GNNs approach. At the same time, applications that require structured sequencing modelling can utilise the CNNs' identification of spatial structures in graph data and RNNs' capability of capturing dynamic patterns (Ma and Mei, 2021).

Similarly, an integrated sensor network or a multidimensional social network can benefit from an integrated, cohesive model using all three architectures where CNNs can be used to understand the spatial layout of the network, RNNs to understand the flow of traffic over time, and GNNs to analyse the relationships and dependencies between different nodes in the network. Additionally, in social media analysis, GNNs can analyse the social network graph, CNNs can process visual content like images and videos, and RNNs can handle sequential data like time-stamped user interactions (Bloemheuvel et al., 2021).

2.4 Cybersecurity Forensics

Cybersecurity forensics, or digital forensics, involves investigating digital devices and networks to uncover and analyse evidence of cybercrimes, unauthorised activities, or security breaches (Gupta et al., 2020). It plays a significant role in understanding how a cybercrime was committed and gathering evidence for legal proceedings. Accordingly, it encompasses several activities ranging from data collection and preservation, data analysis, tracing the sequence of activities and reporting findings that can be used in legal proceedings (*What Is Computer Forensics*, n.d.).

Data collection and preservation involve safely securing evidence from computers, servers, smartphones, and network logs while maintaining the integrity of the evidence for legal admissibility. The subsequent data analysis phase entails extracting pertinent information from the collected data by decrypting data, scrutinising networks, examining malware, and recovering deleted files. The following phase focuses on tracing the activities that led to this particular cybercrime by identifying attack methodologies, exploited vulnerabilities, the extent of the damage, and potentially identifying the perpetrators responsible for the cyber incident. Insights of these analyses are responsible for thwarting future attacks, patching vulnerabilities, and enhancing security protocols. All these steps utilise the different learning paradigms and neural network architectures like CNNs, RNNs, LSTMs, and GNNs to handle spatial, sequential, and intricately complex data (Reedy, 2023).

Cybersecurity forensics has become a crucial component of organisational security strategies and law enforcement due to the rise in cybercrimes. Accordingly, this requires technical expertise, analytical skills, legal knowledge, and highly advanced algorithms.

3. CHALLENGES IN DEEP LEARNING FORENSICS

Integrating deep learning into forensic science represents a significant advancement offering enhanced capabilities in analysing large, complicated datasets and detecting intricate patterns relevant to forensic investigators. However, there are difficulties with this integration, which are particularly evident in areas concerning data availability and quality, as well as privacy and ethical concerns (Solanke and Biasiotti, 2022), as illustrated in Figure 11.3.

3.1 Data Availability and Quality

One of the key challenges in deep learning-based forensics is the limited access of high-quality, relevant forensic data. Since forensic datasets are essential for training and refining deep learning models, the presence of sensitive, confidential, or proprietary information renders them largely inaccessible by many researchers, industry practitioners, and professionals in the field. Given the potential risks to individual privacy and data confidentiality, it makes sense that there would be reluctance to make such data publicly accessible. However, in the forensic domain, this caution causes hindrances in developing and validating deep learning models (Thurzo et al., 2021).

The Nature of Forensic Data: Forensic data, by definition, is complex and multidimensional as it includes a wide range of data types, each with unique characteristics and challenges. For example, digital forensics involves data from multiple sources, such as network logs, mobile devices, and computer systems, each requiring a unique extraction and analysis methodology. Similarly, biometric data used in forensic investigations, such as fingerprints or DNA, requires high accuracy and precision in processing since it directly affects the course of legal proceedings. This complex and sensitive data necessitates stringent guidelines for handling, processing, and analysis, further complicating its availability for deep learning applications (Marturana and Tacconi, 2013).

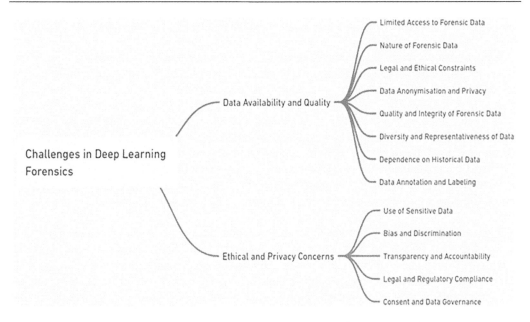

Figure 11.3 The mind map diagram illustrating the challenges in deep learning forensics

Legal and Ethical Constraints: An additional challenge affecting data availability is exist-ing legal and ethical constraints. Rightly so, these laws governing data protection, privacy, and evidence handling are strict to ensure individuals' rights and privacy. However, these necessary legal and ethical constraints make acquiring forensic data for training deep learn-ing models difficult. Thus, finding a careful balance between innovation and compliance is necessary while attempting to develop effective forensic tools (Ducato, 2020).

Data Anonymisation and Privacy: A possible solution to the data availability problem is the anonymisation of data, where identifying information is removed. However, this process is particularly challenging as it might make the training data less effective and efficient. For example, in biometric data, anonymising data by altering facial features in an image to protect the privacy and identity of individuals and prevent re-identification might strip away essential critical data crucial for forensic analysis. Similarly, masking specific genetic markers for privacy in DNA data can compromise the dataset's utility for forensic practices. The same can be seen in digital forensics, where anonymising too much data can make the data useless, while retaining too many details can cause privacy breaches (Aufschläger et al., 2023).

Quality and Integrity of Forensic Data: Beyond the availability of data, the quality and integrity of data are essential aspects as deep learning models need to be trained on accurate, comprehensive, and bias-free data. Such inconsistencies can corrupt forensic data, result-ing in error-prone outcomes. Additionally, biases in the annotation and collection of data can result in models unintentionally reinforcing these learnings in their outcomes (Yaacoub, Noura, and Salman, 2023).

Diversity and Representativeness of Data: For the development of unbiased and generalis-able deep learning models in biometric forensic analysis, it is essential to use training datasets that contain diversity in ethnicity, age, and gender. For example, a dataset lacking diversity and representativeness can make less accurate and discriminatory decisions for the under-represented groups. Similarly, in digital forensics, a dataset focusing on malware analysis must include various types of malware, from viruses to trojans and ransomware, each with unique behavioural patterns to train and utilise deep learning models effectively (Hazırbaş et al., 2021).

Dependence on Historical Data: Because of the advancements in criminal techniques and technologies, criminal techniques and technologies are constantly evolving, making historical data potentially outdated or unrepresentative of current realities. This becomes a big issue when deep learning models are trained on data that are no longer relevant, making them ill-equipped to recognise and respond to emerging cyberthreats. Additionally, the rapid advancement in digital technologies, such as the emergence of new devices or network architecture, will lead to gaps in the models' understanding of contemporary digital environments. Furthermore, the learning process of the model may be distorted by potential biases that exist in historical datasets, which may result from the particular circumstances and settings in which the data was gathered, impacting the models' efficacy and generalisability (van Giffen et al., 2022).

Data Annotation and Labeling: In forensic science, data annotation involves tagging data with labels that help deep learning models understand and learn from the data. However, this poses significant challenges due to the complexity of the data and the sensitivity of the data. Notably, the complexity is increased by the expertise required for accurately labelling data, including intricate and sensitive details, such as network logs in digital forensics or biometric data. The challenge is further compounded by the sheer volume of data required for annotation in forensic applications, which makes the process time-consuming and laborious. So, maintaining quality control in annotation is essential because erroneous or inconsistent labelling can result in poorly-trained models, which can produce biased or unreliable predictions (Li et al., 2022).

By addressing all these challenges represented in Figure 11.4, deep learning models can be better equipped to handle the intricate and vital tasks required in forensic science, leading to more effective and trustworthy outcomes.

3.2 Ethical and Privacy Concerns

The use of deep learning has unquestionably improved the capabilities of forensic science. However, this development raises several ethical issues and privacy concerns that must be addressed appropriately. These concerns are specifically relevant considering the high stakes in forensic applications, where decisions from deep learning applications can significantly impact individual lives and legal proceedings.

Use of Sensitive Data: (Sarabdeen, 2022) Deep learning models in forensic science necessitate handling highly sensitive data, such as personal biometric data (fingerprint, DNA profiles, facial recognition data), private communications (email, text messages, social media posts), and confidential information (financial records, medical history, or other privileged information). Using such personal data in deep learning models for forensic applications raises questions about consent and the right to privacy. Another factor is the risk of sensitive information being leaked or exposed during the handling process, which leads to privacy breaches (Sarabdeen, 2022).

Bias and Discrimination: In integrating artificial intelligence and deep learning forensic science applications, there is the inherent risk of bias and potential for discrimination. The most common sources of this are data-driven bias and bias from how the algorithm is constructed and designed. The latter might result from the developers' unconscious prejudices or preferences or due to the attributes or data points the model chooses to assign more weight to in the neural network architecture. These biases can result in problems like erroneous identification in criminal investigations or uneven scrutiny of particular demographic groups (P. Chen et al., 2023).

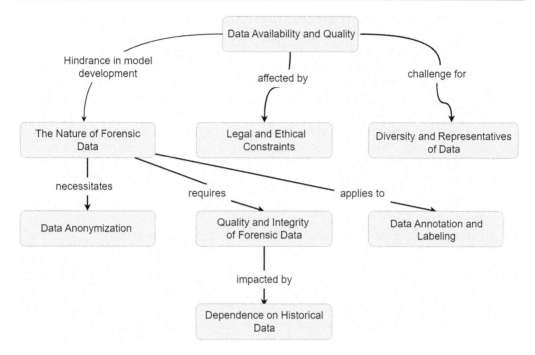

Figure 11.4 The class diagram illustrating the different aspects of data availability and quality in the context of deep learning-based forensics

Transparency and Accountability: Deep learning models have intricate, complex internal mechanisms, especially those involving neural network architecture. The multiple layers of computations and transformations performed on input data render it impossible to explain precisely how a conclusion is reached. This is called the 'black box' nature of many deep learning models and challenges forensic science because of its lack of interpretability (Saleem et al., 2022).

Legal and Regulatory Compliance: Legal regulations governing the use of artificial intelligence in forensics can differ significantly from one jurisdiction to another. This variance may be found in rules governing the use of technology in law enforcement, criteria for the admission of evidence in court, and data privacy legislation. These variances may also present extra hurdles for organisations operating internationally or dealing with cross-border data. They then have to navigate the intricacies of international law and ensure compliance with a wide range of legal requirements (Miller, 2023).

Consent and Data Governance: As part of investigations, personal data is frequently gathered involuntarily, which calls into question the appropriate use of the person's data in deep learning forensic applications and the consent of the individual. Furthermore, many legal systems offer exceptions from the need for consent for data acquisition in criminal investigations. However, care must be taken to ensure that these exceptions are carefully weighed against the rights and privacy of individuals (*Forensic DNA Phenotyping: Privacy Breach, Bias Reification and the Pitfalls of Abstract Assessments of Rights – Margaux Coquet, Nuria Terrado-Ortuño, 2023*, n.d.).

These challenges in deep learning-based forensics highlight the complexities of integrating advanced artificial technologies. Addressing these challenges involves technical solutions, ethical guidelines, legal frameworks, and a commitment to transparency and accountability.

4. DEEP LEARNING-BASED ANTI-FORENSICS

In deep learning, anti-forensics represents a significant challenge between forensic analysis and evasion techniques. The term "anti-forensics" refers to methods and techniques intended to obstruct, hinder, or manipulate forensic investigations. As forensic analysis powered by deep learning technologies becomes increasingly sophisticated, anti-forensic techniques become more and more advanced in their ability to target and neutralise these models. However, while anti-forensic techniques are not inherently unlawful, they may be employed with malevolent intentions. This generates an ongoing cycle of progress and resistance between forensic experts and individuals utilising anti-forensic methodologies. It is thus essential to comprehend the nature and ramifications of these strategies in an era of ever-improving technology (Stamm and Zhao, 2022).

4.1 Understanding Anti-Forensics: Methods and Motivations

Nature of Anti-forensics: Anti-forensics aims to build barriers that lessen the effectiveness of forensic tools and processes. In the past, anti-forensics was limited to relatively straightforward methods like file deleting or disk formatting. However, with the progression of digital forensic techniques, countermeasures to attack them have also progressed. This might include more sophisticated strategies like encrypting sensitive data or actions as basic as deleting files. The primary aim is thus either to completely erase digital footprints or obscure them, making the path of digital investigation immensely difficult (Majed et al., 2020).

Motivations Behind Anti-forensics: The use of anti-forensic techniques is motivated by a wide range of factors, from good intentions to evil deeds. On the one hand, people may use anti-forensic techniques to protect their privacy and autonomy in a world where intrusive monitoring technologies are becoming increasingly prevalent. Accordingly, some people who want to retain control over their digital presence and personal data may regard anti-forensics as an essential defence against the widespread surveillance of their digital footprints. On the other hand, criminals and corrupt individuals use anti-forensic techniques for various illicit and illegal purposes. These can include attempts to evade law enforcement in digital crime and deleting digital evidence that might connect them to illegal activities. In cybersecurity, such anti-forensic techniques are employed by hackers and cybercriminals to hide their identities during and after cyberattacks (Nisioti et al., 2021).

Furthermore, anti-forensics can be used to hide a specific entity or nation-state's involvement in cyber operations within the context of corporate espionage or state-sponsored cyber activities. By effectively erasing or camouflaging digital footprints, they aim to conduct operations covertly, avoiding diplomatic or political repercussions.

Another motivation behind anti-forensics is the growing concern over government overreach and degradation of civil liberties in the digital age. Accordingly, some individuals and organisations employ anti-forensic techniques as a means of resistance or protest against what they perceive as unfair monitoring tactics. This is particularly evident in authoritarian countries where political repression is achieved through government surveillance. In such situations, anti-forensics becomes crucial in upholding the right to free speech and safeguarding human rights (Horsman and Errickson, 2019).

In addition to these motivating factors, the need for intellectual challenge and technical improvements also drives the creation and application of anti-forensic techniques. Accordingly, some people experiment with anti-forensics to test the reliability of forensic techniques and investigate the boundaries of technology. This also includes researchers and hobbyists who try to identify vulnerabilities in digital systems and contribute to the body of knowledge on digital forensics and cybersecurity.

In summary, there are many different and intricate reasons for anti-forensics, ranging from the defense of individual privacy to illegal activity and evading cybersecurity. Thus, understanding the motivations behind anti-forensics is crucial to developing effective strategies to counter anti-forensic techniques and managing ethical and legal ramifications (Yaacoub, Noura, Salman, et al., 2023).

4.2 Evasion and Obfuscation Techniques

In the ever-changing field of cybersecurity, evasion techniques are getting more complex as attackers create new strategies to bypass sophisticated tools, including artificial intelligence-driven security systems. Understanding these evasion techniques is crucial to developing more effective cybersecurity strategies.

Figure 11.5 shows that these attacks are possible for the deep learning model, even though it does not establish direct associations between the adversarial attack and malware modification. Though not a direct association, the hidden directional dashed line suggests possible actions that might take place following the model's training.

Adversarial Attacks: An important technique is adversarial attacks that entail making minuscule, frequently undetectable modifications to data inputs after the model has been trained, which causes the deep learning models to produce inaccurate results. Adversarial attacks can then easily transform the model's greatest strength, which is the capacity to evaluate massive amounts of data and draw conclusions from it, into a vulnerability by deceptively altering data. Such attacks are sometimes challenging to identify since altering data is done in ways that are invisible to humans but cause the deep learning models

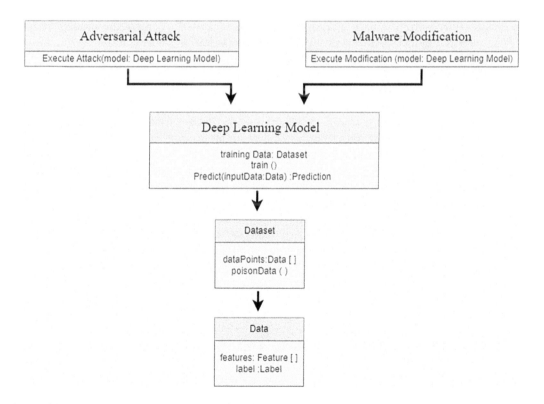

Figure 11.5 Deep learning model possibility of an attack during its training phase

to draw incorrect solutions. Researchers have shown that in the context of these models, minor changes to stop signs in photographs might render them undetectable by driverless cars, presenting severe safety concerns (Wang et al., 2022; Gnanasambandam et al., 2021).

Modifying Malware Code: A common and advanced cybercrime tactic is changing malware code to avoid artificial intelligence-based security systems detecting it. Attackers might redesign their malware by comprehending how artificial intelligence models recognise dangers to avoid detection. The techniques include changing the malware's code structure or integrating benign code segments to confuse the models. Additionally, key malware components can be encrypted, preventing malware recognition. Another technique is to alter the malware signature so that it becomes unrecognisable compared to known threats in the databases. Other techniques involve polymorphic and metamorphic techniques, which involve the malware altering its code at every iteration. While the former can change its code through encryption, the latter can rewrite its malware code entirely. Such techniques exploit specific artificial systems weaknesses, such as training limitations. Some attackers even use artificial intelligence-driven tools to create and develop the malware, automating the testing and modification process (*How Security Analysts Can Use AI in Cybersecurity*, 2023).

Additionally, techniques like obfuscation, which entails purposely confusing the malware code, hampers the models' ability to accurately identify and recognise the malware's true intent. Also, attackers can evade behavioural techniques by designing malware that alters its behaviour under scrutiny or by remaining dormant until it bypasses detection, known as the timing-based evasion technique.

Data Poisoning: In the context of cybersecurity, data poisoning is a subtle, indirect, and effective way to compromise deep learning models. This approach skews the model's learning process by purposefully contaminating the training data used to create the model. Attackers can alter the model's comprehension and interpretation of data by adding erroneous or misleading data to the training set, decreasing the model's ability to recognise and react to threats like malware (Gupta et al., 2023). These assaults range from simple injections of incorrect labels or features in the training dataset to more complex strategies that involve creating inputs to exploit the weaknesses in the learning algorithm.

Thus, data poisoning aims to take advantage of the deep learning systems' fundamental dependence on their training data since it depends on large datasets to learn how to identify patterns, anomalies, and accurately classify inputs. The model's capacity to generate accurate predictions or identifications is severely hampered when the training data is contaminated with errors or misleading information, leading to biased, inaccurate and error-prone deep learning models (Shinde et al., n.d.).

Often, attackers might use a combination of different techniques to create a more complex and challenging attack chain. This dynamic of evolving cybersecurity measures and deep learning advanced models against the developing cybercriminal's evasion techniques is similar to a cat-and-mouse game, wherein each security development inspires a new form of evasion. This cycle of innovation and adaptation in cybersecurity is critical, as it ensures that defences continue to be successful against ever-evolving threats.

5. DEEP LEARNING IN COUNTERING ANTI-FORENSICS

As anti-forensics tactics get more sophisticated in digital forensics, it is imperative to understand the different anti-forensics tactics mentioned in Table 11.1 and create solutions that address each of these challenges and limitations.

Table 11.1 Aspects of deep learning in forensics

Aspect of deep learning in forensics	Description	Citations
Pattern recognition	Deep learning algorithms excel in identifying and classifying patterns in forensic data, crucial for recognising evidence and anomalies.	(Reedy, 2023)
Adversarial attack detection	Utilising deep learning to detect and counter adversarial attacks that aim to manipulate or evade forensic analysis.	(Qiao et al., 2022)
Anomaly detection	Leveraging deep learning for identifying irregularities or anomalies in data, which are often indicative of forensic interest.	(Landauer et al., 2023)
Training with diverse data	Enhancing the robustness of deep learning models by training them with diverse and representative datasets.	(Y. Zhang et al., 2023)
Network traffic analysis for cybersecurity	Applying deep learning to analyse network traffic, aiding in the detection of cyberthreats and malicious activities.	(Abbasi et al., 2021)
Strengthening conventional forensic instruments	Integrating deep learning to improve the efficiency and accuracy of traditional forensic tools and methods.	(Del Mar-Raave et al., 2021)
Real-time analysis	Employing deep learning for the real-time analysis of data; crucial for timely forensic investigations.	(Kebande et al., 2020)
Minimising false positives	Using deep learning to reduce the rate of false positives in forensic analysis, thereby increasing reliability.	(Landauer et al., 2023)
Automated response systems	Implementing deep learning in automated systems for immediate response to forensic findings.	(Bollé et al., 2020)
Explainability and transparency	Focusing on making deep learning models in forensics more explainable and transparent for legal and ethical compliance.	(Solanke, 2022)
Collaborative frameworks and shared knowledge	Developing collaborative frameworks using deep learning to share knowledge and insights across forensic domains.	(Himeur et al., 2023)

5.1 Detection of Anti-Forensic Activities and Enhancing Resilience

By training deep learning models on extensive datasets that cover a variety of cyberattack patterns, these algorithms can be trained to detect subtle anomalies or manipulations indicative of such threats as shown in Figure 11.6.

Pattern Recognition: Deep learning algorithms are particularly good at identifying patterns in large, complicated datasets. These algorithms analyse vast amounts of network traffic or user activity data to find patterns typical of particular assaults. This entails identifying known malware fingerprints, network intrusion patterns, or anomalous data flows that point to a breach. These obfuscating or changing data can be detected by fine-tuning deep learning models, especially those trained on pattern recognition training. In picture forensics, for example, this might include identifying anomalous pixel patterns or discrepancies in image information that point to tampering (Aldhaheri et al., 2024).

Adversarial Attack Detection: In the digital realm, one of the primary methods for countering forensic assaults is to identify adversarial attacks on deep learning models. Since these attacks are intended to be undetectable to the human eye and frequently blend in with real data, identifying them is difficult. By learning to identify the minute patterns or abnormalities typical of these assaults, deep learning models may be trained to identify manipulated data or changed inputs (Alkhowaiter et al., 2023).

Anomaly Detection: Data anomalies frequently indicate possible security risks. Training deep learning models to identify "normal" behavior or data patterns in a system is possible. These models can identify anomalies that require more research when they deviate from the predetermined norms. This works especially well for spotting new or developing cyberthreats that don't fit established patterns (Aktar and Yasin Nur, 2023).

Training with Diverse Data: The quality and variety of the training data are critical factors in determining how well deep learning detects assaults. Models trained on various malware kinds, attack pathways, and threat scenarios can better comprehend possible cyber threats. Training on data covering various network contexts, user habits, and attack techniques is part of this. Also, deep learning models must often be updated with fresh data to reflect the most recent threat landscape. This guarantees that the models will continue to recognise novel and developing dangers (Yi et al., 2023).

Network traffic analysis for cybersecurity: Malicious network traffic is frequently hidden using anti-forensic measures. Deep learning models may analyse big data from networks to find patterns pointing to these evasion strategies. This study may involve finding abnormalities in data packet architecture, strange access patterns, or inconsistencies in traffic flow (Sarker, 2023).

Strengthening Conventional Forensic Instruments: Deep learning can strengthen conventional forensic instruments, increasing their potency against countermeasures. For instance, deep learning may be integrated with file analysis tools to improve the instruments' capacity to identify encrypted or hidden data (Reedy, 2023, pp. 2019–2022).

Real-Time Analysis: The capacity to evaluate data in real-time is essential for many cybersecurity applications. The ability of deep learning models to analyse large volumes of data fast makes it possible to detect dangers in real-time. This is essential for minimising possible harm, making it possible to react quickly to security problems (*Artificial Intelligence for Cybersecurity: Literature Review and Future Research Directions – ScienceDirect*, n.d.).

Minimising False Positives: One of the difficulties in cybersecurity is reducing the number of harmless actions that are inadvertently reported as threats. False alarms can be decreased by fine-tuning deep learning models to discern between benign abnormalities and real threats more correctly.

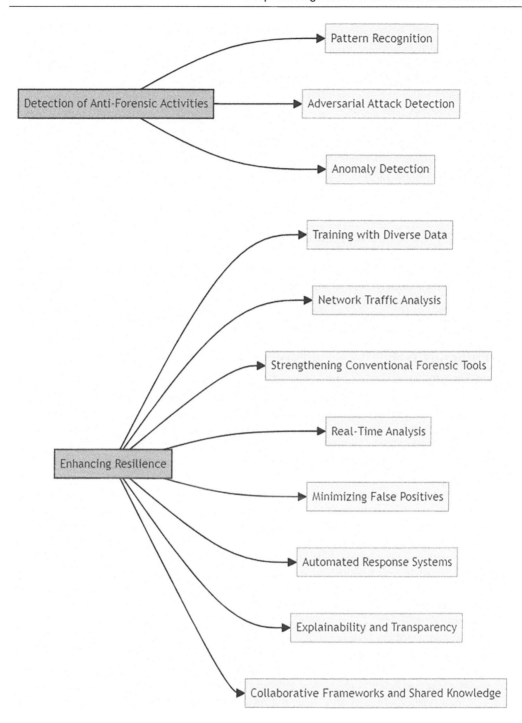

Figure 11.6 Sequence diagram workflow in detecting anti-forensic activities using deep learning

Automated Response Systems: Deep learning models may occasionally be included in automated systems that react to identified hazards. Based on the model's identification, these systems can perform predetermined actions, such as isolating impacted network segments or obstructing malicious traffic. They can adjust and improve their detection skills as they encounter new information and situations, making them more proficient at spotting cyberthreats (Kaur et al., 2023).

Explainability and Transparency: In forensic settings, improving the explainability and transparency of deep learning models is crucial. Models that can rationalise their results in a way that makes sense are more reliable and can be examined more thoroughly for any weaknesses in anti-forensic methods.

Collaborative Frameworks and Shared Knowledge: More powerful forensic tools can result from cooperation between many organisations, including law enforcement, cybersecurity specialists, and artificial intelligence researchers. More robust systems can be aided by exchanging knowledge about cutting-edge AI developments and novel anti-forensic methods (Kaur et al., 2023).

6. FUTURE TRENDS AND DIRECTIONS

With major ethical and legal ramifications and driven by rising technology, the profession of forensic analysis is poised for revolutionary change. This investigation explores the potential trends and paths in forensic analysis going forward, particularly emphasising integrating cutting-edge technologies with the changing moral and legal environment.

6.1 Emerging Technologies in Forensic Analysis

Artificial Intelligence and Machine Learning: Future developments are expected to bring even more profound changes to the field of forensic analysis as these technologies have already started to improve forensic investigations' ability to recognise patterns, making it possible to analyse big data sets more accurately and efficiently. The growth of predictive analytics is one of the most important upcoming trends in this sector as deep learning expedites identifying suspects by analysing large amounts of data from various sources, such as social media and surveillance.

In order to forecast future occurrences, this use of deep learning models includes examining patterns and trends from big datasets, which might entail anticipating crime trends or identifying regions that may be more vulnerable to particular kinds of criminal activity in forensic circumstances. Accordingly, law enforcement organisations might greatly benefit from such predictive powers in terms of resource allocation and strategic planning. Additionally, forensic laboratories can benefit significantly from the application as these technologies can free up forensic specialists to concentrate on more difficult parts of cases by automating mundane operations and analysis (Dakalbab et al., 2022).

Furthermore, the methods for identifying and looking into suspects are going to be completely changed; since these systems can scan and analyse large volumes of data at previously unheard-of rates, they can quickly identify possible suspects from a variety of data sources, such as social media, surveillance footage, and other digital traces. In addition to accelerating the analytical process, this automation will improve its correctness and reduce the possibility of human mistakes. Thus, deep learning models can help to streamline the investigative process by helping to go through massive amounts of evidence to find the most pertinent bits. Also, it has potential applications beyond the investigative stage, such as in legal processes where in-depth evidence analyses might be produced, which would aid in creating more comprehensible and transparent displays of intricate forensic data. This might improve the fairness and efficiency of the judicial process by helping jurors and judges make more informed choices.

Blockchain for Evidence Management: The irreversible and transparent properties of blockchain technology make it a promising tool for revolutionising the management and storage of evidence in forensic contexts. The principal appeal of the technology is its capacity to maintain unalterable documentation, rendering it an ideal platform for safeguarding the integrity and authenticity of forensic data.

Immutable record-keeping: At the core of blockchain technology is its capacity to create records that cannot be modified or deleted since each 'block' of data is time-stamped and linked to the previous block, creating a chronological chain of data. This feature is crucial for forensic evidence as it ensures that once a piece of evidence is recorded on a blockchain, it cannot be tampered with or altered.

Enhanced Chain of Custody: Blockchain has the potential to greatly enhance the management of the digital evidence chain of custody. It establishes an unbreakable and transparent trail from when the evidence is gathered to when it is presented in court by documenting each custody transfer on a blockchain. This procedure ensures that the evidence is uncontaminated throughout its lifespan by adding extra protection and responsibility.

Transparency and Trust: Every transaction or modification can be seen and verified by all parties involved, thanks to the transparent nature of blockchain technology. Since all parties involved may independently confirm the integrity and validity of the evidence, this transparency helps to build confidence in the evidence management process.

Decentralisation of Evidence Storage: Blockchain technology is decentralised, in contrast to conventional centralised databases. Due to its decentralisation, the evidence is more resistant to loss, corruption, and assaults since it is kept throughout a network of computers rather than in a single location.

Reduction of Human Error and Fraud: Blockchain reduces the possibility of fraud and human mistakes. The automated nature of the blockchain's evidence recording and transfer mechanism decreases the possibility of intentional manipulation and human mistake.

Integration with Other Technologies: Artificial intelligence and the Internet of Things (IoT) are two other technologies with which blockchain can be successfully connected. AI may be used to search for patterns and discrepancies in blockchain data, and it can also be used to record evidence gathered by Internet of Things devices directly.

Smart Contracts for Automated Compliance: The smart contract function of blockchain technology enables the automatic enforcement of evidence-handling guidelines and procedures. To ensure adherence to legal requirements, for example, smart contracts can be designed to either permit or limit access to evidence under specific circumstances.

Blockchain technology thus has the potential to become a common tool in evidence management as technological advancements and regulatory frameworks change, providing a more efficient, transparent, and safe means of handling forensic data.

Advanced Biometrics: Modern biometric technologies, which go well beyond conventional techniques like fingerprint and facial identification, are becoming increasingly essential to forensic science. These new technologies cover a broad spectrum of distinctive human traits, providing fresh perspectives on identification and research.

Voice Recognition: Voice biometrics aims to recognise people by their voice traits. These characteristics, which are as distinct as fingerprints, include pitch, tone, and cadence, all analysed by the technology. In situations where vocal exchanges constitute critical evidence, such as in investigations involving recorded communications, voice recognition can be extremely important.

Gait Analysis: Gait recognition is recognising people by their gait patterns. Each individual has a distinct gait that may be recorded via video surveillance. When obstacles or low visibility make facial recognition difficult, gait analysis might be very helpful.

Heartbeat Recognition: Heartbeat recognition is a new biometric that identifies a person based on the distinct patterns of their heart rhythm. This technology can be used for tracking in specialised investigations or high-security settings. It usually involves the use of sensitive scanners or wearable sensors.

Iris and Retinal Scanning: These biometrics, which are based on the eyes, are known for their high accuracy. Retinal scanning examines the blood vessels in the back of the eye, whereas iris recognition examines the coloured ring surrounding the pupil. For safe identification verification, both are being utilised more and more.

Palm Vein and Hand Geometry Recognition: These techniques examine the hand's form or the vein patterns in the palm. They may be employed in many forensic circumstances and are less invasive, especially when confirming identity at crime scenes.

Ear Shape Recognition: Every person has a different ear structure and shape. In forensic analysis, ear shape recognition—which is frequently combined with other face recognition technologies—can be a useful tool, particularly when dealing with cases involving photos or videos.

Behavioral Biometrics: This area of study covers recognition from mouse motions, keyboard stroke patterns, and device interactions, which can be extremely useful in identifying people through their digital activities.

DNA Phenotyping: Using DNA samples, DNA phenotyping goes beyond conventional DNA analysis to estimate physical characteristics and ancestry. When suspects are unknown, this might lead to possible lines of inquiry.

Chemical Biometrics: Analysing chemical indicators in the body, such as breath or perspiration, may be used to track stress levels and detect drug usage, which can be useful in some types of investigations.

Integrating these biometric technologies with artificial intelligence can significantly enhance the capability of deep learning models.

Virtual and Augmented Reality: The fields of forensic science are finding more and more uses for virtual and augmented reality (VR and AR) technology, which provide creative approaches to crime scene reconstruction and analysis. These technologies' immersive qualities greatly improve forensic skills by offering a novel and interactive approach to examining and comprehending crime scenes.

Crime Scene Reconstruction: Detailed, interactive 3D reconstructions of crime scenes may be produced using VR and AR. In difficult situations or when the real location is no longer accessible, investigators and forensic specialists can digitally return and examine the scene.

Improved Evidence Presentation in Courtrooms: It is essential to provide evidence in legal procedures in a straightforward and thorough manner. Virtual reality (VR) and augmented reality (AR) can project digital images of crime scenes or forensic evidence in the courtroom, providing juries and judges with a more realistic and vivid picture of the case.

Training and Education: Forensic specialists can receive realistic training settings thanks to these technologies. Accordingly, by conducting investigations, interacting with simulated crime scenes, and learning procedures in a safe yet realistic environment, trainers may improve their abilities and readiness for real-world situations.

In-depth Examination of the Evidence: VR and AR enable a more detailed examination of evidence. Investigators can zoom in, rotate, and interact with virtual representations of physical evidence, providing a deeper understanding of the crime scene's layout and the spatial relationship between different pieces of evidence.

Collaborative Investigations: These technologies facilitate collaborative investigations, allowing multiple experts to examine a crime scene simultaneously, even in different geographical locations. This collaboration can lead to more comprehensive analyses and quicker resolutions of cases.

Integration with Other Technologies: To provide more precise and in-depth depictions of crime scenes, VR and AR may be combined with other forensic technologies like photogrammetry, drones, and 3D scanning.

Virtual Autopsies and Pathology: Virtual reality (VR) may be utilised in forensic pathology to conduct virtual autopsies, eliminating intrusive procedures by enabling doctors to examine a body in a virtual environment.

Accessibility and Preservation: These technologies offer a way to digitally archive crime scenes for an extended period of time. This might be helpful in lengthy scenarios when the scene could normally alter over time.

Public Engagement and Jury Understanding: Complex forensic evidence may be made easier to access and comprehend for jurors, who might not have a background in forensic science, by utilising VR and AR in courtrooms.

Automation and Robotics: An important development in forensic analysis is the use of automation and robots, which improves productivity, accuracy, and safety—particularly for labour-intensive, repetitive, or dangerous operations.

Streamlining Evidence Processing: Automation technologies greatly accelerate the processing of many kinds of evidence, including forensic evidence. Automation speeds up the process and lowers the chance of human error in jobs like DNA analysis, which typically calls for careful manual labor. This efficiency is essential when managing substantial amounts of evidence and in situations where time is of the essence.

Enhanced Accuracy and Consistency: Forensic analyses are performed with high precision and consistency thanks to automation. Automated systems can execute intricate computations and procedures more accurately, producing more dependable and predictable outcomes. The integrity of forensic investigations and the admissibility of evidence in court cases depend on this uniformity.

Robotics in Hazardous Environments: Robots help inspect crime scenes that provide a risk to human investigators. Scenes involving biological, chemical, or radioactive hazards fall within this category. Personnel health concerns can thus be reduced by using robots with sensors and cameras to traverse these areas, gather samples, and transmit real-time data back to investigators.

Advanced Crime Scene Investigation: Advanced crime scene investigations can use robotics technology. For example, drones may film and take pictures from the air of vast crime scenes or difficult-to-reach locations. Investigators may obtain extensive views and layouts of crime scenes by using ground-based robots to do precise 3D mapping.

Automated Lab Analysis: Automation helps forensic labs simplify several analytical operations, including robotic arms that can handle and examine evidence under controlled settings and automated DNA sequencers and analysers that can process many samples at once.

Data Analysis and Management: Automated solutions are essential for efficient data management and analysis due to the growing amount of data in forensic investigations. Large datasets may be arranged, stored, and analysed with the help of automation software, which also helps to identify important patterns, correlations, and insights from the gathered data.

Robot-Assisted Autopsies and Examinations: In forensic pathology, robotics can help by carrying out or supporting autopsies and exams, increasing process accuracy and lessening the physical burden on pathologists.

Integration with Other Technologies: Automation and robotics perform better in forensic applications when combined with other technologies, such as artificial intelligence and machine learning. Robotic systems in evidence analysis can be guided by AI-driven algorithms, resulting in more intelligent and flexible forensic procedures.

IoT and Smart Devices in Forensics: By presenting smart gadgets and home automation systems as fresh sources of digital evidence, the Internet of Things (IoT) is dramatically changing forensic analysis (Gaurav et al., 2023). These gadgets, which are becoming increasingly common in homes and private areas, include wearables and linked appliances, and they constantly gather and send data that might offer important new information for forensic investigations. The abundance of information gleaned from IoT devices—which mirror people's actions, whereabouts, and interactions—opens up new lines of inquiry by providing forensic specialists with comprehensive digital footprints to examine. Notwithstanding the wide range of devices and platforms, obtaining and evaluating data from them poses distinct difficulties because of the differences in data formats, encryption, and storage techniques. Furthermore, the analysis process is complex and demanding due to the wide and diverse nature of the data created by IoT devices, necessitating the use of advanced data analytics tools and methodologies.

6.2 Future of Ethical and Legal Implications in Advanced Forensics

The development of forensic instruments and technology raises several intricate moral and legal issues requiring careful thought and action. As these instruments become more advanced and sophisticated, they frequently stray into domains that contradict accepted moral and legal standards. For example, collecting biometric data or widespread monitoring creates serious privacy issues and may violate people's rights. Furthermore, concerns of ingrained bias are brought to light by the growing use of artificial intelligence learning paradigms in forensic settings, which may result in false allegations or unfair practices (Kloosterman et al., 2015).

Apart from the technological obstacles, using personal device data in forensic inquiries gives rise to noteworthy privacy and ethical apprehensions, demanding meticulous handling of legal and ethical limits. Another developing issue is the legal admissibility of evidence from IoT devices, with courts considering privacy considerations and data dependability. Therefore, to guarantee the overall quality and dependability of the evidence, careful correlation and verification are necessary when integrating this new type of digital evidence with conventional forensic techniques. This is also significant when different countries have varying data protection laws, making it complicated to access data across borders. Given these circumstances, it is then imperative to carefully navigate international laws and comprehend the legal frameworks governing data access in various regions, Additionally, the rise of sophisticated, complex algorithms in deep learning has exacerbated the 'black-box' problem. This lack of transparency becomes a severe issue in fields where understanding the decision-making process is crucial, such as healthcare, finance, and legal systems, leading to the need for models to show they arrive at their conclusions.

Developing Explainable Artificial Intelligence (XAI): Explainable artificial intelligence focuses on building deep learning models with human-interpretable decision-making processes that are intrinsically more transparent. Applying this concept to forensic applications can bridge the gap between the technical complexity of the model and the need for understandable explanations.

The use cases for creating XAI for deep learning as applied by a forensic analyst are shown in Figure 11.7. It describes the different methods used to attain explainability, the general difficulties encountered in striking a balance between interpretability and model complexity, and the current research and development initiatives in the area (Z. S. Chen et al., 2022).

The two main components of XAI are being able to explain the results and processes in a way that is accessible to humans and making sure that these explanations accurately reflect how deep learning systems work. This covers the model's interpretability (i.e., how it functions) and the findings' explainability (i.e., how the model arrives at a specific conclusion). To achieve this explainability in algorithms, various techniques are employed that are discussed in the following:

Simpler Model Approximations: In this method, the behaviour of sophisticated deep learning models is approximated by employing more comprehensible models, such as decision

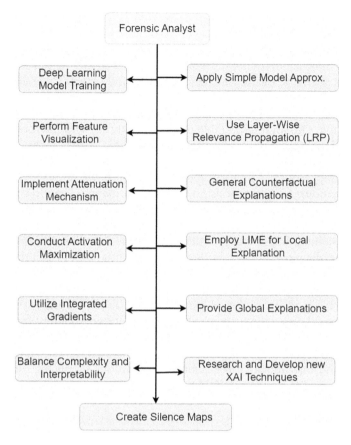

Figure 11.7 The development of Explainable Artificial Intelligence (XAI) deep learning models in forensic applications

trees or linear regressions. These approximations provide a more understandable picture of how neural networks make decisions.

Feature visualisation: This technique helps see and comprehend the characteristics a deep learning model considers necessary when generating judgements. In order to provide insights into what the model "sees" and "learns" from the input data, it entails visualising the features and layers inside neural networks.

Layer-Wise Relevance Propagation (LRP): By backpropagating the prediction value via the neural network layers, LRP is a technique used to explain the predictions of complicated models. This technique aids in determining the input data points that were most important to the model's conclusion.

Attention Mechanisms: Originally designed for tasks related to natural language processing, attention mechanisms in neural networks offer information on the specific segments of the input data that the model prioritises during decision-making. This method has proven essential for comprehending how models make decisions, particularly when doing tasks like picture captioning or translation.

Counterfactual Explanations: This technique entails gently altering the input data and assessing the impact of these modifications on the model's predictions. Understanding which input modifications result in which outputs can provide insight into the model's decision-making process.

Activation Maximisation: In this case, the objective is to identify the input data that optimises the network's activation of specific neurons or layers. This facilitates comprehension of the characteristics or inputs the network searches during decision-making.

Saliency maps: Saliency maps are a useful tool for displaying the salient features of input data that are most crucial to the decisions made by a neural network. These maps indicate the regions of the input data (similar to an image's pixels) that influence the result most.

Local Interpretable Model-Agnostic Explanations (LIME): LIME is a method that uses a local approximation with an interpretable model to faithfully and interpretably explain any classifier's predictions.

Integrated Gradients: This technique offers a more precise knowledge of feature relevance by attributing a deep network's prediction to its input features.

Global Explanations: Some methods go beyond elucidating a model's individual predictions to comprehensively understand the model's general behaviour, which can be done by combining local explanations or examining the model's behaviour over several data subsets.

XAI is thus becoming increasingly critical in various domains. For instance, it helps in understanding the diagnostic and treatment recommendations in healthcare. Similarly, it helps interpret credit scoring models or fraud detection systems in finance. However, there are challenges in implementing XAI, which is the trade-off between model complexity and interpretability. This is evident when a simpler model is contrasted with a complex deep neural network model, since the former will be more interpretable but less accurate. At the same time, the latter will be more accurate but less interpretable. Thus, a significant problem is striking a balance between these two aspects. Therefore, ongoing research aims to provide new techniques and instruments for explainability without sacrificing the functionality of deep learning systems (W. Yang et al., 2023).

7. CONCLUSION

The convergence of forensic science with deep learning represents a revolutionary change in investigation methods, providing unmatched accuracy and analytical power. A new era of efficiency and precision in criminal investigations is heralded by deep learning's use in biometrics, digital forensics, image and video analysis, and predictive policing. The identification of patterns and processing of large datasets has transformed the fields of evidence analysis and identity verification. This technological revolution is, however, not without difficulties. Obstacles to deep learning integration in forensics include restricted data availability, issues with quality and integrity, ethical and legal restraints, and the possibility of prejudice and bias. These difficulties demand that technical innovation and ethical issues be carefully balanced.

An important counterforce is the rise of deep learning-based anti-forensics methods like data poisoning and adversarial attacks. These techniques are designed to impede forensic analysis, necessitating advanced detection and reaction plans. Proactive protection against these changing threats can be provided by deep learning algorithms that are taught to detect minute irregularities and manipulations.

The ongoing integration and adaptation of developing technology will shape forensic science in the future. The industry is expected to transform more using blockchain for evidence management, sophisticated biometrics, virtual and augmented reality, automation and robots, and IoTs. These developments are expected to improve forensic processes' accuracy, transparency, and efficiency.

However, serious worry remains about these technologies' moral and legal ramifications. XAI is needed to address concerns about privacy, data governance, and the 'black box' nature of deep learning models. The goal of XAI is thus to close the gap between the necessity of clear, intelligible forensic procedures and technical complexity.

Conclusively, incorporating deep learning into forensic science signifies a noteworthy advancement, providing improved capacities to scrutinise convoluted patterns and evaluate intricate datasets. It also highlights the necessity of addressing data quality, privacy, ethical issues, and the resistance to cutting-edge anti-forensic methods. Achieving a balance between utilising technical breakthroughs and upholding ethical, legal, and privacy concerns is critical for the future of forensic research. The future direction of forensic science will be significantly influenced by ongoing adaptation and the assimilation of new technology.

REFERENCES

Abbasi, M., Shahraki, A., & Taherkordi, A. (2021). Deep learning for network traffic monitoring and analysis (NTMA): A survey. *Computer Communications*, 170, 19–41. https://doi.org/10.1016/j.comcom.2021.01.021

Abbas, Q., Ibrahim, M. E., & Jaffar, M. A. (2018). Video scene analysis: an overview and challenges on deep learning algorithms. *Multimedia Tools and Applications*, 77(16), 20415–20453.

Ahmed, S. F., Alam, Md. S. B., Hassan, M., Rozbu, M. R., Ishtiak, T., Rafa, N., Mofijur, M., Shawkat Ali, A. B. M., & Gandomi, A. H. (2023). Deep learning modelling techniques: Current progress, applications, advantages, and challenges. *Artificial Intelligence Review*, 56(11), 13521–13617. https://doi.org/10.1007/s10462-023-10466-8

Aktar, S., & Yasin Nur, A. (2023). Towards DDoS attack detection using deep learning approach. *Computers & Security*, 129, 103251. https://doi.org/10.1016/j.cose.2023.103251

Aldhaheri, A., Alwahedi, F., Ferrag, M. A., & Battah, A. (2024). Deep learning for cyber threat detection in IoT networks: A review. *Internet of Things and Cyber-Physical Systems*, 4, 110–128. https://doi.org/10.1016/j.iotcps.2023.09.003

Alkhowaiter, M., Kholidy, H., Alyami, M. A., Alghamdi, A., & Zou, C. (2023). Adversarial-aware deep learning system based on a secondary classical machine learning verification approach. *Sensors (Basel, Switzerland)*, 23(14), 6287. https://doi.org/10.3390/s23146287

Al-Waisy, A. S., Qahwaji, R., Ipson, S., & Al-Fahdawi, S. (2018). A multimodal deep learning framework using local feature representations for face recognition. *Machine Vision and Applications*, 29, 35–54.

Artificial Intelligence for Cybersecurity: Literature Review and Future Research Directions—ScienceDirect. (n.d.). Retrieved November 21, 2023, from https://www.sciencedirect.com/science/article/pii/S1566253523001136

Aufschläger, R., Folz, J., März, E., Guggumos, J., Heigl, M., Buchner, B., & Schramm, M. (2023). Anonymization procedures for tabular data: An explanatory technical and legal synthesis. *Information*, 14(9), Article 9. https://doi.org/10.3390/info14090487

Bansal, S. (2023). *The Anatomy of Web Attacks: Understanding XSS, SQLi, and Other Threats* (p. 1). Insights2Techinfo. https://insights2techinfo.com/the-anatomy-of-webattacks-understanding-xss-sqli-and-other-threats/

Barto, A. G. (1997). Chapter 2—Reinforcement learning. In O. Omidvar & D. L. Elliott (Eds.), *Neural Systems for Control* (pp. 7–30). Academic Press. https://doi.org/10.1016/B978-012526430-3/50003-9

Bloemheuvel, S., van den Hoogen, J., & Atzmueller, M. (2021). A computational framework for modeling complex sensor network data using graph signal processing and graph neural networks in structural health monitoring. *Applied Network Science*, 6(1), Article 1. https://doi.org/10.1007/s41109-021-00438-8

Bollé, T., Casey, E., & Jacquet, M. (2020). The role of evaluations in reaching decisions using automated systems supporting forensic analysis. *Forensic Science International: Digital Investigation*, 34, 301016. https://doi.org/10.1016/j.fsidi.2020.301016

Brayne, S. (2017). Big data surveillance: The case of policing. *American Sociological Review*, 82(5), 977–1008.

Busia, A., Dahl, G. E., Fannjiang, C., Alexander, D. H., Dorfman, E., Poplin, R., . . . & DePristo, M. (2018). A deep learning approach to pattern recognition for short DNA sequences. *BioRxiv*, 353474.

Casino, F., Dasaklis, T. K., Spathoulas, G. P., Anagnostopoulos, M., Ghosal, A., Borocz, I., . . . & Patsakis, C. (2022). Research trends, challenges, and emerging topics in digital forensics: A review of reviews. *IEEE Access*, 10, 25464–25493.

Chai, J., Zeng, H., Li, A., & Ngai, E. W. T. (2021). Deep learning in computer vision: A critical review of emerging techniques and application scenarios. *Machine Learning with Applications*, 6, 100134. https://doi.org/10.1016/j.mlwa.2021.100134

Chen, P., Wu, L., & Wang, L. (2023). AI fairness in data management and analytics: A review on challenges, methodologies and applications. *Applied Sciences*, 13(18), Article 18. https://doi.org/10.3390/app131810258

Chen, Z. S., Kulkarni, P. (Param), Galatzer-Levy, I. R., Bigio, B., Nasca, C., & Zhang, Y. (2022). Modern views of machine learning for precision psychiatry. *Patterns*, 3(11), 100602. https://doi.org/10.1016/j.patter.2022.100602

Chung, H., & Choe, S. (2017). Overview of forensic toxicology, yesterday, today and in the future. *Current Pharmaceutical Design*, 23(36), 5429–5436. https://doi.org/10.2174/1381612823666170622101633

Cvitić, I., Praneeth, G., & Peraković, D. (2021). *Digital Forensics Techniques for Social Media Networking* (p. 1). Insights2Techinfo. https://insights2techinfo.com/digitalforensics-techniques-for-social-media-networking/

Dakalbab, F., Abu Talib, M., Abu Waraga, O., Bou Nassif, A., Abbas, S., & Nasir, Q. (2022). Artificial intelligence & crime prediction: A systematic literature review. *Social Sciences & Humanities Open*, 6(1), 100342. https://doi.org/10.1016/j.ssaho.2022.100342

Del Mar-Raave, J. R., Bahşi, H., Mršić, L., & Hausknecht, K. (2021). A machine learning-based forensic tool for image classification—A design science approach. *Forensic Science International: Digital Investigation*, 38, 301265. https://doi.org/10.1016/j.fsidi.2021.301265

Diallo, B., Urruty, T., Bourdon, P., & Fernandez-Maloigne, C. (2020). Robust forgery detection for compressed images using CNN supervision. *Forensic Science International: Reports*, 2, 100112. https://doi.org/10.1016/j.fsir.2020.100112

Ducato, R. (2020). Data protection, scientific research, and the role of information. *Computer Law & Security Review*, 37, 105412. https://doi.org/10.1016/j.clsr.2020.105412

Dvornek, N. C., & Li, X. (2023). Chapter 13—Deep learning with connectomes. In M. D. Schirmer, T. Arichi, & A. W. Chung (Eds.), *Connectome Analysis* (pp. 289–308). Academic Press. https://doi.org/10.1016/B978-0-323-85280-7.00013-0

Dwivedi, Y. K., Hughes, L., Baabdullah, A. M., Ribeiro-Navarrete, S., Giannakis, M., Al-Debei, M. M., Dennehy, D., Metri, B., Buhalis, D., Cheung, C. M. K., Conboy, K., Doyle, R., Dubey, R., Dutot, V., Felix, R., Goyal, D. P., Gustafsson, A., Hinsch, C., Jebabli, I., . . . Wamba, S. F. (2022). Metaverse beyond the hype: Multidisciplinary perspectives on emerging challenges, opportunities, and agenda for research, practice and policy. *International Journal of Information Management*, 66, 102542. https://doi.org/10.1016/j.ijinfomgt.2022.102542

Dwivedi, Y. K., Kshetri, N., Hughes, L., Slade, E. L., Jeyaraj, A., Kar, A. K., Baabdullah, A. M., Koohang, A., Raghavan, V., Ahuja, M., Albanna, H., Albashrawi, M. A., Al-Busaidi, A. S., Balakrishnan, J., Barlette, Y., Basu, S., Bose, I., Brooks, L., Buhalis, D., . . . Wright, R. (2023). Opinion paper: "So what if ChatGPT wrote it?" Multidisciplinary perspectives on opportunities, challenges and implications of generative conversational AI for research, practice and policy. *International Journal of Information Management*, 71, 102642. https://doi.org/10.1016/j.ijinfomgt.2023.102642

El-Shafai, W., Fouda, M. A., El-Rabaie, E.-S. M., & El-Salam, N. A. (2023). A comprehensive taxonomy on multimedia video forgery detection techniques: Challenges and novel trends. *Multimedia Tools and Applications*. https://doi.org/10.1007/s11042-023-15609-1

Fayyad-Kazan, H., Hejase, A., Moukadem, I., & Kassem-Moussa, S. (2021). Verifying the audio evidence to assist forensic investigation. *Computer and Information Science*, 14, 25. https://doi.org/10.5539/cis.v14n3p25

Forensic DNA Phenotyping: Privacy Breach, Bias Reification and the Pitfalls of Abstract Assessments of Rights—Margaux Coquet, Nuria Terrado-Ortuño, 2023. (n.d.). Retrieved November 20, 2023, from https://journals.sagepub.com/doi/10.1177/14613557231184707

Garfinkel, S. L. (2010). Digital forensics research: The next 10 years. *Digital Investigation*, 7, S64–S73.

Gnanasambandam, A., Sherman, A. M., & Chan, S. H. (2021). Optical adversarial attack. In *Proceedings of the IEEE/CVF International Conference on Computer Vision* (pp. 92–101).

Gupta, B. B., Perez, G. M., Agrawal, D. P., & Gupta, D. (2020). *Handbook of Computer Networks and Cyber Security* (Vol. 10, pp. 3–978). Springer.

Gupta, P., Yadav, K., Gupta, B. B., Alazab, M., & Gadekallu, T. R. (2023). A novel data poisoning attack in federated learning based on inverted loss function. *Computers & Security*, 130, 103270.

Gaurav, A., Gupta, B. B., & Panigrahi, P. K. (2023). A comprehensive survey on machine learning approaches for malware detection in IoT-based enterprise information system. *Enterprise Information Systems*, 17(3), 2023764. https://doi.org/10.1080/17517575.2021.2023764

Gibb, C., & Riemen, J. (2023). Toward better AFIS practice and process in the forensic fingerprint environment. *Forensic Science International: Synergy*, 7, 100336. https://doi.org/10.1016/j.fsisyn.2023.100336

Gulshan, S., Prabhat, K., Gupta, B. B., Suman, B., & Nilanjan, D. (2018). *Handbook of Research on Network Forensics and Analysis Techniques*. IGI Global.

Gupta, B. B., & Agrawal, D. P. (2021). Security, privacy and forensics in the enterprise information systems. *Enterprise Information Systems*, 15(4), 445–447. https://doi.org/10.1080/17517575.2020.1791364

Hardyns, W., & Rummens, A. (2018). Predictive policing as a new tool for law enforcement? Recent developments and challenges. *European Journal on Criminal Policy and Research*, 24, 201–218.

Hazırbaş, C., Bitton, J., Dolhansky, B., Pan, J., Gordo, A., & Ferrer, C. (2021). Towards measuring fairness in AI: The casual conversations dataset. *IEEE Transactions on Biometrics, Behavior, and Identity Science*, 1. https://doi.org/10.1109/TBIOM.2021.3132237

Himeur, Y., Al-Maadeed, S., Kheddar, H., Al-Maadeed, N., Abualsaud, K., Mohamed, A., & Khattab, T. (2023). Video surveillance using deep transfer learning and deep domain adaptation: Towards better generalization. *Engineering Applications of Artificial Intelligence*, 119, 105698. https://doi.org/10.1016/j.engappai.2022.105698

Horsman, G., & Errickson, D. (2019). When finding nothing may be evidence of something: Anti-forensics and digital tool marks. *Science & Justice: Journal of the Forensic Science Society*, 59(5), 565–572. https://doi.org/10.1016/j.scijus.2019.06.004

How Security Analysts Can Use AI in Cybersecurity. (2023, May 24). freeCodeCamp.Org. https://www.freecodecamp.org/news/how-to-use-artificial-intelligence-in-cybersecurity/

Humphries, G., Nordvik, R., Manifavas, H., Cobley, P., & Sorell, M. (2021). Law enforcement educational challenges for mobile forensics. *Forensic Science International: Digital Investigation*, 38, 301129. https://doi.org/10.1016/j.fsidi.2021.301129

Jenis, J., Ondriga, J., Hrcek, S., Brumercik, F., Cuchor, M., & Sadovsky, E. (2023). Engineering applications of artificial intelligence in mechanical design and optimization. *Machines*, 11(6), Article 6. https://doi.org/10.3390/machines11060577

Kaur, R., Gabrijelčič, D., & Klobučar, T. (2023). Artificial intelligence for cybersecurity: Literature review and future research directions. *Information Fusion*, 97, 101804. https://doi.org/10.1016/j.inffus.2023.101804

Kebande, V. R., Ikuesan, R. A., Karie, N. M., Alawadi, S., Choo, K.-K. R., & Al-Dhaqm, A. (2020). Quantifying the need for supervised machine learning in conducting live forensic analysis of emergent configurations (ECO) in IoT environments. *Forensic Science International: Reports*, 2, 100122. https://doi.org/10.1016/j.fsir.2020.100122

Khan, H., Hanif, S., Muhammad, B., Khan, H., Hanif, S., & Muhammad, B. (2021). A survey of machine learning applications in digital forensics. *Trends in Computer Science and Information Technology*, 6(1), 020–024. https://doi.org/10.17352/tcsit.000034

Kloosterman, A., Mapes, A., Geradts, Z., van Eijk, E., Koper, C., van den Berg, J., Verheij, S., van der Steen, M., & van Asten, A. (2015). The interface between forensic science and technology: How technology could cause a paradigm shift in the role of forensic institutes in the criminal justice system. *Philosophical Transactions of the Royal Society B: Biological Sciences*, 370(1674), 20140264. https://doi.org/10.1098/rstb.2014.0264

Kute, R., Vyas, V., & Anuse, A. (2021). Transfer learning for face recognition using fingerprint biometrics. *Journal of King Saud University – Engineering Sciences*. https://doi.org/10.1016/j.jksues.2021.07.011

Landauer, M., Onder, S., Skopik, F., & Wurzenberger, M. (2023). Deep learning for anomaly detection in log data: A survey. *Machine Learning with Applications*, 12, 100470. https://doi.org/10.1016/j.mlwa.2023.100470

Lappas, N. T., & Lappas, C. M. (2021). *Forensic Toxicology: Principles and Concepts*. Elsevier.

LeCun, Y., Bengio, Y., & Hinton, G. (2015). Deep learning. *Nature*, 521(7553), 436–444.

Li, Z., Wang, Y., Zhang, N., Zhang, Y., Zhao, Z., Xu, D., Ben, G., & Gao, Y. (2022). Deep learning-based object detection techniques for remote sensing images: A survey. *Remote Sensing*, 14(10), Article 10. https://doi.org/10.3390/rs14102385

Li, Y. (2017). Deep reinforcement learning: An overview. *arXiv preprint*, arXiv:1701.07274.

Lo Bosco, G., & Di Gangi, M. A. (2017). Deep learning architectures for DNA sequence classification. In *Fuzzy Logic and Soft Computing Applications: 11th International Workshop, WILF 2016, Naples, Italy, December 19–21, 2016, Revised Selected Papers 11* (pp. 162–171). Springer International Publishing.

Ma, Z., & Mei, G. (2021). Deep learning for geological hazards analysis: Data, models, applications, and opportunities. *Earth-Science Reviews*, 223, 103858. https://doi.org/10.1016/j.earscirev.2021.103858

Majed, H., Noura, H. N., & Chehab, A. (2020). Overview of digital forensics and anti-forensics techniques. In *2020 8th International Symposium on Digital Forensics and Security (ISDFS)* (pp. 1–5). https://doi.org/10.1109/ISDFS49300.2020.9116399

Malaca, S., Carlier, J., & Busardò, F. P. (2020). Advances in forensic toxicology. *Current Pharmaceutical Design*, 26(31), 3779–3780.

Marturana, F., & Tacconi, S. (2013). A machine learning-based triage methodology for automated categorization of digital media. *Digital Investigation*, 10(2), 193–204. https://doi.org/10.1016/j.diin.2013.01.001

McCord, B. R., Gauthier, Q., Cho, S., Roig, M. N., Gibson-Daw, G. C., Young, B., . . . & Duncan, G. (2018). Forensic DNA analysis. *Analytical Chemistry*, 91(1), 673–688.

Meijer, A., & Wessels, M. (2019). Predictive policing: Review of benefits and drawbacks. *International Journal of Public Administration*, 42(12), 1031–1039.

Minaee, S., Abdolrashidi, A., Su, H., Bennamoun, M., & Zhang, D. (2023). Biometrics recognition using deep learning: A survey. *Artificial Intelligence Review*, 1–49.

Miller, C. M. (2023). A survey of prosecutors and investigators using digital evidence: A starting point. *Forensic Science International: Synergy*, 6, 100296. https://doi.org/10.1016/j.fsisyn.2022.100296

Nabi, K. N., Tahmid, M. T., Rafi, A., Kader, M. E., & Haider, Md. A. (2021). Forecasting COVID-19 cases: A comparative analysis between recurrent and convolutional neural networks. *Results in Physics*, 24, 104137. https://doi.org/10.1016/j.rinp.2021.104137

Najafabadi, M. M., Villanustre, F., Khoshgoftaar, T. M., Seliya, N., Wald, R., & Muharemagic, E. (2015). Deep learning applications and challenges in big data analytics. *Journal of Big Data*, 2(1), 1. https://doi.org/10.1186/s40537-014-0007-7

Nisioti, A., Loukas, G., Rass, S., & Panaousis, E. (2021). Game-theoretic decision support for cyber forensic investigations. *Sensors*, 21(16), Article 16. https://doi.org/10.3390/s21165300

Qiao, Y., Zhang, W., Tian, Z., Yang, L. T., Liu, Y., & Alazab, M. (2022). Adversarial malware sample generation method based on the prototype of deep learning detector. *Computers & Security*, 119, 102762. https://doi.org/10.1016/j.cose.2022.102762

Reedy, P. (2023). Interpol review of digital evidence for 2019–2022. *Forensic Science International: Synergy*, 6, 100313. https://doi.org/10.1016/j.fsisyn.2022.100313

Ruder, S. (2016). An overview of gradient descent optimisation algorithms. *arXiv preprint*, arXiv:1609.04747.

Saleem, R., Yuan, B., Kurugollu, F., Anjum, A., & Liu, L. (2022). Explaining deep neural networks: A survey on the global interpretation methods. *Neurocomputing*, 513, 165–180. https://doi.org/10.1016/j.neucom.2022.09.129

Sánchez-Hevia, H. A., Gil-Pita, R., Utrilla-Manso, M., & Rosa-Zurera, M. (2022). Age group classification and gender recognition from speech with temporal convolutional neural networks. *Multimedia Tools and Applications*, *81*(3), 3535–3552. https://doi.org/10.1007/s11042-021-11614-4

Sarabdeen, J. (2022). Protection of the rights of the individual when using facial recognition technology. *Heliyon*, *8*(3), e09086. https://doi.org/10.1016/j.heliyon.2022.e09086

Sarker, I. H. (2023). Machine learning for intelligent data analysis and automation in cybersecurity: Current and future prospects. *Annals of Data Science*, *10*(6), 1473–1498. https://doi.org/10.1007/s40745-022-00444-2

Schmidhuber, J. (2015). Deep learning in neural networks: An overview. *Neural Networks*, *61*, 85–117.

Şengönül, E., Samet, R., Abu Al-Haija, Q., Alqahtani, A., Alturki, B., & Alsulami, A. A. (2023). An analysis of artificial intelligence techniques in surveillance video anomaly detection: A comprehensive survey. *Applied Sciences*, *13*(8), Article 8. https://doi.org/10.3390/app13084956

Shinde, R., Patil, S., Kotecha, K., Potdar, V., Selvachandran, G., & Abraham, A. (n.d.). Securing AI-based healthcare systems using blockchain technology: A state-of-the-art systematic literature review and future research directions. *Transactions on Emerging Telecommunications Technologies*, *n/a*(n/a), e4884. https://doi.org/10.1002/ett.4884

Shrivastava, G., Kumar, P., Gupta, B. B., Bala, S., & Dey, N. (Eds.). (2018). *Handbook of Research on Network forensics and Analysis Techniques*. IGI Global.

Solanke, A. A. (2022). Explainable digital forensics AI: Towards mitigating distrust in AI-based digital forensics analysis using interpretable models. *Forensic Science International: Digital Investigation*, *42*, 301403. https://doi.org/10.1016/j.fsidi.2022.301403

Solanke, A. A., & Biasiotti, M. A. (2022). Digital forensics AI: Evaluating, standardizing and optimizing digital evidence mining techniques. *KI – Künstliche Intelligenz*, *36*(2), 143–161. https://doi.org/10.1007/s13218-022-00763-9

Soria, M. L. (2023). The improvements in forensic toxicology and its role in the forensic process (I). *Spanish Journal of Legal Medicine*, *49*(3), 107–117.

Sreenu, G., & Durai, S. (2019). Intelligent video surveillance: A review through deep learning techniques for crowd analysis. *Journal of Big Data*, *6*(1), 1–27.

Stamm, M., & Zhao, X. (2022). *Anti-Forensic Attacks Using Generative Adversarial Networks* (pp. 467–490). https://doi.org/10.1007/978-981-16-7621-5_17

Thurzo, A., Kosnáčová, H. S., Kurilová, V., Kosmeľ, S., Beňuš, R., Moravanský, N., Kováč, P., Kuracinová, K. M., Palkovič, M., & Varga, I. (2021). Use of advanced artificial intelligence in forensic medicine, forensic anthropology and clinical anatomy. *Healthcare*, *9*(11), 1545. https://doi.org/10.3390/healthcare9111545

Van Giffen, B., Herhausen, D., & Fahse, T. (2022). Overcoming the pitfalls and perils of algorithms: A classification of machine learning biases and mitigation methods. *Journal of Business Research*, *144*, 93–106. https://doi.org/10.1016/j.jbusres.2022.01.076

Vidaki, A., Ballard, D., Aliferi, A., Miller, T. H., Barron, L. P., & Court, D. S. (2017). DNA methylation-based forensic age prediction using artificial neural networks and next generation sequencing. *Forensic Science International: Genetics*, *28*, 225–236.

Wang, J., Wang, C., Lin, Q., Luo, C., Wu, C., & Li, J. (2022). Adversarial attacks and defenses in deep learning for image recognition: A survey. *Neurocomputing*, *514*, 162–181. https://doi.org/10.1016/j.neucom.2022.09.004

What is Computer Forensics? (n.d.). IBM. Retrieved November 20, 2023, from https://www.ibm.com/topics/computer-forensics

Yaacoub, J.-P. A., Noura, H. N., & Salman, O. (2023). Security of federated learning with IoT systems: Issues, limitations, challenges, and solutions. *Internet of Things and Cyber-Physical Systems*, *3*, 155–179. https://doi.org/10.1016/j.iotcps.2023.04.001

Yaacoub, J.-P. A., Noura, H. N., Salman, O., & Chehab, A. (2023). Ethical hacking for IoT: Security issues, challenges, solutions and recommendations. *Internet of Things and Cyber-Physical Systems*, *3*, 280–308. https://doi.org/10.1016/j.iotcps.2023.04.002

Yang, G., Ye, Q., & Xia, J. (2022). Unbox the black-box for the medical explainable AI via multi-modal and multi-centre data fusion: A mini-review, two showcases and beyond. *Information Fusion*, *77*, 29–52. https://doi.org/10.1016/j.inffus.2021.07.016

Yang, M., Ling, J., Chen, J., Feng, M., & Yang, J. (2023). Discriminative semi-supervised learning via deep and dictionary representation for image classification. *Pattern Recognition*, *140*, 109521. https://doi.org/10.1016/j.patcog.2023.109521

Yang, W., Wei, Y., Wei, H., Chen, Y., Huang, G., Li, X., Li, R., Yao, N., Wang, X., Gu, X., Amin, M. B., & Kang, B. (2023). Survey on explainable AI: From approaches, limitations and applications aspects. *Human-Centric Intelligent Systems*, *3*(3), 161–188. https://doi.org/10.1007/s44230-023-00038-y

Yi, T., Chen, X., Zhu, Y., Ge, W., & Han, Z. (2023). Review on the application of deep learning in network attack detection. *Journal of Network and Computer Applications*, *212*, 103580. https://doi.org/10.1016/j.jnca.2022.103580

Zhang, D., Song, F., Xu, Y., & Liang, Z. (Eds.). (2009). *Advanced Pattern Recognition Technologies with Applications to Biometrics*. IGI Global.

Zhang, J. X., Yordanov, B., Gaunt, A., Wang, M. X., Dai, P., Chen, Y. J., . . . & Zhang, D. Y. (2021). A deep learning model for predicting next-generation sequencing depth from DNA sequence. *Nature Communications*, *12*(1), 4387.

Zhang, Y., Wang, Z., Jiang, J., You, H., & Chen, J. (2023). Toward improving the robustness of deep learning models via model transformation. In *Proceedings of the 37th IEEE/ACM International Conference on Automated Software Engineering* (pp. 1–13). https://doi.org/10.1145/3551349.3556920

Zhang, Z., Ning, H., Farha, F., Ding, J., & Choo, K.-K. R. (2022). Artificial intelligence in physiological characteristics recognition for internet of things authentication. *Digital Communications and Networks*. https://doi.org/10.1016/j.dcan.2022.10.006

Zou, L., Zhao, M., Gao, Z., Cao, M., Jia, H., & Pei, M. (2018). License plate detection with shallow and deep CNNs in complex environments. *Complexity*, *2018*, c7984653. https://doi.org/10.1155/2018/7984653

Chapter 12

Cyber Synergy
Unlocking the Potential Use of Biometric Systems and Multimedia Forensics in Cybercrime Investigations

Ruchika Thakur, Sudhakar Kumar, Sunil K. Singh, Krishana Singla, Sunil Kr Sharma, and Varsha Arya

I. INTRODUCTION

The synergy between biometrics and forensic science has a deep-rooted historical connection, with early applications focused on biometric measurements for the identification of multiple offenders based on their physiological and behavioral traits [1]. As a matter of fact, the potential for mutually beneficial collaboration between these fields is substantial. Under the broad "Biometrics umbrella," there exist technologies and methods that can be optimized to significantly impact various forensic scenarios and criminal investigations. The shared knowledge and integration of biometric technologies have the potential to revolutionize the landscape of forensic science [2].

In the world of forensic investigation, a noteworthy exploration revolves around the utilization of 2D and 3D face recognition technologies. These technologies present a compelling prospect for elevating the precision in identifying individuals based on facial features. The integration of biometrics into forensic investigations is an ever-evolving landscape, with researchers actively seeking innovative methods and solutions.

Moreover, a promising avenue emerges in harnessing biometric evidence sourced from multimedia content, especially from social networking sites. This form of evidence stands as a valuable resource for forensic investigations and intelligence gathering, offering avenues to enhance diverse forensic processes.

The domain of audiovisual biometrics introduces a fascinating opportunity to capture identity information from various sources, encompassing facial imaging, voice recordings, audio-visual recordings, and gait information [2]. Effectively harnessed, this technology could play a crucial role in forensic investigations, facilitating both individual identification and the validation of recorded media authenticity. An additional intriguing frontier involves the incorporation of "soft biometrics," encompassing attributes like age, gender, ethnicity, height, weight, and distinguishing features such as moles, freckles, birthmarks, scars, marks, and tattoos [3]. While these attributes may not serve for individual authentication, they provide ancillary information supporting forensic evaluations. The fusion of such information with traditional biometrics holds the potential to fortify forensic analyses, particularly in scenarios where only partial strong biometric data is available [3].

Moreover, the emerging field of forensic behavioral biometrics allows for the inference of not just individual identities but also behavioral patterns, particularly in crowd behavioral analysis. This aspect of biometrics is crucial for identifying unusual or criminal activities, adding a proactive dimension to forensic investigations [4]. The synergy between different biometric modalities and other forms of forensic evidence, such as latent fingerprints, palmprints, and written documents, is another area of exploration. Biometric technologies can significantly contribute to the analysis of evidence collected from crime scenes, enhancing the efficiency and accuracy of investigations [5].

DOI: 10.1201/9781003207573-12

This chapter further delves into the intriguing concept of amalgamating multimodal biometrics with other forensic evidence, emphasizing the integration of data from diverse sensory channels. Whether these channels relate to distinct traits or involve the same trait obtained from various devices, this multidisciplinary approach seeks to establish a seamless synergy. By aligning techniques from different fields, the aim is to bolster forensic cases robustly, all while upholding privacy and adhering to legal requirements [6]. In the subsequent sections, the chapter meticulously explores the intricate challenges, potential solutions, and promising opportunities inherent in the fusion of biometrics with forensic science. This journey holds the promise of unveiling a dynamic landscape where technology, science, and investigation converge, potentially ushering in a revolution in the broader field of forensic science.

2. EXPLORING BIOMETRIC MODALITIES IN DIGITAL FORENSICS

Digital forensics stands as a pivotal process in the scrutiny of cybercrimes and the preservation of electronic evidence in the contemporary digital landscape. Biometric modalities, encompassing fingerprint and palmprint analysis, iris and retina recognition, facial and expression recognition, voice and speaker identification, along with behavioral biometrics, have emerged as formidable tools in the world of digital forensics [7]. These biometric technologies play a distinctive role in augmenting digital forensic investigations, ensuring the unwavering integrity of electronic evidence. The symbiosis between biometrics and digital forensics not only furnishes crucial insights into cybercrimes but also facilitates the identification of digital malefactors. By leveraging biometric modalities, investigators can verify individuals based on distinctive physiological and behavioral traits, thereby significantly enhancing the overall efficacy of digital forensic investigations. In the ensuing exploration, we delve into some of the commonly employed biometric modalities as shown in Figure 12.1.

2.1 Fingerprint and Palmprint Analysis

The intersection of biometrics and forensic sciences has ushered in a novel era of investigative tools. Notably, fingerprint recognition, one of the earliest biometric methods, plays an

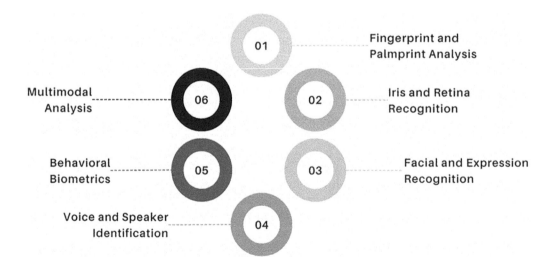

Figure 12.1 Biometric modalities in digital forensics

indispensable role in digital forensics. This integration of technology involves a series of intricate technical processes.

It commences with the acquisition of fingerprint images through methods such as optical scanners, capacitive scanners, and ultrasonic scanners. Post-acquisition, the images undergo various pre-processing steps to enhance their quality, including normalization, enhancement, and segmentation. Feature extraction procedures, such as identifying minutiae points and ridge counts, extract unique fingerprint characteristics. These characteristics are subsequently employed to formulate a mathematical template, which is securely stored in a database. Matching processes are fundamental, encompassing both 1:1 and 1:N matching techniques for verification and identification purposes. Technical considerations, including parameters like the False Acceptance Rate (FAR) and False Rejection Rate (FRR), are pivotal. The choice of sensors and hardware, coupled with algorithm selection, considerably influences the system's performance [8, 9]. Additionally, the incorporation of liveness detection techniques is crucial to prevent fraudulent attempts. The amalgamation of fingerprint biometrics with access control systems necessitates seamless integration with the pertinent hardware and software components. It is vital to emphasize that legal and privacy aspects are paramount to guarantee the secure handling of biometric data [10].

In Figure 12.2, the fingerprint biometrics framework represents a complex system that encompasses the acquisition, pre-processing, feature extraction, template generation, and matching of fingerprint data. This technology finds diverse applications, from bolstering smartphone security to aiding criminal investigations. The technical intricacies inherent in this process contribute to the precision and dependability of the system, all while adhering to privacy and legal imperatives. The intersection of biometrics and digital forensics furnishes critical insights into cybercrimes, thereby enhancing the efficiency of investigative procedures.

2.2 Iris and Retina Recognition

In the world of digital forensics, where the identification of individuals is pivotal, Iris and Retina Recognition have surfaced as distinct biometric techniques. These methods leverage

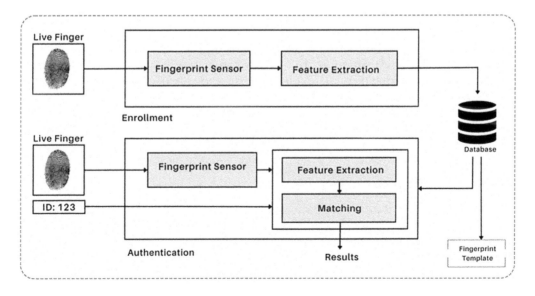

Figure 12.2 Framework for fingerprint biometric authentication

the unique physiological attributes of the eye to establish a person's identity, augmenting security and authentication in cyber investigations. Iris recognition, focusing on the intricate patterns in the colored part of the eye, and retina recognition, which examines the intricate pattern of blood vessels at the back of the eye, have gained prominence in digital forensics [7, 11]. The iris boasts complex and unique patterns, including crypts, furrows, and freckles, rendering it a reliable biometric for individual identification. Similarly, retina recognition capitalizes on the intricate network of blood vessels in the eye's retina, offering a high level of individualization as the vascular pattern remains stable and resists tampering throughout a person's life. These techniques often employ advanced deep learning models, such as Convolutional Neural Networks (CNNs), for more accurate feature extraction and recognition, bolstering the precision of digital forensic investigations [7, 12].

Furthermore, in the context of digital forensics, Optical Character Recognition (OCR) techniques play a crucial role in converting printed or handwritten text from images into machine-readable text, employing algorithms like hidden Markov models (HMMs) and neural networks. Similarly, Automatic Speech Recognition (ASR) systems transcribe spoken language into text, leveraging techniques like deep neural networks and HMMs [13]. These diverse recognition technologies extend beyond eye-based modalities and are instrumental in the analysis of various types of data, enhancing the efficiency of digital forensic investigations.

2.3 Facial and Expression Recognition

Facial recognition techniques encompass a range of methods and technologies for identifying individuals based on their facial features. These techniques have evolved significantly in recent years, with many relying on state-of-the-art deep learning approaches for enhanced accuracy and performance. This fusion of modalities presents a comprehensive approach to individual identification and verification, cementing their indispensable role in the world of cyber investigations.

Some of the fundamental facial recognition techniques include traditional feature-based methods, which identify facial features like eyes, nose, and mouth, using geometric measurements to create unique templates. Eigenfaces, another technique, uses Principal Component Analysis (PCA) to represent faces as a linear combination of eigenfaces, derived from a training dataset [14].

Modern facial recognition heavily relies on Convolutional Neural Networks (CNNs) for feature extraction and classification [15]. CNNs automatically learn hierarchical features from facial images, making them more robust and accurate [16]. Additionally, 3D facial recognition captures unique facial contours using 3D depth information, making it less affected by variations in lighting and poses [17, 18]. In simple words, these facial recognition techniques, ranging from traditional methods to deep learning approaches, collectively reinforce their crucial role in digital forensics and cybersecurity [19].

2.4 Voice and Speaker Recognition

Voice and speaker identification are essential components of modern biometric systems, serving as critical tools in digital forensics and cybersecurity. Recent research in this field has led to the development of innovative techniques that enhance their capabilities, providing robust security measures against fraudulent activities. Notable advancements include optical ciphering schemes designed to secure cancellable speaker identification systems, significantly improving the protection of voice data from malicious attacks, ensuring the integrity of speaker identification in various applications.

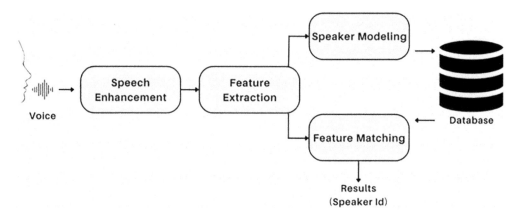

Figure 12.3 Flow for voice recognition biometric

Deep learning approaches have emerged as a powerful tool in combating deepfake audio, a growing concern in the digital age [20]. By leveraging Mel-frequency cepstral coefficient (MFCC) features, these techniques enable the effective detection of manipulated audio content, preserving the reliability of voice-based evidence in cyber investigations. The integration of advanced biometric voice verification into two-factor authentication systems has reinforced web application security. This two-pronged security approach ensures that individuals accessing sensitive data or systems are genuinely authenticated, making it considerably more challenging for unauthorized users to gain access.

Voice comparison techniques have also received substantial attention, with ongoing efforts to improve their forensic applications. These advancements enhance the ability to compare and identify voices, a crucial element in voice-based cyber investigations. Additionally, the application of convolutional neural networks in speech recognition for speaker identity verification stands as a significant breakthrough [21]. These networks leverage deep learning to deliver highly accurate voice matching, further strengthening the role of voice and speaker identification in preserving the integrity of digital evidence and bolstering the cybersecurity landscape.

2.5 Behavioral Biometrics

Behavioral biometrics, a critical facet of digital forensics and cybersecurity, harnesses distinctive behavioral patterns for authentication and identification. This field delves into the analysis of how individuals type, focusing on their unique rhythm, keystrokes, and even the pressure applied to keys. This data generates individualized biometric profiles that are incredibly challenging to replicate, making them highly valuable for access control systems that ensure only authorized users gain entry [4]. For example, a gender classification system based on behavioral biometric modalities, particularly focusing on writing styles, represents an innovative approach at the intersection of biometrics and digital forensics [3, 22]. This system analyzes the distinctive writing styles of individuals to classify their gender, offering valuable context and potentially aiding in identifying the author of documents in forensic investigations. It extends the boundaries of behavioral biometrics, exploring the nuances of writing styles as a unique behavioral signature for gender classification, contributing to document analysis in forensic applications.

Mouse dynamics, another component of behavioral biometrics, scrutinize the way people interact with their computer's pointing devices. Characteristics such as the speed, acceleration, and clicking patterns serve as personalized markers that are effective in recognizing users and detecting unauthorized access. Behavioral biometrics extends its scope to mobile devices, where touchscreens become key identifiers. The pressure, speed, trajectory of gestures on the screen, and even the device's orientation provide valuable biometric information, assuring secure access and data protection.

Gait analysis is an emerging field within behavioral biometrics, delving into an individual's unique walking style, which remains remarkably consistent over time. It considers factors like stride length, walking speed, and body movements to enhance security measures across various applications, from mobile device access to surveillance systems [23]. Additionally, voice recognition as a behavioral biometric is gaining prominence in cyber investigations. By scrutinizing speech patterns, vocal characteristics, and the distinct way individuals articulate words, voice biometrics offer secure access to voice-controlled systems and ensure the protection of voice-based digital evidence. In summary, behavioral biometrics adds an extra layer of authentication, leveraging unique behavioral patterns, and is crucial in preserving digital evidence's security while allowing access only to authorized users. In an ever-evolving digital landscape, these biometric methods are invaluable tools for safeguarding sensitive information and ensuring the privacy and security of individuals.

3. BIOMETRIC DATA ACQUISITION AND SECURE STORAGE

In addressing the escalating challenge of managing electronic evidence, the focus sharpens on the secure acquisition and storage of biometric data. This exploration delves into advanced techniques and challenges inherent in the ethical and legal management of data within the digital forensics landscape. The conversation covers topics such as the ethical considerations of web scraping, extracting data from wearable devices, the intricacies of multimodal biometrics, RF fingerprinting intricacies, and the delicate balance between privacy and security [23, 24]. A collaborative approach involving law enforcement, legal experts, and the technology industry becomes imperative to navigate this intricate landscape successfully.

Several advanced techniques contribute to enhancing the security of biometric data acquisition and storage. As shown in Figure 12.4, distributed data storage, for instance, involves

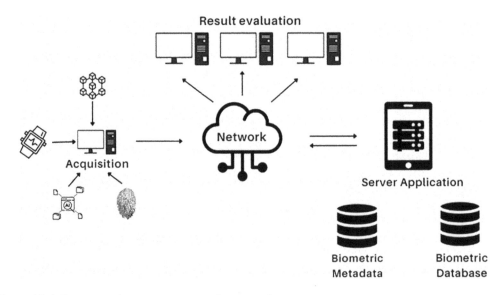

Figure 12.4 Biometric data acquisition and storage flow

storing biometric data in multiple locations, making it more challenging for attackers to access as they would need to compromise multiple systems. Another notable technique is the utilization of multimodal biometrics. These systems combine various biometric modalities, such as fingerprints, facial features, and voice recognition, to elevate the accuracy and security of authentication.

While advanced techniques offer strides in bolstering the security of biometric data, challenges persist and require attention. Ethical considerations surrounding web scraping and the extraction of data from wearable devices present a notable challenge, emphasizing the importance of collecting biometric data in compliance with applicable laws and regulations. The nuances of implementing and managing multimodal biometrics systems add complexity compared to traditional biometric systems, requiring careful design to safeguard against spoofing attacks. The intricacies of this landscape underscore the need for a holistic and collaborative approach to address evolving challenges and ensure the ethical and secure management of biometric data [23, 24].

3.1 Advanced Biometric Data Capture Techniques and Challenges in Secure Biometric Data Storage

In the world of digital forensics, safeguarding the integrity and security of data stands as a paramount concern, particularly as experts grapple with the ever-expanding complexity of electronic evidence. This section delves into the multifaceted challenges and notable advancements linked to ethical and legal data management within this field. Central to this exploration are key facets of secure data management.

Ethical Web Scraping: Researchers must adhere to legal and ethical standards when using web scrapers to collect data from websites, respecting data protection and privacy regulations [25].

Wearable Device Challenges: Extracting and preserving data from wearable devices, like smartwatches, requires overcoming encryption barriers and ensuring data authenticity in forensic investigations [23].

Blockchain and Multimodal Biometrics: Combining blockchain technology with advanced multimodal biometrics, such as 3D face and ear recognition, provides enhanced security for safeguarding sensitive biometric data in digital forensics [17, 18].

Radio Frequency Fingerprinting: Achieving accurate RF fingerprinting for device identification in cyber-physical systems is essential, even in adversarial environments [26].

Balancing Privacy and Security: Striking a balance between privacy and security in regulating cyber technologies is crucial to conduct digital forensics within the bounds of the law while respecting individual privacy rights [27].

In the world of digital forensics, secure data management is paramount as investigators grapple with a growing volume of electronic evidence. A key challenge is navigating stringent data privacy regulations, such as the General Data Protection Regulation (GDPR), while upholding legal compliance and individual privacy rights [28]. Encryption and access control pose formidable hurdles, requiring forensic experts to decrypt data and access devices without compromising evidence integrity. This entails overcoming complex encryption algorithms and robust access controls. The vast and diverse digital data landscape complicates investigations, necessitating the extraction, processing, and analysis of various data types from multiple sources. Equally critical is preserving data integrity to prevent tampering and ensure evidence admissibility. The management of data stored in the cloud and remote servers presents unique legal and jurisdictional challenges, while secure data transfer, up-to-date forensic toolsets, and authentication of digital evidence remain persistent concerns. Cross-border and jurisdictional complexities, resource constraints, big data analytics, data retention policies, counter-forensic tactics, and investigations involving blockchain and cryptocurrencies add to the multifaceted challenges [29].

Integrating biometrics into various technologies like Vehicular Ad Hoc Networks (VANETs) with high-performance computing, cloud resources, and distributed systems, including grid clustering, fortifies cyber investigations. This comprehensive approach ensures secure identity verification for connected vehicles, enhances network security, and optimizes data processing and storage efficiency [30–33].

Navigating this intricate landscape requires adaptability to evolving technologies, legal requirements, and data sources, as well as collaborative efforts among law enforcement, legal experts, and the technology industry to advance the field of digital forensics and ensure secure data management practices.

3.2 Safeguarding Biometric Data: Security and Privacy Measures

Safeguarding biometric data is a multifaceted task that demands preserving data integrity, upholding privacy, and adhering to legal standards. Achieving these objectives involves implementing a comprehensive set of security and privacy measures and best practices for secure data storage in the world of digital forensics. Firstly, strict access control is vital, requiring robust authentication mechanisms, strong passwords, two-factor authentication, and role-based permissions to limit access to authorized personnel. Secondly, employing end-to-end encryption is paramount. This ensures that biometric data is protected during both transmission and storage by using secure communication protocols and encryption algorithms [34]. Regular security audits and vulnerability assessments should be conducted to promptly identify and mitigate potential weaknesses in the biometric data storage infrastructure.

Data minimization practices involve collecting and storing only the necessary biometric data for forensic investigations, thereby reducing privacy risks and exposure in case of a breach. Data anonymization techniques are essential to protect sensitive information within biometric data, minimizing the risk of data breaches and ensuring individual privacy [10]. Effective data lifecycle management strategies encompass defining data retention and disposal policies, determining the duration of biometric data storage, and ensuring secure data disposal when no longer needed. To ensure data availability and reliability, the implementation of secure backup and disaster recovery solutions, along with regular testing of these processes, is indispensable. Preparedness is key, as organizations should develop a well-defined incident response plan outlining procedures for managing data breaches and unauthorized access incidents. This plan should also encompass communication protocols and legal requirements. Personnel handling biometric data should receive comprehensive security awareness training to understand the significance of privacy, best security practices, and the potential consequences of data mishandling. Remaining compliant with evolving data protection regulations, both at international and regional levels, is essential. Regular audits of data practices help maintain compliance.

Conducting privacy impact assessments is a valuable practice to evaluate potential privacy risks associated with biometric data storage and address any identified risks to enhance data privacy [35]. By applying these security and privacy measures in concert, biometric data remains protected from unauthorized access, data breaches, and privacy violations, ensuring the ethical and secure management of sensitive information in digital forensics.

3.3 Best Practices for Biometric Data Storage

Safeguarding biometric data is essential for preserving its integrity and ensuring privacy and legal compliance. To achieve this, consider key security and privacy measures for biometric data storage in digital forensics:

Crafting a robust data management strategy necessitates the meticulous classification of biometric data contingent upon its sensitivity and criticality. Employing sophisticated multi-layer encryption methods is imperative to safeguard data at rest, in transit, and during processing. Furthermore, data segregation based on cases, investigations, or individuals enhances control over the information. A secure storage infrastructure must be instituted, consistently updated with patches to mitigate vulnerabilities [36]. As shown in Figure 12.5, storing biometric data involves multiple measures to ensure privacy and security of data, so implementing stringent authentication mechanisms, such as role-based access control and two-factor authentication, becomes important. The adoption of secure, encrypted channels for data transmission is paramount. Proactive security measures involve the judicious development and automation of data retention policies, ensuring data redundancy, and conducting routine data audits to validate information accuracy [10]. A comprehensive monitoring and tracking system, encompassing audit trails to monitor interactions with biometric data, is crucial. User training and awareness initiatives align personnel with legal and ethical compliance. Ongoing testing and validation serve as fundamental pillars, enabling continuous security assessments through rigorous testing and vulnerability assessments.

By adhering to these best practices, organizations can secure, ethically manage, and efficiently store biometric data in digital forensics, ensuring data integrity, privacy, and value for investigative purposes.

4. MULTIMEDIA FORENSIC ANALYSIS TECHNIQUES

Multimedia forensic analysis techniques play a crucial role in uncovering digital evidence from various forms of multimedia content. These techniques aid investigators in identifying, analyzing, and authenticating multimedia data to support legal cases. From image and audio analysis to video and metadata examination, multimedia forensic methods are diverse and indispensable.

4.1 Digital Image and Video Analysis

Digital image and video scrutiny stands as a crucial element in the world of multimedia forensic analysis. This field encompasses a diverse array of methods, incorporating image processing, computer vision, and deep learning to scrutinize and extract crucial details from

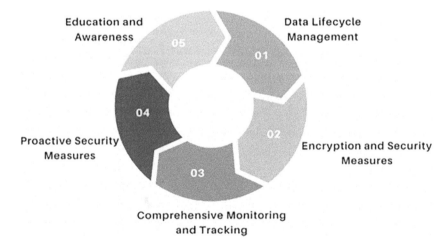

Figure 12.5 Key security and privacy measures for biometric data storage in digital forensics

digital media. The primary aim is to detect potential tampering, assess the credibility of digital content, and recover crucial metadata. Additionally, the text can be transformed into an image for further scrutiny. This summary provides an insight into the methodologies and recent developments in digital image and video analysis in the context of multimedia forensics.

Various techniques are utilized in digital image and video analysis. ELA examines error levels in images, particularly those in JPEG format, to identify potential alterations. It generates ELA maps for digital forensic examinations. This method determines the origin of video content by using features like motion vectors, creating a unique video signature for source identification. Deep learning, specifically Convolutional Neural Networks (CNNs) whose example is shown in Figure 12.6, excels in automatic feature extraction and pattern recognition in digital media [15]. It is crucial for tasks like detecting image tampering, identifying deepfakes, and performing facial recognition in multimedia forensics [3]. Beyond facial recognition, this technique employs deep learning to analyze spatiotemporal aspects of video frames, aiding in detecting video forgeries and discrepancies. Models like Generative Adversarial Networks (GANs) are used to identify deepfake videos and images by comparing content patterns, ensuring multimedia data authenticity [20].

These methods represent just a subset of the diverse approaches utilized in digital image and video analysis for multimedia forensic examination. They play a pivotal role in guaranteeing the authenticity and dependability of multimedia content across various applications, including law enforcement and digital forensics. Recent strides in digital image and video analysis for multimedia forensic analysis have been geared toward enhancing accuracy and efficiency.

In contemporary multimedia forensic analysis, several innovative techniques are enhancing the field. Blockchain integration ensures the secure and immutable storage of digital media, preserving the chain of custody and safeguarding against tampering [19]. Metadata scrutiny, which includes Exif data and geolocation information, plays a pivotal role in verifying the origin and history of multimedia content, providing critical evidence in legal proceedings. Additionally, the application of advanced AI algorithms for multimedia data recovery has become indispensable. These algorithms can restore tampered or deleted content, even after manipulation, greatly facilitating comprehensive analysis.

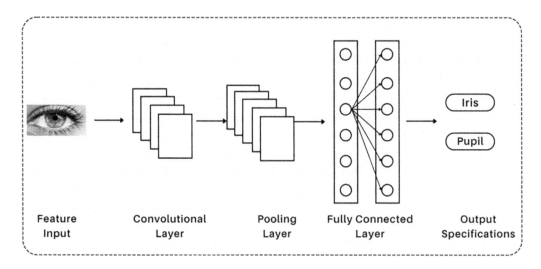

| Feature Input | Convolutional Layer | Pooling Layer | Fully Connected Layer | Output Specifications |

Figure 12.6 Structure of convolutional neural network for biometric analysis

Despite the advancements in digital image and video analysis, challenges persist. Digital adversaries continue to develop sophisticated methods for media manipulation. Therefore, forensic experts need to adapt and improve their techniques continuously.

Future research directions include the development of hybrid techniques that combine multiple forensic methods to enhance the overall reliability of digital media analysis. Moreover, research should focus on addressing the threats posed by emerging technologies such as deepfakes and exploring more robust and efficient algorithms for multimedia analysis.

4.2 Audio Forensics and Voice Profiling

In the field of audio forensics, there have been significant strides that have revolutionized various aspects, including speaker identification, voice profiling, transcription, and voice comparison techniques. These advancements are particularly crucial in addressing the challenges posed by intricate audio recordings. Recent studies have refined methods, employing sophisticated analyses such as spectrogram analysis, pitch modulation, and formant characteristics [21]. The implementation of enhanced algorithms has notably improved transcription and voice comparison processes, contributing to more effective speaker identification and the elucidation of critical evidence.

Forensic voice comparison has undergone a considerable transformation, incorporating advanced techniques like acoustic and phonetic analyses, machine learning, and statistical modeling. These developments have resulted in increased accuracy and reliability [37]. Despite these notable achievements, challenges persist within the world of audio forensics and voice profiling. Adversaries continually devise new techniques to disguise their voices, necessitating ongoing research to counteract such attempts. Additionally, the legal framework surrounding voice evidence must evolve to accommodate the latest forensic techniques and practices.

Looking ahead, future research in audio forensics should prioritize enhancing real-time analysis of audio data, developing more robust algorithms tailored for speaker identification in noisy environments, and ensuring the admissibility of audio forensic evidence in legal proceedings. This forward-looking approach will contribute to the ongoing evolution of audio forensics and its critical role in legal investigations and proceedings.

4.3 Metadata Examination

Metadata examination is a critical element in multimedia forensic analysis, aiding in determining the origin and authenticity of digital content. Recent advancements have highlighted its significance. Metadata, often embedded in multimedia files, provides valuable information about timestamps, device data, geolocation, and editing history. It's used for verifying digital content's authenticity and admissibility as evidence. Additionally, metadata-based forensic analysis in web environments helps trace the origin of web-based multimedia content. Forensic video analysis using metadata allows experts to scrutinize video files for tampering. Handling heterogeneous big data in multimedia forensic analysis presents challenges, but automated approaches assist in metadata examination from various sources like images, videos, and audio recording [38]. Future research should address metadata manipulation, advanced automated metadata analysis, and ensuring the admissibility of metadata-based evidence in legal proceedings [39].

4.4 Detecting and Decoding Steganography

Steganography, the practice of concealing information within seemingly innocuous digital media, presents a significant challenge to multimedia forensic analysts. Its significance lies in its deceptive nature, allowing for the covert embedding of sensitive data, whether for legitimate privacy reasons or malicious purposes. Detecting and decoding steganography are vital tasks in unveiling concealed information, making it a crucial component of digital forensics. In an age where data privacy and cybersecurity are of paramount concern, comprehending the methods for identifying and decoding steganography is essential for preserving the integrity of digital content.

Detecting steganography involves a multifaceted approach, wherein forensic analysts employ a range of techniques to unveil hidden data. Visual inspection, while basic, remains an effective method, involving the examination of media files for visible anomalies, distortions, or patterns that might suggest the presence of concealed information. Statistical analysis is another valuable tool, encompassing the scrutiny of statistical properties within digital media, such as color channels, histograms, and frequency distributions, to identify any deviations from expected patterns. Additionally, techniques like comparing file sizes and examining metadata offer valuable insights for identifying potential instances of steganography. By utilizing these methods, forensic analysts can address various forms of steganography used by individuals and cybercriminals, contributing to both digital security and investigative efforts [40].

Despite the significance of steganography detection in digital forensics, challenges persist. The ongoing cat-and-mouse game between steganography and forensic analysts endures, with steganography techniques progressively growing in sophistication. These advancements render the detection and decoding of steganography more intricate, demanding ongoing adaptation and innovation from digital forensic experts. Looking ahead, the field should prioritize the development of advanced steganalysis methods, machine learning algorithms, and artificial intelligence tools capable of keeping pace with emerging steganographic practices. Additionally, international collaboration among digital forensic experts is imperative, as cybercrimes often transcend borders, requiring a collective effort to address the global nature of steganography in the digital age. As the battle between those concealing information and those striving to reveal it continues, staying ahead of evolving techniques will be pivotal in the field of multimedia forensic analysis, ensuring the preservation of digital integrity and the pursuit of justice.

4.5 AI and Deep Learning for Multimedia Analysis

In the domain of artificial intelligence (AI), recent advancements have ushered in a new era characterized by intelligent machines and data-driven decision-making. Notably, machine learning algorithms, particularly deep learning models, have empowered computers to process extensive datasets, identify intricate patterns, and make informed predictions with remarkable precision [41]. This transformative technology finds applications across diverse sectors, ranging from healthcare, where AI aids in disease diagnosis and drug discovery, to finance, where it enhances investment strategies and risk assessment. AI's capacity to emulate human intelligence and adapt to evolving data positions it as a potent tool for addressing intricate challenges in the contemporary world [42].

The healthcare industry has undergone a profound transformation through the integration of AI and data analytics [43]. These technologies are harnessed to enhance patient care, optimize healthcare operations, and propel medical research forward. AI-driven algorithms demonstrate exceptional precision in analyzing medical images, including X-rays and MRI scans, contributing to early disease detection and diagnosis. Electronic health records are now managed more efficiently, enabling healthcare providers to access critical patient information instantaneously. Furthermore, AI is shaping the future of personalized medicine by tailoring treatment plans to an individual's genetic profile and medical history, opening up new possibilities for more effective and targeted therapies.

Despite the remarkable progress in AI within the healthcare sector, challenges persist, particularly in the worlds of data privacy and ethical considerations. As the healthcare industry increasingly relies on AI for patient data analysis, safeguarding sensitive information and ensuring the responsible use of AI technologies become paramount [21]. It's vital to make AI-driven decisions in healthcare transparent and easy to understand to earn the trust of both healthcare professionals and patients. The future of AI in healthcare looks promising, especially with improvements in understanding medical records through natural language processing and the potential for AI to enhance robotic surgeries [44]. However, the industry must continue to address regulatory and ethical concerns to unlock AI's full potential in revolutionizing patient care and medical research.

4.6 Advancements in Multimedia Data Recovery

In the ever-evolving landscape of technology integration into our daily lives, significant advancements have fundamentally transformed the way we engage with the digital world. From the ubiquitous presence of smartphones to the emergence of smart cities and the Internet of Things (IoT), the impact of technology is undeniably profound. As we continue to witness the revolutionary potential of innovation, it becomes increasingly evident that our reliance on technology is continually strengthening, fundamentally altering how we work, communicate, and even think [24].

In this era of extensive technological integration, data has risen to become the cornerstone of our modern society. Our online activities, spanning from interactions on social media to digital purchases, generate an astonishing volume of data. This data, often likened to the new "oil," fuels machine learning algorithms, tailoring our online experiences and shaping the digital landscape. As data-driven decision-making gains greater prominence, it raises critical questions regarding data privacy and ethical considerations.

While navigating this data-centric digital world, the necessity for robust policies and ethical frameworks becomes abundantly clear. Striking a balance between innovation and privacy, fostering transparency in data collection and utilization, and addressing potential biases in AI algorithms are pivotal challenges that demand our collective attention [43]. The responsible and sustainable integration of technology into our society necessitates a comprehensive approach that considers the repercussions for individuals, organizations, and governments. As such, our capacity to harness the benefits of technology while mitigating its associated risks hinges on our adaptability and ability to evolve within the ever-changing technological landscape.

5. THE SYNERGY OF BIOMETRICS AND MULTIMEDIA FORENSICS: A TECHNOLOGICAL PARADIGM

In the dynamic field of digital investigations, the fusion of biometrics and multimedia forensics represents a seismic shift, offering unparalleled opportunities for enhancing the accuracy, depth, and capabilities of investigative processes. At its core, this integration combines the rich spectrum of biometric modalities with multimedia forensics, ushering in a new era of technology-driven investigative techniques.

5.1 Cross-Modal Biometrics and Advanced Techniques

The implementation of cross-modal biometrics encompasses a sophisticated array of technologies designed to redefine identity verification and enhance multimedia evidence analysis.

In the field of cross-modal biometrics, a key technique called feature-level fusion is making strides. This method blends features from different biometric sources for a comprehensive analysis. For instance, combining facial features with voice patterns enhances the accuracy of identity verification. Another important aspect is sensor integration, where advanced technologies smoothly capture and synchronize data from various sensors. These technologies, equipped with sophisticated sensors, play a crucial role in ensuring accurate and reliable biometric data, forming a strong foundation for a secure identity verification system.

Central to the efficacy of cross-modal biometrics are pattern recognition algorithms. These algorithms, spanning dimensions of machine learning, deep learning, and pattern recognition, are instrumental in matching and analyzing biometric data from diverse sources. Their sophisticated capabilities significantly augment the precision and overall effectiveness of cross-modal biometric systems. As we transition into exploring advanced techniques in multimedia forensics, a parallel suite of technologies enriches the field. Steganalysis, a technique focused on detecting hidden data within digital media, stands at the forefront of multimedia forensics. Employing advanced tools that leverage statistical analysis, machine learning, and deep learning, steganalysis unveils concealed information within multimedia files, playing a crucial role in uncovering covert data and potential threats [40]. Metadata examination takes center stage in the world of multimedia forensics. This technique involves analyzing the metadata associated with multimedia content, utilizing machine learning techniques to unearth valuable information about the origin and history of media files. The insights gained from metadata examination provide a contextual understanding that enhances the credibility of multimedia evidence. By revolutionizing multimedia forensics, blockchain technology offers immutable records of media content [5]. By providing a secure and tamper-resistant ledger, blockchain verifies data integrity and authenticity [18, 43]. This integration reinforces the trustworthiness of multimedia evidence, establishing a robust foundation for its admissibility in legal proceedings.

The seamless integration of these technologies within cross-modal biometrics and multimedia forensics marks a transformative juncture in the worlds of identity verification and evidence analysis. As feature-level fusion, sensor integration, and pattern recognition algorithms redefine identity authentication, steganalysis, metadata examination, and blockchain integration contribute to the credibility and integrity of multimedia evidence [40]. This convergence of technologies not only represents a paradigm shift in the fields of biometrics and

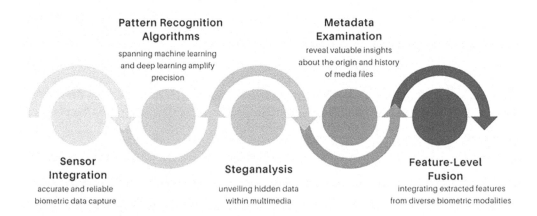

Figure 12.7 Cross-modal biometrics and advanced techniques

multimedia forensics but also underscores the comprehensive solutions available for identity verification and evidence analysis in the intricate landscape of today's digital world.

5.2 Multimodal Biometric Fusion and Deep Learning

Multimodal biometric fusion serves as a pivotal enhancement in the world of identity verification, augmenting reliability and accuracy by combining an extensive array of biometric modalities. This inclusive approach integrates fingerprint and palmprint analysis, iris and retina recognition, facial and expression recognition, voice and speaker identification, along with behavioral biometrics [18]. The fusion of these diverse traits not only expands the dimensions of identification but also ensures the establishment of a more comprehensive and nuanced digital identity.

The technological foundation supporting multimodal biometric fusion encompasses a range of sophisticated technologies. In the world of multimodal biometric fusion, deep learning models are the driving force, using neural networks to autonomously learn from raw data and enhance identification and verification processes [6, 8]. Convolutional Neural Networks (CNNs) play a key role, excelling in processing image-based biometrics like facial and iris recognition [3, 21]. They extract features from visual data for precise analysis of facial features and iris patterns, contributing to robust identification. Recurrent Neural Networks (RNNs) are crucial for voice and speaker identification, capturing temporal dependencies in voice recordings to enhance accuracy [45, 46]. Ensemble learning techniques, including Random Forests and Gradient Boosting, collaborate to improve accuracy in multimodal fusion [6]. These technologies, anchored by pattern recognition algorithms in machine learning and deep learning, represent a significant leap in identity verification capabilities, showcasing the synergy of diverse modalities for a comprehensive digital identity.

5.3 Challenges and Opportunities in Convergence

While the synergy of biometrics and multimedia forensics presents numerous advantages, it concurrently introduces a set of challenges and promising opportunities. A significant challenge lies in ensuring the privacy and security of biometric data when integrated with multimedia content. Striking the right balance between rigorous security measures and the protection of individual privacy rights becomes paramount for researchers and practitioners alike. Additionally, the integration of diverse data formats and sources can pose hurdles to achieving seamless convergence [24].

To address these challenges, the adoption of standardized data formats, the development of interoperable systems, and the utilization of cross-modal biometrics emerge as crucial strategies. These measures contribute to overcoming obstacles and fostering a harmonious integration of biometrics and multimedia forensics.

This convergence not only poses challenges but also opens up compelling opportunities for advancing digital investigations. It enables the discovery of hidden evidence, verification of the authenticity of multimedia content, and the enhancement of identity verification accuracy. Furthermore, the field benefits from continuous advancements in machine learning and deep learning technologies, playing a pivotal role in optimizing the fusion of biometric data with multimedia evidence. These advancements promise groundbreaking developments in the efficiency and precision of digital forensic processes

6. LEGAL AND ETHICAL CONSIDERATIONS IN BIOMETRICS AND MULTIMEDIA FORENSICS

The integration of biometrics into digital investigations, combined with multimedia forensics, brings forth a spectrum of legal and ethical considerations that require meticulous attention.

This section delves into three pivotal aspects that guide the usage of biometrics and multimedia forensics within the framework of legal and ethical standards.

6.1 Legal Frameworks for Biometric and Multimedia Data Usage

In the complex landscape of digital investigations, the interplay of biometric and multimedia data is orchestrated by a web of legal frameworks, regulations, and guidelines. These pivotal laws delineate the intricate dance of data, defining the rules for collection, storage, and utilization across diverse jurisdictions [18]. Among these, the General Data Protection Regulation (GDPR) in the European Union commands attention, setting stringent standards for personal data, including biometrics and multimedia content [22]. Its emphasis on explicit consent, robust data security, and individual control charts the rhythm for ethical data handling. Across the Atlantic, the Fourth Amendment to the United States Constitution takes center stage, safeguarding privacy rights concerning biometric and multimedia data in criminal investigations. Closer to home, the Aadhaar Act of 2016 in India governs the collection and use of biometric data through the Aadhaar identity system, placing a spotlight on data protection and privacy rights. As we unravel these legal intricacies, a clearer picture emerges of the global legal ballet that guides and challenges the seamless integration of biometric and multimedia data in digital forensics. Table 12.1 summarizes some of the major laws and regulations across the world that govern biometric and multimedia data usage.

6.2 Privacy and Informed Consent Issues in Biometric and Multimedia Data

Privacy is at the core of navigating the intricate legal and ethical landscape surrounding the use of biometric and multimedia data. When dealing with these sophisticated data types, it's crucial to ethically handle individual privacy rights. The foundational principle here is informed consent, ensuring that individuals willingly provide their biometric and multimedia data [21, 24].

Informed consent requires individuals to have a clear understanding of how their data will be used, giving them the choice to opt in or out. Transparency in data collection is key, with crucial details like the purpose, duration, and security measures governing data usage communicated clearly. Failing to adhere to these principles raises significant ethical and legal concerns. The use of biometric and multimedia data heightens privacy considerations, highlighting the importance of robust safeguards and informed consent.

Moving into the Internet of Things (IoT), the convergence of biometric and multimedia data adds layers of complexity. Security in IoT applications becomes crucial to prevent unauthorized access and potential breaches. As interconnected devices collect and exchange sensitive data, it becomes imperative to safeguard against cyberattacks. Implementing robust encryption protocols, ensuring secure communication channels, and regularly updating security measures are essential to mitigate risks associated with IoT in the context of biometric and multimedia data [47].

In the metaverse, challenges expand with personalized avatars, demanding careful consideration of virtual identity ownership and usage implications [48]. The blending of biometric and multimedia data with IoT technologies emphasizes the need for comprehensive security measures to protect individual privacy in this ever-evolving digital landscape.

6.3 Ethical Concerns in Deploying Biometrics in Investigations

The deployment of biometrics and multimedia forensics in investigations raises ethical questions concerning accuracy, fairness, and potential for misuse. These ethical concerns have significant implications for technology developers, investigators, and policymakers.

Table 12.1 Relevant laws and regulations

S no.	Laws	Jurisdiction	Key principles and focus
1.	General Data Protection Regulation (GDPR)	European Union	1. Sets formidable standards for meticulous collection and processing of personal data. 2. Emphasizes explicit consent, fortified data security measures, and individual empowerment.
2.	International Covenant on Civil and Political Rights (ICCPR)	International	1. UN adoption designed to uphold civil and political rights 2. Universal stance on the protection of fundamental rights, resonating across biometric and multimedia data usage.
3.	Fourth Amendment to the United States Constitution	United States	1. Defends individual privacy rights against unwarranted searches and seizures. 2. Shapes how biometric and multimedia data are gathered and employed in criminal investigations.
4.	Aadhaar Act, 2016	India	1. Governs biometric data, particularly through the Aadhaar identity system. 2. Focuses on data protection and privacy rights, guiding biometric governance in India's digital landscape.
5.	California Consumer Privacy Act (CCPA)	California, USA	1. Fortifies privacy rights and consumer protection. 2. Regulates collection and utilization of personal information, including biometric data. 3. Empowers consumers with control over their personal information.
6.	China's Cybersecurity Law	China	1. Obligations for network operators and data localization requisites. 2. Influences handling of biometric data within China's digital domain. 3. Prioritizes safeguarding personal information and important data, reflecting China's stance on cybersecurity

One of the most prominent ethical concerns is algorithmic bias. Certain biometric and multimedia systems may exhibit inaccuracies in identifying individuals from specific racial or ethnic backgrounds, leading to discriminatory outcomes. These biases are a critical concern, highlighting the need for fairness and accuracy in biometric and multimedia technologies, especially within the context of advanced technologies like machine learning and deep learning models [49].

Additionally, the impact of biometric and multimedia technology on marginalized communities is a matter of ethical consideration. The deployment of these systems can disproportionately affect vulnerable groups, amplifying existing inequalities. Ethical analysis is required to address these disparities, emphasizing the need to consider the societal implications of technology implementations.

The potential for mass surveillance is another significant ethical concern. The indiscriminate and extensive collection of biometric and multimedia data can infringe on individuals' rights to privacy and freedom from constant surveillance. Striking the right balance between technological capabilities and ethical considerations is essential to ensure the responsible use of biometric and multimedia forensics in the digital investigations landscape.

7. BIOMETRIC AND MULTIMEDIA FORENSICS IN ACTION: REAL-WORLD APPLICATION AND CASE STUDIES

Biometric and multimedia forensics have substantially impacted various fields of investigation, demonstrating their role in real-world applications. In this section, we delve into the practical utilization of these technologies, emphasizing their significance and the technologies that enable their success.

7.1 Leveraging Biometric Systems in Cybercrime Investigations

The utilization of biometric systems has evolved as a cornerstone in cybercrime investigations, providing a robust tool to enhance the investigative process, bolster digital forensics, and deter potential cybercriminals. Biometric systems, spanning modalities such as fingerprint recognition, facial recognition, and iris scanning, offer forensic experts and law enforcement agencies an unprecedented advantage in cybercrime investigations [8].

7.1.1 Behavioral Analysis of Cybercrime

Behavioral analysis in cybercrime is a multidisciplinary approach scrutinizing behavioral patterns exhibited by cybercriminals and victims in digital environments. Understanding and predicting cybercriminal actions, motivations, and tactics is crucial for developing advanced policing strategies. Studying the modus operandi of cybercriminals, identifying recurrent patterns in attacks, and proactively strategizing defense are fundamental aspects of behavioral analysis [50]. It also plays a crucial role in cybercriminal profiling, categorizing potential suspects based on behavioral traits, narrowing suspect lists, and prioritizing investigations. Furthermore, behavioral analysis delves into understanding the motives behind cybercrimes, helping identify vulnerabilities and supporting public awareness campaigns. The analysis extends to studying victim behavior and their digital traces, aiding investigators in identifying attacks and providing support to victims.

Facial recognition technology ascends as a formidable tool in criminal identification, harnessing biometric data from individuals' facial characteristics to establish identity [19]. Applications include matching known individuals with facial images, identifying suspects, verifying individuals in databases, and locating missing persons. The technology offers expeditious and unobtrusive identification, making it invaluable in public spaces and high-traffic areas. While adaptable to varying appearances, it raises privacy, ethical, and bias concerns, necessitating regulation for responsible implementation.

These technologies significantly contribute to law enforcement and digital forensics, enhancing public safety and aiding in criminal investigations. However, balancing their benefits with privacy and ethical considerations remains a crucial challenge.

7.1.2 Combining Blockchain and Biometrics: A Survey on Technical Aspects and a First Legal Analysis

The combination of blockchain technology and biometrics presents an innovative approach to enhancing security and privacy in digital transactions, identity management, and authentication. Leveraging the decentralized and immutable nature of blockchain for secure storage of biometric data makes it resistant to tampering and unauthorized access. This fusion incorporates cryptographic techniques to transform biometric data into an irreversible cryptographic representation before storing it on the blockchain, ensuring enhanced security and data protection [51].

This integration results in the creation of secure digital identities anchored on the block-chain, using biometric data as a foundation. These digital identities enable secure access to various digital services while guaranteeing data integrity and trustworthiness. However, this union presents legal challenges, particularly in complying with data protection laws like the GDPR, which impose strict regulations on biometric data collection and storage. Addressing these legal and regulatory concerns is essential to ensure ethical and lawful implementation of blockchain and biometrics for enhanced security in the digital era.

7.1.3 Biometrics for Digital Identity Verification

Biometrics has emerged as a crucial component of digital identity verification in response to escalating cybercrimes related to identity theft and fraud. These biometric systems employ various modalities, such as fingerprint recognition, facial recognition, and iris scanning, to provide the solutions for digital identity authentication. These modalities rely on acquiring and analyzing unique physiological or behavioral traits.

Fingerprint recognition examines patterns in fingertip ridges and valleys and is known for its accuracy and simplicity [9]. Facial recognition assesses distinct facial features like eye spacing, nose contours, and jaw shape, which are compared with reference databases for verification [17, 19]. Iris scanning examines intricate patterns in the iris, offering high accuracy and security. Biometric digital identity verification surpasses traditional methods like usernames and passwords. Biometric traits are inherently unique and challenging to forge, and dynamic modalities such as behavioral biometrics, capturing traits like keystroke dynamics and voice patterns, further enhance security [4].

For law enforcement and cybersecurity professionals, biometrics play a critical role in authenticating the identities of individuals linked to digital evidence. They can use biometric data, either explicitly provided or extracted from digital artifacts, to verify the identities of suspects, victims, and other relevant parties [50]. This verification is vital for preserving the credibility of digital evidence in legal cases.

Biometric systems are indispensable in the worlds of cybersecurity and digital foren-sics. Through various modalities, they offer high-level security and accuracy for digital identity verification, strengthening the ability to authenticate identities, protect digital evidence, and combat identity-related cybercrimes. In the face of growing cyberthreats, biometric systems provide robust authentication and access control, replacing vulnerable methods like passwords. Biometrics, including fingerprint, facial, and voice recognition, offer unique advantages. Combining these modalities enhances security and reduces unau-thorized access risks. Biometrics safeguard digital evidence and ensure access to sensitive data is restricted to authorized individuals, preserving integrity and credibility. Unlike tra-ditional credentials, biometric traits are unique, difficult to replicate, and integral to an individual's identity. This evolution in digital security is pivotal in deterring cybercriminal activities.

7.2 The Role of Biometric and Multimedia Forensics in Investigations

In the world of criminal investigations, the integration of biometric and multimedia foren-sics has emerged as a cornerstone, providing investigators with powerful tools to unravel complex cases and ensure justice. These technologies find application in diverse domains, showcasing their versatility and impact.

One such critical domain is counterterrorism, where biometric data, encompassing finger-print, facial, and iris recognition, serves as a linchpin for identifying and tracking individuals involved in acts of terrorism. The swift matching of biometric data against watchlists and databases plays a crucial role in preventing terrorist threats and facilitating the apprehension of suspects. Another pivotal application lies in cybercrime investigations, where multimedia forensics revolutionizes the field. It aids in tracking down cybercriminals, identifying the sources of cyberattacks, and providing essential evidence for prosecuting individuals involved in digital crimes. Additionally, biometric technologies play a vital role in resolving cold cases, breathing new life into previously unsolved crimes such as homicides and sexual assaults. Through DNA profiling, fingerprint comparisons, and various other biometric evidence, investigators can identify and prosecute culprits, offering closure to the families of victims and exemplifying the enduring impact of biometric and multimedia forensics on criminal justice.

7.3 Case Study: Unraveling a Complex Cybercrime Network

In the dynamic landscape of digital investigations, the fusion of biometric and multimedia forensics stands as a linchpin for unraveling sophisticated cybercrimes. This case study, illuminating a recent high-profile cybercrime, showcases the practical application of advanced forensic technologies in exposing an organized online fraud syndicate. The narrative not only underscores the evolution of investigative practices but also highlights how technological advancements redefine our approach to combating cyberthreats.

The cybercriminals orchestrated a multifaceted plan involving fraudulent websites, phishing emails, and identity theft, inflicting substantial financial losses on financial institutions and online platforms. As these criminal activities transcended borders, collaborative efforts of law enforcement agencies and cybersecurity experts became imperative, marking a watershed moment in the intersection of technology and cybercrime investigation.

At the technological forefront of this investigation were three key components: Biometric Voice Analysis, Multimodal Analysis, and Machine Learning and Deep Learning Models. Voice biometrics and speaker recognition algorithms in the analysis of recorded phone calls identified unique vocal patterns, exposing inconsistencies and enabling the identification of pivotal individuals. The multimodal approach, integrating voice analysis with multimedia evidence scrutiny, provided a nuanced perspective, enriching the investigation by tracing physical locations and authenticating content [24]. Machine learning and deep learning models processed vast datasets, detecting intricate patterns, identifying phishing email origins, and linking seemingly unrelated incidents [19, 50].

This integration of biometric and multimedia forensics with advanced machine learning models yielded crucial breakthroughs, uncovering vocal signatures, revealing operation centers, identifying victims, and exposing the full extent of the fraud. The success of this case study underscores the pivotal role that technological advancements play in the field, making traditional methods pale in comparison. Voice analysis, facial recognition, and speaker recognition technologies have become integral, enhancing accuracy and efficiency. The seamless integration of modalities provides a comprehensive perspective, enriching the depth and effectiveness of investigations. As we navigate digital threats, the symbiotic relationship between technology and forensic investigation stands as a beacon of progress in our quest for a secure digital future.

7.4 Case Study: Unraveling a Cyber Extortion Ransomware Attack

In this deep-dive case study, we delve into the intricacies of a substantial cybercrime investigation, showcasing how biometric and multimedia forensics played a crucial role in untangling a sophisticated cyber extortion ransomware attack. This real-world example underscores the importance of advanced forensic technologies in navigating the complexities of modern cybercrime investigations [11].

The cyber extortionists behind this elaborate scheme executed a ransomware attack with surgical precision, targeting the critical infrastructure of a multinational corporation. Their method involved encrypting sensitive corporate data and demanding a hefty cryptocurrency ransom for the decryption key. The case study meticulously dissects the technological aspects vital to the investigation, shedding light on the challenges posed by cyber threats in our contemporary digital landscape.

In the initial investigative phase, a close examination of biometric access logs emerged as a pivotal element. This encompassed using biometric data like fingerprint and iris scans to trace the initial breach and identify potential insider involvement [50, 52]. Techniques for decrypting multimedia data were then employed, utilizing advanced voice and facial recognition algorithms for a comprehensive analysis. Additionally, behavioral biometrics, such as scrutinizing keystroke dynamics and mouse movements, played a pivotal role in profiling the attackers and revealing their distinctive behavioral patterns [4].

Within the context of the cyber extortion ransomware attack outlined in this case study, it's important to note that the investigative process encountered challenges beyond encryption. The looming threat of a Denial of Service (DoS) attack, with the intent of disrupting critical systems and services, added another layer of complexity. This aspect underscores the multi-faceted nature of modern cyber threats and the critical role played by comprehensive forensic technologies in addressing them [53].

The investigative journey unfolded with a meticulous reconstruction of the timeline of the cyber extortion attack through biometric data analysis [54]. This chronological mapping proved crucial in pinpointing potential vulnerabilities and understanding the sophisticated methods employed by the attackers. A significant breakthrough was achieved with the successful decryption of multimedia files through multimodal analysis, offering crucial insights into the motive behind the attack and disclosing key individuals orchestrating the operation.

Behavioral biometrics profiling significantly contributed to creating a comprehensive profile of the attackers. By identifying distinct patterns in keystroke dynamics and mouse movements, forensic experts narrowed down potential suspects, aiding law enforcement agencies in their pursuit. The collaborative efforts of these experts, combined with the strategic use of biometric and multimedia forensics, culminated in the successful identification and subsequent prosecution of the cyber extortionists.

This in-depth case study serves as a testament to the dynamic landscape of cybercrime investigations and emphasizes the indispensable role played by technological advancements [11]. The precision and efficiency demonstrated by biometric and multimedia forensics surpasses traditional forensic methods, highlighting the breadth and depth of technology-driven investigative methodologies. As cyber threats continue to evolve, the strategic integration of biometric and multimedia forensics into investigative practices becomes essential for building a resilient and secure digital future.

8. FUTURE HORIZONS AND EMERGING TECHNOLOGIES

The future of biometric and multimedia forensics is on the brink of transformative changes in how investigations are carried out, evidentiary standards are upheld, and technological innovations are utilized. In this section, we delve into emerging technologies, trends, and challenges that will shape the landscape of biometric and multimedia forensics in the coming years.

8.1 Technological Advancements and Trends

Quantum computing holds both opportunities and challenges in the world of biometric cryptography. Researchers are actively exploring its potential to enhance encryption and decryption algorithms, strengthening the security of biometric data against unauthorized access [55]. Integrating quantum-resistant algorithms into biometric security systems is crucial to ensure the protection of sensitive biometric information. Simultaneously, blockchain technology is set to revolutionize data management in the field of biometric and multimedia forensics [24]. Its decentralized and tamper-proof nature enhances the integrity of biometric databases, offering a reliable solution for preserving the chain of custody in forensic investigations.

Another intriguing development is the integration of cognitive biometrics and neurotechnology. This involves measuring brain activity and cognitive responses as unique identifiers for authentication. Brainwave patterns and responses to stimuli offer a high level of security and reliability in identity verification. On a different front, the combination of edge computing and the Internet of Things (IoT) is set to play a pivotal role in securing IoT devices and networks [56–58]. Edge devices equipped with embedded biometric capabilities will process and analyze biometric data locally, reducing latency and enhancing privacy [24] [50]. This technology proves invaluable in scenarios demanding real-time decision-making and minimal data transmission, marking a significant stride in the evolution of biometric and multimedia forensics.

The integration of Vehicular Internet of Things (VIoT) with biometrics is poised to reshape the landscape of cyber investigations and fortify digital security in the world of smart cities [59]. This collaboration serves as a pivotal advancement, facilitating seamless communication and secure interactions among vehicles in an interconnected urban environment. Embracing the tenets of Industry 4.0, this integration contributes to the evolution of industrial processes, automation, and the interconnectedness of devices, laying the foundation for more intelligent and secure transportation networks [44].

Within this paradigm, the fusion of VIoT and biometrics promises to revolutionize hardware efficiency in vehicular systems, ushering in an era of heightened connectivity and security [60]. The incorporation of blockchain technology further reinforces this alliance, ensuring the integrity and trustworthiness of data transmitted within these connected environments [61]. As we peer into the future, this collaborative approach sets the stage for the emergence of advanced robotics within the automotive landscape, ushering in a new era of precision and accountability [44].

Beyond technological integration, this convergence addresses the evolving landscape of cyber threats, guaranteeing the resilience and security of connected vehicular ecosystems. It signifies a proactive step towards cultivating secure, intelligent, and interconnected vehicular networks, aligning seamlessly with the principles of Industry 4.0 [62]. This synthesis of VIoT and biometrics encapsulates a forward-looking vision for the future of smart cities, where technology converges for the betterment of urban living and digital security [63].

8.2 AI and Machine Learning in Forensics

Artificial intelligence (AI) and machine learning are dynamic forces at the forefront of revolutionizing biometric and multimedia forensics. Their evolving algorithms promise heightened accuracy and efficiency in handling vast datasets, particularly in the context of cybercrime investigations. The integration of Explainable AI is pivotal, ensuring transparency in forensic tool decisions and fostering trust, especially when these technologies have a direct impact on judicial outcomes. Deep learning models, a subset of machine learning, play a vital role in automating biometric and multimedia data analysis, demonstrating proficiency in recognizing intricate patterns in facial expressions, gait, and voice [12, 23]. Beyond traditional applications, these models enhance textual content analysis through features like speech-to-text transcription and sentiment analysis. Looking ahead, AI's role extends to neural networks with the capacity not only to identify the content of multimedia files but also to discern context and relevance in an investigation [64]. This holistic approach, including the assessment of visual elements, capture details, and potential digital alterations, reflects the increasing sophistication of AI in the field of forensic investigations. Furthermore, AI and machine learning's facilitation of predictive modeling empowers investigators to anticipate criminal activities, contributing to effective crime prevention strategies and bolstering overall security measures [55].

8.3 Achieving Universality and Ethical Considerations

The future of biometric and multimedia forensics envisions universality through the development of methods applicable across diverse populations and technological landscapes. This ambitious goal, aimed at mitigating biases and errors in reliance on specific biometric traits, necessitates international standardization. Collaboration among governments, law enforcement, technology companies, and international bodies is essential to establish norms for data formats, biometric database interoperability, and cross-border data sharing. Ethical considerations become increasingly crucial as these technologies proliferate, addressing privacy concerns and ensuring responsible data use. Ethical frameworks guide their development, focusing on individual rights, preventing discrimination, and ensuring robust data security. In human rights investigations, these technologies play a significant role, uncovering evidence of abuses, fostering accountability, and ensuring justice with stringent safeguards for privacy and security [65]. Global collaboration becomes crucial in shaping the future trajectory of biometric and multimedia forensics. International agreements and treaties are imperative to navigate ethical dimensions, combat cybercrime, and share expertise, data, and resources. Collaborative research endeavors involving academics, scientists, and practitioners from diverse nations are instrumental in addressing challenges [66]. In essence, AI-driven progress, the pursuit of universality, and ethical considerations shape the future of biometric and multimedia forensics, with global collaboration ensuring responsible technology use while advancing security, accuracy, and fairness in the digital age.

9. CONCLUSION

In the extensive exploration of biometric and multimedia forensics within this chapter, a resounding theme emerges—technology stands as the cornerstone propelling transformative advances in investigative landscapes. The integration of diverse biometric modalities, driven by technologies like artificial intelligence and machine learning, underscores the pivotal role of technology in shaping the progress of this domain. Real-world applications, spanning counterterrorism and cybercrime resolution, vividly illustrate the tangible impact of biometric and multimedia forensics on societal security. Despite this noteworthy progress, persistent challenges emphasize the paramount importance of legal and ethical considerations in navigating complex issues such as data privacy and individual rights. Gazing into the future, the brilliance of emerging technologies like multimodal biometric fusion and AI-driven analyses illuminates a path where technology remains the driving force behind advancements in the field.

Guiding practitioners and researchers through this dynamic landscape involves advocating for multimodal approaches, unwavering adherence to legal and ethical standards, proactive mitigation of algorithmic bias, prioritization of data privacy, staying abreast of technological

advancements, and nurturing an ethical and accountable environment. These guiding principles not only ensure investigative accuracy but also maintain ethical integrity and compliance with legal frameworks. The final thoughts resonate with the intertwined destiny of
biometric and multimedia forensics, where technology, ethics, and legal standards converge.
As these fields continue to evolve, the key lies in the continuous adaptation to technological
advancements and collaborative efforts across disciplines. This promises a brighter future
where technology and ethics harmoniously unite to uphold justice, fairness, and accuracy in
the digital age.

REFERENCES

[1] Abdel-Latif, M. A., & El-Sayed, M. A. (2023). Achieving information security by multi-modal
iris-retina biometric approach using improved mask R-CNN. *International Journal of Electrical
and Computer Engineering Systems*, 14(6), 657–665.

[2] Nagwanshi, K. K. (2022). Cyber-forensic review of human footprint and gait for personal identification. *arXiv preprint*, arXiv:2204.09344.

[3] Kumar, S., Rani, S., Jain, A., Verma, C., Raboaca, M. S., Illés, Z., & Neagu, B. C. (2022). Face
spoofing, age, gender and facial expression recognition using advance neural network architec-
ture-based biometric system. *Sensors*, 22(14), 5160.

[4] Sarkar, G., & Shukla, S. K. (2023). Behavioral analysis of cybercrime: Paving the way for effective
policing strategies. *Journal of Economic Criminology*, 100034.

[5] Gomathi, C., & Jayasri, K. (2023). Rain drop service and biometric verification based blockchain
technology for securing the bank transactions from cyber crimes using weighted fair blockchain
(WFB) algorithm. *Cybernetics and Systems*, 54(4), 550–576.

[6] Rajasekar, V., Saracevic, M., Hassaballah, M., Karabasevic, D., Stanujkic, D., Zajmovic, M., . . . &
Jayapaul, P. (2023). Efficient multimodal biometric recognition for secure authentication based on
deep learning approach. *International Journal on Artificial Intelligence Tools*, 32(03), 2340017.

[7] MK, M. H., & Kumari, M. S. (2023). Performance analysis of deep learning models for iris recognition. *Semiconductor Optoelectronics*, 42(1), 113–123.

[8] Sedik, A., El-Latif, A. A. A., Wani, M. A., El-Samie, F. E. A., Bauomy, N. A. S., & Hashad, F. G.
(2023). Efficient multi-biometric secure-storage scheme based on deep learning and crypto-map-
ping techniques. *Mathematics*, 11(3), 703.

[9] Jeong, J. Y., & Jeong, I. R. (2023). Effect of smaller fingerprint sensors on the security of fingerprint authentication. *IEEE Access*, 11, 97944–97951.

[10] Ikegwu, A. C., Nweke, H. F., & Ugwu, G. E. Digital fingerprint and forensic examination as a
technology for cybercrime detection and prevention in Nigeria. *The SIJ Transactions on Industrial, Financial & Business Management (IFBM)*, 5(5), 76–82.

[11] Garea-Llano, E., & Morales-Gonzalez, A. (2023). Framework for biometric iris recognition in
video, by deep learning and quality assessment of the iris-pupil region. *Journal of Ambient Intelligence and Humanized Computing*, 14(6), 6517–6529.

[12] Minaee, S., Abdolrashidi, A., Su, H., Bennamoun, M., & Zhang, D. (2023). Biometrics recognition
using deep learning: A survey. *Artificial Intelligence Review*, 1–49.

[13] Isaac, S., Haruna, K., Ahmad, M. A., & Mustapha, R. Deep reinforcement learning with hidden
Markov model for speech recognition. *Journal of Technology and Innovation*, 3(1), 1–5.

[14] Yan, L., Shi, Y., Wei, M., & Wu, Y. (2023). Multi-feature fusing local directional ternary pattern
for facial expressions signal recognition based on video communication system. *Alexandria Engineering Journal*, 63, 307–320.

[15] Kaur, P., Singh, S. K., Singh, I., & Kumar, S. (2021, December). Exploring convolutional neural
network in computer vision-based image classification. In *International Conference on Smart
Systems and Advanced Computing (Syscom-2021)*. Springer.

[16] Peng, J., Yang, B., Gupta, B. B., & Abd El-Latif, A. A. (2021). A biometric cryptosystem scheme
based on random projection and neural network. *Soft Computing*, 25, 7657–7670.

[17] Sanil, G., Prakash, K., Prabhu, S., Nayak, V., & Sengupta, S. (2023). 2D-3D facial image analysis for identification of facial features using machine learning algorithms with hyper-parameter optimization for forensics applications. *IEEE Access*, 11, 82521–82538.

[18] Kaur, V., Bhatt, D. P., Tharewal, S., & Tiwari, P. K. (2023, May). Blockchain-based secure storage model for multimodal biometrics using 3D face and ear. In *2023 International Conference on Advancement in Computation & Computer Technologies (InCACCT)* (pp. 860–865). IEEE.

[19] Gokulakrishnan, S., Chakrabarti, P., Hung, B. T., & Shankar, S. S. (2023). An optimized facial recognition model for identifying criminal activities using deep learning strategy. *International Journal of Information Technology*, 1–15.

[20] Altalahin, I., AlZu'bi, S., Alqudah, A., & Mughaid, A. (2023, August). Unmasking the truth: A deep learning approach to detecting deepfake audio through MFCC features. In *2023 International Conference on Information Technology (ICIT)* (pp. 511–518). IEEE.

[21] An, H. (2023, May). Speech recognition of speaker identity based on convolutional neural networks. In *International Conference on Computer Graphics, Artificial Intelligence, and Data Processing (ICCAID 2022)* (Vol. 12604, pp. 653–659). SPIE.

[22] Singhal, A., & Sharma, D. K. (2023). Low resource language analysis using deep learning algorithm for gender classification. *ACM Transactions on Asian and Low-Resource Language Information Processing*.

[23] Mason, R., Pearson, L. T., Barry, G., Young, F., Lennon, O., Godfrey, A., & Stuart, S. (2023). Wearables for running gait analysis: A systematic review. *Sports Medicine*, 53(1), 241–268.

[24] Lin, L., Zhao, Y., Meng, J., & Zhao, Q. (2023). A federated attention-based multimodal biometric recognition approach in IoT. *Sensors*, 23(13), 6006.

[25] Logos, K., Brewer, R., Langos, C., & Westlake, B. (2023). Establishing a framework for the ethical and legal use of web scrapers by cybercrime and cybersecurity researchers: Learnings from a systematic review of Australian research. *International Journal of Law and Information Technology*, eaad023.

[26] Alhazbi, S., Hussain, A., Sciancalepore, S., Oligeri, G., & Papadimitratos, P. (2023). Challenges of radio frequency fingerprinting: From data collection to deployment. *arXiv preprint*, arXiv:2310.16406.

[27] Rebe, N. (Ed.). (2023). *Regulating Cyber Technologies: Privacy Vs Security*. World Scientific.

[28] Johnson, G. A., Shriver, S. K., & Goldberg, S. G. (2023). Privacy and market concentration: Intended and unintended consequences of the GDPR. *Management Science*, 69(10), 5695–5721.

[29] Aggarwal, K., Singh, S. K., Chopra, M., & Kumar, S. (2022). Role of social media in the COVID-19 pandemic: A literature review. In *Data Mining Approaches for Big Data and Sentiment Analysis in Social Media* (pp. 91–115).

[30] Gupta, A., Sharma, A., Singh, S. K., & Kumar, S. (2017). Cloud computing & fog computing: A solution for high performance computing. In *Proceedings of the 11th INDIACom*. IEEE.

[31] Rastogi, A., Sharma, A., Singh, S., & Kumar, S. (2017). Capacity and inclination of high-performance computing in next generation computing. In *Proceedings of the 11th INDIACom*. IEEE.

[32] Singh, S. K., Kaur, K., Aggarwal, A., & Verma, D. (2015). Achieving high performance distributed system: Using grid cluster and cloud computing. *International Journal of Engineering Research and Applications*, 5(2), 59–67.

[33] Gupta, B. B., Perez, G. M., Agrawal, D. P., & Gupta, D. (2020). *Handbook of Computer Networks and Cyber Security* (Vol. 10, pp. 3–978). Springer.

[34] Yang, W., Wang, S., Cui, H., Tang, Z., & Li, Y. (2023). A review of homomorphic encryption for privacy-preserving biometrics. *Sensors*, 23(7), 3566.

[35] Dewani, N. D., Khan, Z. A., Agarwal, A., Sharma, M., & Khan, S. A. (Eds.). (2022). *Handbook of Research on Cyber Law, Data Protection, and Privacy*. IGI Global.

[36] Rudrakshi, P. G., & Hatture, S. K. M. (2014, September). A model for secure information storage and retrieval on cloud using multimodal biometric cryptosystem. In *2014 International Conference on Computer and Communication Technology (ICCCT)* (pp. 169–174). IEEE.

[37] Mengi, G., Singh, S. K., Kumar, S., Mahto, D., & Sharma, A. (2021, September). Automated machine learning (AutoML): The future of computational intelligence. In *International Conference on Cyber Security, Privacy and Networking* (pp. 309–317). Springer International Publishing.

[38] Chopra, M., Singh, S. K., Aggarwal, K., & Gupta, A. (2022). Predicting catastrophic events using machine learning models for natural language processing. In *Data Mining Approaches for Big Data and Sentiment Analysis in Social Media* (pp. 223–243). IGI Global.

[39] Praneeth. (2022). *Cloud Forensics: Open Issues, Challenges and Future Research Opportunities* (p. 1). Insights2Techinfo.

[40] Reinel, T. S., Raul, R. P., & Gustavo, I. (2019). Deep learning applied to steganalysis of digital images: A systematic review. *IEEE Access*, 7, 68970–68990.

[41] Singh, I., Singh, S. K., Singh, R., & Kumar, S. (2022, May). Efficient loop unrolling factor prediction algorithm using machine learning models. In *2022 3rd International Conference for Emerging Technology (INCET)* (pp. 1–8). IEEE

[42] Gupta, A., Singh, S. K., & Chopra, M. (2023). Impact of artificial intelligence and the internet of things in modern times and hereafter: An investigative analysis. In *Advanced Computer Science Applications* (pp. 157–173). Apple Academic Press.

[43] Jayapriya, P., Umamaheswari, K., & Sathish Kumar, S. (2023). Biometrics with blockchain: A better secure solution for template protection. *Artificial Intelligence for Sustainable Applications*, 311–327.

[44] Aggarwal, K., Singh, S. K., Chopra, M., Kumar, S., & Colace, F. (2022). Deep learning in robotics for strengthening industry 4.0.: Opportunities, challenges and future directions. *Robotics and AI for Cybersecurity and Critical Infrastructure in Smart Cities*, 1–19.

[45] Gupta, A., Singh, S. K., Gupta, B. B., Chopra, M., & Gill, S. S. (2023). Evaluating the sustainable COVID-19 vaccination framework of India using recurrent neural networks. *Wireless Personal Communications*, 1–19.

[46] Cvitić, I., Praneeth, G., & Peraković, D. (2021). *Digital Forensics Techniques for Social Media Networking* (p. 1). Insights2Techinfo.

[47] Gupta, B. B., and Quamara, M. (2020). *Internet of Things Security: Principles, Applications, Attacks, and Countermeasures*. CRC Press.

[48] Singh, M., Singh, S. K., Kumar, S., Madan, U., & Maan, T. (2021, September). Sustainable framework for metaverse security and privacy: Opportunities and challenges. In *International Conference on Cyber Security, Privacy and Networking* (pp. 329–340). Springer International Publishing.

[49] Smith, M., & Miller, S. (2022). The ethical application of biometric facial recognition technology. *Ai & Society*, 1–9.

[50] Malathi, C., & Padmaja, I. N. (2023). Identification of cyber attacks using machine learning in smart IoT networks. *Materials Today: Proceedings*, 80, 2518–2523.

[51] Ghafourian, M., Sumer, B., Vera-Rodriguez, R., Fierrez, J., Tolosana, R., Moralez, A., & Kindt, E. (2023). Combining blockchain and biometrics: A survey on technical aspects and a first legal analysis. *arXiv preprint*, arXiv:2302.10883

[52] Kumar, R., Singh, S. K., & Lobiyal, D. K. (2023). UPSRVNet: Ultralightweight, privacy preserved, and Secure RFID-based authentication protocol for VIoT networks. *The Journal of Supercomputing*, 1–28.

[53] Mishra, A., Gupta, B. B., Peraković, D., Yamaguchi, S., & Hsu, C. H. (2021, January). Entropy based defensive mechanism against DDoS attack in SDN-cloud enabled online social networks. In *2021 IEEE International Conference on Consumer Electronics (ICCE)* (pp. 1–6). IEEE.

[54] Gupta, B. B., Sahoo, S. R., Bhatia, V., Arafat, A., & Setia, A. (2020). Auto fill security solution using biometric authentication for fake profile detection in OSNs. In *Handbook of Research on Intrusion Detection Systems* (pp. 237–262). IGI Global.

[55] Kumar, S., Singh, S. K., & Aggarwal, N. (2023). Speculative parallelism on multicore chip architecture strengthen green computing concept: A survey. In *Advanced Computer Science Applications* (pp. 3–16). Apple Academic Press.

[56] Gaurav, A., Gupta, B. B., & Panigrahi, P. K. (2023). A comprehensive survey on machine learning approaches for malware detection in IoT-based enterprise information system. *Enterprise Information Systems*, 17(3), 2023764.

[57] Singh, R., Singh, S. K., Kumar, S., & Gill, S. S. (2022). SDN-aided edge computing-enabled AI for IoT and smart cities. In *SDN-Supported Edge-Cloud Interplay for Next Generation Internet of Things* (pp. 41–70). Chapman and Hall/CRC.

[58] Saini, T., Kumar, S., Vats, T., & Singh, M. (2020). Edge computing in cloud computing environment: Opportunities and challenges. In *International Conference on Smart Systems and Advanced Computing (Syscom-2021)*. Springer.

[59] Kumar, R., Sinngh, S. K., & Lobiyal, D. K. (2023, April). Routing of vehicular IoT networks based on various routing metrics, characteristics, and properties. In *2023 International Conference on Computational Intelligence, Communication Technology and Networking (CICTN)* (pp. 656–662). IEEE.

[60] Kumar, R., Singh, S. K., & Lobiyal, D. K. (2023). Communication structure for vehicular internet of things (VIoTs) and review for vehicular networks. In *Automation and Computation* (pp. 300–310). CRC Press.

[61] Singh, S. K., Sharma, S. K., Singla, D., & Gill, S. S. (2022). Evolving requirements and application of SDN and IoT in the context of industry 4.0, blockchain and artificial intelligence. In *Software Defined Networks: Architecture and Applications* (pp. 427–496). Wiely.

[62] Kumar, S., Singh, S. K., Aggarwal, N., Gupta, B. B., Alhalabi, W., & Band, S. S. (2022). An efficient hardware supported and parallelization architecture for intelligent systems to overcome speculative overheads. *International Journal of Intelligent Systems*, 37(12), 11764–11790.

[63] Chopra, M., Kumar, S., Madan, U., & Sharma, S. (2021, December). Influence and establishment of smart transport in smart cities. In *International Conference on Smart Systems and Advanced Computing (Syscom-2021)*. Springer.

[64] Peng, J., Yang, B., Gupta, B. B., & El-Latif, A. A. A. (2021). Correction to: A biometric cryptosystem scheme based on random projection and neural network. *Soft Computing*, 25, 7657–7670.

[65] Ducey, I. (2022). Biometric data collection and big tech: Imposing ethical constraints on entities that harvest biometric data. *Seattle Journal of Technology, Environmental & Innovation Law*, 12(2), 2.

[66] Kaur, M. (2022, March). Cyber security challenges in the latest technology. In *Proceedings of Third International Conference on Communication, Computing and Electronics Systems: ICCCES 2021* (pp. 655–671). Springer Singapore.

Index

Note: Page numbers in *italics* indicate a figure and page numbers in **bold** indicate a table on the corresponding page.

For Product Safety Concerns and Information please contact our EU
representative GPSR@taylorandfrancis.com
Taylor & Francis Verlag GmbH, Kaufingerstraße 24, 80331 München, Germany

www.ingramcontent.com/pod-product-compliance
Ingram Content Group UK Ltd.
Pitfield, Milton Keynes, MK11 3LW, UK
UKHW051828180425
457613UK00007B/248